D1554578

"Before you even go to trial, you could be held legally in jail for years. More shocks like that are in this book. In it, the author informs in order to transform. Matt Martens is a Christian, the son of a pastor, a husband and father, a church member, and an accomplished lawyer. He has worked in both the private and the public sectors for decades. In these pages, he takes the reader on a tour of what really happens when a crime is alleged. Martens provides definitions and historical context for terms familiar to the average reader, gives examples of current challenges, and raises concerns about how we actually practice justice. This book is more than informative—it is engaging to the point of being disturbing. Martens is trying to serve us by helping us get in 'good trouble.'"

Mark Dever, Pastor, Capitol Hill Baptist Church, Washington, DC

"*Reforming Criminal Justice* is a book for our polarized times. Guided by classical Christian sources and a biblical vision of love's relation to justice, Martens draws on his considerable legal experience to offer a critical yet constructive evangelical approach that is at once theologically sensitive and historically informed. Highly recommended for the church and anyone concerned about the lived realities of the American criminal justice system as an urgent moral and political issue."

Eric Gregory, Professor of Religion, Princeton University

"*Reforming Criminal Justice* is a superb tutorial on the criminal justice system, and it's much more. An experienced criminal justice lawyer—as a prosecutor and then as a defense attorney—Martens is also a trained theologian. He offers simple, biblically grounded principles for assessing American criminal justice and doesn't shy away from the issue of race. Highly recommended."

David Skeel, S. Samuel Arsht Professor of Corporate Law, University of Pennsylvania Carey Law School

"A book like this is long overdue and vitally important. Combining theological training, many years of legal experience, and authentically evangelical convictions, Matt Martens is just the person to write it. In part 1 he provides a biblical framework that connects criminal justice with Christian love in light of just war reasoning. In part 2 this framework helps us to appreciate certain features of America's criminal justice system while identifying an urgent need for reform. As a result, this book will make us better citizens of both Christ's kingdom and our earthly cities."

Daniel J. Treier, Gunther H. Knoedler Professor of Theology, Wheaton College; author, *Introducing Evangelical Theology*

"In a climate in which so many of our positions and policies on matters of criminal law and social justice are driven by party and politics, we need more of the biblical insights and applications Matt Martens offers in this book. *Reforming Criminal Justice* is a rich resource of wisdom, experience, and knowledge that will serve the church and our nation."

Karen Swallow Prior, author, *The Evangelical Imagination: How Stories, Images, and Metaphors Created a Culture in Crisis*

"This extraordinary work embraces three or four books in one, all beautifully and clearly written, deeply researched, and organically knit together. Its gift to readers includes the profound framework author Matt Martens builds to examine the Christian requirements of justice and 'social justice' and his subsequent use of that framework to explore America's criminal justice system. This would be an ideal book for a season-long study by an adult Sunday school class or a community reading group. Matt Martens guides readers step-by-step through his thinking, often sharing vivid personal vignettes in a confessional voice. Yet the depth of his scholarship is remarkable; he's at home not only in the Gospels, the Pauline Letters, and the Old Testament Scriptures but also in the writings of Augustine, Thomas Aquinas, John Calvin, Martin Luther, Reinhold Niebuhr, and Martin Luther King Jr.—learning he wears lightly but employs deftly to support his most important conclusions. A work of love and grace."

John Charles Boger, Former Dean and Professor of Law, The University of North Carolina at Chapel Hill School of Law

"Drawing on his mastery of law and theology, Matt Martens has crafted a marvelous theory of criminal justice. His major theses—that the gospel demands social justice and that justice is grounded in love—originate in insightful biblical exegesis supported by historical theology and generate solid legal principles. While some will quibble at points, every reader, from the responsible voter to the professional magistrate, will feel profoundly compelled to love more tangibly. For this ameliorating service to our image-bearing neighbors, victims and criminals alike, we all stand in Martens's debt."

Malcolm B. Yarnell III, Research Professor of Theology, Southwestern Baptist Theological Seminary; Teaching Pastor, Lakeside Baptist Church, Granbury, Texas; author, *The Formation of Christian Doctrine*

"Martens is a practicing attorney with experience as a prosecutor and as a defense attorney. In this book, he argues that justice must be rooted in love and mercy. He lays out a compelling case for the need to reexamine the reality of injustice in the American justice system. The system is broken and in need of repair. The evidence he presents is compelling. The argument he makes is convincing. The case he makes is compassionate. It is hard to imagine anyone reading this book and not being angered, saddened, and motivated to act for justice. Love demands it."

Glenn R. Kreider, Professor of Theological Studies, Dallas Theological Seminary

"Everywhere, criminal justice reform continues unabated, higgledy-piggledy. Usually animated by a cliche ('defund the police'), it is unintelligible. What is required is a return to first principles. That is Martens's project—from a Christian perspective. Mercifully, he does it in a single volume written in a way that is not sectarian but more general; its appeal, in fact, should be universal."

G. Robert Blakey, William J. and Dorothy K. O'Neill Professor of Law Emeritus, Notre Dame Law School

"Matt Martens's book represents careful research and is an excellent primer on the biblical view of justice. I found the claim that true justice is love in action particularly insightful and well argued. Martens explains well the biblical view of justice, comparing and contrasting it with current practices in the United States. We know these matters are complicated and lack easy answers, but Martens's research helps us chart a way forward as we consider what it means to enact justice in the United States."

Thomas R. Schreiner, James Buchanan Harrison Professor of New Testament Interpretation, The Southern Baptist Theological Seminary

"Matt Martens shows great courage, as well as biblical and legal depth, in tackling the controversial and sometimes toxic subject of criminal justice in the United States. The research is meticulous, the historical perspectives helpful, and the impact of his sweeping presentation convicting! This book can't be ignored by those in the political and legal worlds or by anyone else who cares for a just society."

John H. Munro, Pastor, Calvary Church, Charlotte, North Carolina

Reforming Criminal Justice

Reforming Criminal Justice

A Christian Proposal

Matthew T. Martens

WHEATON, ILLINOIS

Reforming Criminal Justice: A Christian Proposal

© 2023 by Matthew T. Martens

Published by Crossway
    1300 Crescent Street
    Wheaton, Illinois 60187

Cover design: Spencer Fuller, Faceout Studio

First printing 2023

Printed in the United States of America

Hardcover ISBN: 978-1-4335-8182-3
ePub ISBN: 978-1-4335-8185-4
PDF ISBN: 978-1-4335-8183-0
Mobipocket ISBN: 978-1-4335-8184-7

Library of Congress Cataloging-in-Publication Data

Names: Martens, Matthew T., 1972- author.
Title: Reforming criminal justice : a Chrisitian proposal / Matthew T. Martens.
Description: Wheaton, Illinois : Crossway, [2023] | Includes bibliographical references and index.
Identifiers: LCCN 2022026015 (print) | LCCN 2022026016 (ebook) | ISBN 9781433581823 (hardcover) | ISBN 9781433581830 (pdf) | ISBN 9781433581854 (epub)
Subjects: LCSH: Christianity and justice. | Love—Religious aspects—Christianity. | Criminal justice, Administration of—United States.
Classification: LCC BR115.J8 M3845 2023 (print) | LCC BR115.J8 (ebook) | DDC 261.8—dc23/eng/20230211
LC record available at https://lccn.loc.gov/2022026015
LC ebook record available at https://lccn.loc.gov/2022026016

Crossway is a publishing ministry of Good News Publishers.

LB		32	31	30	29	28	27	26	25	24	23
15	14	13	12	11	10	9	8	7	6	5	4	3	2	1

For my children,
may they know the one who does justly,
loves mercy, and walked humbly for our salvation

Contents

Foreword

WOULD YOU IMAGINE SOMETHING WITH ME for a moment? Here's the setting. You and your four closest friends are on a boat: it's not a Tiger Woods yacht, but after twenty years in corporate America as an executive, you were able to buy your dream boat. You're enjoying the ocean off the Florida Keys, still laughing at the same jokes you told one another in college. The storytelling has now stretched from fact to fiction. The only thing better than the surf-and-turf dining is the deepening of your friendships. Jay is cancer free now. Alex is finally married to Gabby. Jacob is still a serial entrepreneur looking to start the next big thing. Craig is six years sober. At this stage of life, you realize that peace and love are what matter most. You're just happy to be with your friends.

As the sun begins to set, the winds pick up, and the seas get choppy. According to the weather report, all you should have expected was sunshine and smooth sailing. But seemingly out of nowhere, clear, blue skies fade into angry, dark rain clouds that start pouring buckets. The calm seas become rough, and your fun turns into fear. Dense fog rolls in, covering the seas. You feel lost. You can't see land. Your anxiety levels are spiking now. Intrusive thoughts like, *We aren't going to make it back,* crowd your mind. The once laughter-filled boat is overflowing with emotional despair.

Then your wisest friend, Craig, in a calm, confident, clear voice says, "Bros, look up to the lighthouse! The lighthouse will guide us home." One by one, instead of looking at the rough seas and fog, you look to the light. The more you look to the lighthouse, the more hope begins to rise. Cries of fear morph into shouts of courage. The seas didn't stop being rough. The fog didn't dissipate. The wind still shouts. But the light from the lighthouse guides you home. Now you have a new story to tell.

Since the time of the ancient Egyptians, the lighthouse has served as a navigational tool that led sailors home. The book you are reading by Matthew Martens, *Reforming Criminal Justice: A Christian Proposal*, is a lighthouse that will guide you home as you sail the rough seas of reforming criminal justice. As a course-plotting tool, I want to use the acronym LIGHTHOUSE so that you will know where the adventure you are embarking on is taking you.

Love

Matthew is going to challenge you to reexamine your beliefs about love. God in Christ calls us to love our neighbors. This love is sacrificial and unconditional for the victim of a crime and for *the perpetrator of a crime*. "'Love your neighbor as yourself.' Love does no wrong to a neighbor. Love, therefore, is the fulfillment of the law" (Rom. 13:9-10 CSB).

Insights

Matthew is a lawyer. His brain is a supercomputer. In 1996, he was first in his class at the University of North Carolina School of Law. He then served in Washington, DC, as a law clerk for a federal court of appeals judge. After that, he served as a law clerk to Chief Justice William H. Rehnquist at the US Supreme Court. That's a big deal.

For nine years, he was a federal prosecutor, and for eleven years, he was a criminal defense attorney. Matthew has worked every type of criminal case you can imagine, including "capital murder, securities fraud, drug trafficking, firearms violations, child pornography, mortgage fraud, voter fraud, and public corruption."[1]

In 2010, he decided to attended Dallas Theological Seminary, where he graduated first in his class with a master's degree in biblical studies. The man knows what he is talking about legally and theologically. His insights are breathtaking. I learned so much in this book. And so will you.

Grace

To have a more just society, we need to be a more gracious society. After you read this book, your grace for people in the criminal justice system will

---

1   See https://matthew-martens.com.

increase. The criminal justice system is complex and nuanced. This book will help you become less judgmental and more compassionate. Grace tends to do that to people.

History

History is a great teacher if we'd only heed her lessons. Matthew, like a skilled tour guide, takes you on a journey of American legal history and historical theological reflection. It's quite brilliant. Of all people on earth, followers of Jesus must desire to have a kingdom-of-God perspective of criminal justice. Matthew anchors us in the kingdom of God, not Democratic or Republican politics.

Trust

Your trust is a gift that will be safe with Matthew. He doesn't have a partisan axe to grind or a political agenda to spread. His work is well researched— historically, legally, and biblically. Regardless of your politics, you are going to be challenged, stretched, and educated.

Hope

If it were not for Jesus's resurrection from the dead, and his launching of the new heaven and new earth (Rev. 21:1-4), I would not have hope. One day, all the broken pieces will be put back together again; all the hurt will be healed; all the wrongs will be made right. But until that glorious day, God's people, who are presently a new creation (2 Cor. 5:17), are to be living advertisements that bear witness to the soon-coming King. Criminal justice reform is a way that we can point the world to our King. This is a hope-filled book!

Obedience

This book is going to challenge you to do something with what you read. The last chapter, "What Can You Do?," is your call to action. As a former NFL player, I love the call to action. Matthew includes this short poem by Edward Everett Hale:

I am only one,
But still I am one.

I cannot do everything,
But still I can do something;
And because I cannot do everything
I will not refuse to do the something that I can do.

Matthew writes, "Stop thinking, 'They're animals.' Instead, think like a Christian. Remember that those accused and even those convicted are people, fellow humans made in God's image." He adds, "Stop thinking that prosecutors are above reproach. Instead, think like a Christian. Remember that Scripture speaks at length about the injustices of rulers and that accuracy demands accountability when the wrongdoer is the state."

Understanding

"Whoever is patient has great understanding, but one who is quick-tempered displays folly" (Prov. 14:29 NIV). We live in a culture of quick-temperedness. The words of this book will give you an understanding of criminal justice that will enable you to respond in a measured, patient, kind manner. To reform criminal justice requires people who are patient, wise, and loving. I believe we can be such people.

Stand

Criminal justice and all the political baggage that goes into it can cause us to stumble. Matthew helps us to stand in the kingdom of God. Read this book slowly, prayerfully, and with people you disagree with on criminal justice.

Express

Matthew writes, "My goal in writing this book is both to tell a history and to offer a hope. I have sought to recount accurately and fairly the legal history of my nation's struggle toward justice, and, against the backdrop of that history, I want to leave you with hope for justice."

I believe that he accomplishes his vision. I'm grateful for his hard work. I am a better follower of Jesus as a result of reading his book. The church I cofounded and serve as lead elder-pastor will be better as a result as well.

Hey, friends, look to the lighthouse; it will guide you home.

The LORD is my light and my salvation—
whom should I fear?
The LORD is the stronghold of my life—
whom should I dread? (Ps. 27:1 CSB)

Dr. Derwin L. Gray
COFOUNDER AND LEAD PASTOR, TRANSFORMATION CHURCH
AUTHOR, *HOW TO HEAL OUR RACIAL DIVIDE*

Acknowledgments

IT ALL BEGAN AT SWEETWATER TAVERN.

In the fall of 2014, my wife and I had dinner with Isaac Adams (one of the pastoral staff members at our church) and his wife. During that dinner, which occurred only months after the events in Ferguson, Missouri, Isaac urged me to write a book on how to think about criminal justice as a Christian. He was convinced that a book of that sort could be helpful to believers who were, in that moment, wrestling with the issues of criminal justice and policing that were roiling the nation. I said I would think about it. I did for a bit. But I was busy.

Nearly six years later, in the summer of 2020, George Floyd was murdered in Minneapolis, and, amid the national unrest that ensued, another pastor friend of mine, Garrett Kell, pushed me to write a book on criminal justice. This time, I agreed to give it a try. The turmoil gripping the country was distressing to me, and I thought that perhaps I could help in some small way. But I had no idea whether anyone would be interested in reading what I had to say, much less whether anyone would be interested in publishing it.

Garrett put me in touch with Justin Taylor at Crossway, and, to my surprise, Justin was interested in receiving a proposal about my book idea. I say "surprise" because I had no experience writing a book and no profile that would be useful in selling a book. But Justin thought the content could be edifying to the church, so he took a chance that an obscure and entirely unproven author could deliver something readable. I'm grateful for the opportunity that Crossway provided to share with others thoughts on a topic about which I am passionate.

It turns out that writing a book is hard. Like, really hard. I organized my thoughts and wrote the 140,000 words that make up this book in about ten months, all as a part-time endeavor while working my regular full-time job. This was only possible because of many other people.

First and foremost, my family tolerated my absence and endured my obsession. They have heard me talk about this book so much that there is little need for them to read it. My wife jokes that she could stand in for my speaking engagements at this point, and that's probably true. But had they not allowed me room to write and served as sounding boards with whom to ruminate, this project could never have happened.

I am also indebted to the innumerable other people who discussed my ideas, cheered me on, and read drafts of the book. My pastor, Mark Dever, read the entire manuscript and provided me detailed comments on a chapter-by-chapter basis. This was an enormous gift from one of the busiest people I know. I'll be forever grateful. Having my pastor read the manuscript was important to me because, as a Christian, I understand myself to be under the spiritual authority of my church. I write not as an individual Christian but as a member of the Christian church, guided by and subject to its teachings as understood and passed on by the community of faith. In writing this book, I've done my best to remain faithful to that teaching, and Mark's feedback was to me an important check in that regard.

Many other people also devoted precious hours of their time to reading and commenting on portions of the manuscript, including Jonathan Leeman, Kurt Meyers, John Onwuchekwa, Jaclyn Moyer, Garrett Kell, Charles Hedman, Aaron Griffith, Rachel Barkow, Glenn Kreider, Mark Vroegop, Justin Taylor, Samuel James, and my dad (Ted Martens). The entire board of elders at my church read one of the chapters, discussed it as a group, and provided helpful feedback.

Several academics who didn't know me and (most of) whom I have still never met took time to field questions I had about their written work. Daniel Strand engaged with me about Augustine's political writing. Nigel Biggar answered questions about just war theory. Seth Kotch pointed me to sources related to his writing about the death penalty. Other professors reviewed the historical analysis in chapter 9.

I was also greatly aided by a trio of research assistants. Raleigh Clay and Park Lukich (both then students at Dallas Theological Seminary) helped me with theological research. Meredith Yates (a law student at the University of North Carolina School of Law) was tireless in her legal research, locating the most obscure of sources with amazing speed.

When I began thinking about a foreword, I wanted someone who would read the book and, after doing so, believed in what I was doing. Derwin Gray has been that and more. He has been enthusiastic about this project from the outset and, despite his busy schedule, read the book before agreeing to participate. I am honored by his words and thankful for his integrity, his encouragement, and his friendship.

I am also extraordinarily grateful to my editor, Chris Cowan. He was patient when I missed deadlines (which happened more than once) and delivered a manuscript twice the length expected. His insightful edits preserved my voice, corrected my errors, and refined my thoughts. The book you have before you is what it is because a rookie author had an experienced guide.

Despite all this help, it is possible that I have erred in certain respects. If so, the errors are mine. But I trust that, in the end, the core argument of the book is true and that it will prompt a discussion on which others can expand, perhaps correct, and certainly improve. My goal in writing was that we would all better love our neighbors as ourselves. If I have contributed anything to that effort, it is only because many others have loved me as themselves.

Introduction

YOU HAVE HEARD IT SAID THAT JUSTICE DELAYED is justice denied. But I tell you that justice denied is love denied. And love denied to *either* the crime victim *or* the criminally accused is justice denied. This, I hope to persuade you, is not merely my view but also Christ's.

This book is born of recent events in the United States. Long-simmering racial tensions have been forced to the surface in the context of our criminal justice system. The series of deaths of Black children and men, often at the hands of police, some caught on video, usually by smartphones, have been streamed into living rooms across the country and even the world. The names of many of those men and boys have become part of our cultural lexicon: Trayvon Martin, Michael Brown, Eric Garner, Tamir Rice, Walter Scott, Alton Sterling, Philando Castile, Elijah McClain, Ahmaud Arbery, George Floyd, Patrick Lyoya. Their killings, and the resulting protests, have birthed slogans that provoke passion on all sides: Hands up, don't shoot. I can't breathe. Law and order. White privilege. Systemic racism. Black lives matter. Blue lives matter. All lives matter. Merely to recite these names and phrases is to invoke events and stir accompanying emotions.

If you're reading this book, I assume it's because you have some interest in the ongoing national conversation about criminal justice. Perhaps your natural tendency has been to approach issues of this sort as a political conservative or political liberal. That's not surprising, as criminal justice is commonly thought of as purely political or ideological. Maybe you've never thought about what it means to approach criminal justice from a religious perspective. Or you may have wondered what the Christian view is on the issue, but you're at a loss to discern what Scripture has to say about it. In the pages that follow, I'll try to show you that the Bible does speak to the issue of criminal justice and that the root of the biblical concept of justice is love.

I approach this issue and write this book as someone who is both seminary trained and has practiced law for more than twenty-five years. The focus of my study in seminary was historical theology, and that experience embedded in me the simple but vital truth that I am neither the first nor the smartest person ever to read the Bible. We risk serious error if we approach the Scriptures and the Christian life without a firm grasp of the teachings of believers who have come before us. I'll seek to tap the wisdom of our spiritual forebears in the pages that follow.

I'll also draw on my own experience and training as a lawyer. Most of my time as an attorney has been devoted to the practice of criminal law. I spent more than nine years as a federal prosecutor and spent slightly longer as a criminal defense attorney. As a prosecutor, I worked in various ways on numerous capital murder cases. As a defense attorney, I represented an accused murderer. I have handled virtually every type of criminal case imaginable on one or the other side of the "v." And throughout my quarter century as a lawyer, I have spent a significant amount of time thinking about what it means to practice criminal law as a Christian.

As I've watched the national conversation concerning criminal justice play out among evangelicals in recent years, I've observed two roadblocks to meaningful dialogue and charting a way forward. First, many of the loudest voices on this issue are not particularly well-informed about how the American criminal justice system operates. The resulting discussion has not been a critique, or even an analysis, of the features of the criminal justice system. Instead, the focus has been either on the system's inputs or on its outputs. By this I mean that much of the criticism of our criminal justice system has revolved around statistics about either crime or incarceration rates.

Some participants in the criminal justice discussion focus on the fact that violent crime rates in the United States are unusually high compared to western Europe. In 2020, there were an estimated 22,000 homicides in the United States, or approximately 6.5 homicides for every 100,000 people.[1]

---

1 "FBI Releases 2020 Crime Statistics," Federal Bureau of Investigation, September 27, 2021, https://www.fbi.gov/; Crime Data Explorer, Federal Bureau of Investigation, accessed April 10, 2023, https://cde.ucr.cjis.gov/LATEST/webapp/#/pages/explorer/crime/crime-trend (choosing "Homicide" under "Crime Select").

By contrast, the homicide rate that year was 1.4 in France, 1.0 in England, 0.9 in Germany, 0.6 in Spain, and 0.5 in Italy.[2] Likewise, the rates of other violent crimes (rape, robbery, aggravated assault, burglary, theft) in the United States were generally much higher than in those countries.[3] And the combined arrest rate in the United States for these crimes is only about 10 percent.[4] From statistics like these, some argue that what the United States needs is a tougher approach to crime control.

Other participants in the criminal justice conversation focus on what has come to be called "mass incarceration" and, in particular, the racial disparity of the American prison population as compared to the population at large. The United States is the world's largest jailer, as others have frequently observed, accounting for approximately 19 percent of the world's prisoners but only 4.25 percent of the world's population.[5] Even removing all drug crimes from the calculus, our country has the highest incarceration rate among Western countries by a wide margin.[6] And the percentage of Black people imprisoned in the United States is five times higher than that of White people.[7]

These jarring statistics about the justice system's input (crimes) and output (imprisonment) are certainly relevant to the conversation. More telling, in my view, are these statistics: 40 percent of murders in the United States go unsolved while, since 2000, 1,039 men and women have been exonerated of murders for which they were convicted.[8] Thousands of guilty wander free

2   "Intentional Homicide," United Nations Office on Drugs and Crime, accessed October 29, 2022, https://dataunodc.un.org/; "Homicide in England and Wales: Year Ending March 2021," Office for National Statistics, February 10, 2022, https://www.ons.gov.uk/.

3   "Violent and Sexual Crime," United Nations Office on Drugs and Crime, accessed October 29, 2022, https://dataunodc.un.org; "Corruption and Economic Crime," United Nations Office on Drugs and Crime, accessed October 29, 2022, https://dataunodc.un.org/.

4   Shima Baradaran Baughman, "How Effective Are Police? The Problem of Clearance Rates and Criminal Accountability," *Alabama Law Review* 72, no. 1 (2020): 86, https://dc.law.utah.edu/scholarship/213/.

5   Helen Fair and Roy Walmsley, *World Prison Population List*, 13th ed. (London: Institute for Crime and Justice Policy Research, 2021), 6, 17, https://www.prisonstudies.org. The authors report that, as of 2019, the United States had 2.07 million of 10.77 million worldwide prisoners.

6   Rachel Elise Barkow, *Prisoners of Politics: Breaking the Cycle of Mass Incarceration* (Cambridge, MA: Harvard University Press, 2019), 120.

7   E. Ann Carson, *Prisoners in 2019* (Bureau of Justice Statistics, October 2020), 10, https://bjs.ojp.gov/.

8   Baughman, "How Effective Are Police?," 95; "Clearance Rates," Murder Accountability Project, accessed October 1, 2022, https://www.murderdata.org; "Exonerations by State," The National

while more than a thousand were wrongly imprisoned. This suggests that something in the American criminal justice system is broken.

But these statistics cannot tell us *what* is broken. To answer that question, an analysis of the design and operation of the features, procedures, actors, and laws that make up the system is required. We need an examination of the machinery, not merely the product, of the criminal justice system. We need to understand how the system was intended to function, and we need to inspect how it is actually running. Are the justice system's outputs a by-product of a machine that has malfunctioned (or worse, has been designed to function) in an unjust way? This analysis has been largely missing from the evangelical conversation. In fact, it's been mostly missing from the secular national conversation too. Conducting the needed analysis to make a competent diagnosis requires an understanding of how the machinery of criminal justice operates and why it operates that way. What happens at the various stages of a real-life criminal prosecution? Whether the system is just can only be answered with that factual understanding.

Which brings me to a second roadblock I have observed—namely, that much of the discussion occurs without reference to a comprehensive Christian ethic of criminal justice. Rather, much of the current Christian engagement on this issue sounds more like political talking points than a biblical framework. To be sure, reference is made here and there to Scripture's teaching that we are all made in the image of God. And that is a relevant theological consideration. But it is not alone sufficient.

The criminal justice system is, by definition, state-sponsored violence. Every criminal law, even a just one, is an authorization for the state to use physical force against an image bearer if he or she fails to comply with the law's mandate. Most Christians do not believe that the Bible either forbids or condemns such violence. It is expressly sanctioned by Scripture in several passages, the most notable of which is Romans 13. This means that the sight of the criminal justice system at work, even in entirely appropriate ways, will be often violent. And viewing physical force brought to bear on another human is upsetting. What is disturbing, however, is not always unjust.

Registry of Exonerations, University of Michigan, accessed April 8, 2023, https://www.law.umich.edu/special/exoneration/Pages/Exonerations-in-the-United-States-Map.aspx.

The question that has largely gone unanswered in the dialogue concerning criminal justice reform is what biblical framework we should employ in evaluating those uses of governmental force. A few writers have offered an ethical framework for the remedial and punitive goals of the criminal justice system.[9] I have yet to come across any resource that attempts to offer a Christian ethical framework with which to evaluate the system's day-to-day operation. In the pages that follow, I will propose one.

In short, I hope to demonstrate from Scripture that justice is, most fundamentally, an issue of love. What the Bible teaches is that justice is an act of love. That which is loving is no less than that which is just. As professor Christopher Marshall, a leader in the restorative justice movement, puts it, "Love requires justice, and justice expresses love, though love is more than justice."[10] For the Christian, love is an issue of the highest order. It is foundational to the Christian ethic. Love is—or should be—of utmost importance to Christians because it is of utmost importance to Christ. The implication of Jesus's teaching is that everything about life turns on love (Matt. 22:37–40). And justice is no exception. Get love right, and you will get justice right. But you will never set the justice system straight without a proper understanding of love.

Some have objected that all this discussion about justice—social justice generally and criminal justice in particular—distracts Christians from what really matters, namely, the gospel. "Just preach the gospel," some say. But what is the gospel—the good news—if not a gracious promise and provision of justice? The best news you will ever hear is this promise from the one who sits on the throne of the universe: "Behold, I am making all things new" (Rev. 21:5). Peter encourages us

---

9   Charles Colson, *Justice That Restores* (Carol Stream, IL: Tyndale, 2001); Christopher D. Marshall, *Beyond Retribution: A New Testament Vision for Justice, Crime, and Punishment* (Grand Rapids, MI: Eerdmans, 2001); James Samuel Logan, *Good Punishment? Christian Moral Practice and U.S. Imprisonment* (Grand Rapids, MI: Eerdmans, 2008); Amy Levad, *Redeeming a Prison Society: A Liturgical and Sacramental Response to Mass Incarceration* (Minneapolis: Fortress, 2014); Howard Zehr, *The Little Book of Restorative Justice*, rev. ed. (New York: Good Books, 2015); Andrew Skotnicki, *Conversion and the Rehabilitation of the Penal System: A Theological Rereading of Criminal Justice* (New York: Oxford University Press, 2019). For a Christian ethical reflection on policing, see Tobias Winright, *Serve and Protect: Selected Essays on Just Policing* (Eugene, OR: Cascade, 2020).

10   Marshall, *Beyond Retribution*, 24.

to look forward to "new heavens and a new earth in which righteousness dwells" (2 Pet. 3:13). As Christians have confessed for centuries,
we "look for the resurrection of the dead, and the life of the world to
come."[11] In other words, the renewal for which we watch and wait with
anticipation is a world of justice. Dutch Reformed theologian Herman
Bavinck captures well the thrust of these texts: "All that is true, honorable, *just*, pure, pleasing, and commendable in the whole of creation, in
heaven and on earth, is gathered up in the future city of God—renewed,
re-created, boosted to its highest glory."[12]

The good news we proclaim as Christians is that in the re-created and
righteous world to come, in that new earth, in that world where everything
is boosted to its highest glory, all tears and pain from injustice will be "no
more . . . for the old order of things has passed away" (Rev. 21:4 NIV). The
injustice will be undone. "Everything sad is," in J. R. R. Tolkien's famous
words, "going to come untrue."[13] The unjust order of things that vexes us
now every day will be made new. And only righteousness will dwell in that
new earth.

Anglican ethicist Oliver O'Donovan rightly observes, "It is the task
of Christian eschatology to speak of the day when [divine] justice shall
supersede all other justice."[14] Our eternal hope as Christians is found in
the answer to Abraham's rhetorical question, "Shall not the Judge of all
the earth do what is just?" (Gen. 18:25). Indeed, Christ posed—and answered—that same question in his parable of the persistent widow: "Will
not God give justice to his elect, who cry to him day and night? Will he
delay long over them? I tell you, he will give justice to them speedily"
(Luke 18:7–8).

Some might respond that while our ultimate hope is a just world to
come under the only just King, we have no such promise in this present
world. And that is true. We will not see perfect justice on this side of eter-

11 "The Nicene Creed," in *Creeds, Confessions, and Catechisms: A Reader's Edition*, ed. Chad Van
Dixhoorn (Wheaton, IL: Crossway, 2022), 18.
12 Herman Bavinck, *Holy Spirit, Church, and New Creation*, vol. 4 of *Reformed Dogmatics*, ed. John
Bolt, trans. John Vriend (Grand Rapids, MI: Baker Academic, 2008), 720 (emphasis added).
13 J. R. R. Tolkien, *The Return of the King: Being the Third Part of The Lord of the Rings* (London:
Houghton Mifflin, 2001), 930.
14 Oliver O'Donovan, *Resurrection and Moral Order: An Outline for Evangelical Ethics*, 2nd ed.
(Grand Rapids, MI: Eerdmans, 1994), 75.

nity. Earthly politics have a "provisional task of bearing witness to God's justice" fully realized only in the eschaton, O'Donovan reminds us.[15] The danger, however, is that our pessimism is overactive and our eschatology is under-realized.

I think this is a particular danger for Protestants of the Reformed variety. We rightly emphasize that Christ declares us just, but we tend to underemphasize that he is making us into people who live justly as well. We fail to see that we glorify the God who is just and who has declared us just when we, as his image bearers, do justly. As more and more justified people do justly, it makes for a more just, or at least less unjust, world. Our prayer even now is that God's will for justice "be done, on earth as it is in heaven" (Matt. 6:10). As a result, "social injustice must always be denounced, even if its ultimate abolition awaits Christ's return."[16] And as we live justly in this life, we point to that day of ultimate justice in the life to come. "Our membership in the kingdom of God may be transcendent," O'Donovan writes, "but it can be gestured towards in the way we do our earthly justice."[17]

As my pastor, Mark Dever, puts it, "The gospel is the joyous declaration that God is redeeming the world through Christ."[18] *Is* redeeming. Even today. "The kingdom of heaven is at hand," Jesus proclaimed (Matt. 4:17). He thought that was good news. So do I. Each far too infrequent instance of justice in this world is, to borrow author Philip Yancey's phrasing, a "rumor of another world."[19] Every glimmer, however faint, of justice in this life is God's kingdom breaking through, a reminder that cloaked in fog, just around the bend, perfect justice is on the march. One day soon, he will dwell with us (Rev. 21:3).

And all of that is true because of love. His love. For us.

This is a book about that love and what it means for the American criminal justice system. Crime is conflict. It is a product of a fallen world. God ordained government to address that conflict, and a criminal justice system is one facet of that conflict management enterprise gifted to us by God for

---

15 O'Donovan, *Resurrection and Moral Order*, 72.

16 Craig L. Blomberg, *Neither Poverty nor Riches: A Biblical Theology of Possessions* (Downers Grove, IL: InterVarsity Press, 1999), 160.

17 Oliver O'Donovan, *The Ways of Judgment* (Grand Rapids, MI: Eerdmans, 2005), 215.

18 Mark Dever, "The Gospel," Sunday Morning Bulletin, Capitol Hill Baptist Church, January 30, 2022.

19 Philip Yancey, *Rumors of Another World* (Grand Rapids, MI: Zondervan, 2003).

our use until that day when conflict is no more. The question I set out to answer in this book is how to conform such a system to Scripture—which is to say, how to do criminal justice justly. In sum, my answer is that a criminal justice system marked by Christ's love for accused and victim alike is, in a fallen world, a crucial element of what Augustine of Hippo (AD 354–430) called the "tranquility of order" (*tranquilitas ordinis*) and President Lincoln much later called "a just and lasting peace among ourselves."[20]

The issue of race and the role it plays in the criminal justice system will be a topic occasionally discussed in the pages that follow. This is not a book about race, but race cannot be avoided in an honest conversation about criminal justice in America. Race has been a recurring theme in the history of criminal justice in the United States, so I will not shy away from this hard topic to make the discussion more comfortable.

But the failings in the American criminal justice system go well beyond race into issues of class, wealth, power, and pride. To frame the failings of the criminal justice system as primarily an issue of racism is, in my estimation, to overlook much of the injustice that plagues the system. In significant part, what drives our approach to criminal justice is fear. Politicians play on it. News media sell it. And we have acted on it. In doing so, we have built a criminal justice system based on a fear of "other" people who, we think, will never include us as the accused, much less as the convicts.

Much of the story of American criminal justice has been a story of "us versus them." In a sense, the us-versus-them approach to criminal justice has intuitive appeal. Each criminal prosecution is, after all, the People versus the Defendant. It is the "versus," however, that frames the problem. It is the "versus" that highlights the conflict that makes love for both victim and accused seem out of reach or, worse yet, unnecessary. We too often fall prey to thinking that the "versus" of criminal justice means that there is a "them," an accused, a defendant, who is unentitled to our love. That conclusion—or, perhaps, simply an unchallenged assumption—is wrong. It is unbiblical. It is unloving. It is unjust. It is sin. The story of biblical criminal justice is a

---

20 Augustine, *The City of God*, trans. Marcus Dods (Peabody, MA: Hendrickson, 2009), 624 (19.13); "Lincoln's Second Inaugural Address" (March 4, 1865), Lincoln Memorial, National Park Service, last modified April 18, 2020, https://www.nps.gov. I am grateful to Paul Miller for drawing this connection between the words of Augustine and Lincoln. Paul D. Miller, *Just War and Ordered Liberty* (New York: Cambridge University Press, 2021), 18.

story of "we." For the Christian, the defining slogan of the criminal justice system should not be "law and order" but "love your neighbor."

This book will proceed in two parts. In part 1, I propose a Christian ethic of criminal justice by which we can measure our, or any other, criminal justice system. Our just God has ordained government. And like all that God created, he ordained government for our good and to be good. The rulership for which we were created and the dominion that we were assigned by God prior to the fall were among the things that God looked on and declared "good" in Genesis 1.

Like everything, that dominion and our capacity to exercise it were marred by the fall. At the historical moment of Genesis 3, everything in creation broke. The curse of God because of our sin went all the way down to the dirt (the foundation, if you will), affecting everything between the highest and lowest points of creation, including government. But as we see throughout the pages of Scripture, God's plans are not frustrated. Government is still God's intended good for us, and he has explained to us in Scripture the principles of truly good government. What I will attempt to surface from Scripture are those principles that bear on the construction of a system of criminal justice.

In part 2, I unpack how the criminal justice system—or, more properly, systems—in America operates today. To be clear, this is not a book about policing. My focus is, consistent with my background, on the prosecution of criminal offenses, beginning with indictment and continuing through sentencing. For many Americans, their understanding of how a criminal prosecution works is the product of television and movie dramas, which bear little resemblance to reality. I want to display for you how criminal prosecutions play out. In the real world, American image bearers suffer daily injustice at the hands of lawyers, judges, and juries. And the hands dispensing that injustice are our hands as well. They operate, in a democracy, at our behest. We tend to avert our eyes while they work. I think it important to stare at what we have wrought. And in doing so, I will compare our system with the biblical principles of justice laid out in part 1.

I recognize that some readers might think this book entirely unnecessary. While I was discussing with a friend my vision for this book, he asked a question that you might have: Whatever the faults with the American system of criminal justice, isn't it the finest the world has ever known? Is there another country, past or present, that has done it better? I certainly understand the heart behind that question. But in my view, the question we should be asking is not whether anyone else has done better, but whether we can do better. We are a particular people, in a particular moment, with particular resources. We have been given a particular stewardship that no other people have been given. The question is what we are doing with it, not what other people have done with theirs. And the measure against which we will be judged as faithful or unfaithful in that stewardship is justice as God defines it. The standard is justice. Given our nation's resources—financial, scientific, technological, sociological, political, and ethical—is it within our reach to fashion a criminal justice system more in line with biblical teaching? This is the question that I intend to explore in this book.

I am grateful that you have chosen to join me in that quest.

PART 1

A CHRISTIAN ETHIC OF CRIMINAL JUSTICE

1

The Gospel and Social Justice

"I HAVE HEARD SO MANY MINISTERS SAY, 'those are social issues with which the gospel has no real concern.'" The Reverend Dr. Martin Luther King Jr. penned those words on April 16, 1963, from a jail cell in Birmingham, Alabama. He had been arrested four days earlier, on Good Friday, for his role in the economic boycotts and marches against the city's system of segregation. In his "Letter from Birmingham Jail," King lamented that, though nearly one hundred years had passed since the Civil War's end, the criminal justice system was still regularly misused to oppress Black Americans. Some, however, preferred that King stick to the gospel.[1]

Did King's critics have a valid point? Is a concern for social issues like criminal justice a distraction from the gospel? Or is justice, including social justice, in some way bound up with the true gospel? The answer to these questions depends, of course, on what one means by "social issues" and how one understands the "gospel." So, as we seek to work out a Christian understanding of criminal justice, our discussion must begin with first principles, namely, "What is the gospel?" In his letter to the Ephesians, the apostle Paul referred to "the gospel of your salvation" (Eph. 1:13). The good news, according to Paul, is that we are saved from something. This would suggest that one way to tackle the questions at the heart of the dispute between King and his antagonists is to start with a definition of our salvation.

---

1 Martin Luther King Jr., "Letter from Birmingham Jail," April 16, 1963, The University of Alabama Libraries Special Collections, accessed June 8, 2022, 15, http://purl.lib.ua.edu/181702.

Since the Reformation, Protestants have been clear in their teaching that Christ's salvific work is one of both declaring us just in our standing before God (justification) and making us just in our living toward God and with others (sanctification). The good news is that God in Christ has saved us both from sin's penalty and from sin's power. The gospel is not either/or but rather both/and. It is good news that God has "forgiven us all our trespasses, by canceling the record of debt that stood against us with its legal demands" (Col. 2:13–14). But it is no less good news that we have been raised with Christ to walk in newness of life, no longer slaves of sin (Rom. 6). None of this is novel. It is traditional Protestant doctrine.

Other books have explored what this new life looks like in various areas of social life. This book focuses on what it means to walk in newness of life when it comes to participation in a system of criminal justice. And, as will become clear in the pages that follow, we are participants in that criminal justice system, at least to the extent that we live in a democratic nation. This places on us an obligation to determine what it means to live justly and to walk righteously as a participant. *What sanctification looks like for the Christian participant in the criminal justice system is the subject of this book.*

Questions of social justice are addressed in part within a branch of Christian theology known as political theology, which seeks to answer how we should think about politics (meaning, governance) as Christians.[2] An example of political theology is just war theory, which provides a Christian framework for evaluating when and how the state may use lethal military force. Also within the realm of political theology is the theology of criminal justice, which seeks to answer when and how the state may use punitive force against its citizens. My effort here is to articulate a theology of criminal justice that Christians can use to analyze the questions concerning criminal justice that currently divide not only our nation but also our churches. In simpler terms, I want to offer a Christian ethic to guide our thinking about criminal justice issues.

But let me be clear at the outset: the framework I propose for evaluating a system of criminal justice is not only consistent with, but is grounded in,

2   Elizabeth Philips, *Political Theology: A Guide for the Perplexed* (London: T&T Cark, 2012).

my faith in the historic, orthodox Christian understanding of the gospel. As Oliver O'Donovan puts it, "Christian ethics must arise from the gospel of Jesus Christ. Otherwise, it could not be *Christian* ethics."[3] To be sure, neither an ethic of social justice generally nor criminal justice specifically is the gospel. But the true Christian gospel is for the here and now as much as it is for the hereafter. The Christian gospel is so comprehensive that it offers both forgiveness in the end and new life in the present. The gospel both declares us just before God and empowers us to live justly with others.

The Gospel as the Story of New Life

I still remember the moment. It was Thursday morning, January 10, 2008. I was working as a federal prosecutor, but the prior summer I had begun attending seminary on a part-time basis. I was in Dallas in early January for a weeklong intensive class on the doctrines of sin, man, and angels. I had never heard anyone explain the Bible like my professor, Glenn Kreider. To him the Bible was one long interconnected story.

For most of the week, I just sat silent, listening and processing. That Thursday morning, it was like a light bulb went on. And, apparently, the light bulb went on for another student as well. I was sitting in the back right of the classroom. A student on the front left raised his hand and commented, "So what you're saying is that the Bible is the story of redemption." Kreider walked over, shook his hand, and remarked, "You got it." At that moment, I got it too.[4]

The gospel is a story. The gospel is more—though not less—than a proposition or a doctrine. The gospel runs further than the "Romans Road" and is more expansive than the "Sinner's Prayer." The gospel is more than a systematic arrangement of truths about salvation. The good news, like most news, is a narrative. The gospel is the story about how a holy God, through Christ's sacrificial death and resurrection, is redeeming a world wrecked by sin, and how God has by sheer grace invited us to live in that renewed world. The gospel is the story of how, though this world is permeated by sin and all its devastating effects, God's original plan for a good creation

---

3 Oliver O'Donovan, *Resurrection and Moral Order: An Outline for Evangelical Ethics*, 2nd ed. (Grand Rapids, MI: Eerdmans, 1994), 11.

4 For more on Kreider's understanding of the story of the Bible, see Glenn R. Kreider, *God with Us* (Phillipsburg, NJ: P&R, 2014).

occupied by men and women ruling in obedience to him—living justly, you might say—will not be frustrated.

The story of the Bible, and thus the gospel, is a story of justice. It begins with God who is perfectly good and just in all that he is and all that he does. In the first two chapters of Genesis, we learn that God created a good world. It was a sinless world where all was right and just. Man and woman alike were created in God's image and given a job: to govern. "Have dominion," God instructed them (Gen. 1:28). Because man and woman were created as imagers of God, they were to exercise this dominion in a way that portrayed God's perfectly just character.

But, we are told in Genesis 3, Adam and Eve corrupted this good world through their sin. Their sin was a rebellion, an insurrection against God. The result was that their nature, the very core of who they were, became sinful (Rom. 5:12), and injustice became their way of life (Isa. 59:8). The destruction was comprehensive, passed on to their offspring and shattering all of creation. The infection of sin went all the way down to the foundation of creation (Gen. 3:17).

The result of the fall was not merely that the material world was affected by sin (though it was) but also that the moral order and coherence of creation were upended.[5] Things were and are no longer the way they were supposed to be.[6] Only a chapter later we read of history's first crime—a murder (Gen. 4:8)—followed by another killer writing a poem celebrating the murder he had committed (Gen. 4:23–24). Things, you might say, escalated quickly.

God had warned Adam that if he ate the forbidden fruit, he would die that very moment (Gen. 2:17). Death is the absence of life. And, as promised, Adam and Eve died the day they ate. They lost the good and just lives that God had created them to live. There was no going back. They were driven from the garden, east of Eden, blocked from reentry (Gen. 3:24). They would continue to exist physically, but their existence would not be life. True life—the life that God had offered them, the life in a just world—was absent from the remainder of their days on this earth. The day Adam ate he was a dead man walking.

---

5   O'Donovan, *Resurrection and Moral Order*, 31.
6   Cornelius Plantinga Jr., *Not the Way It's Supposed to Be: A Breviary of Sin* (Grand Rapids, MI: Eerdmans, 1995).

The good news, though, is that the story didn't end there. In another sense, Adam and Eve didn't die that day. Genesis 5 displays God's mercy: Adam would not die physically for more than nine hundred years (Gen. 5:5). And buried in the wreckage of Genesis 3 was a glimmer of hope, a foreshadowing that somehow this mess would be resolved. Theologians call it the *proto-evangelium*—that is, the first good news (Gen. 3:15).

In the unfolding narrative, God held out his just law with the invitation to obey and live (Deut. 5:33). This wasn't an offer of life on the condition of just living. It was a definition of life *as* just living. Ruling creation justly according to God's law would be living life as it was meant to be. Doing justly would be to experience life again as it was created. Obedience was life, and the invitation was to "choose life" (Deut. 30:19–20).

What followed instead looked more like a crime spree. Murder and rape. Kidnapping and assault. Theft and prostitution. Crooked judges and corrupt kings. The rich oppressing the poor, the widows, and the orphans. Everybody oppressing the foreigners. Injustice in the courts. Injustice in the economy. Wickedness by political and religious leaders alike. Each person did what was right in his or her own eyes (Judg. 21:25). This was no way to live. In fact, it wasn't living at all. It was death. Everything was broken.

And yet along the way, God kept offering good news. He kept holding out a way to life. He established sacrifices to make atonement for the people's sins. Sin required a sacrifice; unjust living could not go unaddressed. Yet, at the same time, God kept inviting people to "pursue justice" (Deut. 16:20 CSB), to judge in accord with God's righteous revelation. And he promised that his good plan for creation would not be frustrated forever. He assured his people of a coming day of good government ruled by a prince whose reign would be marked by unending peace (Isa. 9:6–7). He promised that this prince, whom God also called his servant, would "bring forth justice to the nations" and establish "justice in the earth" (Isa. 42:1, 4). The subjects in that servant-prince's kingdom would be just too. They would be people with new hearts (Ezek. 11:19) and with the law written on those hearts (Jer. 31:33). New hearts to give new life to the dead, and the law written on those hearts so that they could obey and live. Because obedience is life. Obedience is the good life as it was created to be.

Against that backdrop, Jesus of Nazareth stepped onto the pages of history two thousand years ago. His birth was both obscure, occurring in a stable, and yet remarkable, heralded by angels with promises of peace on earth (Luke 2:7, 13–14). When he was grown, he traveled his home country both claiming to be life (John 14:6) and offering eternal life to those who would follow him (John 3:16). Because life is what dead people need.

We tend to think of the eternal life that Christ offered as *eternal* life— that is, life enduring forever. And it is certainly true that through Jesus Christ we have hope in the resurrection of the dead, never to die again (John 11:25). But the point of eternal life is as much its quality as its duration. As the psalmist rejoiced, the new life is "fullness of joy," and it is "forevermore" (Ps. 16:11). Christ's offer of eternal life wasn't merely an offer of endless existence but an offer of never-ending life as it was meant to be. It is the good life restored. It is renewed life in a world marked by righteousness (2 Pet. 3:13). Jesus said that he came so that we could not only have life but "have it to the full" (John 10:10 NIV). The offer of life "abundantly," as some translations put it, wasn't only an offer of a lot of life (though it was that), but more importantly an offer of a new type of life. New life. Truly living again. The invitation that Christ made was not just *eternal* life, but eternal *life*.[7]

The same Jesus who made this offer supplied all that is needed for its acceptance. In his crucifixion, he paid the penalty for my disobedience. He was the final atonement, the sacrifice to end all sacrifices (Heb. 10:12). On the cross, Christ put death to death. In his resurrection, he gave life to those dead in their sins. Rightly summarizing Christ's work on the cross, the modern hymn declares, "Death is crushed to death; / life is mine to live."[8] He freed us from slavery to sin (Rom. 6:8–11). We can obey again, and by obeying, life is ours to live again (Rom. 6:22). The gospel is not a command to obey but rather a promise that God, in Christ, will remake you into someone who obeys. Eternally. Jesus, through the greatest act of love the world has ever known, graciously provided eternal *life*.

---

7   Herman Bavinck, *God and Creation*, vol. 2 of *Reformed Dogmatics*, ed. John Bolt, trans. John Vriend (Grand Rapids, MI: Baker Academic, 2004), 565, writes that "Holy Scripture . . . sums up all the blessedness associated with the doing of God's commandments in the word 'life,' eternal life."

8   "The Power of the Cross" by Keith Getty and Stuart Townend, Thankyou Music, 2005.

And the best part is that eternal *life* starts now. "The darkness is passing away," John writes, "and the true light is already shining" (1 John 2:8). The first Easter was, in the words of one biblical scholar, "the day the revolution began."⁹ The resurrection set in motion a revolt against the old order of things, an overthrow of an unjust world ruled by death. We were dead in our sins (Eph. 2:1) because a life of sin robs us of life as it was meant to be. Christ's sacrificial death paid the penalty for our sins and provided forgiveness while his resurrection made us alive now too (Rom. 6:4; Eph. 2:4–5). This new life means a new way of living, a true way of living.

As people graciously given new life, we cannot look away when confronted with the injustice around us (James 2:14–16; 1 John 3:17). We were made to image God's just rule, created to exercise dominion as extensions of his justice in this world, and, in Christ, we can do so again (Heb. 10:26; 1 John 2:3–5). To be made just through Christ's sanctifying work means that, by the work of the Holy Spirit, we live justly. Justice as God defines justice becomes our ethic, and our Spirit-fueled just living can change the world. Not entirely, not permanently, but nonetheless meaningfully. The world as experienced by others can be a more just place because we live lives of justice as followers of Jesus. The kingdom of that promised Prince of Peace is at hand (Matt. 4:17).

In another sense, however, that eternal life isn't here quite yet. The darkness is passing away, but it's not yet gone. Things still seem broken. Things *are* still broken. Injustice is still far too prevalent. My own unjust behavior still dogs me. While I can now obey and live again as God intended, the lure of death is weirdly strong (Rom. 7:21–23). The world around me constantly screams that the unjust get ahead (Ps. 73). During this life, I must fight to obey. Each day is a choice to live justly. Every day is another day of faith, another day of trusting that to follow Jesus is to live life as it was meant to be lived. For now, we walk by faith, believing that the life Christ offers is truly life even when the evidence at times seems to the contrary (2 Cor. 5:7).

And one day soon, that faith will be sight. "He shall come again, with glory," the Nicene Creed reminds us, and his "kingdom shall have no end."¹⁰ In that kingdom, we "will reign with him" (Rev. 20:6). Life again. Eternal

9   N. T. Wright, *The Day the Revolution Began* (New York: HarperOne, 2016).
10 "The Nicene Creed," in *Creeds, Confessions, and Catechisms: A Reader's Edition*, ed. Chad Van Dixhoorn (Wheaton, IL: Crossway, 2022), 18.

life. Not just unending physical existence but truly living in a world where things are completely remade as they were meant to be and where we are doing what we were created to do. All wrong will be set right. Perfect justice will prevail. Everything will be made new. The pain of injustice will pass. The broken way of things will be no more (Rev. 21:4–5).

But we are warned, God's eternal justice will come in two forms. Justice will be perfectly restored in the end for those who take hold by faith of the gracious gift of eternal life in the new earth. For those who turn from the just new world offered as a gift, however, justice of a different sort will be eternally extracted in hell. "The Lord is righteous in all his ways," the psalmist says. He "preserves all who love him, but all the wicked he will destroy" (Ps. 145:17, 20).

"The arc of the moral universe is long," King said, "but it bends toward justice."[11] He was right. The story of the Bible tells me so. That story of God's justice is a long story. It's a story still ongoing. It's a story of ultimate justice in the end. But it's also a story of true life, good life, life lived in the image of God, life lived justly, eternal *life*—that starts now. It's a story where we as Christ's followers play a part, leaving for our fellow travelers signposts of justice along the way. That story is great news. That story is the gospel.

The Gospel Promise of New Life

That the salvation proclaimed by the gospel includes our walk in newness of life is central to the New Testament's teaching. As the apostle Paul explains, Christ's resurrection secured both our justification (Rom. 4) and our sanctification (Rom. 6). By grace we have been united with Christ in his death and resurrection so that "we too might walk in newness of life" (Rom. 6:4). That resurrection freed us from sin's slavery to a life of increasing sanctification (Rom. 6:22).

Paul rejoices that we can obey again as people with new hearts (Rom. 6:17). In fact, Paul opens (Rom. 1:5) and closes (Rom. 16:26) his letter to the church at Rome with a reminder of the gospel's point: "the obedience of faith." The apostle Peter writes similarly that we were "ransomed from the futile ways" (1 Pet. 1:18) and chosen by God "for obedience" (1 Pet. 1:2). In

11 Martin Luther King Jr., "Where Do We Go from Here?," in *A Testament of Hope: The Essential Writings of Martin Luther King, Jr.*, ed. James M. Washington (New York: HarperCollins, 1991), 252.

Peter's view, the very reason "the gospel was preached" (1 Pet. 4:6) was so that we would cease "from sin, so as to live . . . for the will of God" (4:1–2). Moses previewed this in Genesis 18:19 when he wrote of Abraham as a man "chosen . . . that he may command his children and his household after him"—that is, all true followers of Jesus (see Gal. 3:7, 29)—"to keep the way of the Lord by doing righteousness and justice."

One helpful and oft repeated formulation of salvation is that we have been saved from the penalty of sin (justification), are being saved from the power of sin (sanctification), and will be saved from the presence of sin (glorification). No one of these elements of salvation is alone the gospel; they together comprise the totality of the good news of Jesus and his kingdom.

We were, as Paul puts it, "created in Christ Jesus for good works" (Eph. 2:10). It is not the case that "created in Christ Jesus" is the gospel and "for good works" is some knock-on effect of the gospel. It's all of a piece. It is good news that because of my re-creation in Christ Jesus I am now free from sin's penalty to do good works. "Jesus arose with our freedom in hand," the song reminds us, and "that's when . . . my life began."[12] I am no longer a slave to sin, Paul says (Rom. 6:18). That's good news! It's as much the gospel that I am now free from the penalty of sin as it is that I am now free to obey. Both are products of God's grace to us in Christ. To borrow the words of another hymn writer, we need Christ's work as "a double cure" not only to save us from wrath but also to make (not only declare) us pure.[13]

The centrality of sanctification to our salvation was a major theme in the writing of John Calvin (1509–64). He argues that living justly in obedience to God is not just an outgrowth of the gospel but is part of the gospel. The "sum of the Gospel," Calvin writes, is "repentance and forgiveness of sins," explaining that by "repentance" he means "real conversion of our life unto God."[14] To Calvin, "a complete summary of the Gospel" is twofold in that "the Lord justifies his people freely, and at the same time renews them to true holiness by the sanctification of his Spirit."[15] We receive a "double

12 "Death Was Arrested," featuring Seth Condrey, by Ryan Heath Balltzglier, Brandon Coker, Adam Kersh, Paul Taylor Smith, track 2 on North Point Worship, *Nothing Ordinary*, Centricity Music, 2017.

13 Augustus Toplady, "Rock of Ages," 1763.

14 John Calvin, *Institutes of the Christian Religion*, trans. Henry Beveridge (Peabody, MA: Hendrickson, 2008), 386 (3.3.1), 388 (3.3.5).

15 Calvin, *Institutes*, 397 (3.3.19).

grace" in Christ: "Being reconciled to God through Christ's blamelessness, we may have in heaven instead of a Judge a gracious Father; and secondly, that sanctified by Christ's spirit we may cultivate blamelessness and purity of life."[16] It would "rend the gospel" to separate this justification and sanctification.[17] In sum, Calvin's teaching was that "sanctification is *salvation*, just as much as justification is *salvation*."[18]

The essence of Calvin's teaching was reaffirmed by Herman Bavinck (1854–1921), one of the great theologians of the twentieth century. Like Calvin, Bavinck understood both justification and sanctification to be "according to the principles of the gospel."[19] Sanctification, Bavinck explains, is re-creation, and this "re-creation has a specific purpose"—namely, "the good works which believers do."[20] In other words, sanctification is ethical living.[21]

This sanctification "is God's means of actualizing in forgiven sinners his original creative purpose"[22]—that is, imaging God. Having received new life, we can again reflect what God is like by pursuing (1 Tim. 6:11) and practicing (1 John 3:7) "righteousness."[23] It is God's righteousness that gives shape to the human justice that we are to mirror.[24] And as we will see in the

16 John Calvin, *Institutes of the Christian Religion*, ed. John T. McNeill, trans. Ford Lewis Battles, 2 vols. (Philadelphia: Westminster, 1960), 725 (3.11.1).
17 John Calvin, *Acts of the Council of Trent with the Antidote*, in *Tracts Relating to the Reformation*, vol. 3, trans. Henry Beveridge (Edinburgh: Calvin Translation Society, 1851), 116.
18 Jonathan H. Rainbow, "Double Grace: John Calvin's View of the Relationship of Justification and Sanctification," *Ex Audito* 5 (1989): 104; see also Cornelius P. Venema, "Calvin's Understanding of the 'Twofold Grace of God' and Contemporary Ecumenical Discussion of the Gospel," *Mid-America Journal of Theology* 18 (2007): 69–70, https://www.midamerica.edu/up loads/files/pdf/journal/venema18.pdf. More recently, John R. W. Stott likewise writes of the "two gospel promises"—namely, "forgiveness of our past" and "new life in the present through the regeneration and indwelling of the Holy Spirit." John R. W. Stott, *Christian Mission in the Modern World* (Downers Grove, IL: InterVarsity Press, 1975), 52.
19 Herman Bavinck, *Our Reasonable Faith*, trans. Henry Zylstra (Grand Rapids, MI: Eerdmans, 1956), 482.
20 Bavinck, *Our Reasonable Faith*, 479.
21 James Eglinton, "On Bavinck's Theology of Sanctification-as-Ethics," in *Sanctification: Explorations in Theology and Practice*, ed. Kelly M. Kapic (Downers Grove, IL: IVP Academic, 2014), 184.
22 Bruce Demarest, *The Cross and Salvation* (Wheaton, IL: Crossway, 1997), 385.
23 The concepts of justice and righteousness are linked in the Hebrew Old Testament. See Bavinck, *God and Creation*, 221–22. "The pervasiveness of the concept of justice in the Bible can be veiled from the English reader by the fact that the original terms most approximating justice have been frequently translated in English as 'righteousness' and 'judgment.'" *Harper's Bible Dictionary*, ed. Paul J. Achtemeier (San Francisco: Harper, 1985), 557.
24 Paul Ramsey, *Basic Christian Ethics* (Louisville: Westminster John Knox, 1950), 4–8.

THE GOSPEL AND SOCIAL JUSTICE 23

coming chapters, "the kind of holiness that reflects God's own holiness is thoroughly practical. It includes . . . integrity in judicial processes."[25]

The Old Testament law demanded just living in obedience to God's original righteous design; the good news is that God, in Christ, has both paid the penalty for our failure to live justly and has re-created us so that we can live justly as we were originally created to do as images of God's righteousness.[26] As Bavinck puts it, "We are only truly human to the extent that we display God,"[27] and that element of our humanity lost in the fall is retrieved for us through Christ's sanctifying work. God in his grace makes us alive again as the just people that he originally created and that he has again declared and called us to be. This "conversion" into renewed imagers of God is, as Sinclair Ferguson puts it, "a life-long transformation with a once-and-for all beginning."[28]

For our purposes, the key point is that our salvation is more than merely forensic; it is transformational. Or as Bavinck sums it up, "In justification, Christ is granted to us juridicially; in sanctification, ethically."[29] In Christ, we are forgiven legally *and* we are remade ethically. This is what Paul means when he says that, by the Spirit, we "are being transformed into the same image" as Christ (2 Cor. 3:18)—we are saved from the power of sin and made into a people who live according to Christ's ethic. The "gospel ethic," as the Princeton religion professor Paul Ramsey (1913–88) calls it,[30] to which we are now being conformed is an ethic grounded in love for neighbor, an ethic by which we image the God revealed to us in the righteous (i.e., just) life of Christ.

In short, you cannot separate Christian ethics from the Christian gospel, pretending that there is a coherent way in which to discuss the latter without including the former. "Excluding sanctification (and its fruit in a

---

25 Christopher J. H. Wright, *Old Testament Ethics for the People of God* (Downers Grove, IL: IVP Academic, 2004), 39.

26 Bavinck, *God and Creation*, 532, observes that, "underlying Ephesians 4:24 and Colossians 3:10 . . . is the idea that humankind was originally created in God's image and in the re-creation is renewed on that model."

27 Herman Bavinck, *Created, Fallen, and Converted Humanity*, vol. 1 of *Reformed Ethics*, ed. John Bolt (Grand Rapids, MI: Baker Academic, 2019), 40.

28 Sinclair B. Ferguson, *Let's Study Ephesians* (Edinburgh: Banner of Truth, 2005), 142.

29 Herman Bavinck, *Holy Spirit, Church, and New Creation*, vol. 4 of *Reformed Dogmatics*, ed. John Bolt, trans. John Vriend (Grand Rapids, MI: Baker Academic, 2008), 244.

30 Ramsey, *Basic Christian Ethics*, 185.

life of justice) from the gospel would be to 'rend Christ asunder,' as Calvin says."[31] We cannot call people to the only true gospel without calling them to obey God. As the old hymn puts it, "Trust and obey, for there's no other way."[32] There is, in fact, no biblical way to trust God that does not include obedience to him through ethical living.

But—and this is the critical point for answering both King's critics and those who today wish to treat talk of justice as a distraction from the gospel—we cannot call people to obey God without telling them what obedience is. We cannot tell people what obedience is without explaining to them that it includes doing justly (Mic. 6:8). And what it means to do justly requires a definition. Justice—including just living—is definitional to the gospel. Just living does not save us, but just living in obedience to God and in the image of his Son is to what we are saved (Eph. 2:8–10).

The Gospel and Justice

Where things get sticky for some Christians is when the just living to which we are called by the gospel is referred to as "social justice." I understand the discomfort because the term "social justice" has been co-opted today by progressive politics and thus carries ideological baggage.[33]

At the same time, no less an evangelical than the Anglican pastor John R. W. Stott (1921–2011) insisted that "the community of the cross should concern itself with social justice."[34] Elsewhere he explains that Christians should be concerned with "the quest for better social structures in which peace, dignity, freedom, and justice are secured for all."[35] Decades ago, Baptist minister Carl F. H. Henry (1913–2003) was writing about "social injustice," "structural evil," and "institutional sin."[36] More recently, Presbyterian pastor Timothy Keller has explained

31 J. Todd Billings, *Union with Christ: Reframing Theology and Ministry for the Church* (Grand Rapids, MI: Baker Academic, 2011), 117.
32 John H. Sammis, "Trust and Obey," 1887.
33 To take one example, the right to elective abortion is claimed by some on the political left to be a matter of "social justice."
34 John R. W. Stott, *The Cross of Christ* (Downers Grove, IL: InterVarsity Press, 1986), 285.
35 Stott, *Christian Mission in the Modern World*, 30.
36 Carl F. H. Henry, *A Plea for Evangelical Demonstration* (Grand Rapids, MI: Baker, 1971), 14; "Interview with Carl F. H. Henry: A Summons to Justice," *Christianity Today* 36, no. 8, July 20, 1992, 40, https://www.christianitytoday.com/; Carl F. H. Henry, "Perspective for Social

that the meaning of the two Old Testament terms for justice, when used together, is best captured by the English expression "social justice."[37] And the term "social justice" has been part of the official teaching of the Roman Catholic Church since at least 1931 and appears in Catholic writing a century earlier than that.[38] The language of social justice is not a twenty-first-century addition to Christianity.

What is important, however, is to define our terms. When I use the term "social justice," I mean nothing more than justice in the structuring of a society.[39] I am referring to the design of a society in a way that treats all its members justly. A society is a group of people who live together in some ordered way.[40] That ordering may be the result of laws, or it may simply be the result of social customs. In either event, some sort of "rules" govern how a group of people live and interact with one another.[41] Those rules can be just or unjust. Ambrose (ca. 339–397) believed that it was the justice (along with kindness) of those rules that "holds society together."[42] Others too have recognized "justice as a predicate of societies and of their actions

Action (Part II)," *Christianity Today* 3, no. 9, February 2, 1959, 14, https://www.christianity today.com/.

37 Timothy Keller, *Generous Justice: How God's Grace Makes Us Just* (New York: Viking, 2010), 14. Two Southern Baptist professors have made a similar observation: "Normally, in prose, when the words 'justice' and 'righteousness' are coordinated, they form a single concept or idea: social justice." Peter J. Gentry and Stephen J. Wellum, *God's Kingdom through God's Covenants* (Wheaton, IL: Crossway 2015), 124. Anglican Old Testament scholar Christopher Wright is of the same view. Wright, *Old Testament Ethics for the People of God*, 257.

38 Pius XI, *Quadragesimo Anno* [Encyclical Letter on Reconstruction of the Social Order] May 15, 1931, sec 57, http://www.vatican.va. It is believed that the term "social justice" was coined in 1837 in the writings of Antonio Rosmini Serbanti, an Italian Roman Catholic priest and philosopher. Robert P. Kraynak, "The Origins of 'Social Justice' in the National Law Philosophy of Antonio Rosmini," *The Review of Politics* 80, no. 1 (Winter 2018): 6, https://doi.org/10.1017 /S0034670517000754.

39 This is a typical definition of "social justice." See, e.g., Brian Matz, *Introducing Protestant Social Ethics: Foundations in Scripture, History, and Practice* (Grand Rapids, MI: Baker Academic, 2017), 184; John Rawls, *A Theory of Justice*, rev. ed. (Cambridge, MA: Harvard University Press, 1999), 6, 47.

40 This is both the dictionary definition and the standard conception of a society used by sociologists. Georg Simmel, *Sociology: Inquiries into the Construction of Social Norms*, vol. 1, trans. and ed. Anthony J. Blasi, Anton K. Jacobs, and Mathew Kanjirathinkal (Boston: Brill, 2009).

41 Bavinck, *God and Creation*, 568–69, writes that "all social cooperation . . . is ultimately grounded in a covenant, that is, in reciprocal fidelity and an assortment of generally recognized moral obligations."

42 Ambrose, *De Officiis Ministrorum*, vol. 1, ed. and trans. Ivor J. Davidson (Oxford: Oxford University Press, 2002), 130 (1.28).

and institutions."[43] By using the term "social justice," I am referring to an ordering of society based on rules that are just as God defines justice. A socially just world is the good world that God created in the garden, and it is the just world that God will renew in the end. And a more socially just world is one for which we as believers must, in obedience to God, strive even now.

Justice occurs in a society when people in that society live justly, whether in their individual or collective endeavors. A society's justness can be furthered or hindered by its laws, by its institutions, by its culture, and by individual behavior. When our government leaders enact or enforce good laws, they create a more just society for us all. Bad laws do the opposite. When businesses treat their employees fairly, when schools teach their students truth, when legislatures forbid murder, and when homeless shelters provide housing for the poor, these institutions make our society more just. Bad businesses, schools, legislatures, and charities can have the opposite effect. When we as a community observe certain moral traditions or conventions, we together can make our society a just one. Different moral traditions and conventions can make society unjust. And my daily obedience to God's law can bring justice to those in my circle of influence. Or my disobedience can work injustice. The same is true of you. Both in our individual and collective work, we decide each day whether we will heed the gospel and its offer of new life and walk by faith in Christ's promise that the just life is *life*.[44]

In a sense, all justice is social because all justice is an issue of our actions toward others. But in using the term "social justice" in this book, I am focused on justice in the structure of a society. Christian philosopher Nicholas Wolterstorff likewise distinguishes between "social justice" and "justice in personal relationships."[45] My country's laws prohibit robbery. In that limited respect at least, the legal structure is just. If I were to rob you at gunpoint in violation of the law, it would be an act of injustice,

---

43 Gene Outka, *Agape: An Ethical Analysis* (New Haven, CT: Yale University Press, 1972), 75.

44 As British theologian Lesslie Newbigin (1909–98) puts it, Christian discipleship requires that we "challenge the assumptions which govern the world of politics, economics, education, and culture." Lesslie Newbigin, *The Gospel in a Pluralist Society* (Grand Rapids, MI: Eerdmans, 1989), 220.

45 Nicholas Wolterstorff, *Justice in Love* (Grand Rapids, MI: Eerdmans, 2015), 70. Others have drawn a similar distinction. See Outka, *Agape*, 75, who distinguishes "social justice" from "commutative justice (involving rights between two individuals)."

but that type of injustice isn't a structural one. Rather, I would be acting in violation of the just legal structure governing my society. By contrast, there was a time when my country's laws permitted chattel slavery. Slavery is an injustice for a number of reasons, including that it allows the theft of another person's labor. The laws of my country that legalized slavery created a structural injustice. Those laws organized society in a way such that people could lawfully commit unjust acts without fear of legal sanction. This is what I'm referring to when I use the terms "social justice" or "social injustice."

The prophet Isaiah warned against this type of social or structural injustice when he pronounced woe on those who "make unjust laws" (Isa. 10:1 NIV). In other words, the leaders denounced by Isaiah were "mak[ing] their exploitative practices technically legal."[46] The psalmist too denounced as wicked those rulers who "frame injustice by statute" (Ps. 94:20) and prayed for God to instead "give the king your justice" so that he would rule with such (Ps. 72:1–2). Solomon similarly acknowledged that by divine wisdom "rulers decree what is just" (Prov. 8:15), implying that a ruler's decrees can conversely decree injustice. Even when laws are just, those laws can go unenforced and thus allow injustice to flourish. The prophet Jeremiah warned against this type of structural injustice when he admonished the king of Judah to "do justice" by "deliver[ing] from the hand of the oppressor him who has been robbed" (Jer. 22:3).

The Enlightenment philosopher Jean-Jacques Rousseau (1712–78) maintained that people are naturally good but become corrupted by society's institutions.[47] Scripture teaches otherwise. We are sinners, and we corrupt society's institutions.[48] Unjust laws don't spring from the ether; those laws are the result of unjust decisions by voters, legislators, governors, presidents, and judges. These actors create the legal structure. Numerous other actors fashion additional elements of a society's structure.

---

46 Wright, *Old Testament Ethics for the People of God*, 273.
47 Christopher Bertram, "Jean Jacques Rousseau," *The Stanford Encyclopedia of Philosophy*, September 27, 2010, last modified May 26, 2017, https://plato.stanford.edu/.
48 As Herman Bavinck argues, "If the ills of humanity were caused by culture, they could certainly be cured in no way other than by culture." Herman Bavinck, *Sin and Salvation in Christ*, vol. 3 of *Reformed Dogmatics*, ed. John Bolt, trans. John Vriend (Grand Rapids, MI: Baker Academic, 2006), 327. For a further discussion of the notion that we are corrupted by society, see Bavinck, *Our Reasonable Faith*, 225–28.

That structure, including its institutions, can be either just or unjust. It is this structural element of justice that, like Stott, I am attempting to capture with the term "social justice."[49] But ultimately, the point isn't the term we use. The point is that *the social structure itself—including its laws and the ways those laws are enforced—can be unjust*, as Scripture acknowledges and condemns.

In one sense, I agree with those who claim that the way to true social justice is through the gospel. But that is true because people coming to trust and follow Christ will do justly not only in an individual one-on-one sense, but also in how they contribute to the structuring of the societies in which they live. They will walk in newness of life. As God sanctifies me, I will live more justly, not only by refusing to rob people at gunpoint but also by refusing to condone the structuring of society in a way that permits robbery. I will seek to ensure that people are given their due in myriad other respects that are affected by society's structure.

Given the democratic form of government in my country, this means that I will exercise my rights to vote, petition, and protest with an eye toward the enactment of laws that organize society in a more biblically just way. The prophet Jeremiah urged his readers, even during their exile in an unbelieving land and without the benefit of democratic means, to "seek the welfare of the city" in which they lived (Jer. 29:7). There is likewise a moral obligation on believers today to do the same, and one of the ways we can do so is through voting. I will return to this topic in chapter 3 when I discuss the idea of moral proximity. For now, it is enough to say, as Stott did, that as Christians "we cannot evade our political responsibility to share in changing the structures that inhibit development."[50]

But the way that we as Christians do justly in our social situations involves more than casting votes. Justified people should advocate for more just laws. Justified people should conduct more just prosecutions (cf. Luke 3:14). Justified people should render more just verdicts. Justified people should impose more just sentences. Justified people should run more just prisons. Justified people should operate more just

---

49 Stott, *The Cross of Christ*, 285, referring to social injustices as "the structures that inhibit development"; Stott, *Christian Mission in the Modern World*, 30.
50 Stott, *The Cross of Christ*, 285.

businesses. Justified people should educate children about justice. Justified people should inspire us, through the arts, to pursue justice.[51] Justified people should persuade their acquaintances to act more justly.[52] Justified people should do justly. And they should do all this now. "The salvation we claim," Stott says, "should be transforming us in the totality of our personal and social responsibilities."[53] The revolution has already begun. And so we must be declaring, by word and deed, the fact that the kingdom of heaven is already at hand.

Whether or not they think of it in this way, innumerable Christians regularly live out the truth that the gospel obligates us to pursue social justice. Thousands of pro-life evangelicals, for example, pursue social justice each January when they march in Washington, DC, in support of life, calling on Congress to pass just laws protecting the unborn. These Christians rightly desire justice under law in our society, and they work to achieve it. This is the work of social justice. The Christians who march for life also build institutions that advance the cause of life. They staff adoption agencies and they volunteer at crisis pregnancy centers in

51 "Art in all its works and ways conjures up an ideal world before us, in which the discords of our existence on earth are purged in a gratifying harmony. Thus a beauty is disclosed which in this fallen world has been obscured." Bavinck, *Our Reasonable Faith*, 21.

52 "Christian citizens should use their religious freedom to publicly advocate ways for a public order that is more just, life-giving, and God-honoring." Bruce Riley Ashford and Dennis Greeson, "Modern Political Ideologies," in *Reformed Public Theology: A Global Vision for Life in the World*, ed. Matthew Kaemingk (Grand Rapids, MI: Baker Academic, 2021), 133. Professor Robert Benne has provided a useful discussion of the range of approaches that Christians have taken to implementing their religious convictions in public life. At one end of the spectrum is what he calls "the ethics of character" or an "unintentional and indirect influence." Under this approach, the organized church does not advocate in the political realm for particular policies. Rather, "religious communities are capable of forming a powerful ethos among people who participate. These people then shape the world about them, as voters and political leaders." Robert Benne, *Good and Bad Ways to Think About Religion and Politics* (Grand Rapids, MI: Eerdmans, 2010), 83.

53 John R. W. Stott, "Lausanne Occasional Paper 3: The Lausanne Covenant: An Exposition and Commentary" (Lausanne Commitee for World Evangelization, 1975), sec. 5, https://lausanne .org. See also Craig G. Bartholomew and Michael W. Goheen, *The Drama of Scripture: Finding Our Place in the Biblical Story* (Grand Rapids, MI: Baker Academic, 2004), 201: "When we grasp that the salvation of the kingdom restores the creation, and all of it, we see that witness to God's kingdom is as wide as creation. Witness will mean embodying God's renewing power in politics and citizenship, economics and business, education and scholarship, family and neighborhood, media and art, leisure and play. It is not just that we carry out evangelism in these areas. Again, this is important but not enough. It means that the way we live as citizens, consumers, students, husbands, mothers and friends witnesses to the restoring power of God."

hopes of saving unborn lives from premature death. This is the work of social justice. At the same time, many of these Christians seek daily to create a culture of life in society, speaking and writing against attitudes and actions by fellow citizens that cheapen human life. They use their skills in journalism, science, medicine, education, and law to change minds so that their fellow citizens view life in a more just way. This too is the work of social justice. And many of these people individually seek justice for the unborn, whether in their own responses to unexpected pregnancies or in their personal assistance to others facing such. All of this is the work of social justice, which is the work of obedience to God. It is work that values all human life as God values human life. It is the work of a life lived as God made life to be lived. And, as such, it is work born of the gospel.

I've never met anyone who views elective abortion as unjust and yet also believes that nothing should be done in the reordering of social institutions to bring about its end. I know of no one who says, "There is simply nothing I should do to end the injustice of abortion because, ultimately, only God can change lives through the gospel." Such a response would be confused and confusing. God has called us in the gospel to live justly, and part of that just living is using our resources—from voting to advocacy skills to financial means—to seek justice for others (Isa. 1:17). Part of our sanctification, you might say, is doing the work of social justice.

For those of us who view elective abortion as a grave injustice against the unborn, we of course hope to see more and more people come to know the truth of the gospel and to turn from their sins. But I, for one, have never thought that evangelism was alone a sufficient response to abortion. In the face of a structural injustice in our society that legalizes killing of the unborn, I as a Christian must act. Obedience to God demands it. And here is the crucial point: what is true of our obligation to live justly in response to abortion is no less true of our obligation to live justly in the many other areas in which our society is unjust.

But somewhere along the way, many conservative evangelical Christians in the United States became uncomfortable with talk of social justice. A recent online petition concerning social justice—a petition signed by thousands of evangelical Christians—declared that "the obligation to live justly in the world" is "not [a] definitional componen[t] of the gospel."[54] I appreciate the desire of the signatories to affirm and defend the Protestant doctrine of salvation by grace through faith alone, but in doing so their statement went too far and drifted into error. Christ's salvific work includes our sanctification, which the same petition affirms.[55] But what is sanctification if not Christ's conforming us to live justly in this world? A gospel that calls people to trust and obey must, of necessity, tell people that obedience means to live justly as God has defined justice. To excise from the gospel the just way of life that through Christ we can now live again is to, as Calvin said, "rend the gospel" in two.

A true and complete understanding of the gospel extends beyond a promise of forgiveness to include a promise that we are being renewed to live justly in the world. "Social justice is not," Henry argues, "simply an appendage to the evangelistic message; it is an intrinsic part of the whole, without which the preaching of the gospel is truncated."[56] The Christian gospel includes the good news that God is making us an ethical people, both in our individual and our social lives, whether within the church or without. Or as O'Donovan puts it, "A belief in Christian ethics is a belief that certain ethical and moral judgments belong to the gospel itself."[57] Just living in obedience to God is definitional to the gospel, not as an obligation extracted from us but rather as a gift conferred on us. "Command what you will," Augustine pleaded of the Lord, but "grant what you command."[58] God has commanded us to live justly, and now through God's grace in Christ he has given to us the obedience that he commanded. He has graciously freed us to *live*.

We can, like the Reformers, both deny that our obedience *merits* salvation and at the same time affirm that our obedience *is part of* the salvation (from the power of sin in our lives) that God in Christ graciously provides. Christ declares us just before God, and he enables us to truly live again by, as he demands, doing justly in our society. It's all the gospel.

54 "The Statement on Social Justice and the Gospel," sec. 6 (Gospel), accessed April 28, 2021, https://statementonsocialjustice.com.

55 "The Statement on Social Justice and the Gospel" sec. 7 (Salvation), accessed April 28, 2021, https://statementonsocialjustice.com.

56 Carl F. H. Henry, *God, Revelation, and Authority*, vol. 4 (Wheaton, IL: Crossway, 1999), 551.

57 O'Donovan, *Resurrection and Moral Order*, 12.

58 Augustine, *Confessions*, trans. Henry Chadwick (New York: Oxford University Press, 2008), 202 (10.29.40).

We need to avoid a theology of overcorrection. In medieval times, the church drifted into gospel error, claiming that our obedience merits salvation.[59] We risk overcorrecting into an error of our own, denying the truth that the obedience God graciously provides is salvation. In the early twentieth century, Walter Rauschenbush veered into a different gospel error known as the Social Gospel, claiming that the gospel consisted entirely of liberation from societal injustice.[60] We risk overcorrecting again, denying the truth that living justly in our societies is a gospel issue. We need to hold the wheel of the gospel steady, rather than veering from theological ditch to theological ditch. God's gracious provision of justice, in all its forms and manifestations, marks the center of the gospel road.

Of course, agreement that following Jesus entails a life of justice still necessitates a definition of "justice." For much of modern history, justice has been defined in a utilitarian way. Utilitarianism holds that what is moral is that which brings the greatest happiness to the greatest number of people in a society.[61] Utilitarianism defines justice based entirely on results and does so from an aggregate, rather than an individual, point of view. If an action inflicts an enormous amount of undeserved harm on a single individual but the result is an even more enormous benefit for the society as a whole, then utilitarianism would deem that action moral. In his monumental work titled *A Theory of Justice*, moral philosopher John Rawls offered a competing conception of justice. He argued that "the main idea of justice is fairness,"[62] which sounds appealing but also misses the biblical mark.

---

59 General Council of Trent: Sixth Session, canon 32, accessed July 31, 2022, http://traditional catholic.net/, states, "If anyone saith, that the good works of one that is justified are in such manner the gifts of God, as that they are not also the good merits of him that is justified; or, that the said justified, by the good works which he performs through the grace of God and the merit of Jesus Christ, . . . does not truly merit increase of grace, eternal life, and the attainment of that eternal life, . . . let him be anathema." See also Catechism of the Catholic Church, part 3, sec. 1, chap. 3, art. 2, III (Merit), 2010, accessed June 2, 2022, http://www.vatican.va, which states, "Moved by the Holy Spirit and by charity, we can then merit for ourselves and for others the graces needed for our sanctification, for the increase of grace and charity, and for the attainment of eternal life."

60 Walter Rauschenbusch, *Christianity and the Social Crisis* (New York: McMillan, 1913).

61 Norman L. Geisler, *Christian Ethics: Contemporary Issues and Options*, 2nd ed. (Grand Rapids, MI: Baker Academic, 2010), 411.

62 Rawls, *A Theory of Justice*, 3.

At the risk of getting ahead of myself, my goal here is to reclaim the biblical conception of justice as an act of love. That which is just is that which is loving, the Bible teaches. As we'll see, justice is giving people their due, and what we owe people is love (Rom. 13:8). God is love. He created a world to be ruled by humans acting in love in his image, and one day he will come again to remake the world in his image—in love. In the meantime, he has called us to image his love in a broken world. As Oxford theologian Nigel Biggar puts it, "One cannot reflect God without loving the world that God loves."[63] As we grow in sanctification, we grow in our love for the world that God loves. This is a promise of the gospel. "Love of neighbor and, consequently, justice are folded in as an essential feature of the Spirit's work of regeneration."[64] And "the life of love" is, even now, "a true participation in the restored order of creation."[65]

This calling to love applies as much to our individual lives as it does to our collective lives. We owe people love not only in our direct interactions but also in our structuring of society. We should not commit injustice by breaking the law, but we must also refrain from "mak[ing] unjust laws" (Isa. 10:1 NIV). Love requires individual and social justice. This teaching is as ancient as Augustine, who said that "both the individual just man and the community and people of the just, live by faith, which works by love, by that love with which a man loves God as God ought to be loved, and his neighbor as himself."[66] The duty to love our neighbors is God's ideal social justice. And so, what I am proposing in the pages that follow is an ethic of justice—specifically, criminal justice—premised on love.

My sense is that the resistance among some Christians to talk of "social justice" springs from a legitimate concern that much of what is today being passed off as justice is no justice at all. I share that concern. But the answer to injustice mislabeled as "social justice" is not to abandon the pursuit of social justice altogether. True social justice belongs to the church. A real social justice—accomplished imperfectly now through our sanctification and perfectly in the end through our glorification in the new earth—is a crucial purpose of the gospel.

63 Nigel Biggar, *In Defence of War* (New York: Oxford University Press, 2013), 330. Reproduced with permission of the Licensor through PLSclear.
64 Billings, *Union with Christ*, 107.
65 O'Donovan, *Resurrection and Moral Order*, 248.
66 Augustine, *The City of God against the Pagans*, ed. and trans. R. W. Dyson (New York: Cambridge University Press, 2002), 959 (19.23).

Concerns about gospels of false justice are no reason to abbreviate the true gospel, stripping it of its promise of new life, an obedient life, a just life. Instead, we should provide people with a biblical picture of social justice. Doing so is of gospel importance. We can't call people to follow Jesus if we can't tell them what obedient following looks like. You can't call others to the whole gospel if you can't tell them what God's ideal for just living in their society looks like. You yourself cannot embrace the whole gospel, repenting of your unjust acts and turning toward true justice in your daily life, if you cannot define what justice toward your fellow citizens means. What that justice looks like is a topic we will explore in the pages that follow.

In his provocatively titled book, *Heaven Is a Place on Earth*, Michael Wittmer argues that a world restored to the "flourishing" for which it was created is the good news. As he puts it, "caring for culture"—or, you might say, caring about social justice—"is not a distraction from the gospel. It is the gospel in all its fullness, a gospel that not only saves our souls but also restores the rest of us—and the rest of the world—to their original goodness. This is a compelling gospel to share—and live."[67] More than a century earlier, Bavinck said it like this: "The Gospel is a joyful tiding, not only for the individual person but also for humanity, for the family, for society, for the state, for art and science, for the entire cosmos, for the whole groaning creation."[68] That is truly joy to the world!

You cannot have a whole gospel without a vision of God's social justice.

---

67 Michael E. Wittmer, *Heaven Is a Place on Earth: Why Everything You Do Matters to God* (Grand Rapids, MI: Zondervan, 2004), 219.
68 Herman Bavinck, "The Catholicity of Christianity and the Church," trans. John Bolt, *Calvin Theological Journal* 27, no. 2 (November 1992): 224, https://bavinckinstitute.org/.

2

Criminal Justice as Social Justice

CRIMINAL JUSTICE IS AN ELEMENT of social justice. If social justice is justice in the structuring of society, the criminal law is one of many ways in which we structure society. Criminal laws put boundaries on the range of acceptable societal conduct and impose penalties on those who transgress those boundaries. The state, US Supreme Court justice Clarence Thomas has explained, "enforce[s] societal norms through criminal law."[1]

But there are a multitude of other ways in which we fashion a society, including through educational institutions, family structures, government regulatory agencies, news media, the arts, stigma and shame, and social customs. The list goes on and on. Reasonable people, including faithful Christians committed equally to biblical principles of justice, can disagree about which of these means should be used and to what degree they should be used to shape the social structure. At the same time, Christians should be united in their commitment to a just social order. And to the extent that the criminal law is used to shape a society, its use should be a just one.

Unlike other elements of social justice, criminal justice is not something we can safely outsource to the private sector, at least not in its entirety. Criminal justice is a governmental function because a central element of any criminal justice system is the authority to use physical force against wrongdoers. The criminal law sets the rules for when the government can use physical force against citizens. Because this authorized physical force

---

1 Shinn v. Ramirez, 142 S. Ct. 1718, 1731 (2022).

is an enormous power and because the abuse of that authority could result in severe harm, we generally don't delegate that authority to private parties and institutions. As Thomas Aquinas (1225–74) put it, a "private person . . . has no coercive power, such as the law should have"; rather, "this coercive power is vested in the whole people or in some public personage, to whom it belongs to inflict penalties."[2] Herman Bavinck likewise held that justice (in contrast to morality) is "the terrain of the state" and "ought to and may be maintained with violence and coercion."[3]

Whatever you believe about the competence of private charity or industry as compared to that of government generally, there are few today who would dispute that criminal justice falls within the exclusive domain of the state. In fact, a primary object of a criminal justice system is to replace individual acts of vigilante "justice" with an orderly system in which the government acts on behalf of the people as a whole to seek measured justice for the wronged.[4]

Don't miss this point: although criminal justice is one element of social justice, a criminal justice system is state-sponsored *physical force*. As a general matter, Scripture deems physical violence by one human being against another immoral. But as with any rule, there are exceptions. I noted in the last chapter that just war theory seeks to answer for Christians when lethal military force against others is morally justified. Similarly, Scripture makes clear that the government's use of physical force in response to criminal acts can be morally permissible. The key words are "can be." Knowing when Scripture authorizes the government's use of physical force against an accused or convicted criminal, and when it does not, must be answered if Christians are to, in obedience to God, do justly in the realm of criminal justice. It's to that question we now turn.

---

2   Thomas Aquinas, *Summa Theologica*, trans. Fathers of the English Dominican Province (New York: Benziger Bros, 1947), 1–2.90.3, http://www.ccel.org.

3   Herman Bavinck, *Created, Fallen, and Converted Humanity*, vol. 1 of *Reformed Ethics*, ed. John Bolt (Grand Rapids, MI: Baker Academic, 2019), 225. More recently, theologian Emil Brunner observed that "it belongs to the essence of the State that it should have the power to compel obedience." Emil Brunner, *The Divine Imperative*, trans. Olive Wyon (Philadelphia: Westminster, 1979), 445.

4   Oliver O'Donovan, *The Ways of Judgment* (Grand Rapids, MI: Eerdmans, 2005), 123, writes, "It is the task of all government to bring grievance out of the sphere of private action into the field of public judgment; and if its judicial and penal arrangements fail to do that, informal vendettas will take their place."

The Government as Physical Violence

The notion that the criminal justice system is state-sponsored physical force may come as a surprise to you. But political theorists have long recognized that the state operates by physical coercion. English philosopher Thomas Hobbes (1588–1679) argued in his book *Leviathan* that the sovereign, by the consent of the governed, has the right to use coercive force.[5] Max Weber (1864–1920), one of the fathers of modern sociology, famously said that a state "lays claim to the monopoly of legitimate physical violence within a certain territory."[6] More recently, John Rawls (1921–2002), who was perhaps the most influential moral philosopher of the twentieth century, observed that "political power is always coercive power" because "government alone has the authority to use force in upholding its laws."[7] Legal philosopher John Austin (1790–1859) is known for his command theory, which defined law as the command of the sovereign backed by sanctions.[8] Five hundred years before Austin, Aquinas similarly argued that "the notion of law contains two things: first, that it is a rule of human acts; secondly, that it has coercive power."[9]

5 Thomas Hobbes, *Leviathan: Or the Matter, Forme, and Power of a Commonwealth, Ecclesiasticall and Civill*, ed. A. R. Waller (Cambridge: Cambridge University Press, 1904), 115–19. As Nicholas Wolterstorff explains, it is not that the state has a monopoly on coercive power, but rather on "certain forms of coercive power"—namely, coercion by physical force. Nicholas Wolterstorff, *The Mighty and the Almighty: An Essay in Political Theology* (New York: Cambridge University Press, 2014), 59. Paul Ramsey similarly explains that, while "every community pursues a common good . . . the legitimate use of decisive physical power distinguishes political community from . . . other communities in the formation of the life of mankind." Paul Ramsey, *The Just War: Force and Political Responsibility* (Lanham, MD: Rowan and Littlefield, 1983), 7.

6 *Weber: Political Writings*, ed. and trans. Peter Lassman and Ronald Speirs (Cambridge: Cambridge University Press, 1994), 310. Weber further states that "the modern state can only be defined sociologically in terms of a specific means, which is peculiar to the state . . . namely physical violence" (310). O'Donovan disagrees that physical violence is foundational to the state. Rather, he argues that "the state's claim to monopolize legitimate force is secondary; it derives from the harnessing of the power to the service of right and tradition." O'Donovan, *The Ways of Judgment*, 141.

7 John Rawls, *Political Liberalism*, expanded ed. (New York: Columbia University Press, 2005), 136. For a further discussion of the notion that government is inherently physically coercive, see Jonathan Leeman, *Political Church: The Local Assembly as the Embassy of Christ's Rule* (Downers Grove, IL: IVP Academic, 2016), 60–62.

8 John Austin, *The Province of Jurisprudence Determined*, ed. Wilfred E. Rumble (Cambridge: Cambridge University Press, 1995), 117–18.

9 Aquinas, *Summa Theologica*, 1–2.96.5.

In the same vein, Herman Bavinck said that "law is not law unless it is enforced, if necessary, by coercion and punishment."[10] While philosophers debate whether Austin's command theory is a fair characterization of all types of law,[11] there is little doubt that it accurately captures how the criminal law operates. The renowned Cambridge criminologist Lawrence Sherman put it this way: "Force is the essence of criminal justice, just as the monopoly on the legitimate use of force is the essence of the nation state."[12] Every criminal law is a threat that the state will use physical force against you if you fail to do what the state demands or do something the state forbids.[13] And, at least in democracies, that threat is being leveled on behalf of and with the authorization of the citizenry. The state is threatening you with physical violence because your fellow citizens have requested—even demanded—that the state do so.

This likely is not how you think of government. The term "criminal justice system" can sanitize what a government does through the criminal law. We view trials on television or in a movie, or maybe even observe a real-life trial, and see people politely handcuffed and walked out of the courtroom after the guilty verdict is read. Rarely do we see the arrest. And even more rarely does the trial end with the convicted defendant attempting to flee the courtroom while the sheriff's deputies wrestle him to the ground. It happens. But it's rare, and when it does occur, we rarely see it. On the off chance we did see it, we would think of it as an aberration from what the criminal justice system really is. But, in fact, those seemingly rare physical altercations are vivid demonstrations of the essence of criminal justice— actual or threatened physical force.

What has been so jarring, at least about *some* of the videos of violent arrests that have captured our nation's attention, is that prior to the advent

---

10 Herman Bavinck, *God and Creation*, vol. 2 of *Reformed Dogmatics*, ed. John Bolt, trans. John Vriend (Grand Rapids, MI: Baker Academic, 2004), 228.

11 H. L. A. Hart, *The Concept of Law* (Oxford: Oxford University Press, 1962), 20–25.

12 Lawrence W. Sherman, *Ethics in Criminal Justice Education* (Hastings-on-Hudson, NY: Hastings Center, 1982), 37.

13 The Swiss theologian Emil Brunner argued that the law is not merely the power to use force but also "the power to kill." Brunner was not speaking of the death penalty, but rather that the government must ultimately be willing to use deadly force to enforce compliance with the law. "Without the will to enforce the law if necessary by killing the person who resists the authority of the State, every one who came to the point of killing could effectively evade the law." Brunner, *The Divine Imperative*, 453.

of smartphones we were largely shielded from the violent reality of criminal justice. And so it has not been obvious to us that the criminal law is not only a threat of physical violence but also the application of violent physical force to our fellow citizens. Physical force is precisely what the criminal law authorizes.

Let me try to help you visualize this more clearly. Imagine with me an individual in your home state indicted for a horrific murder. The indictment is merely an accusation that triggers the right to a trial to determine whether the accused is guilty of the charge. A trial requires, under the US Constitution, the presence of the defendant at trial.[14] Most people accused of crimes, and certainly most accused murderers, don't waltz into the local police station and surrender themselves for trial. Instead, almost every indictment is followed by an arrest. So what is an arrest?

Frequently, an arrest begins with an arrest warrant issued by a court based on a judicial finding of probable cause that the person committed the crime.[15] "Probable cause" is a fancy way of saying that there is reasonable ground for believing that the defendant committed the crime.[16] If the government presents evidence of probable cause, a judge will issue an arrest warrant. An arrest warrant is literally a court order commanding law enforcement officers to "arrest" the person and "bring" him or her before the court.[17]

In the case of *California v. Hodari D.*, the late US Supreme Court justice Antonin Scalia explained that an "arrest" occurs with either an "application of physical force" or a suspect's submission to an officer's "assertion of authority."[18] In other words, some arrests require physical force to subdue the suspect, usually because he or she resists the arrest and flees or fights back against the police officer. But other arrests don't require physical force because the suspect, for example, complies with a command to "stop" or "put your hands up" or "put your hands behind your head."

14 Hopt v. Utah, 110 U.S. 574, 579 (1884); Crosby v. United States, 506 U.S. 255, 261 (1993).
15 There are also circumstances under which a law enforcement officer is entitled to make an arrest without a warrant. Following a warrantless arrest, the suspect is promptly brought before a judicial officer who will determine whether probable cause exists.
16 Brinegar v. United States, 338 U.S. 160, 175 (1949) (defining probable cause as "a reasonable ground for belief of guilt").
17 "Arrest Warrant," United States Courts, https://www.uscourts.gov/.
18 California v. Hodari D., 499 U.S. 621, 626 (1991).

Make no mistake, however, that those seemingly nonviolent arrests occur only because the suspect knows that the assertion of authority is real. If the suspect doesn't comply with the command, then actual physical force will be brought to bear.

But the arrest is not the end of the state-sponsored physical force, actual or threatened, in the criminal justice system. The use or threat of physical force continues all the way through release from prison after the sentence is completed. Think of it this way: once the suspect is arrested, he or she will very often be held in jail until the trial occurs and, if convicted, will often be sentenced to time in prison. It is theoretically possible that, after arrest, police officers could themselves physically detain the suspect for months until trial and for years after conviction. That wouldn't be especially practical, but it would illustrate for us the reality that the criminal law is an authorization for the state to apply physical force to someone.

A jail cell serves as a stand in for the officer's use of physical force.[19] The jail cell is, in effect, the physical force applied. Metal bars and cement walls are used as a physical means to detain the suspect. If the suspect refuses to enter the cell, physical force will be applied to put him in the cell. If the suspect attempts to escape, physical force will be applied to stop him. And, as noted, the walls and bars of the cell itself are physical means to prevent the accused's movement. All of this is the application of physical force to restrain the suspect bodily. The more the suspect resists the restraint, the more physically violent force is brought to bear. Ultimately, the force used may rise to the level of deadly force even if the offense charged isn't an offense that carries the death penalty. When a state passes a criminal law, it is threatening that this physical force will be used against violators.

The criminal law's threat of physical force is seen most clearly in the phrasing of the federal criminal code. Many state criminal codes separate the definition of the crime from the potential sentence that can be imposed on someone found guilty of the offense. Federal law is different; it is written in the form of the threat that all criminal laws are. To take one example, the federal criminal statute outlawing counterfeiting reads like this: "*Whoever,*

19 For thoughts by a prisoner on how the bars of a prison represent the state's use of force against him, see Billy Neal Moore, *I Shall Not Die: Seventy-two Hours on Death Watch* (Bloomington, IN: AuthorHouse, 2005), 2.

CRIMINAL JUSTICE AS SOCIAL JUSTICE 41

with intent to defraud, falsely makes, forges, counterfeits, or alters any obligation or other security of the United States, *shall be* fined under this title or *imprisoned* not more than 20 years, or both."[20] Written this way, the threat is obvious. Whoever counterfeits securities of the United States (i.e., money) shall be punished. It's a threat.

What is less obvious is that the threat is one of physical violence because the phrase "shall be imprisoned" sanitizes the threat. But there is no doubt that the threat is one of physical force; the only way someone is imprisoned is if law enforcement officers use physical force to cram the person into the cell or, in the face of an implicit threat that force will be used, he or she submits and walks into the cell. As O'Donovan puts it, "The prisoner walks into the cell on his own two legs because the prospect of being manhandled is too painful, but his choice in the matter is limited to the means."[21] Actual or threatened physical force by the state—that's what the criminal law is.

Now, let me be clear: none of what I am describing so far is necessarily a criticism of the application of physical force by the state against either an accused or a convict. In fact, you likely believe, as do I, that these uses of physical force are justified in the case of the hypothetical murder that I asked you to imagine. But it's worth keeping in mind that the same threat of physical force is leveled for offenses much less serious than murder, which raises real questions about whether the threat is morally justified in those instances. We'll return to that topic later. For now, what I've attempted to do is simply describe a reality. As I said in the introduction to this book, we tend to be shielded from what the criminal justice system does on our behalf. A fair evaluation of that system requires that we observe and understand clearly what is occurring so that we can measure it against Scripture. And what is occurring is the use or threat of physical force.

The Morality of Government Force

The fact that the criminal law is state-sponsored physical force raises this question: When, if ever, is the state morally authorized to use physical force against people? Your initial answer might be, "Whenever a person violates

---

20 18 U.S.C. § 471 (emphasis added).
21 O'Donovan, *The Ways of Judgment*, 129.

a law of the state." That may be the (mostly) correct legal answer, but that certainly cannot be the correct moral answer, at least not for a Christian.

As a general rule, Scripture quite clearly prohibits one person from intentionally taking the life of another person, the most obvious example of this prohibition being the sixth commandment: "You shall not murder" (Ex. 20:13; see also Gen. 4:8–12; 9:6; Lev. 24:17; Num. 35:16–19; Deut. 17:8; 19:11–12). That biblical prohibition applies to people wearing police uniforms and to civilians like you and me. But as explained earlier, law enforcement will use deadly force if needed to make an arrest or subdue an escaping suspect. What is the moral authority for that use of deadly force? What, if anything, makes the killing of another human being to stop him from escaping a prison morally justifiable?

In a similar vein, Scripture generally prohibits the use of physical violence against another human being (Ex. 21:18–19; Lev. 19:16; 24:19–20; Deut. 17:8; 19:21; 27:24). This biblical prohibition applies to people wearing judicial robes too. But judges necessarily authorize the use of physical force when they issue arrest warrants. And if you refuse to submit to an attempted arrest, the police will use physical force against you. If you resist entry into your jail cell after arrest, the sheriff will use physical force to jam you into the cell. And, as discussed, the cell itself is the application of physical force to restrict your movement. If my neighbor locked me in a room for ten years, we would call that kidnapping or false imprisonment. If a police officer, prosecutor, and judge work together to use a threat of physical violence to lock me in a cell, we call it law and order. Why? What, if anything, makes the government's use of physical force morally permissible?

The answer is not found merely in the fact that the government, rather than a private citizen, applied the physical force. The government may have a monopoly on the use of physical force, but that monopoly is not without moral limits. To say that physical violence is morally justifiable simply because it is used by the government would be to say that the government is unable to act immorally. We know that's not correct. To take an extreme example, Nazi Germany used physical force—indeed, deadly force—against millions of its citizens both to arrest and then murder them in concentration camps. Those uses of physical force were not somehow rendered moral because they were committed by the German Secret State Police rather than by a random ruffian on the street. To the contrary, those already gravely immoral acts were all the more immoral because government actors committed them.

At the same time, we know that government is justified, at least in some circumstances, in the use of physical force against its citizens. The apostle Paul says as much in his letter to the Romans, where he explains that government is ordained by God to "bear the sword" on his behalf (Rom. 13:4), a clear reference to the state's use of physical force against the citizenry.[22] Swords are instruments of physical violence. They are used to kill. Paul acknowledges what I discussed earlier, namely, that government operates through physically violent coercion. And Paul tells us that this is God-ordained. Accordingly, we know that it is morally permissible for the government to, in some circumstances, use physical force against its citizens.[23]

The question for the Christian is what principle(s) should guide that use of force. In *City of God*, Augustine answers this question by posing a rhetorical question: "Justice removed, then, what are kingdoms but great bands of robbers?"[24] Stated differently, might does not make right when it comes to government.[25] Nor, for that matter, does a majority vote. Actions are not moral merely because they are performed by a sovereign state or authorized by a vote of its citizens. Augustine claimed that what distinguishes good government from bad government, what differentiates moral governance from mob violence, is justice.[26] In other words, government is not just merely because it is government. Governance (and, in particular, government's use of physical force to enforce its edicts) is moral only if it is just. Which presents the question: When, and under what circumstances,

22 I recognize that Paul was more likely thinking in terms of sovereigns and subjects than states and citizens. I don't think that distinction alters the analysis here.

23 In fairness, not all Christians agree with this. During the Reformation, Anabaptists recognized that the state operated by coercive physical force and thus their pacifist position led them to oppose not only military service but also service as government magistrates. Brian Matz, *Introducing Protestant Social Ethics: Foundations in Scripture, History, and Practice* (Grand Rapids, MI: Baker Academic, 2017), 109–10.

24 Augustine, *The City of God against the Pagans*, ed. and trans. R. W. Dyson (New York: Cambridge University Press, 2002), 147 (4.4).

25 Augustine argued against the notion that might makes right when it comes to war in *City of God*, 950 (19.21), denying the "definition" of justice as "the interest of the stronger."

26 Picking up on Augustine's reference to robbery, Pope Benedict XVI argues that "a state that . . . constructs justice only on the basis of majority opinions inherently sinks down to the level of the robber band." Joseph Ratzinger, *A Turning Point for Europe? The Church in the Modern World: Assessment and Forecast*, 2nd ed., trans. Brian McNeil (San Francisco: Ignatius, 2010), 137.

is it just for a government to use physical force against its citizens? This is the question that a Christian ethic of criminal justice must address.

Earlier, I mentioned just war theory, which dates back at least to Plato but was developed from a Christian perspective by Ambrose and Augustine and, almost a millennium later, Aquinas.[27] Perhaps its most elaborate Protestant articulation is found in the writing of Hugo Grotius (1583–1645), a Dutch political theorist and lawyer.[28] As its name suggests, just war theory seeks to answer the question of when it is just for a government to use lethal military force. It seeks to reconcile three seemingly conflicting truths:

1. Killing is morally wrong;
2. governments have a moral duty to protect their citizens from injustice; and,
3. to protect their citizens from injustice, governments sometimes need to use lethal violence.

In its effort to resolve this conundrum, just war theory addresses the circumstances under which the use of military force is justified (*jus ad bellum*) and, if justified, by what moral means a war may be fought (*jus in bello*). In other words, just war theory asks both *when* and *how* war may be conducted consistent with Christian morality.

Just war theory provides a useful analogy in fashioning a Christian ethic of criminal justice. Aquinas implied as much in his writing.[29] Gratian, a twelfth-century Italian monk who is considered the father of canon law,

---

27 Plato, *Republic*, trans. Robin Waterfield (New York: Oxford University Press, 1993), 189 (5.471); Ambrose, *De Officiis Ministrorum*, vol. 1, ed. and trans. I. J. Davidson (Oxford: Oxford University Press, 2002), 1.29.140; Augustine, *Contra Faustum Manichaeum*, in *Nicene and Post-Nicene Fathers*, First Series, vol. 4, ed. Philip Schaff (New York: Christian Literature, 1896), 22.74–77; Aquinas, *Summa Theologica*, 2–2.40.1–4. For a discussion of the origin of Christian just war theory, see Paul Ramsey, *Basic Christian Ethics* (Louisville: Westminster John Knox, 1950), 172; Paul D. Miller, *Just War and Ordered Liberty* (New York: Cambridge University Press, 2021), 18–52.

28 Hugo Grotius, *The Law of War and Peace*, trans. Francis W. Kelsey (Indianapolis, IN: Bobbs-Merrill, 1925). For more information, see Jon Miller, "Hugo Grotius," in *Stanford Encyclopedia of Philosophy*, December 16, 2005, last modified January 18, 2021, https://plato.stanford.edu.

29 "And just as it is lawful for [those who are in authority] to have recourse to the sword in defending that common weal against internal disturbancess, . . . so too, it is their business to have recourse to the sword of war in defending the common weal against external enemies." Aquinas, *Summa Theologica*, 2–2.40.1.

CRIMINAL JUSTICE AS SOCIAL JUSTICE 45

saw war as analogous to judicial activity.[30] More recently, Baptist just war theorist Paul Miller observed that "soldiers are part of the same system of justice as judges, jailers, and executioners,"[31] while Catholic ethicist Edward Malloy and Anglican ethicist Nigel Biggar have both recognized the applicability of just war theory to criminal justice.[32] A system of criminal

30 Frederick H. Russell, *The Just War in the Middle Ages* (Cambridge: Cambridge University Press, 1977), 62–63, writes, "The importance of Gratian's conflation of war and justice is that it emphasised the similarity between a judicial process and the just war. Both recourses to force were means of correcting an unjust situation: the one an ordinary procedure; the other an extraordinary measure warranted by extreme circumstances." Several Christian theologians in the sixteenth and seventeenth centuries likewise argued for a relationship between just war theory and criminal justice. Nigel Biggar, *In Defence of War* (New York: Oxford University Press, 2013), 157–58, 162.

31 Miller, *Just War and Ordered Liberty*, 32–33. Other Early English and American Baptist ministers made similar observations. Thomas Helwys, "Of Magistracy," in Joe Early Jr., *The Life and Writings of Thomas Helwys* (Macon, GA: Mercer University Press, 2009), 138; Andrew Fuller, "Christian Patriotism; or the Duty of Religious People towards Their Country," in Andrew Gunton Fuller, *The Complete Works of Andrew Fuller, with a Memoir of His Life* (London: Henry G. Bohn, 1859), 577; John Leland, "Free Thoughts on War," in *The Writings of the Late Elder John Leland*, ed. L. F. Greene (New York: G. W. Wood, 1845), 457–58.

32 Edward A. Malloy, *The Ethics of Law Enforcement and Criminal Punishment* (Washington, DC: University Press of America, 1982), 24; Biggar, *In Defence of War*, 58, writes, "The doctrine of just war . . . does not prohibit the publicly legitimate use of violent force by police or soldiers. On the other hand, it insists that lethal violence may only ever be used with the intention of securing a just peace (or reconciliation)." Reproduced with permission of the Licensor through PLSclear. In our personal correspondence, Professor Biggar said that "'just war' is a form of criminal justice" and there is a "close analogy" between just war and "the operations of police and courts." Nigel Biggar, email to author, August 6, 2022.

    Princeton religion professor Eric Gregory views the theology of criminal justice as derivative of just war theory: "Th[e] logic of the just war tradition . . . can and should be applied 'back' to domestic politics." Eric Gregory, *Politics and the Order of Love: An Augustinian Ethic of Democratic Citizenship* (Chicago: University of Chicago Press, 2008), 188. Professor Ralph Potter, of Harvard Divinity School, suggests the same, describing just war theory as a "mode of thinking for assessing the use of domestic police power." Ralph B. Potter, *War and Moral Discourse* (Richmond, VA: John Knox, 1969), 49–50. By contrast, Oliver O'Donovan understands just war theory as derivative of the theology of civil government. Oliver O'Donovan, *In Pursuit of a Christian View of War* (Bramcote, UK: Grove, 1977), 14, explaining that "the basic concept" of Augustinian just war theory "is to interpret war as an act of responsible magistracy." See also John Calvin, *Institutes of the Christian Religion*, trans. Henry Beveridge (Peabody, MA: Hendrickson, 2008), 977 (4.20.11).

    Whichever came first, they are closely related. Cf. Grotius, *The Law of War and Peace*, 18 (prolegomena), who writes, "War is directed against those who cannot be held in check by judicial processes. For judgements are efficacious against those who feel that they are too weak to resist; against those who are equally strong, or think that they are, wars are undertaken. But in order that wars may be justified, they must be carried on with not less scrupulousness than judicial processes are wont to be." Wolterstorff, *The Mighty and the Almighty*, 90, notes that the government protects the public both through the justice system and the military. Esau

justice, like the prosecution of a war, is the governmental use of physical force against other human beings. Typically, the force used by the criminal justice system is less than lethal force, but at times even it too uses deadly force. Like just war theory, a Christian theory of criminal justice seeks to reconcile the claims that

1. physical violence is morally wrong;
2. governments have a moral duty to protect their citizens from injustice; and,
3. to protect their citizens from injustice, governments sometimes need to use physical violence.

As Wolterstorff puts it, "States in our world cannot exist without exercising the police function; but exercising the police function inevitably involves doing violence and harm to others."[33] As with military force, the use of physical violence by a legal system poses two questions of justice for the Christian: *When* is that violence justified, and, if justified, *how* may it be used?

Just war theory is an apt analogy for resolving moral questions posed by a system of criminal justice because crimes, at least violent crimes, are like small wars. In a war, one group of people acting on behalf of a nation-state uses physical force against a group of people from another nation-state. The people of a nation-state that is attacked use physical violence in return, both to defend themselves and in hopes of ending the violence. Just war theory tells us when each nation-state may use physical force and the conditions under which that force may be used. Similarly, a crime occurs when one person engages in physical violence against another person. Assault, murder, robbery, and rape are examples. When that occurs, the government steps in to use physical force against the original perpetrator to defend the person

---

McCaulley, *Reading While Black: African American Biblical Interpretation as an Exercise in Hope* (Downers Grove, IL: IVP Academic, 2020), 29, argues that, with regard to Romans 13, "scholars neglect the overlapping role of soldier and police officer in ancient Rome." For an application of just war theory to policing, see Tobias Winright, *Serve and Protect: Selected Essays on Just Policing* (Eugene, OR: Cascade, 2020).

33 Wolterstorff, *The Mighty and the Almighty*, 29. Emil Brunner notes the "paradoxical nature of the State," asserting that "the State is a contradiction of the law of love." "Thus for love's sake, the possession of force by the State is necessary, although, in itself, the use of force is," Brunner maintains, "opposed to love." Brunner, *The Divine Imperative*, 445, 469. For reasons that I set forth in the pages to come, I believe that Brunner is incorrect in this respect.

attacked, to punish the attacker, and to discourage future violence. As with just war theory, a Christian theory of criminal justice needs to answer for us when the government may justly intervene with physical force of its own and in what ways it may justly do so. These are the questions that I hope to answer, or at least begin to answer. And since I'm a Christian, the teachings of Jesus are a good place to start.

Government as Love

A lawyer had a question. In Luke 10, we read that Jesus was speaking privately with his disciples when a lawyer interrupted. His inquiry wasn't a genuine one, we are told by Luke. The lawyer was not truly perplexed. Rather, he wanted to play a trick.

"Teacher," he asked, "what shall I do to inherit eternal life?" (Luke 10:25). What made this seemingly innocent question a ploy was that it was posed by a lawyer—literally, an expert in the law. His query wasn't born of ignorance of the law's requirements. He knew full well what the law demanded that one "do." He was asking the question to test whether Jesus would stumble in the answer, perhaps offering a response inconsistent with the law.

Luke reveals that the lawyer knew the answer to his own question because, when Jesus turned the quiz back on him, the lawyer quickly answered, "You shall love the Lord your God with all your heart and with all your soul and with all your strength and with all your mind, and your neighbor as yourself" (Luke 10:27). The lawyer didn't pull this answer out of thin air. His answer came from the Jewish law—the first part from Deuteronomy 6:5 and the second part from Leviticus 19:18.

What's fascinating is Christ's response: "Do this, and you will live" (Luke 10:28). Do. And you will live. In one sense, Christ was laying before the lawyer the impossibility of the law's demand if he wished to achieve eternal life by doing. Perfection was the standard. Christ doesn't invite an honest effort, a sincere attempt, or a good college try. Do—the unstated implication is *do perfectly*—and you will live (cf. Lev. 18:4–5). And because obedience will always be imperfect, obedience will never be such that it can merit eternal life.

But in another sense Christ was, by connecting doing and living, invoking the Old Testament definition of life as obedience. Obedience to God was the good life offered in the beginning, squandered in the fall, and now graciously reoffered through faith in the Son of Man. Jesus was not teaching that obedience would earn salvation. He was repeating what the story of the Old Testament had long taught: obedience is that to which we are saved. Again, this is not an offer of life on the condition of just living. It is a definition of life *as* just living.

It is unclear whether the lawyer understood the latter sense in which obedience is life. But he certainly understood the former sense of perfect obedience required. Grasping the impossibility of the law's demand, he sought to "justify himself." "Who is my neighbor?" he asked (Luke 10:29). There would need to be some narrowing of the definition of "neighbor" if he was to accomplish obedience, perfect obedience, to the law. In that day, some Jews excluded certain groups such as Samaritans, foreigners, apostates, and resident aliens from the command to love one's neighbor.[34] So perhaps the lawyer was hoping Jesus would endorse such teaching. Regardless, the lawyer knew that some redrawing of the neighborhood boundary was needed. And so he asked, "Who is my neighbor?"

We will return in the next chapter to Jesus's answer to the lawyer's second question. For now, let's pause on the lawyer's answer to his original question. He plucked two commands—love God and love neighbor—from the entire Old Testament law and deemed those two verses alone the keys to eternal life. And Jesus agreed. The command of Leviticus 19:18 to "love your neighbor as yourself" is repeated verbatim seven times in the New Testament (Matt. 19:19; 22:39; Mark 12:31; Luke 10:27; Rom. 13:9; Gal. 5:14; James 2:8). In six of those instances, we are told that the whole law is captured, in some sense, in that one small phrase. The Old Testament contains page after page of commands; the New Testament tells us that the essence of all those mandates can be captured in a sound bite.

What does any of this have to do with a Christian ethic of criminal justice? The key point is this: the Old Testament law was based on love (Matt. 22:40). Its foundation was love. Its central premise was love. All its commands—forbidding all manner of conduct and declaring penalties for offenders—were a manifestation of love. Everything about God's law was

---

34 Darrell L. Bock, *Luke 9:51–24:53*, Baker Exegetical Commentary on the New Testament (Grand Rapids, MI: Baker Academic, 1996), 1035–36; Thomas R. Schreiner, "Luke," in *ESV Expository Commentary* (Wheaton, IL: Crossway, 2021), 888.

based on love; in particular, love for God and likewise love for neighbor. To obey the law is to live life as it is meant to be lived, and the entire law is about love of God and neighbor. To live, truly live, then is to love.[35]

Every command of the law is a way to love God and neighbor alike. The details of the law are simply applications of the command to love. The command not to murder is a command to love your neighbor. The command not to steal is a command to love your neighbor. The command not to commit adultery is a command to love your neighbor and his or her spouse. Our just God's good law can be summed up in what is, in effect, one command: love God and your neighbor as yourself. God's just law embodied love for others. That's what just laws do.

Later, Paul discusses the command to "love your neighbor as yourself" in Romans 13. This passage is most frequently cited for the obligation of citizens to their government. Our governing authorities act on behalf of God, Paul tells us, and we are morally obliged to obey them (Rom. 13:1; Titus 3:1). Often overlooked in Romans 13 is that the government Paul envisions is a good government. God ordained government "for your good" (Rom. 13:4), Paul writes, echoing the good dominion that God assigned to man in Genesis 1. Government rulers are God's servants or ministers (Rom. 13:4, 6) "not [as] a terror to good conduct, but to bad" (Rom. 13:3). Peter echoes that the role of government officials is "to punish those who do evil and to praise those who do good" (1 Pet. 2:14). They are intended by God to promote what is good for our good.[36]

Both Paul and Peter, then, tell us that God ordained an institution—government—administered by men and women, many of them unregenerate, to work God's justice in this world. Government officials who act rightly are doing God's work of justice. The unavoidable implication is that individual conversion through gospel proclamation is not God's sole means of accomplishing justice in this life. Preaching the gospel and seeing people come to faith in Christ is *a* means, but not the *only* means, that God uses to promote the good and restrain the evil today. God's love is displayed as well

35 For a beautiful reflection on loving as truly living, see Matthew Myer Boulton, "Samaritan Justice: A Theology of 'Mercy' and 'Neighborhood,'" in *Doing Justice to Mercy: Religion, Law, and Criminal Justice*, ed. Jonathan Rothchild, Matthew Myer Boulton, and Kevin Jung (Charlottesville, VA: University of Virginia Press, 2007), 137–39.

36 John R. W. Stott, *The Cross of Christ* (Downers Grove, IL: InterVarsity Press, 1986), 297: "I find it extremely impressive that Paul writes of both the 'authority' and the 'ministry' of the state."

in his common grace of government. Faithfulness to Scripture requires that we affirm the God-ordained role of human legal institutions to bring about some measure of justice, however imperfect, for those who suffer wrongs. Our answer to the injustice experienced by our fellow image bearers cannot be "just preach the gospel" because God's answer is not "just preach the gospel." His answer is also a just government.

Obviously, just government is not descriptive of what government has always, or even usually, been. History is replete with examples of governments that were precisely the opposite, celebrating or perpetrating evil acts and punishing conduct that is good and honorable. What the apostle Paul is describing in Romans 13 is the ideal. Or better, it's the God-assigned "job description."[37] His reference point is good, moral government, which all too frequently is not the government we have. But that is no reason to abandon God's description of good government any more than my moral failures are reason to abandon pursuit of increasing sanctification. We should strive for God's ideal, both individually and collectively. And what Paul holds out in Romans 13 is an obligation not only of obedience by citizens to government but also an obligation of goodness by government toward its citizens. Government is intended to do good for those whom it governs.

Notice also that Paul tells his audience that a citizen who does good will receive the government's approval (Rom. 13:3). Again, this is obviously not always how government has functioned. Today, as in Paul's day, governments murder Christians for practicing their faith. Today, as in Paul's day, governments celebrate and promote acts that are wicked. What Paul is describing is neither the way things were in his time nor the way things are today, but rather the way things should be. He has in view the good, the ideal, the job description. Paul's vision for government is that its laws will give approval to the good behavior of its citizens, and then Paul reminds his audience that the good behavior of those citizens can be "summed up in this word: 'You shall love your neighbor as yourself'" (Rom. 13:9).

In other words, Paul has in mind a just government with laws that approve of the good. And what does Paul mean by "good"? Loving your neighbor as yourself. That's the sum of the law, as Jesus told us. Both the government and

---

37 Jonathan Leeman, *Authority: How Godly Rule Protects the Vulnerable, Strengthens Communities, and Promotes Human Flourishing* (Wheaton, IL: Crossway, 2023), 198.

its subjects are to be seeking the same good end—love of neighbor. This is a critical point for our purposes. Paul expects the Christians at Rome to love their neighbors as themselves. But just as importantly, Paul has in mind a government with good laws that likewise advance the love of neighbor more than self. In this just society that Paul envisions, the citizenry will have no reason to fear government. The laws will be written with love of neighbor in mind, and the citizenry will live out that love of neighbor the law demands. In this arrangement of mutual love, the government will be a threat only to those who fail to display neighborly love, not to those who exemplify that love.

Paul also includes an admonition we must not overlook if we are to rightly understand justice. He instructs the believers at Rome to "owe no one anything, except to love each other" (Rom. 13:8). In other words, love is something we owe our neighbor. We tend to think of love as a gift; Paul viewed love as an obligation. Our neighbors are entitled to our love. They have a claim on our love. Love is their right—you might even call it their civil right. It is not within our discretion to dispense and withhold our love as we see fit.

This insight is crucial to a biblical conception of just government. Augustine defined justice as "giv[ing] everyone his due."[38] This definition of justice has persisted, in Christian thought at least, for two millennia.[39] What Paul contributes to this definition of justice is the startling declaration that what our neighbors are due is our *love*. If we understand that love of neighbor is a command not an option, if we grasp that love is obligatory not voluntary, then we see that a government that embodies love for neighbor does so not merely as an act of charity but as an act of justice.

Government that acts on the principle of love for neighbor is government to which the citizenry is due as a matter of justice. A government that does less than love its citizens—all of them—is a government that is less

---

38 Augustine, *City of God*, 951 (19.21). Cf. Augustine, *On the Free Choice of the Will, On Grace and Free Choice, and Other Writings*, ed. and trans. Peter King (Cambridge: Cambridge University Press, 2010), 22: "Justice is but the virtue by which each receives his due." Aquinas defines justice similarly. Aquinas, *Summa Theologica*, 2–2.58.1. This definition of justice also appears in the writings of Aristotle. John Rawls, *A Theory of Justice*, rev. ed. (Cambridge, MA: Harvard University Press, 1999), 9.

39 Bavinck, *God and Creation*, 226, who defines justice as "the constant and perpetual desire to grant every person his or her due," quoting the *Institutes* of Justinian I, part of the sixth-century Byzantine emperor's effort to codify Roman law.

than completely just. For a government to do justice by giving its citizens their due, its decrees, its laws, its rulings, and its judgments must exemplify love for the entire body politic. So while Romans 13 certainly states our obligation as citizens to obey government authorities, the passage is also a reminder to those who have a hand in governing that they act on behalf of a good God who requires that they do justice by promoting love of neighbor. Good and just government, in other words, is government that operates on the principle of neighbor love.[40]

Augustine, Aquinas, and Calvin each confirm this understanding of government as operating on the principle of love of neighbor. In *City of God*, Augustine laid out a detailed argument for what he understood to be God's ideal for a society, contending that justice rooted in love of God and neighbor is essential.[41] He elsewhere put it more succinctly: "Justice is love . . . ruling well."[42] The essence of a just law is that it seeks the good of others—what Aquinas called the "common good."[43] Similarly, Calvin saw in Romans 13 a connection between the power of government authorities and the law of love. The requirement to obey rulers is "nothing more than what all the faithful ought to do, as demanded by the law of love," Calvin explains, because "magistrates are the guardians of peace and justice." Thus, to obey the government authorities is to love one's neighbor by furthering peace, safety, and respect of rights for all. In all of this, Calvin assumed that government authorities were "not to rule for their own interest, but for the public good."[44]

Government understood as love of neighbor points to a solution to the conundrum the believer faces when it comes to criminal justice. Scripture tells us that physical violence against fellow human beings is immoral, yet God has ordained government to use physical force (the "sword"). What

---

40   Reinhold Niebuhr argues that love is both the fulfillment and negation of justice. Perfect love is what justice requires, and yet principles of justice would be unnecessary if love were perfect. See Reinhold Niebuhr, *The Nature and Destiny of Man: A Christian Interpretation*, vol. 1 (Louisville: Westminster John Knox, 1996), 295.

41   Augustine, *City of God*, 959 (19.23).

42   Augustine, "On the Morals of the Catholic Church," in *The Works of Aurelius Augustine, Bishop of Hippo*, vol. 5, ed. Marcus Dods (Edinburgh: T&T Clark, 1872), 17 (15.25).

43   Aquinas, *Summa Theologica*, 1–2.96.4.

44   John Calvin, *Commentaries on the Epistle of Paul to the Romans*, ed. and trans. John Owen (Edinburgh: Calvin Translation Society, 1849), 481, 484, 486. Calvin elsewhere states that the duty to obey the government is not limited to those instances when the government acts justly. Calvin, *Institutes*, 984–85 (4.20.25).

Paul's teaching in Romans 13 offers is a way to reconcile this seeming conflict: the state's use of physical force can be moral when its use is both motivated *and* restrained by the principle of neighborly love. Paul's teaching in Romans 13 has in view what is, in effect, a governmental system of criminal justice that punishes wrongdoers with physical force, and Paul believes that this governmental use of physical force can be moral when used in service of neighbor-love. "That is, love motivates a concern for the innocent and vulnerable that subsequently justifies . . . state coercion on their behalf."[45] And this use of coercive force is also justified by love for the wrongdoer. Commenting on Romans 13, Augustine observes that those "who cause fear [i.e., governing authorities] are ordered to render love to those who fear [i.e., wrongdoers]" and they do so by using "fear to check the evil deeds of men."[46]

Thus, Paul envisions the criminal justice system as itself governed by the law of love. As Wolterstorff puts it, "Political authority mediates divine authority while at the same time being limited and placed under judgment by divine authority."[47] Citizens wrongfully inflict harm on others; so do government leaders. Thus, "sin must be checked in every one, ruler and ruled alike."[48] Even laws themselves, Calvin says, "are always to be tested by the rule of charity."[49] The principle of neighbor love serves as a check on government through its "boomerang effect" back against the public official.[50] Wolterstorff captures this in his summation of Romans 13:

> If God commissions government to exercise governance over the public for the purpose of executing wrath on wrongdoers, then obviously God does not authorize government to itself become a wrongdoer. . . . God does not *permit* the government to issue directives or employ forms of coercion that constitute wrongdoing on the part of the government.[51]

45 Gregory, *Politics and the Order of Love*, 188.
46 Augustine, "Letter 153," in *From Irenaeus to Grotius: A Sourcebook in Christian Political Thought*, ed. Oliver O'Donovan and Joan Lockwood O'Donovan (Grand Rapids, MI: Eerdmans, 1999), 127.
47 Wolterstorff, *The Mighty and the Almighty*, 16.
48 Ramsey, *Basic Christian Ethics*, 331.
49 Calvin, *Institutes*, 979 (4.20.15).
50 Jonathan Leeman, *How the Nations Rage: Rethinking Faith and Politics in a Divided Age* (Nashville: Thomas Nelson, 2018), 111.
51 Wolterstorff, *The Mighty and the Almighty*, 92.

Rather, both governor and citizen must act in love, and when the government fails to do so, it exceeds its moral authority notwithstanding its political power. "Christian love provides the ground for the legitimacy of resort to force. But neighbor-love simultaneously limits this force."[52] Or as the Baptist minister Isaac Backus (1724–1806) observes, the first ten verses of Romans 13 "clearly shew that the crimes which fall within the magistrate[']s jurisdiction to punish, are only such as work ill to our neighbor."[53] The good of our neighbors guides and restrains the proper reach of the government. This is the idea of social justice that I introduced in the prior chapter. Individuals can act unjustly but so can governments. In either case, the injustice is a failure of love, and the remedy in each instance is the application of love. The absence of love works injustice that only the application of love can remediate. Or as King puts it, "Justice is love correcting that which revolts against love."[54] Insufficient love of neighbor works injustice; love of neighbor requires government force to restore justice; and love of neighbor restrains government force to prevent injustice.

———

Just criminal justice, then, operates according to love. The criminal justice system, like all of government, must love our neighbors to be just because our neighbors are due our love. The Bible doesn't exempt the criminal law from this obligation of love. The law—all of it—must find its foundation in love. For the criminal law, as with all law, that which is just is no less than that which affords our neighbors the love they are owed, which means that

---

52 Gregory, *Politics and the Order of Love*, 187. Paul Ramsey likewise argues that, for the Christian, just war theory operates on the principle of love, which both requires the use of force and constrains its use: "Love for neighbors threatened by violence, by aggression, or tyranny, provided the grounds for admitting the legitimacy of the use of military force. Love for neighbors at the same time required that such force be limited." Ramsey, *The Just War*, 144–45. See also Paul Ramsey, *War and the Christian Conscience: How Shall Modern War Be Conducted Justly?* (Durham, NC: Duke University Press, 1961), 59: "Christian men felt themselves impelled out of love to justify war and by love severely to limit war."

53 Isaac Backus, *An Appeal to the Public for Religious Liberty, against the Oppressions of the Present Day* (Boston: John Boyle, 1773), 11–12. See also Isaac Backus, *An Appeal to the People of the Massachusetts State, against Arbitrary Power* (Boston: Benjamin Edes and Sons, 1780), 3.

54 Martin Luther King Jr., "Montgomery Bus Boycott," December 5, 1955, accessed June 6, 2022, https://www.digitalhistory.uh.edu.

the criminal justice system, to live up to its name, must manifest love for our neighbors as ourselves.

And, if we read Leviticus 19 carefully, we will see that the connection between love and justice was present all along. The Israelites were told not to steal (Lev. 19:11), not to testify falsely (19:12), not to withhold the wages of workers (19:13), not to do injustice in the courts (19:15), not to slander (19:16), but instead to love their neighbors as themselves (19:18). In other words, the "various ways of treating the neighbor justly are cited as examples of loving one's neighbor."[55] To love your neighbor is to do justice to your neighbor because your neighbor is owed your love.

So when it comes to criminal justice, who then are our neighbors?

---

55 Nicholas Wolterstorff, *Justice in Love* (Grand Rapids, MI: Eerdmans, 2015), 83.

3

My Neighbors

WHEN CRIMINOLOGISTS AND CRIMINAL LAW scholars debate the proper objectives of the criminal law, they typically focus on retribution, rehabilitation, deterrence, and incapacitation. Criminal justice can repay a wrong with a fitting penalty (retribution), reform an offender to a law-abiding way of life (rehabilitation), discourage future acts of lawlessness (deterrence), or prevent a perpetrator from committing future criminal acts (incapacitation). These are the purposes consistently identified as legitimate ends of a criminal justice system.

The Christian Scriptures, however, frame the purpose of a criminal justice system differently. They teach that the end of the law is love, and a legal system is just only to the extent that it is loving. To render biblical justice is to love your neighbor, and this is true not only for justice at the individual level but also at the collective level. Government acts justly only when it acts lovingly. God ordained government and authorized it to punish crime by use of physical force, but he demanded that it do so with love as its goal even when physical coercion is its means. The whole law, including the criminal law, hangs on love.

And yet, precious little is written on what it means for a criminal justice system to love. Scholars have analyzed whether criminal laws deter and how those laws could be further refined to more effectively do so. Academics have studied the types of prison programming that best rehabilitates offenders. The voting public cheers on politicians who ramp up criminal sentences to further incapacitate career criminals. And moral theorists have debated the just deserts for a given crime. Virtually nobody is talking about how the criminal justice system can love better. But Christians should be asking, and encouraging the society at large to ask, that very question. To center the criminal justice debate on any other inquiry is a recipe for injustice.

To ask how a justice system can love is actually to ask two questions. The first question is this: *How*, exactly, does a criminal justice system go about distributing neighbor love? We'll turn to specifics of the how question in subsequent chapters. For now, I want to consider the second of the two questions: *Whom* does a criminal justice system love? Or perhaps I should say, whom *should* a criminal justice system love? To rephrase the question in scriptural terminology, when it comes to criminal justice, who is my neighbor?

As we consider the "who" question in this chapter, I will draw out three points. First, thinking biblically about criminal justice requires acknowledging the presence of two neighbors in the criminal justice system—the crime victim and the criminally accused. Second, these two neighbors are in conflict with each other. It's that conflict that has brought them together in a single criminal case. One of the neighbors stands accused of harming the other. One neighbor has leveled an accusation against the other, demanding that a penalty be imposed and relief be provided. A vs. B. A winner and a loser. A conviction or an acquittal. It seems like a zero-sum game. In that situation, the idea of loving both neighbors seems impossible. Having two neighbors in conflict leads to the third point of this chapter: you will likely relate to one of those two neighbors more than the other depending on your station in life, and that positional bias can prevent you from loving well both of your criminal justice neighbors.

A Parable of Neighborly Love

In one of my favorite snippets in the Scriptures, the lawyer, after receiving from Jesus confirmation that he rightly understood the law's demand to love "your neighbor as yourself" (Luke 10:27), sought to justify himself by requesting a definition. "And who is my neighbor?" the lawyer snapped back at Jesus (Luke 10:29). He was asking, in effect, "Whom do I have to love?"

The lawyer pressed this question, we are told, in an effort to justify his stinginess of heart. He grasped the seemingly impossible demands of the law of neighbor love, and he understood himself to be on the wrong side of the law unless that law could be shrunken down to size. Loving is hard enough when it comes to family and friends. But loving my neighbor as myself? That is possible, if at all, only with a cramped definition of "neighbor." The next-door neighbor is fine. Even next door on both sides. The backyard neighbor too. But surely there must be a limit to the command to love my neighbor as myself, the lawyer hoped. This applies only to an exclusive enclave of the neighborhood, right? The lawyer was hoping that Christ's demand that he love his neighbor was not, as it seemed, a demand to love *all* of his neighbors. Certainly, loving the entire cul-de-sac would be sufficient.

In response to the lawyer's second question, one born of miserly love, Jesus told what has become perhaps his most famous story of all. He spins that story—the parable of the good Samaritan—in the most shocking of ways, touching on a deep ethnic hatred in that culture to impress on the listeners how radical the command was. This parable can, if we let it, help us untie the knot of criminal justice.

The story opens with a man about whom Christ tells us nothing. We don't know whether he was good or bad, honorable or evil, responsible or foolish. We don't know about his educational background, his occupation, his upbringing, or his social status. No details are provided that would make him especially worthy or unworthy of our love. He is whomever you want him to be—or don't want him to be. He is the person you envision as deserving of your love, and he is the person not at all deserving of your love. He is, in a sense, "everyman," representing the best and the worst of humanity. He is a typical human being, just another face in the crowd. The key attribute of this man for our purposes is his ordinariness in the fullest sense of fallen humanity's ordinariness.

Though we are told nothing about this man, we are told what happened to him. He was traveling along the road from Jerusalem to Jericho when he suffered a serious injustice—an assault and robbery. But injustice takes many forms. The particulars are not central to the point of the story. The key detail is that he was the victim of an injustice.

Into this story of injustice, Jesus introduced two additional characters. By all appearances, the two men who arrive on the scene of the crime were good and honorable: a priest and a Levite. Neither committed or contributed to the injustice the traveler suffered. They showed up after the injustice was perpetrated and stumbled on the crime scene by happenstance. When these two men spotted the victimized man in his helpless condition, they did nothing to exacerbate the injustice he had suffered. They didn't further assault him. They didn't steal his remaining money or goods as he lay battered on the side of the road. Rather, the two men simply ignored him. They left him be. They minded their own business. They passed by the aftermath of injustice in which they played no role, declining to intervene. They opted not to be, as we say today, "good Samaritans."

Jesus then tells of a third man, a Samaritan, who also happened on the scene of the injustice. The Samaritan saw what had occurred, felt compassion, and did something about it (Luke 10:33–34). It's interesting that Jesus tells us that the Samaritan felt sympathy for the victimized man. But the Samaritan didn't stop at warm feelings. He acted. He intervened. He helped. The Samaritan had done nothing to contribute to the injustice. And yet, he helped remedy the injustice. He invested his own time, money, and energy to provide whatever measure of redress he could for the injustice suffered by another.

With that, Jesus turned back to the lawyer with a question of his own: "Which of these three, do you think, proved to be a neighbor to the man who fell among the robbers?" The lawyer had asked, "Who is my neighbor?" Christ responded by asking, in effect, "Who acted as a neighbor?" As the Danish theologian Søren Kierkegaard (1813–55) observed, "Christ does not talk about knowing one's neighbor, but about one's self being a neighbor, about proving one's self a neighbor."[1] The question isn't "Who are *they*?" but "Who are *you*?" when it comes to those in need. We are called, Christ says, *to be neighbors* to those in need with whom we cross paths when it is within our means. It is what they are due from us; we have an obligation to them.[2] "Neighbourliness," Dietrich Bonhoeffer observed, "is not a quality in other people, it is simply their claim on ourselves."[3]

As we see in Jesus's parable, when we are in a position to help, it is no answer to say that we played no role in causing the wrong that gives rise to the need. To narrow the obligation to love based on our role, or lack thereof,

---

1 Søren Kierkegaard, *Works of Love*, trans. David F. Swenson and Lillian Marvin Swenson (Princeton: Princeton University Press, 1946), 19.

2 Our ability to help is, of course, constrained by our finite resources (Prov. 3:27), and our allocation of those limited resources is a question of moral proximity, discussed shortly.

3 Dietrich Bonhoeffer, *The Cost of Discipleship* (New York: Touchstone, 1995), 78.

in the injustice is to play the lawyer, circumscribing the boundaries of the neighborhood of affection. Neighborly love is not a love of culpability but a love of compassion. Whether or not we are responsible for committing the wrong does not determine whether we are responsible for remedying it. The law of love that Christ commended was more than a command to "do no harm" and, if need be, to correct the harm we cause. To love as Jesus commanded is to desire someone else's good as an end in itself.[4] Christ suggests that our obligation to love means we must fix some messes we did not cause and cure injustices for which we may not be responsible. Christian love is proactive, affirmative, and interventionist. Christian love jumps in to help.

Why is the law of love so broad? Why does it reach so far? Why is my responsibility to help not constrained by my role in perpetrating the harm? Why am I the keeper of not only my brother but also my neighbor? Jesus hints at the answer in Matthew 22 when another lawyer tested Jesus with what that lawyer too believed was a trick question: What is the greatest commandment? This time, there was no question about how to inherit eternal life. Rather, the questioner sought a ranking of obligations. What is the single greatest commandment? At first, Jesus responded somewhat predictably: "You shall love the Lord your God with all your heart and with all your soul and with all your mind. This is the great and first commandment" (Matt. 22:37–38). But then, with a twist, Jesus volunteered that "a second is like" the first. That lawyer hadn't asked for a second commandment, but Jesus offered one anyway: "Love your neighbor as yourself" (22:39).

Notice the important connection that Jesus made between the two commandments. The second was, in his rendering, "like" the first. The similarity is not only that they are both commands to love but also that, while the first commandment is to love God, the second commandment is to love the image of God—humankind. Men and women are made in God's image (Gen. 1:27–28), so loving God's image bearers is like loving God himself. We must love without regard to our definitions of worthiness because

4   Thomas Aquinas, *Summa Theologica*, trans. Fathers of the English Dominican Province (New York: Benziger Bros, 1947), 1.20.3, http://www.ccel.org, writes that "to love a thing is to will it good." See also Nicholas Wolterstorff, *Justice in Love* (Grand Rapids, MI: Eerdmans, 2015), 23; Gene Outka, *Agape: An Ethical Analysis* (New Haven, CT: Yale University Press, 1972), 8–9; Timothy Keller, *Forgive: Why Should I and How Can I?* (New York: Viking, 2022), 107.

worth is determined by God's having made others in his image. Thus, to love those in need is like loving God himself. In fact, to love others is to love the Lord himself (Matt. 25:40). Or as the disciple whom Jesus loved put it, "He who does not love his brother whom he has seen cannot love God whom he has not seen" (1 John 4:20). In short, justice understood as loving our neighbor rests on a foundation of the dignity of our neighbor as an image bearer of God.[5]

A Problem of Two Neighbors

As noted earlier, what makes criminal justice a challenging context in which to implement Christ's law of neighbor love is that the justice system necessarily involves two neighbors. But more than that, these two neighbors are in conflict. Someone has committed a wrong, and someone has been wronged. The criminal defendant and the crime victim. One wants an acquittal while the other wants a conviction.

It is this conflict that necessitates justice. "It is only because life is in conflict with life . . . that we are required carefully to define schemes of justice," the American theologian Reinhold Niebuhr (1892–1971) observes.[6] And yet, while doing justice between the two in opposition, both must be loved because each bears God's image. Love is due them both, and so to do justice to both is to love them each. As Paul Ramsey puts it, justice is "what Christian love does when confronted by two or more neighbors."[7]

To make neighbor love all the more difficult in the criminal justice context is the fact that the justice system involves not simply two neighbors in conflict but tens of thousands. The sheer enormity of the criminal justice system compounds the difficulty of delivering on our obligation to love. The "neighborhood" is so populous as to render its residents effectively invisible to us. In 2020, 1.6 million Americans were victims of

---

5 Brian Matz, *Introducing Protestant Social Ethics: Foundations in Scripture, History, and Practice* (Grand Rapids, MI: Baker Academic, 2017), 185.

6 D. B. Robertson, ed., *Love and Justice: Selections from the Shorter Writings of Reinhold Niebuhr* (Louisville: Westminster John Knox, 1957), 49. In *Federalist*, no. 10 (1787), accessed June 15, 2022, https://guides.loc.gov/, James Madison argues that the entire point of government generally, not just the criminal law, was addressing the conflicts between what he called "factions."

7 Paul Ramsey, *Basic Christian Ethics* (Louisville: Westminster John Knox, 1950), 243.

violent crimes,[8] while the police made more than 7.5 million arrests for crimes of all sorts.[9] Hundreds of thousands of Americans commit crimes each year. In New York, for example, about 10,000 adults were convicted of felony charges in 2020, while nearly 14,000 more were convicted of misdemeanors.[10] That same year, just short of 80,000 adults were convicted of felony offenses in California.[11] At the end of 2020, Indiana had nearly 24,000 adult prisoners in the state's Department of Correction facilities.[12] Colorado had more than 16,000.[13] The most sensational of the crimes and the most heinous of the offenders make appearances on the evening news. But for every crime featured on *Dateline NBC*, thousands more churn through the system without attracting interest by the public. They're not even names or faces. They're merely numbers, data points, crime statistics, prison population figures, and state budget expenses. They are out of sight and, therefore, out of mind.

The criminal justice machinery hums along so quietly that, unlike the priest and the Levite, we don't even realize that we are passing neighbors by. Perhaps you know where the county courthouse is located. You may even drive past it every day, but you likely give no thought to what happens behind the granite walls and Greek columns. You need not even avert your eyes. The conveyer belt of the criminal justice machinery converts tens of thousands of our fellow citizens—fellow humans—into convicts and applies actual or threatened physical force without disturbing our sensibilities in the process. Along the way, some of the many crime victims get justice. Many others don't. Their agonized cries are also out of earshot, their pain beyond our line of sight. None of them are our concern. We

8   Rachel E. Morgan and Alexandra Thompson, *Criminal Victimization, 2020* (Bureau of Justice Statistics, October 2021), 1, https://bjs.ojp.gov/.
9   "Law Enforcement and Juvenile Crime," Statistical Briefing Book, Office of Justice Programs, U.S. Department of Justice, accessed August 6, 2022, https://www.ojjdp.gov/ojstatbb/crime/ucr .asp?table_in=2.
10 "Dispositions of Adult Arrests (18 and Older) 2017–2021," Division of Criminal Justice Services, New York State, accessed January 14, 2023, https://www.criminaljustice.ny.gov.
11 *Crime in California 2020* (California Department of Justice, July 1, 2021), 53, https://openjustice .doj.ca.gov.
12 *Offender Population Report* (Indiana Department of Correction, January 2021), 5, https://www .in.gov/.
13 "End-of-Month Inmate Population," Dashboard Measures, General Statistics, Colorado Department of Corrections, accessed January 2, 2022, https://cdoc.colorado.gov/.

avoid the entire sordid situation without even crossing the road to pass by. Ignorance is bliss.

The invisibility of these neighbors—perpetrators and victims alike— makes love for them nearly inconceivable, much less a weighty obligation. But our love they are due. To put a finer point on this, every single criminal defendant who has passed through the criminal justice system in your home state this year is entitled to love, and every single crime victim in your home state this year is entitled to love. Not just somebody else's love. Your love. And as if that neighborhood were not large enough, every last one of the criminal defendants charged in federal court anywhere in the country, and every victim of each of those federal crimes is due your love. You may not have realized it, but the neighborhood of criminal justice is a sprawling one. And yet we—you—must love all the neighbors.

Moral Proximity

Now, you may be wondering why any of this is your problem. Perhaps you agree that *someone* must love these participants in the criminal justice system. But why you? You may be willing to concede that those who encounter the mess, like the priest and Levite, are compelled by the law of love to render aid. But many, perhaps most, of you are not prosecutors or policemen, judges or jailers. So you may find this discussion interesting enough for lawyers but not really that relevant for laymen. You may wonder how the story of the good Samaritan applies if you never even encounter the battered man or woman in the courtroom.

It is certainly correct that the story of the good Samaritan assumed that the duty of the priest and the Levite to love was dependent on their physical proximity to the man on the roadside. The point of the parable is not that you and I have an obligation to intervene to assist anyone and everyone in need in the entire world. The parable was not intended to create an unrealistic universal philanthropic obligation.

Key to understanding the command implicit in the parable is Christ's description of the physical proximity of the priest, the Levite, and the Samaritan to the wounded man (Luke 10:31–33).[14] Each of them, because of their

14 Oliver O'Donovan, *Resurrection and Moral Order: An Outline for Evangelical Ethics*, 2nd ed. (Grand Rapids, MI: Eerdmans, 1994), 240.

travels, encountered the man in need. Each was, by dint of circumstance, in a position to assist. They were near and aware, and so they were able to help. Their geographic position gave rise to a responsibility. Because they were neighbors in a locational sense, they were obligated to be neighborly.[15] Christ's point is that the priest and Levite could have helped given that they happened upon the scene of the crime, but they chose not to. The Samaritan too was able to help, and he did. Christ's command—"go, and do likewise" (Luke 10:37)—requires that we, like the Samaritan, render aid to those in need when our circumstances and resources are such that we can.

The point of the good Samaritan story isn't to draw a distinction between the robbers (who are *not* neighbors we must love) and the robbed (who *is* a neighbor we must love). The story isn't one of excusing obligation to the unlovable but rather of confirming and defining that obligation. The point is that we must be neighbors by, consistent with our means, loving *those in need whose paths we cross.* Sometimes we cross paths with crime victims. Sometimes we cross paths with the criminally accused or even convicted. Sometimes we cross paths with both. Sometimes the person with whom we cross paths is or has been both. The point of the story is that we owe neighbor love to whomever we encounter.

But physical proximity does not alone define the borders of the neighborhood. Your obligation to love the participants in the criminal justice system does not turn on how close to the local criminal courthouse you venture on your drive to work or church. Duty is born of what theologians and philosophers refer to as "moral distance" or "moral proximity." The idea is that "distance, both physical and relational, makes a significant difference in our obligations to help others."[16]

Moral proximity recognizes that I cannot be a neighbor, or at least not the same neighbor, to everyone. I don't travel every road. I don't know of every injustice. And even if I did, I am a person of limited means bound by time and space. Martin Luther King Jr. famously wrote, "Injustice anywhere is a threat to justice everywhere."[17] But I cannot be anywhere and everywhere and do everything all the time. The principle of moral proximity

15   Jeremy Waldron, "Who Is My Neighbor? Humanity and Proximity," *The Monist* 86, no. 3 (July 2003): 343, https://doi.org/10.5840/monist200386324.

16   Deen K. Chatterjee, "Moral Distance: Introduction," *The Monist* 86, no. 3 (July 2003): 327, https://doi.org/10.5840/monist200386316.

17   Martin Luther King Jr., "Letter from Birmingham Jail," April 16, 1963, The University of Alabama Libraries Special Collections, accessed June 8, 2022, 2, http://purl.lib.ua.edu/181702.

recognizes my finiteness. It acknowledges a hierarchy of obligation. Some needs and some injustices have a stronger claim on me. Certain injustices rightly demand more of my attention than others. This is the essence of the concept of moral proximity.

We see the idea of moral proximity in a variety of passages in Scripture. In the Old Testament law, moral proximity is embedded in the law's description of the differing obligations to one's family, to one's tribe, to fellow Israelites, and then to other nations.[18] In the New Testament, Paul similarly writes of our obligation to provide for our relatives, "especially for members of [our] household" (1 Tim. 5:8). Relatives have greater claim on our assistance than strangers. But even among relatives there is an ordering; immediate family is especially entitled to assistance. Paul recognizes a hierarchy of obligation defined not only by physical proximity but also by relational proximity. As Augustine would later explain, "All men are to be loved equally. But since you cannot do good to all, you are to pay special regard to those who, by the accidents of time, or place, or circumstances, are brought into closer connection with you."[19]

As an American, I have a responsibility for those—victim and accused— affected by the American criminal justice system because democracy is a type of relationship that creates a moral proximity.[20] Consider, by way of compari- son, a monarchy. Scripture makes clear that, appearances notwithstanding, kings and queens reign at God's discretion alone: "He removes kings and sets up kings" (Dan. 2:21). The authority of monarchs is only that which God has given, and unjust exercises of that authority are morally illegitimate. But in a monarchy, the subjects have no say (apart from violent revolt) in who serves as king or queen and how he or she rules. If a ruler acts unjustly, the onlooking

18 Kevin DeYoung and Greg Gilbert, *What Is the Mission of the Church? Making Sense of Social Justice, Shalom, and the Great Commission* (Wheaton, IL: Crossway, 2011), 184.

19 Augustine, *On Christian Doctrine*, trans. J. F. Shaw (Mineola, NY: Dover, 2009), 19 (1.28.29). For a helpful discussion of how finitude, moral proximity, Christian love, and friendship relate, see Gilbert C. Meilander, *Friendship: A Study in Theological Ethics* (South Bend, IN: Notre Dame University Press, 1981).

20 Emil Brunner, *The Divine Imperative* (Philadelphia: Westminster, 1979), 462, writes, "There was a great difference between the monarchical system of government . . . and the republican government. . . . For good or for evil: today we are all responsible, and even if we do not exercise our political rights we cannot evade our responsibility." Jonathan Leeman argues that Genesis 9:5–6 "*obligate* all human beings, as a matter of obedience to God, to ensure that a reckoning for crimes against humans occurs" within their given society. Jonathan Leeman, *Political Church: The Local Assembly as the Embassy of Christ's Rule* (Downers Grove, IL: IVP Academic, 2016), 187. Democracy provides a means for all humanity to play a role in fulfilling that mandate.

subjects can do nothing about it but pray (1 Tim. 2:2). In that system, there is a world of distance between ruler and subject, and that relational distance means the subject has little if any moral responsibility for the injustices the ruler commits. However grieved the subject may be at those inequities, he or she lacks the means to stop them. To use the analogy of the parable of the good Samaritan, the subject in a monarchy may be aware of injustices, but he or she is, as a practical matter, too far away from the scene of the robbery to lend aid. The subject is, metaphorically speaking, simply not on the same road as the man being battered by the monarch.[21]

In the American democratic (or, more precisely, republican) system of government, however, "we the people" (as the preamble to the US Constitution says) have a say in the actions of the authorities. To be clear, I am not suggesting that the governing authority of democratic leaders derives from the people. While the Declaration of Independence makes a theological claim that "Governments . . . deriv[e] their just powers from the consent of the governed,"[22] God has declared otherwise. "There is no authority except from God, and those that exist have been instituted by God" (Rom. 13:1). With or without the consent of the governed, God grants governments authority. Whether in a monarchy or a democracy, government leaders derive their authority to act justly from God and God alone.[23]

At the same time, the *means* God uses to install governing authorities in a democracy is the consent—expressed by vote—of the people. Our role in this selection process is an important one for purposes of moral proximity. God alone confers *authority* on governing officials, but you and I play a morally responsible role in granting *power* to those government leaders. As we saw earlier, the criminal law is the actual or threatened application of physical force, and the power to threaten and apply that force is power that we, as

---

21 This is not to say that those living in a monarchy have no obligation to their neighbors who are harmed by the king's injustice. While subjects may lack the ability to work through the system of government to achieve justice, they can work outside the system to provide relief. Thus, for example, Scripture tells us to "remember those who are in prison, as though in prison with them" (Heb. 13:3).

22 "Declaration of Independence: A Transcription" (July 4, 1776), National Archives, accessed May 24, 2022, https://www.archives.gov.

23 "Even a procedural arrangement such as democracy can become idolatrous when the voice of the people is equated with the voice of God." Bruce Riley Ashford and Dennis Greeson, "Modern Political Ideologies: A Reformed Alternative" in *Reformed Public Theology: A Global Vision for Life in the World*, ed. Matthew Kaemingk (Grand Rapids, MI: Baker Academic, 2021), 127.

voters, play a role in supplying to the government officials. Every few years, we select who among us will carry the sword for us. We decide who will exercise a power to kill that we have conferred. The power we give them may be unjust and thus morally illegitimate in God's eyes, or the power we as voters grant may be misused by our elected officials in unjust ways. Either way, if those we select commit unjust acts, we the people have means to stop them.

This brings us back to the discussion of individual versus social justice. As with the good Samaritan, individual acts of kindness are certainly within the scope of our duty to love our neighbors. So too are structural acts of kindness that shape the social systems within which our neighbors live. Being the neighbors Christ calls us to be means evidencing a concern for the social institutions—including the criminal justice systems—that we empower to affect our neighbors. As Nicholas Wolterstorff puts it, "Seeking the flourishing of one's fellow human beings requires that one seek to promote the flourishing of a wide variety of social entities of which those individuals are members." Our neighbors live in societies, not in isolation, and the justice or injustice of the social systems in which those neighbors live and operate has a dramatic influence on their well-being. Thus, "care about one's neighbor has inescapable civic and political implications."[24]

The important point for the Christian in a democratic system is that, because government officials exercise power that we played a role in giving them, our duty to love carries with it a moral obligation to supervise the exercise of governmental power we conferred. We must do what we can to ensure that this conferred power is exercised justly.[25] You cannot simply walk by someone battered and bruised by prosecutors, police officers, judges, and jailers who abused and misused the power you voted to give them (or declined to vote to deny them). You and I have a political relationship, and thus a moral proximity, to the situation. When the local courthouse commits assaults— the actual or threatened uses of physical force—those acts are done in your name.[26] The relationship between voters and elected officials in a democracy

---

24 Wolterstorff, *Justice in Love*, 134.
25 Nicholas Wolterstorff, *The Mighty and the Almighty: An Essay in Political Theology* (New York: Cambridge University Press, 2014), 76, who argues that the duties to restrain the king—duties that Calvin assigned to "lesser magistrates"—are, in a democratic system of government, the responsibility of voters.
26 Oliver O'Donovan, *The Ways of Judgment* (Grand Rapids, MI: Eerdmans, 2005), 158: "The representative acts for the people, and in his action the people acts [*sic*]."

renders the voters morally proximate to those officials who act on the voters' behalf *and* thus to those harmed by the officials acting on the voters' behalf. The power to vote means that, like the priest, Levite, and Samaritan, you are traveling the same road as those on whom the justice system operates. The franchise creates proximity. As a result, you have a moral obligation to intervene through its exercise. Justice demands it. Love requires it.[27]

———

The good Samaritan displays for us that the power Christianity brings to bear on social problems is neighborly love—a love for others inspired by and born of Christ's transforming love for us. That love is the firm foundation for a truly just response to crime. A just legal system must be one designed to love our neighbors, both the victim and the accused, by seeking their good.

At the same time, God has not left us entirely to ourselves to define what is good for those neighbors. All the law was founded on love, but the law also contains particulars that spell out what love looks like. The law tells us, even if at some level of generality, what is good for our neighbors and for us. And while Scripture does not (for the most part) dictate particular criminal justice policies, Scripture does define for us in some respects what love demands of us in the context of a legal system.[28] We are told both what is good and how to seek that good for our neighbors when a crime is committed. We turn now to examine five biblical pillars of justice—accuracy, due process, accountability, impartiality, and proportionality—that stand on the foundation of neighborly love.

27 Of course, a voter's moral obligation to restrain government officials through voting is complicated by the fact that voting for a candidate implicates moral issues in addition to criminal justice. My point here isn't to resolve how one must weigh the myriad issues but rather to establish that criminal justice is one of the issues that the Christian has a moral obligation to consider in weighing how to vote.

28 Situational ethics holds that the law of love alone controls in every situation even to the point of overriding moral rules or principles: "All laws and rules and principles and ideals and norms, are only contingent, only valid if they happen to serve love." Joseph Fletcher, *Situation Ethics: The New Morality* (Louisville: Westminster John Knox, 1997), 30. That is not my view, for reasons that are beyond the scope of this book. For a helpful summary of the criticisms of situational ethics, see Outka, *Agape*, 104–12. Suffice it to say that I believe Scripture does lay down rules, or at least controlling principles, that dictate what love looks like in the context of a legal system.

4

Accuracy

REVEREND JOSEPH W. PARKER (1805–87) served as the second pastor
of Capitol Hill Baptist Church in Washington, DC (of which I am a member), from 1879 through October 1882. Born in Vermont, Parker was an
abolitionist and, in his day, one of the most accomplished and respected
Baptist ministers in the country. After the Civil War, he devoted himself to
establishing schools for recently emancipated slaves and founded several
schools to train Black preachers.[1]

From 1859 through 1865 Parker served as pastor of Shawmut Avenue
Baptist Church of Boston, Massachusetts. While he was pastoring in Massachusetts, a member of his congregation, Franklin W. Smith, was charged
by court-martial with defrauding the US Navy. The trial on these charges
was to be held in Philadelphia in 1864 while the American Civil War was
still raging. Parker was convinced that his parishioner was innocent, believing that Smith had been charged in retaliation for exposing a fraud by
other members of the Navy. Deeply distressed by what he perceived to be a
serious injustice, Parker secured an audience with President Lincoln at the
White House in July 1864 to press his claim of Smith's innocence.[2] During

---

1 "Rev Joseph Whiting Parker," 1805–1887, Memorials, Find a Grave, maintained by KBSteward-
   Family, last modified January 16, 2017, accessed December 30, 2021, https://findagrave.com;
   Caleb Morell, "A Light on the Hill: The Story of Capitol Hill Baptist Church, 1878–Present"
   (unpublished manuscript, November 15, 2022), Microsoft Word.
2 Joseph W. Parker, Alumni File, Special Collections and Archives, Union College, https://digital
   works.union.edu/; Caleb Morell, "A Light on the Hill"; Curtis Dahl, "Lincoln Saves a Reformer,"
   American Heritage, October 1972, https://www.americanheritage.com; J. W. Parker, "Joseph

that meeting, Lincoln was moved by Parker's plea and assured him that he would personally review any guilty verdict:

> Let your friend be tried by the method proposed. I will review the case in person. Justice shall be done to Mr. Smith. I have practiced law for twenty-seven years and if there is false witness or perversion of right in the case I know I can find it. I don't care if the devil tries the case, I can find his tracks. Come to me after the court is through with its work. Your friend shall have justice done him![3]

This was not the response that Parker had hoped would come from the meeting, but he had at least succeeded in bringing Smith's predicament to President Lincoln's attention and had secured a promise of intervention if needed. And Lincoln agreed to move the trial back to Boston.[4]

Smith's case proceeded to trial by a court-martial in Massachusetts in September 1864. It was a lengthy trial, lasting through the fall and into the winter, with a verdict returned on January 13, 1865. As Parker feared, Smith was convicted and sentenced to two years in prison and a fine of $20,000—the equivalent of about $365,000 in 2022.[5]

Smith's trial was a bit of a cause célèbre at the time, with several US Senators and Congressmen weighing in on the matter. Now, more than a century and a half later, the story has long been forgotten. But Parker's appeal to President Lincoln in the summer of 1864 offers two insights into how a Christian should think about biblical justice. What initially motivated Parker was a concern for accuracy, and as we will see in the next chapter, he understood that accurate outcomes depend on fair process.

Actual Guilt

The primary feature of any biblically just legal system is that it judges accurately. To achieve accuracy—or, you might say, truth—is the core of what it means to love in the administration of justice. As we saw earlier,

Whiting Parker Sr.'s Memoirs," 1880, MSS 14909, Special Collections, University of Virginia Library, Charlottesville, VA, 113, 132, 141, 148.

3   Parker, "Joseph Whiting Parker Sr.'s Memoirs," 142.

4   Morell, "A Light on the Hill"; Parker, "Joseph Whiting Parker Sr.'s Memoirs," 142–43; Dahl, "Lincoln Saves a Reformer."

5   Dahl, "Lincoln Saves a Reformer."

the theological conundrum of criminal justice is that physical violence against others is (as a general matter) morally wrong, that the government is obliged to protect its citizens, and that sometimes the government must use physical force to protect its citizens. Scripture's solution to this ethical puzzle is found in recognizing that a government, when it bears the sword on God's behalf, is itself bound to act in accord with Christ's law of love. The government's use of physical force can be moral but only if it too is guided and constrained by the obligation to love. Whatever else it means to act with neighborly love in the context of a criminal justice system, it certainly means that the government will punish only those who are in fact wrongdoers. The law of love demands accuracy.

This insistence on accuracy appears throughout Scripture. It is implied in passages like Romans 13 where Paul says that the governmental sword is to be a terror to "the wrongdoer" (Rom. 13:4). Likewise, Peter describes the role of government as punishing "those who do evil" (1 Pet. 2:14). In Genesis 9, God authorizes the death penalty for "whoever sheds the blood of man" (Gen. 9:6). In Deuteronomy 25:1–3, Moses records God's authorization of corporal punishment against those who have harmed others.

Nowhere does Scripture permit humankind to use physical force as punishment of a person who is accused of—but who has not actually committed—an offense. In every instance in which Scripture authorizes the use of punitive force, it does so only for those who are guilty of wrongdoing. Moses makes this explicit: "Keep far from a false charge, and do not kill the innocent and righteous" (Ex. 23:7). To wield the punitive sword of government against those who are innocent goes beyond the authorization of Scripture. In other words, accuracy is a prerequisite for morally legitimate governmental punishment.

Accuracy is essential for punishment to be morally legitimate because accuracy is essential for that punishment to be loving. "To love is to want to benefit," Nigel Biggar says, "and to love sincerely is to *try* to benefit."[6] To strive for accuracy in our judgments is to desire and attempt to benefit both the accused and victimized neighbor. No one is loved when the innocent are punished. For the accused who is wrongly convicted, the failure of love is obvious. The innocent man who languishes for years or decades

---

6   Nigel Biggar, *In Defence of War* (New York: Oxford University Press, 2013), 330. Reproduced with permission of the Licensor through PLSclear.

in prison has been denied his due—physical freedom—in payment of a debt he did not owe. He has borne a burden that was not his to bear. For the innocent convict, the system both battered him while he traveled life's road and then daily passes him by as he is left for dead in its ditch. At the same time, wrongful convictions are a failure of love for the crime victim. To punish the wrong person is to mislead the victim. The actual thief or rapist or killer still walks free while the crime victim is led to believe that justice has been served. There is only a façade of redress. In truth, the wrong has not been remediated, for whoever paid owed nothing. And further still, the guilty man or woman who goes unpunished because of the wrongful conviction of the innocent is deprived of the corrective force of the law. Wrongful convictions are a failure by the government to adhere to the law of love and, thus, a miscarriage of justice because the falsely accused, the crime victim, and the truly guilty all fail to receive their due.

The story of George Stinney Jr. provides a jarring example of this tripartite injustice. Stinney, a fourteen-year-old Black youth, was executed in 1944 for the murder of two White girls in Alcolu, South Carolina. Stinney's conviction was obtained under circumstances that a court determined—long after his execution—ran afoul of the constitutional guarantee of due process. The injustice to Stinney is obvious. Barely a teenager, his life was snuffed out for a crime he did not commit. But Stinney was not the only one wronged by his false conviction. As the late historian Eli Faber observed, "If in fact it was not George Stinney who committed the murders, then the injustice he suffered extended to [the victims], whose murderer simply walked away, disappearing down the railroad tracks of Alcolu," escaping corrective discipline.[7]

This latter point warrants emphasis. Justice does require punishing the guilty, a topic that is the focus of chapter 8. For all the talk of "mass incarceration," the American justice system does an exceedingly poor job of holding to account those who commit the most serious of crimes. A recent academic study concluded that, in the United States, "97% of burglars, 88% of rapists, and over 50% of murderers get away with their crimes."[8]

---

7   Eli Faber, *The Child in the Electric Chair: The Execution of George Junius Stinney Jr. and the Making of a Tragedy in the American South* (Columbia, SC: University of South Carolina Press, 2021), 126.

8   Shima Baradaran Baughman, "How Effective Are Police? The Problem of Clearance Rates and Criminal Accountability," *Alabama Law Review* 72, no. 1 (2020): 55, https://dc.law.utah.edu /scholarship/213/.

This is an astounding rate of injustice to hundreds of thousands of crime victims and criminals across the United States each year. Neither neighbor receives his or her due. Most of this injustice is the result of a failure of policing rather than an epidemic of inaccurate "not guilty" verdicts, as data shows that police are "not solving most crimes."[9] But whatever the cause, an accurate system of criminal justice should, to achieve biblical justice, be one that punishes those who are in fact guilty. Each unsolved crime or unprosecuted offender is an injustice to—a failure to love—a crime victim and an uncorrected criminal.

Few, if any, would disagree with the notion that justice, biblical or otherwise, demands that a system of criminal justice be committed to accuracy. And at first blush, this principle of accuracy—the moral obligation to punish the guilty but only the guilty—may seem straightforward. But what do we mean by *guilty*? Guilty of what? And even if we agree on what offenses deserve our condemnation, how certain must we be of the defendant's guilt? Can we tolerate any error? If so, how much error can we morally tolerate? And if the system misfires and convicts an innocent man or woman, what does justice demand of those responsible for the system's errors? Each of these questions requires further examination.

True Verdicts

As I noted above, a criminal justice system operating according to the law of love should punish those, but only those, who are guilty of a wrong. When I refer to this actual guilt requirement, your mind likely turns to the verdicts a criminal justice system renders, and it is certainly the case that the actual guilt requirement means that we punish those who are convicted at trial and not those who are acquitted. It is not enough, however, that the justice system punish only those adjudged guilty after trial. Juries get it wrong sometimes. A guilty verdict, and the resulting punishment of the person convicted, is not just—as the Bible defines justice—if the person did not actually commit the offense of which he or she is convicted.

While we would like to believe that these miscarriages of justice don't occur, we know that they do. In the United States, *thousands* of convicted prisoners, many of whom have been imprisoned for decades, have later been

9   Baughman, "How Effective Are Police?," 70.

exonerated.[10] A conservative estimate is that at least 1 percent of the United States prison population, meaning approximately 20,000 people, is incarcerated as the result of wrongful convictions.[11] Other estimates are higher.[12] We *know*, for example, that at least 2 percent of capital sentences returned since 1973 were of people who were innocent of the crime for which they were sentenced to death.[13] Even if we look only at those sentenced to death in the last 25 years, already 1 percent of them have since been exonerated.[14] This

---

10 As discussed further in chap. 6, from 1989 through 2022, there were 3,272 confirmed exonerations in the United States amounting to 28,917 years of wrongful imprisonment. "Exonerations by State," The National Registry of Exonerations, University of Michigan, accessed April 8, 2023, https://www.law.umich.edu/special/exoneration/Pages/Exonerations-in-the-United-States-Map.aspx.

11 Samuel Gross, "What We Think, What We Know and What We Think We Know about False Convictions," *Ohio Journal of Criminal Law* 14, no. 2 (2017): 785, https://repository.law.umich.edu/articles/1882. For a contrary view that the rate of wrongful convictions is much lower, see Paul G. Cassell, "Overstating America's Wrongful Conviction Rate? Reassessing the Conventional Wisdom about the Prevalence of Wrongful Convictions," *Arizona Law Review* 60, no. 4 (2018): 815-63, https://arizonalawreview.org/pdf/60-4/60arizlrev815.pdf.

12 Charles E. Loeffler, Jordan Hyatt, and Greg Ridgeway, "Measuring Self-Reported Wrongful Convictions among Prisoners," *Journal of Quantitative Criminology* 35, no. 2 (2019): 259–86, https://doi.org/10.1007/s10940-018-9381-1.

13 Out of the 8,790 people sentenced to death in the United States from 1973 through 2022, 184 have been exonerated. "Death Sentences in the United States since 1977," Death Penalty Information Center, accessed January 13, 2023, https://deathpenaltyinfo.org; "2022 Death Sentences by Name, Race, and County," Death Penalty Information Center, accessed January 13, 2023, https://deathpenaltyinfo.org; "Innocence Database," Death Penalty Information Center, accessed January 13, 2023, https://deathpenaltyinfo.org; Phillip Morris, "Sentenced to Death but Innocent: These Are Stories of Justice Gone Wrong," *National Geographic*, February 18, 2021, https://www.nationalgeographic.com. Thankfully, a 2 percent error rate in death sentences has not resulted in a similar error rate in actual executions. Litigation after the sentencing has resulted in nearly two hundred exonerations prior to execution. However, statisticians have estimated based on the exonerations to date that more than 4 percent of people on death row are innocent and "it is all but certain that several" innocent people have been executed since 1977. Samuel R. Gross, Barbara O'Brien, Chen Hu, and Edward H. Kennedy, "Rate of False Conviction of Criminal Defendants Who Are Sentenced to Death," *Proceedings of the National Academy of Sciences* 111, no. 20 (May 20, 2014): 7234–35, https://doi.org/10.1073/pnas.1306417111.

14 From 1997 through 2021, 2,966 people were sentenced to death in the United States. "Death Sentences in the United States since 1977: National Death Sentences by Year," Death Penalty Information Center, accessed January 13, 2023, https://deathpenaltyinfo.org. Thirty of them were later exonerated of the crimes for which they were sentenced to death. Of the 122 death row inmates exonerated since 1997 (many sentenced to death prior to 1997), more than 60 of them waited 15 years or more for their exoneration. "Description of Innocence Cases," Death Penalty Information Center, accessed January 13, 2023, https://deathpenaltyinfo.org. Thus, of people sentenced to death since 1997 (nearly 40 percent of whom have not yet spent 15 years on death row), the number of exonerations is almost certain to grow beyond the 1 percent who

is a shocking rate of error for a sentence with irreversible consequences. If you're inclined to think that 1 to 2 percent is a low error rate, ask yourself this: Would you willingly enter a room of one hundred people if you knew that one or two of them would be randomly shot and killed? Would you send your children into that room? If not, why is our society sending other people's children into that "room"?

Maybe the answer is that this loss of innocent life is the price we must pay in a fallen world to achieve justice in the other 98 or 99 percent of murder cases. That raises three questions. First, are we morally entitled to accept any loss of innocent life as the cost of achieving justice? Second, and relatedly, are we doing all we can to avoid those wrongful executions? Third, are we willing to accept the risk of wrongful executions because we know that it's not a risk evenly distributed across the population? I'll turn to these questions in later chapters. For now, my point is simply that inaccurate death sentences are a reality and their rate of occurrence is not immaterial.

Even when these wrongful death sentences are detected prior to the actual execution date, the defendants have all too frequently spent decades in prison for crimes they did not commit.[15] The havoc wreaked on those wrongfully convicted and sentenced for lesser crimes is no less tragic. And regardless of whether the crime is a capital one, exonerations are wrenching for crime victims who learn decades later that they have been deceived all along. Love demands that those adjudged guilty be those, but only those, who are in fact guilty of the charges. Juries can and do render incorrect verdicts, and criminal punishment is not morally justified merely because it follows a jury verdict of guilt. A criminal justice system that loves must return verdicts that accurately distinguish the guilty from the innocent.

False Witnesses

The accurate verdicts that biblical justice requires depend, in part, on truthful witnesses. That was true in ancient Israel; it is no less true today.

---

have already been exonerated. One group of academic researchers has concluded, "It is possible that the death-sentencing rate of innocent defendants has changed over time," but "no specific evidence points in that direction." Gross et al., "Rate of False Conviction," 7235.

15 To take one example, in 2021, Kevin Strickland was exonerated after forty-three years in prison in Missouri for a triple murder he was later deemed not to have committed. See Luke Nozicka, "Kevin Strickland Freed after Judge Vacates Conviction in 1978 Triple Murder," *Kansas City Star*, December 19, 2021, https://www.kansascity.com/.

A main, if not the main, reason verdicts go awry is false testimony, whether intentional or unintentional.[16] So it should come as no surprise that Scripture, given its demand for accuracy in a criminal justice system, devotes a great deal of attention to the issue of false witnesses.

The ninth of the Ten Commandments condemns not only lying as a general matter but also highlights a lie that takes the form of false testimony against another. "You shall not bear false witness *against your neighbor*" (Ex. 20:16; Deut. 5:20), the commandment reads, reminding us that bearing false witness is a failure of neighbor love. The courtroom scene brings the accuser and the accused into proximity, and so the obligation to act in love is implicated. False testimony is a failure to love by denying both parties the accurate verdict that they are due; it "makes a mockery of justice" (Prov. 19:28 NLT). This is why our just God hates false witnesses, deeming them an abomination (Prov. 6:16, 19).

Of particular note is the comparison in Proverbs of a false witness to "a war club, or a sword, or a sharp arrow" (Prov. 25:18). Like those weapons, false witnesses kill because, if they are believed and a verdict is returned in reliance on them, the government is then empowered to bear the sword against the convict. False witnesses mobilize the physical violence of the state against the innocent. As one commentator puts it, false witnesses are compared to deadly weapons because they can "result in someone's death."[17] The English minister Charles Bridges (1794–1869) colorfully observed that this verse likens bearing false witness to intentional murder: "Would you shrink with horror at the thought of beating out your neighbor's brains with an hammer, or of piercing his bowels with *a sword, or a sharp arrow*? Why then do you indulge in the like barbarity"?[18] Calvin built on this idea, observing that "a man, in being robbed of his good name [through false testimony], is no less injured than if he were robbed of his goods."[19] But the danger of those who testify falsely is not only to the accused. False witnesses can defraud victims by freeing the guilty. This seems to be the import of

16 A false conviction could also result from entirely truthful testimony from which a jury draws inaccurate inferences. In other words, circumstantial evidence can be truthful but lead to erroneous conclusions.

17 Tremper Longman III, *Proverbs* (Grand Rapids, MI: Baker Academic, 2006), 455–56.

18 Charles Bridges, *An Exposition of the Book of Proverbs* (New York: Robert Carter, 1847), 402.

19 John Calvin, *Institutes of the Christian Religion*, trans. Henry Beveridge (Peabody, MA: Hendrickson, 2008), 261 (2.8.47).

the Mosaic law, which speaks of a "malicious witness" making "common cause with the wicked" (Ex. 23:1 NET).

Perjury, however, is not the only way in which one can run afoul of the ninth commandment. Because trials depend on witnesses, a witness who stands by silently when his or her testimony is relevant to the proceeding can subvert justice. The Westminster Larger Catechism calls this out, deeming "undue silence in a just cause" to be a violation of the ninth commandment.[20] Calvin likewise understood the ninth commandment to require that we "faithfully assist everyone, as far as in us lies, in asserting the truth."[21] It is not at all uncommon for witnesses to seek to avoid testifying in someone else's criminal trial. Testimony is time-consuming, often requiring many idle hours awaiting your opportunity to take the witness stand. And who among us would welcome being cross-examined by a hostile attorney? The desire to avoid the situation entirely is understandable. As a result, people often try to beg off from testifying, refusing to cooperate by feigning poor memory or uncertainty that is not true. The Westminster Catechism speaks directly to that issue, declaring it a violation of the ninth commandment to speak in "equivocal expressions, to the prejudice of truth."[22]

Failing to provide relevant testimony when you could do so is unloving. It subverts the justice that both the victim and the accused are due. Silence can itself bear false witness in violation of the ninth commandment because silence conveys to the jury that no one else can speak to the situation when, in fact, the recalcitrant witness could. "When someone is on trial for his life, speak out if your testimony can help him" (Lev. 19:16 GNT), Scripture commands. Loving your neighbors—both the criminally accused and the crime victim—demands that witnesses to the events testify truthfully to what they know.

Quantum of Evidence

Though Scripture imposes a moral obligation on witnesses to testify and to do so truthfully, the Mosaic law nonetheless required more than a single witness to convict someone of a charge. What the American legal system refers to as proof beyond a reasonable doubt is embodied in ancient Israel's

20 Westminster Larger Catechism, question 145.
21 Calvin, *Institutes*, 260 (2.8.47).
22 Westminster Larger Catechism, question 145.

so-called two-witness rule. In several places, the Old Testament law forbids a guilty verdict on the testimony of only one witness: "A single witness shall not suffice against a person for any crime or for any wrong in connection with any offense that he has committed. Only on the evidence of two witnesses or of three witnesses shall a charge be established" (Deut. 19:15). Elsewhere, the Pentateuch repeats this requirement regarding capital offenses in particular (Num. 35:30; Deut. 17:6).

Picture how this two-witness rule might play out at a trial in ancient Israel. A man is charged with murder. The "prosecutor" calls as his first witness Aaron, the elder brother of Moses and high priest of Israel, who testifies that he saw the defendant commit the murder. The defense doesn't lay a finger on Aaron during cross-examination, unable to call into question the veracity of his testimony. The murder was committed in broad daylight. Aaron observed the crime from only twenty feet away. Aaron had no personal grievance against the accused and no friendship with the victim; thus, he had no motive to provide false testimony. But the prosecutor has no other witnesses, so he rests his case. At that point, the defendant moves to dismiss the charges. And that dismissal is granted. The defendant walks free. That's what the two-witness rule in the Old Testament law required.

This might strike you as a case of a defendant getting off on a "technicality." It might even seem like an injustice. And if the Israelite charged with murder in fact committed the murder, then he has not yet received the punishment due. But the question a trial poses is not only *what* punishment is due but also *who* is authorized to impose it. "All punishment presupposes that the person who pronounces and imposes punishment is clothed with authority over those who have violated the law," Herman Bavinck writes, and "this authority cannot have its origin in humanity alone."[23] Authority, and physically coercive punitive authority in particular, comes only from God (Rom. 13:1). In the absence of divine authorization, we have no right to punish another person.

In the Mosaic law, God expressly withheld that authorization in those instances in which only a single witness was available. To be sure, the Old Testament's two-witness rule meant that some—maybe even many—guilty

---

23 Herman Bavinck, *Sin and Salvation in Christ*, vol. 3 of *Reformed Dogmatics*, ed. John Bolt, trans. John Vriend (Grand Rapids, MI: Baker Academic, 2006), 163.

people would go free. God knew that. Our *just* God knew that. Our *loving* God knew that. And you and I are not more just or loving than he. God seems to have been saying that, in a fallen world in which complete justice is impossible, the Israelites would love their neighbors best if they forewent conviction on the testimony of only one witness.

The application of the two-witness rule even in cases of idolatry (Deut. 17:6) evidences, according to the English Baptist minister John Gill (1697–1771), that "so careful is the Lord of the lives of men, that none should be taken away but upon full and sufficient evidence, even in cases in which his own glory and honor is so much concerned."[24] It would follow that comparable care is in order in the prosecution of less serious crimes directed primarily at man.

That the two-witness requirement is carried over into the New Testament to govern church discipline (Matt. 18:16; 2 Cor. 13:1; 1 Tim. 5:19; Heb. 10:28) suggests that the rule is not an anachronism of the Mosaic law but rather an inherent limitation on human justice. God has not authorized us to pass judgment on one another, whether in the criminal justice context or otherwise, based only on the say-so of a single person. As one Old Testament scholar observes, "The requirement of two or three witnesses is not an infallible guarantee of justice, but it is a foundation stone of any system designed to maintain justice in the human community as it tries to guard against the danger of the system's breaking down through either human fallibility or human sin."[25] That danger of system malfunction due to human fallibility and fallenness is no less true today than in ancient times. And if Scripture sets high evidentiary standards to ensure that judgments among God's people (whether Old Testament Israel or the New Testament church) are accurate, then surely Christians should want no less for their national neighbors today. That is what it means to, as believers, love those neighbors as ourselves.

This isn't to suggest that a single witness is necessarily lying. Nor is it to deny that people are often wronged in secret. The point is simply that God has not authorized us to wield the sword of judgment in that circumstance. The implication of that prohibition seems to be that when one person

---

24 John Gill, *An Exposition of the Old and New Testament*, Sacred-Texts, Deut 17:6, https://www.sacred-texts.com/.

25 Patrick D. Miller, *Deuteronomy* (Louisville: Westminster John Knox, 2012), 144.

claims a wrong was committed and the other party denies the accusation, we are less able than we believe to resolve these one-on-one disputes. We may think that we have the capacity to discern, to sort out who is lying and who is not, but Scripture casts doubt on our self-confidence that we can judge appropriately in these circumstances. Thus, when presented with a he-said-she-said scenario, Scripture appears to say that we are not divinely authorized to impose punishment. As Calvin puts it, "Since too great credulity would often impel the judges to condemn the guiltless, [God] here applies a remedy to this evil, forbidding that the crime should be punished unless proved by sure testimony."[26] An evidentiary requirement like the two-witness rule, while a blunt instrument, can serve to enforce the accuracy requirement and protect against overconfidence in our ability, both as witnesses and as judges, to discern the truth from lies.

That said, the totality of the Mosaic law is not directly applicable to us today. Calvin divided the law into moral, ceremonial, and judicial categories.[27] Relying on this division, both the Westminster Confession of Faith and the Second London Baptist Confession of Faith provide that so-called judicial laws are "not obliging," in a mechanical sense, outside of their original context of ancient Israel. At the same time, both confessions acknowledge that the "general equity" underlying the judicial law is of continuing moral use.[28] In other words, while we are not bound by the letter of the judicial law, its underlying intent still provides moral guidance.[29] For us today, the judicial law offers principles to guide us rather than proscriptions that bind us.

The point of the two-witness rule was to require a degree of certainty greater than a single witness could provide. That core principle still stands. The insufficiency of a single witness to a crime is expressly addressed in the Old Testament, the concept appears repeatedly in the New Testament, and

26 John Calvin, *Commentaries on the Four Last Books of Moses Arranged in the Form of a Harmony*, vol. 3, trans. Charles William Bingham (Grand Rapids, MI: Christian Classics Ethereal Library, 1999), 51, https://www.ccel.org.

27 Calvin, *Institutes*, 979 (4.20.15).

28 "The Westminster Confession of Faith," in *Creeds, Confessions, and Catechisms: A Reader's Edition*, ed. Chad Van Dixhoorn (Wheaton, IL: Crossway, 2022), 213 (19.4); "The London Baptist Confession," in Dixhoorn, *Creeds, Confessions, and Catechisms*, 269 (19.4).

29 Harold G. Cunningham, "God's Law, 'General Equity' and the Westminster Confession of Faith," *Tyndale Bulletin* 58, no. 2 (2007): 312, https://doi.org/10.53751/001c.29241.

there is no reason to think that a single witness today is more reliable than in Bible times. One witness is still insufficient to meet the Bible's demand for accuracy, and we should not pass judgment on that limited evidence. Both then and now, a single eyewitness case with no other corroborating evidence is morally insufficient. Surveying the biblical teaching on this issue, the Calvinist minister George Cheever (1807–1890) concluded that, at least for a capital offense, the two-witness concept still holds and "mere circumstantial evidence [is] not to be relied upon."[30]

But there are forms of evidence available today that were inconceivable in ancient times. For example, DNA evidence may provide more assurance than a second eyewitness. The same is true of a video recording of the events in question. Perhaps there are (or will be) other forms of evidence in which we could have similar confidence.[31] Scripture doesn't speak to those scenarios because they were unimaginable to Moses. What Scripture does impress on us is that accuracy is of paramount importance to God. We are left to apply the principle of accuracy to modern technology, always keeping central in our thinking that we must "render true judgments" (Zech. 7:9).[32]

The principle behind the two-witness rule is that a single witness alone does not produce reliably true judgments. That principle—the "general equity" of the rule—endures. Today, as in ancient days, human memories are too fallible and motives too mixed to allow a single witness to determine another human's fate. Something more is required. That something more could be a second human witness. But, given technological and scientific

---

30 George B. Cheever, Samuel Hand, and Wendell Phillips, "The Death Penalty," *The North American Review* 133, no. 301 (December 1881): 536, https://www.jstor.org/stable/25101016. Cheever was both a slavery abolitionist and a death penalty proponent. Philip English Mackey, "Reverend George Barrell Cheever: Yankee Reformer as Champion of the Gallows," *Proceedings of the American Antiquarian Society* 82, no. 2 (1973): 323–24, https://www.americanantiquarian .org/proceedings/44498047.pdf.

31 As discussed in chap. 16, much of what is passed off in criminal cases today as forensic evidence is of doubtful scientific reliability.

32 The Hebrew word translated as "judgments" in Zech. 7:9 is *mihspat*, which "can describe the whole process of litigation (a case), or its end result (the verdict and its execution)." Christopher J. H. Wright, *Old Testament Ethics for the People of God* (Downers Grove, IL: IVP Academic, 2004), 257. The Hebrew word translated as "true" is *emet*, which means faithful or reliable in the sense of being in conformity with God's righteousness. We are told elsewhere in the Old Testament that God cannot lie (Num. 23:19; 1 Sam. 15:29). Thus, for a judgment to be faithful to God's righteous character it must be factually accurate.

advances, there are other evidentiary options that can provide equivalent, and perhaps even greater, reliability than a second eyewitness. Using evidence of this sort satisfies the principle underlying the two-witness rule even if that evidence is not, as a technical matter, a second person testifying to what he or she observed. In sum, the moral guidance of the two-witness rule is that a single eyewitness should not be enough to convict, but additional evidence (such as DNA or a video-recording) could satisfy the principle of accuracy that motivated the rule in its original ancient context.

There is a word of warning to us all here in a day and age of judgment by Twitter mob. Whatever authority you and I have to judge another human being is a derivative authority. We have no such inherent right, and this is true regardless of what our laws may say. We can judge only if and when God has authorized us to do so.[33] While God has directed us to help the oppressed (Isa. 1:17)—which we can do through a well-functioning criminal justice system—he has not authorized us to judge oppressors whenever we believe the proof of guilt meets our definition of "sufficient." One witness alone, no matter how believable, does not suffice.

It is not hard to imagine how frustrating the two-witness rule or its modern equivalent could prove to be. But what if that frustration is part of the rule's purpose? Justice in this fallen world is an intermediate justice, not an ultimate one, as the two-witness rule so starkly reminds us. Some crimes will go unproven or be unprovable if, to protect the innocent, we insist on two eyewitnesses or other evidence of equivalent reliability. But if we jettison that rule or its underlying principle and instead pursue ultimate justice when, for now, the intermediate must do, we risk committing injustices of our own in the name of justice.

And so, to avoid compounding individual injustice with governmental injustice, some wrongs must go unpunished for now. Will that be disappointing, even maddening, at times? For sure. But we are not without hope. We know that Christ will come again in glory to judge the living and the dead. Wrongdoers will not escape the arm of the Lord even if their time on this earth passes without giving an account. In some cases, acting justly in a fallen world means we must for a time suffer injustice and instead entrust

33 For a further theological discussion of the derivative nature of human authority, see Jonathan Leeman, *Political Church: The Local Assembly as the Embassy of Christ's Rule* (Downers Grove, IL: IVP Academic, 2016), 161–62, 206–7.

the matter to the one who always judges justly and who has promised that, if not now, he will do so in the end.

Just Laws

Scripture's accuracy requirement is about more than accurate verdicts, however. Actual guilt also demands that the law properly distinguish what is morally right from what is morally wrong.

In other words, justice requires that the law rightly draw the line between good and evil, that laws be what Scripture calls "true laws" (Neh. 9:13).[34] Thomas Aquinas made this point when he wrote that "the force of a law depends on the extent of its justice."[35] Juries can err in differentiating the guilty from the innocent, but so can the laws that juries apply. A man-made law can unjustly declare as guilty someone who committed no moral wrong, and conversely the law can declare innocent those who have acted immorally. The prophet Isaiah warned of this, pronouncing woe on "those who call evil good and good evil" (Isa. 5:20), which the Westminster Catechism deems a form of bearing false witness in violation of the ninth commandment.[36] Verdicts can do that on a one-off basis; laws can do that as a category.

Thus, when it comes to biblical justice, violating the law does not necessarily equate to moral guilt. The actual guilt requirement implied in Romans 13 limits the authority of government to punishing one who is not merely a lawbreaker but a moral "wrongdoer"[37]—rendered literally as one who practices evil (Rom. 13:4). Augustine touched on this when he argued that, in the same way that an unjust society is no society at all, "a law that is not just does not seem to me to be a law."[38] As we saw in the previous chapter,

34 The Hebrew world translated as "true" in this passage is the same word used in "true judgments" in Zech. 7:9. Even if a law is "true" in the sense that it rightly divides right from wrong, there are other requirements of a moral legal system, which Harvard law professor Lon Fuller referred to as the "internal morality of the law." For example, laws can be unjust if applied retroactively, if they can't be understood, if they are frequently changed, or if they require people to do things beyond their power. Lon L. Fuller, *The Morality of the Law*, rev. ed. (New Haven, CT: Yale University Press, 1969), 39.

35 Thomas Aquinas, *Summa Theologica*, trans. Fathers of the English Dominican Province (New York: Benziger Bros, 1947), 1–2.95.2, http://www.ccel.org.

36 Westminster Larger Catechism, question 145.

37 Nicholas Wolterstorff, *The Mighty and the Almighty: An Essay in Political Theology* (New York: Cambridge University Press, 2014), 90–95.

38 Augustine, *On the Free Choice of the Will, On Grace and Free Choice, and Other Writings*, ed. and trans. Peter King (Cambridge: Cambridge University Press, 2010), 10.

God has granted to government the authority to enact laws and enforce them through the use of physical coercion, but the government is itself restrained by the moral obligation to love. Thus, what the government has been divinely authorized to adopt and administer with physical force are just laws. If a law is not just, then a violation of that law is not a moral wrong. And if the defendant has not committed a moral wrong, then the authorities are not morally permitted to punish him regardless of what the text of the statute or system of government might empower them to do. A person who violates an unjust law is not a Romans 13 "wrongdoer";[39] therefore, a violation of an unjust law does not render the violator actually guilty of anything that the state is biblically authorized to punish.

Of course, juries may (and do) return verdicts finding a person guilty of violating an unjust law, and the state may (and does) possess the *power* to punish that person. But the state has *no moral authority* to inflict that punishment because the state is divinely authorized to use force only in the cause of justice. An unjust law empowers the state to use physical force against a citizen, but because the law is unjust those who violate that law have committed no wrong for which Scripture authorizes the state to use punitive force. For this reason, Aquinas says that unjust laws "are acts of violence rather than laws."[40]

Remember, the conundrum of criminal justice (and war) is that physical violence against another is, as a general rule, immoral. What makes the use of physical force by the state moral is its use to advance justice. If instead the state uses physical coercion to enforce an unjust law, the government's actions against the morally innocent individual are nothing more than, to paraphrase Augustine, organized crime.[41] Stated another way, the use of physical force is moral not simply because it is employed by the state but only if it is used by the state to accomplish justice. And whether force is used for justice depends on whether the law being enforced is itself just—meaning that the law rightly discerns right from wrong. In sum, the justice, not

---

39 Echoing Augustine, the English Puritan Richard Baxter (1615–91) concludes, regarding our obligation to obey penal laws, that "it is no sin to break a law which is no law, as being against God, or not authorized by him." Richard Baxter, *A Christian Directory: Or, A Body of Practical Divinity, and Cases of Conscience*, vol. 5 (London: Richard Edwards, 1825), 99–100.

40 Aquinas, *Summa Theologica*, 1–2.96.4.

41 Augustine, *The City of God against the Pagans*, ed. and trans. R. W. Dyson (New York: Cambridge University Press, 2002), 147 (4.4).

the text, of a statute determines the moral legitimacy of the government's punishment of the law's violator.

Recently, a new chief prosecutor was elected in the county neighboring mine in northern Virginia. Shortly after taking office, she was asked about what she saw as the shortcomings in our justice system. Her response mirrors the dual concerns I've discussed here: "I think about sorting the people who are innocent from the people who are guilty. But the system also has a problem sorting out what things should be punished from those things that should not." She went on to explain that she "care[s] about truth in both the narrow sense and the broad sense. There is the truth of whether this person did something. But there is another truth about whether we should be putting someone in prison for" whatever it is they did.[42] In other words, she understands that the criminal law itself can be unjust—a social injustice, you might say.

Recognizing that the law can be either just or unjust raises questions about the use of cliches like "law and order" to describe one's theory of criminal justice (e.g., "I'm a 'law and order' conservative"). It's possible that someone using this phrase simply intends it as a shorthand for enforcing just laws fairly, which we should all desire. More likely, to my observation, is that "law and order" is used interchangeably with "tough on crime."[43] If that's what someone means, then it raises the question whether we *should* be tough on crime. The answer depends on whether that toughness is, in context, just. I'll return to that issue in chapter 8. For now, it's worth noting that talk of "law and order" has a checkered history and has frequently been little more than coded language for perpetuating injustice. During the Civil Rights Era, calls for "law and order" were, for all intents and purposes, calls to maintain the status quo by suppressing protest of the unjust legal order. Indeed, Martin Luther King Jr. warned of the man "who is more devoted to 'order' than to justice; who prefers a negative peace which is the absence of tension to a positive peace which is the presence of justice."[44] Oliver

---

42 This prosecutor's comments are recounted in Carissa Byrne Hessick, *Punishment without Trial: Why Plea Bargaining Is a Bad Deal* (New York: Abrams, 2021), 202–3.

43 For a discussion of the history of the evangelical embrace of "law and order" language, see Aaron Griffith, *God's Law and Order: The Politics of Punishment in Evangelical America* (Cambridge, MA: Harvard University Press, 2020).

44 Martin Luther King Jr., "Letter from Birmingham Jail," April 16, 1963, The University of Alabama Libraries Special Collections, accessed June 8, 2022, 9–10, http://purl.lib.ua.edu/181702. King

O'Donovan similarly observes that "'justice' is a moral concept; 'order' is not."[45] Nor, for that matter, is law.

Justice, biblically defined, is the standard against which man-made law, and the order that law brings about, must be measured. If the law is unjust, an appeal to "law and order" is a call to punish unjustly those who are not morally blameworthy. A theory of criminal justice that does no more than invoke the legal status quo is not a theory of justice at all, as it lacks the tools to evaluate the morality of that status quo. Only when man's law aligns with God's justice is the violator of that law guilty—a Romans 13 wrong-doer—such that the state may rightly employ punitive force against him.

———

While Franklin Smith's court-martial was underway in Massachusetts in the fall of 1864, Abraham Lincoln was reelected that November to his second term as president. As the commander-in-chief, President Lincoln had the final say over the verdict handed down in a military court-martial like Smith's. There was good reason to think that Smith had been framed for a crime he did not commit, so following the trial Lincoln requested that the transcript of the proceeding be sent to him and directed that execution of the sentence be delayed until he had a chance to review the case.

In the early morning hours of March 18, 1865, Lincoln drafted by hand an order finding the evidence against Smith insufficient and directing his immediate release.[46] Accuracy, the first principle of justice, was vindicated. This time. Barely.

Twenty-eight days later, President Lincoln was assassinated.

---

may have been echoing Reinhold Niebuhr, who wrote that "order precedes justice in the strategy of government; but . . . only an order which implicates justice can achieve a stable peace. An unjust order quickly invites the resentment and rebellion which leads to its undoing." Reinhold Niebuhr, *The Children of Light and the Children of Darkness* (New York: Charles Scribner, 1960), 181.

45 Oliver O'Donovan, *In Pursuit of a Christian View of War* (Bramcote, UK: Grove, 1977), 8.

46 Dahl, "Lincoln Saves a Reformer."

5

Due Process

WHEN REVEREND PARKER MET with President Lincoln at the White House in July 1864, his ultimate concern was the falsity of the allegation made against his church member. He believed that Franklin Smith was an innocent man framed for a crime he had not committed. Parker was concerned about an inaccurate conviction.

But Parker's more immediate concerns were procedural. Smith's case had been diverted from a civilian court to a military court-martial, a procedural move that Parker feared was designed to facilitate Smith's conviction. To make matters worse, though the supposed crime had occurred in Massachusetts, the trial had been moved to Philadelphia, away from Smith's home, witnesses, and means of defense.[1]

As Parker feared, Smith was wrongfully convicted in the court-martial, an outcome that was rectified only by Lincoln's extraordinary intervention. For this, Parker was certainly grateful. But he preferred that the trial be the means by which Smith was cleared. Accordingly, when Parker met with Lincoln to plead Smith's cause before the trial, Parker's argument wasn't merely that Smith was innocent but also that the process being used to determine his guilt or innocence had been rigged.

Parker understood that accurate outcomes at trial depend on fair procedures to adjudicate the allegations, so he pleaded with Lincoln to correct the procedural maneuver that had landed Parker's case in a court-martial

---

1 Curtis Dahl, "Lincoln Saves a Reformer," *American Heritage*, October 1972, https://www .americanheritage.com/.

far from home. These procedural issues, Parker anticipated, would in combination yield the conviction of an innocent man. To avoid that injustice, Parker implored Lincoln to direct the Secretary of the Navy to reassign the case to a federal criminal court where (unlike in a court-martial) Smith would be tried by a jury of his civilian peers. Lincoln declined to make this move, concerned that it would suggest a lack of trust in the Navy Secretary. Instead, Lincoln moved the case back to Boston for trial and promised intervention after the verdict if the court-martial went awry.[2]

Parker's desire for an accurate verdict, and the relationship of a just verdict and due process, are at the heart of what it means to love in the context of criminal justice. We saw in the last chapter that at the core of divine justice is accuracy: "true laws" (Neh. 9:13) and "true judgments" (Zech. 7:9). In this chapter we will explore how a commitment to fair process is inextricably intertwined with the biblical demand for accuracy.

Procedural Fairness

Though Parker didn't expressly frame his appeal to President Lincoln in biblical terms, underlying his argument was a theological point of central significance to any Christian ethic of criminal justice: the God of truth and love cares about the justice system's accuracy, which depends on the system's process. Whether a system yields accurate verdicts turns on the processes the system employs. This means, to put it in Christ's language, that loving your neighbors as yourself requires designing a criminal justice process that distinguishes those who are actual wrongdoers from those who are not. Substantive justice is inextricably tied to procedural justice. True verdicts require due process.

A simple example might help to illustrate this relationship between accuracy and process. Imagine a criminal justice system claiming that the accused can only be convicted on proof of guilt beyond a reasonable doubt. The jurors are instructed, as the law requires, that they must not convict except on this high standard of proof. This sounds good and just. But then also imagine that this hypothetical justice system denies the defendant an attorney, does not allow for the cross-examination of the prosecution's witnesses, and does

---

2   J. W. Parker, "Joseph Whiting Parker, Sr.'s Memoirs," 1880, MS 14909, Special Collections, University of Virginia Library, Charlottesville, VA, 142–43; Dahl, "Lincoln Saves a Reformer."

not permit the defense to present any evidence. Now how just does it sound? This hypothetical system of justice may, on paper, profess a commitment to accuracy beyond a reasonable doubt. But the system's process tells a different story. The process this hypothetical jurisdiction uses to conduct its trials gives little if any reason to have confidence that the verdicts reflect the truth. The distorted process raises questions—serious questions—about the accuracy of the outcomes. While this example is an extreme one, it serves to illustrate that a justice system's commitment to accuracy runs only as deep as the system's use of processes that ensure accuracy.

We saw in the last chapter that both crime victims and the criminally accused are due accuracy as a matter of biblical justice. If accuracy depends on process, then both crime victims and the criminally accused are also due a justice system with processes designed to yield accuracy. If we owe crime victims and the criminally accused accurate verdicts, then we owe them a process that will yield those verdicts. You can't have accuracy without process. And because our neighbors are *due* a system that reaches accurate results, *love* demands that we provide such a system to our neighbors who are either accused or victimized. Today, we call such a system "due process," and taking seriously the biblical demand for accuracy means taking due process seriously. Achieving accuracy is not happenstance. True verdicts are the by-product of a system with procedures intentionally and thoughtfully designed for truth-seeking.

If you think about it, there really is no way to reach accurate conclusions on a consistent basis without an adequate process. Prior to a trial, we know the accusation that has been leveled; we might even know what a witness claims he or she saw or experienced. What we do not know prior to trial is whether that witness is reliable, nor do we know what the competing evidence might show. Without a trial, we hear *part* of the story. Without a trial, we *may* have suspicions. But without a trial (or some other process), we do not *know* whether a crime occurred and, if so, who committed the crime. And that trial cannot provide a reliable answer to the question of guilt or innocence if its procedures are not of a sort designed to yield accurate results.

When I meet someone new and tell him or her that I'm a criminal defense attorney, at some point I'm usually asked some version of this question: How do you represent someone you know is guilty? My response to this question is always the same: How do I know whether the client is guilty?

The only way I could know the answer to that question is by going through a process. I may ask the client what happened. But I would be foolish if I simply accepted what the client tells me about what happened. The client may be wrong. He or she may misremember the events. The client might even be lying to me about what occurred because he or she is embarrassed or scared or devious. I listen to what the client says, but what the client says is only one piece of evidence that I must weigh in determining what happened. Whether the client claims to be innocent or admits to being guilty, I don't merely accept that representation—I test it. People deny things they did do and (as I will discuss in chap. 11) admit to doing things they didn't do. So I review all of the evidence, as I should if I am seeking the truth.

To gather and analyze all the evidence, I need to undertake an investigative *process*. I need to review documents, interview witnesses, visit the crime scene, and consult with experts. Then I need to compare and weigh these various pieces of evidence. After going through that process, I may conclude that the client has recounted accurately to me what happened, or I may conclude that he hasn't. But it is only after the process of evidence gathering and weighing that I can form an accurate view of what happened so that I can then render legal advice. Without a thorough process for evaluating the evidence, I would be unable to reach an accurate conclusion as to whether the client committed a crime.

My point here isn't that defense lawyers should be the final authorities on guilt or innocence; in fact, I don't think they should be. My point is that none of us *know* whether someone is guilty or innocent until we go through some type of fact-finding process. Even the step of simply interviewing the client about what happened is a process. The question then isn't *whether* a process is necessary to sort out guilt from innocence. The question is *what* fact-finding process is needed in a criminal justice system to reach accurate results on a consistent basis. This is the question of due process, the question of what process is owed the participants in the justice system who are, as a matter of love, entitled to accuracy.

Allowance for Error

When we approach the question of what process is due, we are also addressing a related question (whether we recognize it or not): May a government justly tolerate the conviction and punishment of some number of innocents in the course of convicting the guilty? In other words, how certain must we be that someone is guilty before the state may punish? Given the relationship between accuracy and process, the degree of certainty required and the extent of error we can morally tolerate will dictate the procedures we put in place.

The thought that we might tolerate some number of wrongful convictions may strike you as incomprehensible, especially coming after a chapter arguing that love for neighbor requires a commitment to accuracy. But error is the reality of life in a fallen world. "To err is human," the English poet Alexander Pope reminds us.[3] No criminal justice system in this life will achieve perfection. Acknowledging this isn't resignation to injustice but rather clear-eyed realism that justice will not be fully realized in this life no matter how much we strive for it.[4] In a sin-soaked world we cannot, as they say, let the perfect be the enemy of the good.

To demand absolute accuracy of fallible earthly administrators of criminal justice would be to demand the impossible. Augustine summarized this wretchedness of the human condition in *City of God* where he explained that, because of our fallenness, judgment is a necessary response to humankind's injustice, and yet, because of our fallenness, our judgment will be fallible and thus cause injustice of its own.[5] To insist that the only acceptable system of justice is a system that never yields wrongful convictions would be, for all intents and purposes, to demand the abolition of criminal justice, which is its own injustice. And yet to require that the system never let a guilty man or woman go free would require that the system convict some number of innocents in the process, which is an injustice of the opposite sort.

We have never and will never devise a system that is precisely calibrated to 100 percent accuracy. In this life, there is no perfection. We will err in

3 Alexander Pope, "An Essay on Criticism," part 2, https://www.poetryfoundation.org.
4 This Christian realism, which seeks to balance the seriousness of the second Great Commandment and the reality of life in a fallen world, is most closely associated with Reinhold Niebuhr. See Reinhold Niebuhr, *Christian Realism and Political Problems* (New York: Charles Scribner's Sons, 1953). For an accessible introduction to Christian realism, see Daniel Strand, "Christian Realism: An Introduction," *Providence*, January 31, 2020, https://providencemag.com/.
5 Augustine, *The City of God against the Pagans*, ed. and trans. R. W. Dyson (New York: Cambridge University Press, 2002), 926–28 (19.6).

one direction or the other. As we require more certainty in our verdicts before we punish, the inevitable result will be the exoneration of a greater number of the guilty, which is an injustice against the victims and perpetrators of those unpunished offenses. If, on the other hand, we reduce the needed level of certainty to ensure the conviction of all the guilty, we risk ensnaring a larger number of the innocent in the system. Both "acquitting the guilty and condemning the innocent" work an injustice, and God hates them both (Prov. 17:15 NIV).

The inability to achieve perfection in our justice system means we must decide in which direction we will err. How do we choose between these imperfect and unjust alternatives? Is our choice merely a matter of Christian prudence? Are we as Christians at liberty to construct a system in a way that we know will result in the imprisonment of some number of innocent people to serve the greater good of more punishment of those who are guilty? In short, I don't believe so.

While acquitting the guilty and convicting the innocent are both unjust, they are not *equally* unjust.[6] Recall that the presumption of Scripture is that the use of physical force by one human against another is, as a general rule, immoral. This means that any moral authority we might have to use force against another person requires a divinely granted exception from that general prohibition. In Romans 13, the apostle Paul articulates such an exception, but it is a narrow one: the governing authorities may use punitive force against actual wrongdoers. The baseline presumption of Scripture against the use of physical force against others remains intact, and it means that we must err on the side of not acting lest we employ punitive force against an innocent without divine authorization. Ideally, we should neither acquit the guilty nor convict the innocent. But in a world that is less than ideal, we must "keep far from a false charge" (Ex. 23:7).

It may seem obvious to you that a government should punish the guilty—and only the guilty—and thus design criminal justice procedures

---

6   Martin Luther agrees that to "err in th[e] direction" of "punish[ing] too little is more tolerable, for it is always better to let a scoundrel live than to put a godly man to death." His reasoning, however, differs from mine. His argument is that "the world has plenty of scoundrels anyway and must continue to have them, but godly men are scarce." Martin Luther, "Temporal Authority: To What Extent It Should Be Obeyed," in *From Irenaeus to Grotius: A Sourcebook in Christian Political Thought*, ed. Oliver O'Donovan and Joan Lockwood O'Donovan (Grand Rapids, MI: Eerdmans, 1999), 590.

along those lines, but that is by no means the view of all ethicists. Utilitarian ethics looks at the consequences of an action, defining justice based on the aggregate net good achieved by a particular policy or practice without regard for either the nature of the act or the individualized harm inflicted. Utilitarianism is what moral philosophers call a consequentialist ethic because whether conduct is morally acceptable is determined not by categories of right and wrong, but rather by the consequences of the conduct. Utilitarianism can be thought of as an ends-justifies-the-means ethic.

The utilitarian conception of justice is said to originate with the English legal philosopher Jeremy Bentham (1748–1832), who taught that the ethical course of action is that which brings the greatest happiness to the greatest number of people.[7] Thus, utilitarianism allows for a criminal justice system that punishes innocent people if, for example, the consequence of doing so is to deter others from committing crime and thus result in happiness to the population at large in greater measure than the pain suffered by the wrongly convicted.[8] Or, to take another example, utilitarianism might say that it is morally permissible to convict some number of innocents if the financial consequence of a more reliable justice system would be a cost to taxpayers greater than the cost (however measured) borne by the wrongly convicted innocents.

Christian ethics is not utilitarian. For one thing, utilitarianism's ends-justifies-the-means view of justice runs headlong into Paul's teaching in Romans 3:8. Based on that passage, it has long been a "basic principle in Christian morality . . . that no one should do wrong that good may come of it."[9] What is more, utilitarianism offers a vision of justice that requires some

---

7 Jeremy Bentham, *An Introduction to the Principles of Morals and Legislation*, vol. 1 (London: W. Pickering, 1823), 1–6; Norman Geisler, *Christian Ethics: Contemporary Issues and Options*, 2nd ed. (Grand Rapids, MI: Baker Academic, 2010), 24, 30, 119 (discussing Bentham's utilitarian view of morality); Michael Sandel, *Justice: What's the Right Thing to Do?* (New York: Farrar, Straus and Giroux, 2009), 34–35.

8 Igor Primorac, "Utilitarianism and Self-Sacrifice of the Innocent," *Analysis* 38, no. 4 (October 1978): 194, https://doi.org/10.2307/3327991. Some ethicists contest the claim that utilitarianism allows for punishing the innocent for the greater good of society. See Saul Smilansky, "Utilitarianism and the 'Punishment' of the Innocent: The General Problem," *Analysis* 50, no. 4 (October 1990): 256–61, https://doi.org/10.2307/3328264.

9 Paul Ramsey, *War and the Christian Conscience: How Shall Modern War Be Conducted Justly?* (Durham, NC: Duke University Press, 1961), 51. See also Catechism of the Catholic Church,

members of a society to "take one for the team," so to speak, elevating the interests of the community to such a degree that they obliterate the interests of the individual. Utilitarianism sees people as means to a greater end of communal happiness rather than as ends in themselves with dignity and rights that are inviolable even for good purposes. Scripture, by contrast, sees people as ends in themselves, each of them individually made in the image of God and each entitled to our collective love.[10] Accordingly, a Christian vision of criminal justice cannot be a utilitarian one.

Instead, the Christian conception of justice declares that certain acts are right or wrong without regard to the consequences of those acts. Christian ethics is, in the language of moral philosophers, a deontological system of ethics.[11] It is wrong, for example, to use government force against an innocent person (Ex. 23:7), and it is right and proper to use proportional government force to punish wrongdoers (Rom. 13). As a matter of Christian ethics, these statements are true not because of the consequences these actions yield but because of God's categorical declarations about the propriety or impropriety of those acts.

To say that a Christian ethic of criminal justice cannot be utilitarian does not mean that cost cannot be considered in fashioning a justice system. Not every consideration of cost is utilitarian. In a world of limited resources, choices must be made about how to allocate those resources to achieve the greatest possible justice. But, for the Christian, the justice of an act is not determined by whether its benefits exceed its costs. Christian ethics claims that there are some lines that cannot be crossed regardless of cost and that certain cost arguments are illegitimate.

---

part 3, sec. 1, chap. 1, art. 4, II (Good and Evil Acts), 1756 ("One may not do evil so that good may result from it") and 1759 ("The end does not justify the means"), accessed June 10, 2022, http://www.vatican.va; John Paul II, *Veritatis Splendor*, August 6, 1993, sec 81, http://www.vatican.va.

10 Gene Outka, *Agape: An Ethical Analysis* (New Haven, CT: Yale University Press, 1972), 9: "[Th]e neighbor ought to be cared about for his own sake . . . and not for the sake of benefits to the self." The Catholic theologian Albert Dondeyne (1901–1985) captures this beautifully: "There is, at the origin of Christian moral choice, . . . the constant and effective recognition of the great dignity of every human person, taken not only as an end in himself existing for himself, but also as a child of God. . . . Christianity demands of Christians that this effective recognition . . . be the very breadth of their life, the unwavering inspiration of all their actions, the rule of their conduct everywhere and at all times." Albert Dondeyne, *Contemporary European Thought and Christian Faith*, trans. Ernan McMullin and John Burnheim (Pittsburgh, PA: Duquesne University Press, 1958), 196.

11 Geisler, *Christian Ethics*, 17–18.

Let me try to illustrate this distinction with an example. When I explain the dangers of plea bargaining (a topic I will address in chap. 11), a common response is that we need plea bargaining because it would simply be too expensive to provide trials to every defendant who wants one. In fact, the late Supreme Court Justice Antonin Scalia described plea bargaining as a "necessary evil"—necessary because it would be too "expensive" to give everyone an American-style trial.[12]

Whether this is a morally legitimate argument for the Christian depends on what one means by "too expensive." If "too expensive" means an amount greater than voters are willing to expend because they would rather spend their money on some luxury item that would bring them greater happiness, then the argument is a utilitarian one that is impermissible for the Christian. But if by "too expensive" one means that an American-style trial demands more in the way of financial resources than a state or country has at its disposal, then this may be a type of moral argument that a Christian can properly make. We are finite by nature and limited in our financial (and other) resources and must necessarily make moral decisions as such.

So what is a state or country to do if it lacks the financial resources to provide an American-style process to every criminal defendant? Several options are imaginable, but not everything imaginable is permissible for the Christian. Some options are, as a categorical matter, out of bounds. For example, it might be morally permissible to change the law to reduce the number of crimes to the most serious ones so that resources are available to provide a trial to everyone charged with a crime. But if the crime eliminated from the law books was murder, the result would be an unjust failure of the government to punish the evil of murder. For the Christian, that's a categorical line that cannot be crossed.

Another option to address the shortage of resources might be to streamline the process provided to criminal defendants. We will consider in the second half of this book whether American-style criminal justice provides defendants with all the process they are morally due. But even if it does, this doesn't mean that American-style criminal procedure is the only system that could meet the biblical standard of due process. To evaluate whether the

12 Lafler v. Cooper, 566 U.S. 156, 175, 185 (2012) (Scalia, J., dissenting).

American system or any other justice system satisfies Scripture's procedural demands, we first need to determine what those demands are. Rejecting utilitarianism as the governing ethic requires that we decipher Scripture's categorical lines that cannot be crossed. What process does the Bible teach is due a criminal defendant?

The process due as a matter of Christian ethics is rooted not in society's net happiness from a given legal system (utilitarian) but rather in the defendant's and the victim's biblical right to accuracy. If both the criminally accused and the crime victim are due an accurate determination of guilt, and if procedure A is needed to make an accurate determination of guilt, then both defendant and victim are due procedure A. If 100 percent accuracy was feasible with a society's available resources, then the biblical demand for accuracy would require those procedures needed to achieve 100 percent accuracy. But we don't live in the world of perfection. We live in a world of imperfect outcomes. And therein lies the problem. What process is due in a fallen world?

All Reasonable Means

Notice, however, that I have qualified these statements by reference to feasibility and available resources—admittedly ambiguous concepts. It is here again that just war theory can help sharpen our thinking. As explained earlier, the Christian doctrine of just war addresses not only when it is moral to engage in war (*jus ad bellum*) but also how a just war should be prosecuted (*jus in bello*). As part of the *jus in bello* analysis, Christian thinkers have wrestled with the question of how much collateral damage to innocents (i.e., noncombatants) is morally tolerable in a just war, and this body of thought is useful in evaluating the moral tolerance for error in a criminal justice system.

Theologians and philosophers have long observed that whether a war is justly conducted depends on two core principles: discrimination and proportionality.[13] With regard to the former, "Christian Just War Theory has, at least since the seventeenth century, regarded the immunity of in-

13 Paul Ramsey, *The Just War: Force and Political Responsibility* (Lanham, MD: Rowan and Little-field, 1983), 428; Marc Livecche, "Just War," in *Protestant Social Teaching: An Introduction*, ed. Onsi Aaron Kamel, Jake Meador, and Joseph Minich (Landrum, SC: Davenant, 2022), 78; Elizabeth Philips, *Political Theology: A Guide for the Perplexed* (London: T&T Clark, 2012), 103.

1

nocent human beings as one of its primary concerns."[14] Accordingly, the principle of discrimination—derived from Paul's admonition that we may "not do evil that good may come" (Rom. 3:8)—requires that lethal force be directed only at those who are legitimate targets of attack (i.e., opposing combatants). The evil of *intentionally* killing innocent parties may not be done to achieve the good of a military victory. This is why, as a general rule, it is deemed immoral to intentionally launch military attacks against noncombatant civilians.[15]

For similar reasons, it would be deeply immoral to intentionally prosecute an innocent person, bringing the punitive force of the state to bear on someone who has committed no crime. This is the stuff of banana republics and tyrannical regimes. The criminal justice system is not a play toy to be wielded against political and personal enemies without regard to wrongdoing. To *intentionally* bear the punitive sword of the state against someone who has done no wrong is categorically unjust, a conclusion that every fair-minded person, Christian or not, should agree on.

But turning back to the just war analogy, what if a military attack directed at an opposing combatant would also result in the *unintended* deaths of civilians? What if innocents would be collateral damage of the bombing of a military base, for example? In that instance, would the unintended but foreseeable injury to innocents be morally acceptable? To answer these and similar questions, Christian ethicists have reasoned that the just war principle of discrimination requires that *all reasonable means* be taken to avoid collateral damage to noncombatant innocents from lethal force directed against legitimate military targets.

In a nutshell, the argument for the all-reasonable-means test goes like this. The doctrine of double effect (which is credited to Thomas Aquinas) recognizes that there may be more than one effect of an action—the intended effect and an unintended effect.[16] As discussed above, a person is

14 Camillo C. Bica, "Interpreting Just War Theory's Jus In Bello Criterion of Discrimination," *Public Affairs Quarterly* 12, no. 2 (April 1998): 161, https://www.jstor.org/stable/40441189.
15 Livecche, "Just War," 81.
16 Thomas Aquinas, *Summa Theologica*, trans. Fathers of the English Dominican Province (New York: Benziger Bros, 1947), 2–2.64.7, http://www.ccel.org; Livecche, "Just War," 81. For a more extended discussion of the development and application of the doctrine of double effect, see Ramsey, *War and the Christian Conscience*, 39–59.

100 A CHRISTIAN ETHIC OF CRIMINAL JUSTICE

morally responsible for *the intended effect* of his or her actions. Intended killing of innocent civilians is immoral, even if done for good purposes. That an effect is unintended, however, doesn't necessarily absolve the actor of responsibility for the effect. To answer that question of moral responsibility one must ask whether *the unintended effect* was foreseeable. Christian ethicists have generally concluded that an actor bears moral responsibility not only for intended but also *unintended but foreseeable and avoidable* results of his or her conduct.[17] For example, if I carpet bomb a city with the intent only to kill a single terrorist hiding in the city, it is foreseeable that I will kill untold numbers of innocent civilians in the city in the process. Thus, regardless of my intent to kill only the terrorist through the bombing, I would be morally at fault for the foreseeable civilian deaths that resulted from my bombing and could have been avoided by a more targeted attack. According to just war theory, I have a moral obligation to be discriminating in my use of force, and carpet bombing of this sort would be indiscriminate.

But under the doctrine of double effect, *unexpected or unavoidable* effects of our actions are of a different moral character. One is not morally culpable for effects that were not reasonably foreseeable in light of the precautions taken or were unavoidable given the options available. Or, in the words of the Catechism of the Catholic Church, "for a bad effect to be imputable it must be foreseeable and the agent must have the possibility of avoiding it."[18] Taking military action "to kill the innocent unnecessarily, and when they can be distinguished from the guilty, implies that the motive is malicious"— meaning that the use of lethal force under those circumstances suggests that someone actually intends to kill the innocent regardless of what they might claim.[19] Thus, for example, military action is morally justified so long as its intended and reasonably foreseeable effects are the deaths only of legitimate military targets. Stated conversely, a military actor is not morally culpable if he or she, after taking all reasonable precautions, nonetheless unexpect-

---

17 Nigel Biggar, *In Defence of War* (New York: Oxford University Press, 2013), 96, explains that even if an evil effect is not intended, one is morally responsible for that effect if it was "caused needlessly, in the sense that it could have been avoided." Reproduced with permission of the Licensor through PLSclear.

18 Catechism of the Catholic Church, part 3, sec. 1, chap. 1, art. 3, I (Freedom and Responsibility), 1737, accessed June 13, 2022, http://www.vatican.va.

19 Biggar, *In Defence of War*, 183. Reproduced with permission of the Licensor through PLSclear.

edly or unavoidably kills an innocent civilian.[20] While the civilian death is tragic, if it wasn't intended, wasn't foreseeable in light of the reasonable precautions taken, and wasn't avoidable with other reasonably available precautions, then the military actor did not commit an immoral act even though the act's effect was the death of an innocent.

This all-reasonable-means test is Christian realism at its best. The test is Christian in its respect for life and realistic in its recognition that we live in a fallen world where mistakes happen and not all harm is avoidable. Sometimes the obligation to stop evil will involve unintended and unavoidable harm. This isn't morally culpable. The all-reasonable-means test doesn't insist on impossible perfection. Requiring perfection in a fallen world would oblige us to abandon entirely the pursuit of justice, which would be its own injustice. But while the all-reasonable-means test doesn't demand perfection, it does demand that we do all we reasonably can to avoid error. The test is realist in light of human frailty. And yet the test recognizes that a mistake isn't really a mistake and a harm isn't truly unintended if available precautions weren't taken. That, instead, is immoral recklessness. This is what the doctrine of double effect, worked out over centuries by Christian thinkers, teaches us.

This all-reasonable-means test provides a useful analogy for thinking about what process is due the criminally accused to protect against wrongful convictions. Whether we are considering military force or judicial force, the question for the Christian is essentially the same: When and under what conditions may the state use physical force against another person consistent with the law of love? If love demands that the governing authorities, when using military force, take all reasonable means to avoid collateral damage to innocents, then it would seem that love demands the same regarding the state's use of judicial force. In other words, the all-reasonable-means test, rooted in centuries of Christian thought concerning the government's use of physical force, is the proper one for evaluating our tolerance for error in the justice system.

---

20 Bica, "Interpreting Just War Theory's Jus In Bello Criterion of Discrimination," 161–65; Biggar, *In Defence of War*, 189, writes that the unintentional death of innocents is not morally culpable if "one has done everything feasible to avoid and minimize them." Reproduced with permission of the Licensor through PLSclear. Alison McIntyre, "Doctrine of Double Effect," *Stanford Encyclopedia of Philosophy*, last modified December 24, 2018, https://plato.stanford.edu, sec. 1: it is permissible to cause unintended harm if the "agents strive to minimize the foreseen harm."

To be sure, what constitutes all-reasonable-means will differ in war as compared to the criminal justice system. What is reasonable means will depend on the context in which we are asking the question. The fog of war is different than the deliberation of a jury room. And the twenty-first century is different than the first. The means available to us today differ from the means available to those long ago. Even today, the means available in a wealthy, scientifically advanced community may differ from those in the third world. I will consider in the coming chapters what those reasonable means are in our day and nation. My point here is simply that when the state deploys punitive force by means of the justice system, love demands that all reasonable means be used to ensure that this force is brought to bear only against those guilty of wrongdoing.

We cannot, as Christians, just throw up our hands or shrug our shoulders at the inevitability of erroneous convictions in a fallen world. That errors will occur does not mean that any process will do. Even as fallen creatures, there is some maximum level of accuracy that is reasonably available to us in our context. If we used every procedural and evidentiary tool reasonably at our disposal in our culture with our resources at this moment in time, we could achieve accuracy X percent of the time. Our moral obligation is to use those procedural and evidentiary tools to achieve that maximum level of accuracy. A century from now, perhaps it will be possible to achieve accuracy X+2 percent of the time. If and when that day comes, those living then will have an obligation to steward the resources available to them to reach what is then achievable. But we are not those people. We are stewards of what God has provided in our moment in time, and they will be stewards of what God affords in theirs.[21] For now, the criminal defendant and the crime victim (through the prosecutor) are due all the process available to achieve the maximum level of accuracy feasible today.[22] If we fail to provide that process, we are failing to love—we are sinning.

21 As Augustine explains, justice is not "liable to variation and change" though "the times which it rules over are not identical, for the simple reason that they are times." Augustine, *Confessions*, trans. Henry Chadwick (New York: Oxford University Press, 2008), 45 (3.7.13). Thus, the law "may differ from time to time and from place to place in accordance with circumstances and needs, and these different laws or customs may all conform to what is right and just." Herbert A. Deane, *The Political and Social Ideas of St. Augustine* (New York: Columbia University Press, 1963), 91.

22 As Jonathan Leeman puts it, "Any lack of due diligence in searching for the processes that yield that most 'reckoned' outcomes can therefore be characterized as disobedience to God." Jonathan

This brings me back to the wrongful conviction percentages we considered in the last chapter. One might be tempted to think that 98 or 99 percent accuracy is pretty good. But what if it were within our reach to achieve 99.5 or 99.9 percent accuracy? What if the means reasonably available to us in America today could make the system even more reliable? In that instance, would a failure to make use of those means be a failure of Christian stewardship? I think it would. Our moral obligation is measured against the resources—the reasonable means—with which we have been entrusted. To whom more is given, more is morally required (Luke 12:48).

In sum, the biblical principle of accuracy does not unrealistically demand perfection in a fallen world, but the principle does require that we use all reasonable means to avoid convicting the innocent. The process that is due the participants in a criminal justice system is all the process we can reasonably provide in our context to further the cause of accurate outcomes. What the law speaks of as "due process" is, for the Christian, a moral requirement that we love our neighbors by designing a justice system that includes all the procedures reasonably available to avoid wrongful convictions.

Opportunity to Be Heard

Courts have long recognized that "the opportunity to be heard" is central to the concept of due process.[23] Accuracy requires hearing both sides of the case. "The one who states his case first seems right, until the other comes and examines him," Solomon observes (Prov. 18:17). The Mosaic law similarly provided for the testing of evidence, directing that "judges shall inquire diligently" of a witness to determine if he is testifying truthfully (Deut. 19:18). Even when two witnesses are presented, their testimony is not simply accepted as true. It must be scrutinized.

Sometimes that testing may take the form of cross-examination. But that is not the only way to examine the witness's story and inquire diligently into its truthfulness. Witness testimony can also be examined and tested by the presentation of contrary evidence from other witnesses or through

---

Leeman, *Political Church: The Local Assembly as the Embassy of Christ's Rule* (Downers Grove, IL: IVP Academic, 2016), 188.

23 The US Supreme Court has defined due process as including, at a minimum, notice of the allegation and a meaningful opportunity to be heard in response. Mathews v. Eldridge, 424 U.S. 319, 348 (1976).

physical evidence that contradicts the witness. A witness may claim that the defendant punched her, but a video recording (rather than hostile questioning) may conclusively disprove the allegations. One witness may claim with certainty that John committed the crime, while a witness proffered by the defense may testify that John was at a party with friends at the time. The point of these scriptural passages isn't that the accused must have a chance to conduct American-style cross-examination of accusers. The point is broader: a witness's claims must be tested, *and* the accused must have the opportunity to be heard, to challenge, to push back, to contest those claims. Whatever this opportunity to be heard entails in a given justice system must amount to all the means reasonably needed to reach an accurate determination of the matter.

In most instances, cross-examination will be a central element of biblical due process. Cross-examination has been called "the greatest legal engine ever invented for the discovery of truth."[24] People can testify falsely, even if not maliciously so, but cross-examination serves to ferret out that inaccuracy. A witness who is 51 percent certain in his or her identification of a suspect is of a very different quality than a witness who is 95 percent certain. Either witness can, consistent with his or her oath to tell the truth, testify that it was the defendant who committed the crime. Cross-examination serves to draw out whether that witness is sufficiently reliable to satisfy Scripture's accuracy requirement. Similarly, a witness may testify using a word that is susceptible to multiple meanings. "I was defrauded," the victim claims. But probing on cross-examination might reveal that the so-called victim hadn't read the contract. Cross-examination allows the defense attorney to explore the meaning of what the witness said and clarify ambiguities. Likewise, cross-examination affords the prosecution a chance to test the memories and perceptions of witnesses who purport to provide a criminal defendant with an alibi or attest to his or her moral character. Cross-examination gives the prosecution and the defense alike a tool to use in the pursuit of accurate verdicts.

This is not to say that Scripture demands that every criminal defendant be armed with defense counsel who can conduct withering cross-examination. In Deuteronomy 19, a judge, not a defense attorney, cross-examined the witness. That model is still followed in some Western countries today.[25] The American system of lawyers acting as adversaries—each examining and cross-examining witnesses directly with a neutral third-party (jury or judge) deciding the case—is one system of justice that can meet the biblical criteria of accuracy founded on fair process, but it is not the only system that might satisfy the biblical test. We must keep in mind that Scripture does not mandate the particulars of a justice system. Instead, what Scripture requires is an accurate outcome and, by implication, all the process reasonably needed to present and challenge the evidence in service of that outcome.

Now, this idea of using all *reasonable* means might strike you as a bit unsatisfying. What means are reasonable? The answer is that it depends, which is admittedly an ambiguous response. While Scripture is clear that God cares about what we today call criminal justice, the Bible does not contain a code of criminal procedure. God has not mandated for all time the particular design details of every justice system. And with good reason. Times change. Cultures differ. Resources are not uniform. Science develops. Learning increases. In colonial America, for example, crime victims often initiated and prosecuted their own cases, and defendants likewise defended themselves. Neither side had a lawyer representing them. All of this played out in relatively small communities.[26] Was it unjust that the defendant in that system wasn't represented at trial by an attorney? I don't think so. The principle of accuracy requires something different in a sophisticated legal system with well-funded and exquisitely skilled prosecutors seeking your conviction than the principle of accuracy requires in a less formal and rudimentary legal system. The type of process needed to ensure accuracy in a close-knit community of one hundred people may be different than what is needed in an impersonalized urban area or in a county still plagued by racist sentiments. The evidentiary requirements needed in an age of video cameras and DNA technology is different than in an age or locality with neither. So

25 Harry R. Dammer and Jay S. Albanese, *Comparative Criminal Justice Systems*, 5th ed. (Belmont, CA: Cengage Learning, 2013), 128–29, 149.
26 Stephanos Bibas, *The Machinery of Criminal Justice* (New York: Oxford University Press, 2012), xix, 3–6.

it should come as no surprise that there is no one-size-fits-all criminal procedure mandate in Scripture.[27]

One last point is in order. Inherent in due process is a presumption of innocence. Without a presumption of innocence, a case will be decided before the hearing has even begun. The process would be meaningless. As the Roman emperor Julian (c. 331–363) asked rhetorically, "Can anyone be proved innocent, if it be enough to have accused him?"[28] The answer, of course, is no. The process is rendered meaningless. The accusation alone becomes the verdict, condemning those both rightly and wrongly charged. A presumption of innocence is needed to ensure that the decision is instead the result of a process that includes a right to respond. Accuracy, in other words, requires a presumption of innocence.

This presumption of innocence does not mean that we assume an accuser is lying when he or she claims to be a victim. Rather, the presumption of innocence precludes us from assuming the accuser is telling the truth until we have heard the whole matter. The presumption of innocence shouldn't be used as a tool to deny a hearing to one who claims to be victimized. Rather, it ensures that one who claims to be harmed *and* the one accused of doing harm both get a hearing. The presumption doesn't deny due process; it demands it. It ensures that judgment is reserved until the process has played out. This is the idea embedded in the proverbial warning that it is "folly and shame" to the one who "gives an answer before he hears" (Prov. 18:13).

———

The final decade of the nineteenth century was a period of record numbers of lynchings in the United States—a quintessential denial of due process. As will be discussed in chapter 18, lynching was an all too common response to an allegation of rape by a Black man, especially if of a White woman. In 1898, there were 120 lynchings, 101 of which were of Black men and

---

27 Oliver O'Donovan, *The Ways of Judgment* (Grand Rapids, MI: Eerdmans, 2005), 121, writes, "All these features of the Western penal system are dependent upon social conditions that have not always existed, and which do not exist everywhere today."

28 Ammianus Marcellinus, *Rerum Gestarum*, trans. John C. Rolfe (London: William Heinemann, 1935), 405 (18.1.4).

women. This pace of more than two lynchings a week continued into 1899 and grew to an annual total of 130 lynchings in 1901.[29]

In the summer of 1899, amid this onslaught, Reverend Francis J. Grimké (1850–1937) delivered a series of three sermons on the topic of lynching. At the time, Grimké was the pastor of 15th Street Presbyterian Church, an African-American congregation in Washington, DC. The son of a slave-holder and enslaved woman, Grimké was for decades considered one of the leading Black ministers in the United States. In the second sermon of his series, Grimké explained how fair process as a means to accurate verdicts is what the law of love demands:

> The law assumes that every man is innocent until he is proven guilty; the fact that he is a Negro does not destroy this presumption. The law also provides how his guilt shall be established. It shall be upon the testimony of credible witnesses, before a jury of his peers, and the evidence must be so conclusive as to put his guilt beyond a reasonable doubt. If there is a reasonable doubt, after hearing all the evidence, he is entitled to an acquittal. That is the law in every state in the Union, and it is a good law, based upon reason and common sense, and simple justice. Until the guilt of a prisoner is established according to the forms of law, we have no right to assume that he is guilty; it is unfair to do so; it is treating him, not as we are directed to do by the golden rule, as we would like to be treated ourselves. And yet this grave [rape] charge against the Negro is accepted in violation of every principle of right and justice and fair play, and by men and women, too, even in the North, who profess to be animated not only by the ordinary principles of justice, but by the higher principles of Christianity,—ministers of the gospel, elders and deacons and members of the church, although they know that the alleged Negro rapist is never granted a trial, is denied the sacred right guaranteed to him under the constitution and laws of the land, the right of a fair and impartial trial before a jury of his peers. The Negro is never tried according to the forms of law; is never given an opportunity of confronting his accusers and of rebutting their testimony by witnesses of his own; his guilt is assumed

---

29 Douglas O. Linder, "Lynchings: By Year and Race," University of Missouri-Kansas City School of Law, accessed June 13, 2022, https://famous-trials.com.

on a bare suspicion, or on the uncorroborated testimony of any white woman who chooses to make the charge. . . . So far as I am personally concerned, I do not believe, and never will believe these charges until the Negro is accorded a fair trial before the courts, and his guilt established as the law prescribes. That is the position which every fair-minded man ought to take . . . ; that is the position which the church of Jesus Christ ought to take.[30]

Grimké was right. Due process isn't a "technicality." It's not an obstacle. It is the means by which we protect the biblical principle of accuracy. Fair process is a way to love. And this is, as Grimké said, a principle to which the church of Jesus Christ ought to be committed.

---

30 Francis Grimké, "Lynching: Its Causes—the Crimes of the Negro," in *Addresses*, vol. 1 of *The Works of Francis Grimké*, ed. Carter G. Woodson (Washington, DC: Associated, 1942), 311–12.

6

Accountability

SINCE 1989, 3,272 MEN AND WOMEN across the United States have been exonerated after being convicted and collectively serving 28,917 years in prison for crimes they did not commit. That's an annual average of 96 exonerations, with the rate much higher as of late. During the nine-year period from 2014 through 2022, an average of 172 men and women were exonerated each year—about 3.3 per week. The average exoneree lost nearly nine years in prison before his or her innocence was uncovered. Many spent far longer waiting for justice to arrive.[1]

The criminal charge that has yielded the most wrongful convictions is murder: 1,215 exonerations (or 37 percent of all exonerations) were convicted killers who weren't killers. Drug convictions have yielded the second most exonerations (585, or 18 percent), followed by sexual assault (357, or 11 percent) and child sex abuse (312, or 9.5 percent). Illinois leads the nation with 498 exonerations since 1989, while Texas is a distant second with 447. Of all exonerees, 1,718 were Black. Although Black men and women make up about 33 percent of the US

---

1 "Exonerations by State," The National Registry of Exonerations, University of Michigan, accessed April 8, 2023, https://www.law.umich.edu/special/exoneration/Pages/Exonerations-in-the-United-States-Map.aspx. The first exoneration by means of DNA technology occurred in August 1989. Rob Warden, "First DNA Exoneration: Gary Dotson," Center on Wrongful Convictions, Bluhm Legal Clinic, Northwestern Pritzker School of Law, accessed April 18, 2022, https://www.law.northwestern.edu. Of the more than 3,250 exonerations since, 570 have been in cases where DNA evidence was present. "Exonerations by State," The National Registry of Exonerations.

prison population, they comprise 52 percent of the exonerations in the last thirty-four years.[2]

The stories behind these statistics are both heartrending and maddening. At the center of each of those stories is a person, a man or woman made in the image of God and due our love. Some of these wrongful convictions are merely honest mistakes, the tragic results of criminal justice administered by well-intentioned but finite humans. But some are not. Some—too many—were calculated corruptions of justice. The best available estimate is that 57 percent of wrongful convictions involved some type of government misconduct. Those 1,927 cases involving misconduct resulted in incarceration of men and women for a combined 19,976 years. In biblical terms, the sword of the state was wielded *by wrongdoers* against the innocent.[3]

What almost no one discusses when these exonerations occur is accountability for those wrongdoers, meaning the police officer or prosecutor or judge who misbehaved in some respect. To be sure, in some states, a person wrongly convicted is legally entitled to some amount of financial compensation, typically a pittance in return for the hell they endured. But what of accountability for the individual government official who perpetrated the injustice?

The Boomerang

To consider this issue of accountability, let's review briefly where we are in our analysis of biblical criminal justice. As discussed in chapter 4, the scriptural principle of accuracy demands that the state use its punitive power against, but only against, the morally guilty. Punishing even a criminal defendant who was convicted can be an immoral act if that person was wrongly convicted. Those wrongful convictions can take two forms: a person

---

2   Black inmates make up a larger share of the prison population than of the US population. John Gramlich, "Black Imprisonment Rate in the U.S. Has Fallen by a Third since 2006," Pew Research Center, May 6, 2020, https://www.pewresearch.org; "Exonerations by State," The National Registry of Exonerations. Looking at exonerations for murder, a group of researchers concluded that "differences in homicide rates may explain most of the enormous racial disparity in exoneration rates for murder, but not all." Samuel R. Gross et al., *Race and Wrongful Convictions in the United States 2022* (National Registry of Exonerations, 2022), 4, https://www.law.umich.edu/.

3   "Exonerations by State," The National Registry of Exonerations.

may be (1) convicted of something he or she did not do or (2) convicted of something he or she did do that the law improperly criminalizes.

Chapter 5 unpacked the relationship between process and accuracy. Due process is a means to true verdicts. Thus, to achieve accurate results in a criminal justice system, we must as a moral matter afford both the accused and the accuser all the process reasonably available to reach a correct conclusion about the defendant's guilt or innocence.

This brings us to the next question for our consideration: What must we do, as a moral matter, about those government officials who secure the conviction of an innocent person by means of a criminal justice process that did not employ all reasonably available means to avoid that inaccurate result? The answer turns on recognizing that a government official is, in that circumstance, a moral wrongdoer. If biblical justice requires that governing authorities use all reasonable means to avoid convicting the innocent, and if a government official's failure to do this results in the conviction and punishment of an innocent person, then that official has used the sword of the state unjustly—sinfully, to put a finer point on it. The government official has become a "wrongdoer" about whom Romans 13 speaks and against whom Paul directs that the sword of government should be wielded.

While Paul teaches in Romans 13 that the government is permitted by the law of love to use physical force against the guilty, there is no biblical authorization to use such force against the innocent. Intentionally punishing people known to be innocent would obviously be evil. But so too is "mistakenly" convicting and punishing people by means of an obviously defective justice system. It is unjust—a failure of love—for the government to operate a system of justice that does not use all reasonable means to protect the innocent from a wrongful conviction. If government officials operate such an unjust system and as a result an innocent man or woman is wrongly convicted, then those officials are themselves at moral fault. That wicked act by the authorities must, as a matter of justice and love for those victimized by them, be punished.

In other words, the biblical principle of accuracy demands as a corollary that a government official who contributed to a wrongful conviction be held accountable *if* the government official acted unjustly in securing that conviction. And government officials act unjustly when they operate a justice system that they know (or should know[4]) is defective, meaning the system does not take all reasonable means to avoid wrongful convictions. In that instance, the biblical requirement of accuracy implies that the state and its actors must themselves be held accountable for inaccurate outcomes. The law of love governs both the state and the citizen, both the ruler and the subject. If love demands that the individual citizen who commits an injustice be held accountable, then love demands no less when the perpetrator of injustice is a government official.

This is the import of Romans 13: the government itself is subject to the obligation to love. Irenaeus of Lyon (AD c. 130–c. 202), in his influential work *Against Heresies*, observes that Romans 13 both recognizes the authority of magistrates to bear the sword and also implies that "whatsoever they [the magistrates] do to the subversion of justice, iniquitously, and illegally, and tyrannically, in these things shall they also perish; for the just judgment of God comes equally upon all."[5] This is what political theologian Jonathan Leeman describes as the "boomerang effect" of the law of love that turns back to punish the government actor who exceeds his or her divine mandate.[6] To wield the sword is not only divinely authorized but also divinely constrained. It is serious stuff. If we are to love our neighbor who is the victim of unjust acts by government officials, then those officials too must be held to account when they wield the sword unjustly.

Regardless of whether government actors are held to a higher standard, they are most certainly held by Scripture to the same standard as those whom they judge. Paul's call to the ruler to reward the good and punish the

---

4   The obligation to take all reasonable means to avoid wrongful convictions implies an obligation on the part of government officials to reasonably assure themselves that the justice system they are using against others is not defective. Willfully blinding oneself to the defects in the system is no excuse.

5   Irenaeus, *Against Heresies* 5.24, in *From Irenaeus to Grotius: A Sourcebook in Christian Political Thought*, ed. Oliver O'Donovan and Joan Lockwood O'Donovan (Grand Rapids, MI: Eerdmans, 1999), 17.

6   Jonathan Leeman, *How the Nations Rage: Rethinking Faith and Politics in a Divided Age* (Nashville, TN: Thomas Nelson, 2018), 111. James Madison famously wrote of this need for a check on government itself: "If men were angels, no government would be necessary. If angels were to govern men, neither external nor internal controls on government would be necessary. In framing a government which is to be administered by men over men, the great difficulty lies in this: you must first enable the government to control the governed; and in the next place oblige it to control itself." *Federalist*, no. 51 (1788), accessed June 13, 2022, https://guides.loc .gov/.

bad is not intended to place the ruler *above* such accountability. The ruler too is subject to God's standard of justice. When a police officer, prosecutor, or judge uses the physical force of the state to imprison someone in violation of Scripture's accuracy requirement, he or she has acted, as Irenaeus puts it, "to the subversion of justice." And as Irenaeus argues, that "magistrate" must "perish also" or suffer whatever other punishment is a just response to his or her wrong.[7] The law of love demands accountability.

Whose Fault Is It?

This raises another question: Which government official(s) should be held accountable for a wrongful conviction? No one person can bring about a conviction. There's a reason it is called a criminal justice "system." Legislators pass laws, governors sign them, police arrest suspected violators, district attorneys prosecute them, juries find them guilty, and judges sentence them. And we the people elect some of these government actors. If this system— this collection of people acting on behalf of the rest of us—misfires, whose fault is it? Who bears responsibility? Who must be held accountable?

To answer these questions, we need to keep in mind that the principle of accuracy has two forms that we explored in chapter 4. A law *defining* a crime may be unjust, meaning that it inaccurately delineates the good from the bad. As a result, people who violate a law may not actually be committing a moral wrong. But even a law that accurately defines a wrong may be *applied* inaccurately if someone is convicted of violating that law when he or she hasn't actually done so. A conviction in either scenario can violate the accuracy principle.

Let's start with the first scenario. A wrongful conviction due to the first form of inaccuracy implicates legislators (who write the laws), prosecutors (who enforce those laws), and judges (who impose sentences on those convicted under those laws). A legislature, usually with the concurrence of a governor (at the state level) or the president (at the national level), that enacts an unjust law sets the stage for an unjust conviction because, without that law, there would be no crime for which someone could be convicted.

---

7   Of course, not every act of misconduct by a government official in convicting an innocent person is of equal culpability. The principle of proportionality discussed in chap. 8 should be applied to distinguish between greater and lesser wrongs by government officials and fashion the punishment accordingly.

To take an extreme example from American history, in the infamous case of *Plessy v. Ferguson*, Homer Plessy was convicted of the crime of sitting in a rail car reserved for White passengers. This conviction was possible only because the Louisiana legislature passed an unjust law that required Whites and non-Whites to travel separately.[8]

But the legislature cannot, simply by passing a bill defining a crime, bring about a conviction. The American form of government separates power among different branches. Legislatures pass laws; prosecutors enforce those laws. The Louisiana legislature passed the Separate Car Act, but a conviction under that law required a decision by a prosecutor to charge Homer Plessy with violating the law. A prosecutor must decide what crimes he or she will or won't charge—an exercise of what the law calls prosecutorial discretion.[9] Each day, prosecutors choose not to prosecute certain offenses because no prosecutor has the resources to pursue every violation of the law. In the American justice system, the discretion to charge or not charge an offense is the prosecutor's alone to exercise, and the decision not to prosecute cannot be overruled by either the legislature or the courts.[10]

This means that if a defendant is prosecuted for violating an unjust law it is because the prosecutor too has made an unjust decision to bring that charge. In Homer Plessy's case, a prosecutor made an unjust decision to enforce an unjust law by charging Plessy with violating the Separate Car Act. It is no answer for the prosecutor to say that he or she was "just following the law." If the law is unjust, the prosecutor has an ethical obligation not to enforce it.[11] I say "obligation" because a prosecutor has no moral authority to bring the physical force of the government to bear on someone who has committed no moral wrong. And this is true regardless of what the law

8   Plessy v. Ferguson, 163 U.S. 537, 541 (1896).
9   Police exercise similar discretion in the performance of their duties and prioritize the enforcement of some laws over others. Edward A. Malloy, *The Ethics of Law Enforcement and Criminal Punishment* (Washington, DC: University Press of America, 1982), 7.
10 Heckler v. Cheney, 470 U.S. 821, 831–32 (1985). Of course, a prosecutor's decision not to prosecute someone for violating a just law could also be unjust depending on the reason for not prosecuting.
11 Because a prosecutor takes an oath to enforce the law, he or she may need to resign if confronted with a choice between enforcing an unjust law or violating the oath to enforce the law. The proper response by the Christian in this circumstance is informed by the doctrine of the lesser magistrate. John Calvin, *Institutes of the Christian Religion*, trans. Henry Beveridge (Peabody, MA: Hendrickson, 2008), 988 (4.20.31). I return to this issue in chap. 19.

says. God's law of love is the supreme moral law of the land, and it restricts the state's use of force to those who are Romans 13 wrongdoers. Someone who violates an unjust law is not a Romans 13 wrongdoer; someone who enforces such a law is.

But even a prosecutor unjustly charging someone with a violation of an unjust law passed by a legislature cannot bring about a conviction without the cooperation of still others. A conviction can only occur if the judge, after a jury verdict, enters a judgment of conviction. In other words, convicting a defendant of violating an unjust law requires the complicity of a legislature, a prosecutor, a jury, and a judge. If a criminal defendant is ultimately convicted of violating an unjust law, he or she may be subjected to the punitive force of the state in the form of imprisonment. That imprisonment is unjust violence against the prisoner. The legislators, prosecutors, judge, and jurors who played a role in that unjust use of physical force have each committed a moral wrong. They each caused a moral evil—physical violence against an innocent. They are each Romans 13 wrongdoers.

But let's say the law that a criminal defendant is convicted of violating rightly defines some wrongful act—murder, for example—but the defendant is inaccurately convicted of violating that law because, in fact, he didn't kill anyone. If this occurs, who is at moral fault? The legislature doesn't bear moral responsibility for its definition of the crime since in that sense the criminal law is just. But the legislature could still bear some moral responsibility if it failed to provide by law for all the procedural tools reasonably necessary for a defendant to prove his or her innocence. In other words, the legislature may have designed the procedures of that state's justice system in an unjust way. To take one example that I'll discuss at length in chapter 14, the legislature may have failed to provide adequate funding for the public defender's office to such a degree that the defendant was not reasonably represented. If that failure to provide adequate funding causes a wrongful conviction, then the legislature would be morally responsible for the wrongful conviction that resulted.

Alternatively, the prosecutor could bear moral responsibility if he or she were reckless in fulfilling his or her duty to hand over evidence the police collected that might show the defendant's innocence, an issue that I'll take up in chapter 15. Or maybe the judge is at fault for sloppy legal research that resulted in an erroneous evidentiary ruling that prevented the defendant from introducing important evidence in his defense. The examples are myriad. Numerous factors can contribute to this sort of inaccurate conviction. The point is that, even when the law defining crimes is just, the legislature, prosecutor, or judge can fail to provide for all reasonably available procedures needed to avoid a wrongful conviction, thus making those officials morally responsible if such a conviction occurs.

To put a finer point on this, the police officer or the prosecutor or the judge is morally responsible for any wrongful conviction resulting from his or her actions *if* the criminal justice system that yielded that result and in which he or she participated did not include *all reasonable precautions to avoid wrongful convictions*. In that circumstance, biblical justice demands that those government officials be held to account for the divinely unauthorized physical force (i.e., imprisonment) they wrongly brought to bear on an innocent person.

Reasonableness, Not Perfection

To be clear, none of this is to say that the police and prosecutors and judges should be, as a matter of Christian ethics, held to a standard of perfection. We must be Christian in our approach, which means we must be realists. We live in a fallen world, and we are finite creatures. Even if government officials are acting with the best of intentions and using all reasonable means to ensure accuracy, the justice system will reach inaccurate outcomes in some cases. The conviction of an innocent person, while an injustice to that person, does not *alone* prove that the police, prosecutor, judge, or jury acted immorally.

This is the point of the all-reasonable-means test laid out in chapter 5. A police officer isn't necessarily committing an immoral act by arresting (that is, using actual or threatened physical force) against someone who later turns out to be innocent. The question is whether the officer used all reasonable means to determine the guilt of the person arrested. A prosecutor hasn't necessarily committed an immoral act by prosecuting a case that results in the conviction of someone who is later determined to be innocent. The question is whether the prosecutor used all reasonable means to ensure the accuracy of the verdict. And a judge doesn't necessarily commit an immoral act by sentencing to prison someone who was convicted but, unknown to the judge, was innocent. The question is whether the judge conducted the trial in a way that ensured all reasonable means were employed to reach a true verdict.

The principle of accountability doesn't require the impossible. It requires the reasonable. The question I'm raising here is one of accountability for police, prosecutors, and judges when an innocent person is convicted because the system did *not* use all reasonable means to ensure accuracy. The relevant moral question is whether the legal proceedings that misfired in that one case included all reasonable means to avoid conviction of an innocent person. If the various government officials each used all reasonable means to ensure accuracy, then the inaccurate result is tragic but those officials are not morally responsible for that inaccuracy.

I want to be very clear about what I am and am not arguing here. *If* a criminal justice system is designed and operated so that it takes all reasonable means to avoid wrongful convictions, *then* a government official (whether judge, prosecutor, or police officer) who participates in that system is *not* a Romans 13 wrongdoer *even if* that system results in a wrongful conviction. The man or woman wrongfully convicted in that situation has most certainly suffered an injustice but it was an injustice due to human frailty rather than wrongdoing. In a fallen world, innocents will suffer at times even when the government takes all reasonable steps to prevent that. "The greatest reason for injustice is simply human limitation," Oliver O'Donovan observes.[12]

At the other end of the spectrum, it should be obvious that if a police officer and prosecutor arrested and convicted someone they *knew* was innocent, then those officials should be held accountable. But in the middle are those cases where the police or prosecutor may sincerely believe in the defendant's guilt and thus have a sense of unwarranted moral comfort in obtaining convictions through the use of a flawed judicial system—that is, a system that does not employ all reasonable means to avoid inaccurate results. It's this middle case that I'm especially focused on here. And the point I'm making is that sincerity of the government official's belief in a defendant's guilt does not absolve the official of moral responsibility for erroneous convictions by an unreasonable process.

12 Oliver O'Donovan, *The Ways of Judgment* (Grand Rapids, MI: Eerdmans, 2005), 144.

Again, I'm addressing something more than simply a prosecutor's failure to follow the law during a prosecution. If a legal system is designed
well and yet a wrongful conviction occurs because a prosecutor violates
a procedural rule designed to ensure accuracy, then one can easily see
why we would hold that prosecutor morally responsible in that instance.
But I'm arguing for something more. I'm addressing moral responsibility when a prosecutor follows all the legal rules but those rules are
something short of what is reasonably needed to ensure accurate results
and the shortcomings of the system were knowable in advance. In that
situation, the prosecutor followed the law, and that prosecutor may not
have intended a wrongful conviction. But it is not morally permissible
for a prosecutor to participate in a prosecution that he or she knows (or
reasonably should know) will be conducted in a way that falls below the
all-reasonable-means standard. "I was just following the law" is not a
valid moral defense when the law is known to be procedurally unjust.
And if a prosecutor knowingly elects to participate in a procedurally
unjust prosecution, then he or she is morally responsible if a substantive
injustice in the form of a wrongful conviction results.

This does not necessarily mean that a Christian cannot morally participate in a justice system that fails to use all reasonable means to avoid
convicting an innocent defendant. It may be possible for an individual
prosecutor working in a defective justice system to nonetheless handle
his or her cases in a way that ensures all reasonable means are taken
to avoid wrongful convictions. The same is true for a judge presiding
over a trial or a police officer investigating a crime. But this may not
be possible, either because a supervisor won't allow it or the defect
in the system is outside the prosecutor's or police officer's or judge's
control.[13] In that instance, that government official would bear moral
responsibility for erroneous convictions he or she caused by operating
in that defective system.

Part 2 of this book will consider specific ways in which a criminal justice system can fall short of the obligation to take all reasonable means to
avoid a wrongful conviction. My point for now is that *if* a justice system

---

13 For example, if the defect in the system is a failure to provide for adequate defense counsel
for a poor person accused of a crime (see chap. 14), that is not something that an individual
prosecutor can correct on his or her own.

fails to provide for all such reasonable means, and *if* the police, prosecutor, or judge cannot correct for those deficiencies in an individual case in
which he or she is involved, and *if* the inadequacies of that system result
in the conviction of an innocent person in that case, then the officials who
knowingly chose to participate in that case are morally accountable if a
wrongful conviction results. Why? Because Scripture's accuracy principle
implies that all reasonable means be taken to avoid wrongful convictions.
If a prosecutor or a police officer obtains a conviction in a system without
those precautions, then those authorities are blameworthy—Romans 13
wrongdoers—for making use of a morally defective system to obtain that
conviction.

To put a finer point on it, if the government executes an innocent man,
that may be more than merely a tragic mistake. It is a murder by the
state officials involved in that conviction *if* they knew that the criminal
justice system they used to secure that conviction did not, in its design
and implementation, include all reasonable means to avoid wrongful
convictions. Similarly, if the government imprisons (i.e., uses physical
force against) a woman for a crime she didn't commit, that may be more
than just disastrous. It is a morally unjustified assault by the state officials
if they knowingly used a defective justice system to secure the conviction. Even if a police officer, prosecutor, or judge sincerely believed the
defendant to be guilty, those officials are nonetheless morally culpable
if they convicted an innocent defendant through use of what they knew
(or reasonably should have known) was an unreasonably inadequate
justice process.

What reasonable means are required of the police officer, prosecutor,
and judge may differ for each of them because of the differing roles they
play. My point in this chapter (or even in this book) isn't to sort out what
particular measures must be taken by each state actor at each stage of the
criminal justice process because, as I've explained, the answer can differ
depending on the context. What I am trying to do is establish a framework
for thinking about those issues. And part of that framework requires a re-
orientation of how we think about the moral accountability of those who
operate the machinery of criminal justice on behalf of the state. The justice
system is operated by people, and those people bear moral responsibility
for their roles in its operation. At the same time, that moral responsibility

does not rise to the level of requiring their infallibility. Rather, it requires their use of all reasonable means to achieve accuracy. Reasonableness, not flawlessness, is the moral standard.

Over the course of the last several chapters, I have repeatedly emphasized that (a) the criminal law is the use of physical force, and (b) according to Scripture, the use of physical force against an innocent person is, as a general rule, a morally blameworthy act. These concepts are critical to understanding why government authorities are themselves subject to accountability and punishment for certain wrongful convictions. While Romans 13 permits governing authorities to use physical force, this authorization is an exceedingly narrow one that is morally constrained by the accuracy requirement. The authorization is limited to actual wrongdoers, *and* the accuracy requirement demands that all reasonable means be taken to avoid wrongful convictions. Regardless of what the law may say, if a state official violates the obligation to use all reasonable means to ensure accuracy by participating in a justice system that the official knew (or reasonably could know) was defective, then any resulting conviction of an innocent man or woman is the use of physical force against another person *without divine authorization*. That is a moral wrong. Loving the neighbor wronged by that wrongful use of force requires accountability on the part of the government official who committed that wrong.

Just Following the Law

To summarize where we are so far in this chapter, there are at least nine ways in which government officials can act immorally with regard to a system of criminal justice:

1. Legislators can pass laws that unjustly define a crime.
2. Legislators can fail to enact just processes for the prosecution of crimes.
3. Police can follow lawful but unjust procedures for investigating crime.
4. Prosecutors can prosecute violations of laws that unjustly define a crime.
5. Prosecutors can follow lawful but unjust procedures for prosecuting crime.
6. Judges can preside over a prosecution carried out using lawful but unjust procedures.
7. Police can fail to follow just legal procedures for investigating crime.

8. Prosecutors can fail to follow just legal procedures for prosecuting crime.

9. Judges can fail to follow just legal procedures for presiding over trials.

Love for neighbor, and thus justice, requires that legislators, police officers, prosecutors, and judges be held accountable for these types of immorality when they result in the conviction of innocent people.

But here is the reality: legislators, police officers, prosecutors, and judges who commit the first six of these types of injustice—meaning, they follow a law that is unjust—will never face accountability in the form of a criminal prosecution, at least not in the United States. If the police officer, prosecutor, or judge follows the law, however unjust that law might be, the US Constitution's *ex post facto* clause prohibits the prosecution of those government officials.[14] Only in the last three types of government misconduct—where police, prosecutors, or judges fail to follow the law—is it even theoretically possible to prosecute those officials for their misconduct. For the most part, "just following the law" will be a defense that absolutely precludes criminal prosecution of a government official in the United States.

Why, then, have I spent all this time arguing that justice requires accountability for government officials who engage in any of these nine categories of misconduct? For two reasons.

First, accountability can take forms other than criminal prosecution. Voters can hold wayward government officials accountable by removing them from office for lawful but unjust conduct. The principles of accountability and moral proximity place on voters a moral obligation to hold wayward officials accountable at the ballot box. People rightly lament wrongful convictions when they come to light. Rarely do people vote to oust the prosecutors and judges whose misconduct caused those wrongful convictions. At times, the voters instead promote renegade prosecutors to the judicial bench.[15]

But elections aren't the only way that we could hold government officials accountable. Accountability could also take the form of greater civil liability

14   U.S. Const. art. I, § 9, cl. 3. In short, the *ex post facto* clause prohibits retroactively declaring criminal conduct that the law deemed legal at the time the act was committed.

15   Jimerson v. Payne, 957 F.3d 916, 930 n.10 (8th Cir. 2020).

for those officials who unjustly violate the law. Beginning in the 1950s, American courts invented the doctrine of absolute immunity that protects legislators, courts, and prosecutors from facing federal civil rights lawsuits for their injustices.[16] The police are protected by a qualified immunity that is nearly absolute.[17] Even the government itself—rather than just individual officials—is largely immune from federal civil rights suits.[18] As a result, one federal judge recently observed that "worthy civil rights claims are often never brought to trial . . . because [this] unholy trinity of legal doctrines . . . frequently conspires to turn winnable claims into losing ones."[19] But Congress could change all this if it wanted to—if *we* wanted it to. Greater accountability is only a single federal statute away.

Second, heightening awareness of the ways in which "just following the law" can violate divine justice should serve as a frightening warning to any Christian serving or contemplating service in the criminal justice system. Bearing the sword of the state as ministers of God (Rom. 13:4) carries with it a solemn responsibility to do justly as God, not man-made law, defines justice. Whether or not secular courts can reach the police, prosecutors, or judges who act unjustly, God's divine court can and one day will.

There was a time when people recognized that those who dispense criminal justice bear a moral responsibility before God when it misfires. The history of the "beyond a reasonable doubt" standard of proof in criminal cases reflects a sensitivity to the moral culpability of jurors in wrongful convictions. While today we think of the requirement of proof beyond a reasonable doubt as protecting criminal defendants, that standard originated because of concern that jurors would commit a mortal sin if they returned a guilty verdict while harboring a reasonable doubt about the defendant's guilt. In other words, Christian thinkers in an earlier era recognized that even jurors have a moral obligation to use all reasonable means to avoid wrongful convictions.[20]

16 Tenney v. Brandhove, 341 U.S. 367 (1951) (absolute legislative immunity); Pierson v. Ray, 386 U.S. 547 (1967) (absolute judicial immunity); Imbler v. Pachtman, 424 U.S. 409 (1976) (absolute prosecutorial immunity).
17 Pierson v. Ray, 386 U.S. 547, 557 (1967) (qualified police immunity).
18 Monell v. New York City Dept. of Social Servcs., 436 U.S. 658, 691 (1978).
19 Wearry v. Foster, 33 F.4th 260, 278 (5th Cir. 2022) (Ho, J., dubitante).
20 James Q. Whitman, *The Origins of Reasonable Doubt: Theological Roots of the Criminal Trial* (New Haven, CT: Yale University Press, 2008).

More recently, the late US Supreme Court Justice Antonin Scalia, who was a faithful and outspoken Roman Catholic, acknowledged that a judge is morally accountable for his or her role in the injustices of the legal system over which he or she presides. In an essay written fifteen years after he joined the Supreme Court, Justice Scalia discussed how the morality of the death penalty affected "whether [he] can or should be a judge at all." As a judge, he was part of "the machinery of death" in the sense that his judicial "vote, when joined with four others, is, in most cases, the last step that permits an execution to proceed." Given his role in a death sentence, Justice Scalia was of the view that he "could not take part in that process if [he] believed what was being done to be immoral." His obligation in such a situation "is resignation, rather than simply ignoring duly enacted, constitutional laws and sabotaging death penalty cases."[21]

Of particular interest for our purposes is Justice Scalia's acknowledgment that he "could not take part in the process" *if* what the justice system was doing was "immoral." Ultimately, Justice Scalia concluded that the death penalty is morally permissible, and thus he saw no need to avoid judicial participation in death penalty cases. But what if the justice system was immoral in some other respect? Whether the death penalty is, in the abstract, morally permissible is not the only ethical question presented by the operation of a criminal justice system. What if a criminal justice system doesn't use all reasonable means to avoid inaccurate convictions? That too is immoral. What must a Christian judge do in that situation? Can a Christian participate in "the machinery of death" or even "the machinery of imprisonment" under those circumstances?

As I have been arguing in this chapter and the last, it is also immoral to punish (even in ways far short of death) innocent people whose convictions are obtained by means of a process that does not take all reasonable steps to avoid such unjust outcomes. It makes no difference that the government official followed the law in securing the conviction. Man-made law does not ultimately determine right from wrong. Divine law does. Laws, including legal systems, can be unjust. And as Justice Scalia acknowledged, Christians have an obligation not to participate

21 Antonin Scalia, "God's Justice and Ours," *First Things*, May 2002, https://www.firstthings.com/.

in a legal system to the extent that doing so is contrary to the biblical demands of justice.

If it is immoral to punish an innocent defendant whose conviction is secured by means of a justice system that does not take all reasonable means to avoid that wrongful conviction, then Justice Scalia's argument would suggest that, to use his words, a Christian judge "could not take part in that process." The unreasonably inadequate process is an immoral one. If a judge (or prosecutor or police officer) nonetheless chooses to participate in that immoral prosecution and it yields an erroneous conviction, then he or she will one day stand before God in a moment of ultimate accountability for that injustice. And "it is a fearful thing to fall into the hands of the living God" (Heb. 10:31).

———

Exoneration stories have no happy endings, only less tragic ones. The years, sometimes decades, that the locusts have eaten cannot be restored, at least not by us (Joel 2:25). But when we discover these injustices, however belatedly, we can and must speak accurately, telling the truth both about the wrong done and about who did it. When government officials are the wrongdoers, they are, as Augustine observed, little more than a band of criminals. Justice thus requires that they be held accountable, whether by turning them out of office, subjecting them to civil liability, or, when possible, turning the punitive authority of the state back on them. Accountability is part of what neighbor love demands.

7

Impartiality

WARREN MCCLESKEY WAS BORN in Marietta, Georgia, on March 17, 1946. When McCleskey was nine years old, the US Supreme Court ruled in *Brown v. Board of Education* that America's public schools must be desegregated "with all deliberate speed."[1] But McCleskey, who was Black, attended a racially segregated school through his high school graduation in 1964.[2]

After graduation, McCleskey took a job with Lockheed Aircraft where he worked for five years until he was laid off. He struggled to find new employment and instead turned to a life of crime, eventually pleading guilty to nine armed robberies for which he spent more than seven years in prison. In 1977, McCleskey was paroled and returned to Marietta where he befriended three men, two of whom had been his fellow inmates.[3]

With those friends, McCleskey hatched a plan to rob a Marietta jewelry store on Saturday, May 13, 1978. This wasn't their first robbery together that spring, but it would be their last. McCleskey picked up his three friends that morning and drove to the jewelry store where one of the three surveyed the scene while the others waited. For reasons that are unclear,

1 Brown v. Bd. of Educ., 349 U.S. 294, 301 (1955). A year earlier, the Supreme Court had declared that racial segregation in schooling violated the Fourteenth Amendment's Equal Protection Clause. Brown v. Bd. of Educ., 347 U.S. 483, 497 (1954). The issue in the case a year later was how the unconstitutional segregation should be remedied.
2 Jeffrey L. Kirchmeier, *Imprisoned by the Past: Warren McCleskey and the American Death Penalty* (New York: Oxford University Press, 2015), 12.
3 Kirchmeier, *Imprisoned by the Past*, 13.

they decided against robbing that store and instead cruised around town looking for a better target for their intended crime.[4]

Unable to agree on a target in Marietta, the four of them drove to Atlanta, about twenty-five miles to the south. All four men were armed, one of them with a sawed-off shotgun and the other three, including McCleskey, with pistols. Once in Atlanta, McCleskey parked the car and went to case the Dixie Furniture Store. When he returned, the four of them planned the robbery. McCleskey would enter the front door while the other three would enter through a loading dock in the rear. Once inside the store, McCleskey and his three accomplices rounded up the employees, forced them to lie on the floor, and bound them with tape. But unknown to McCleskey and his friends, one of the store employees had pulled a silent alarm.[5]

Frank Schlatt, a thirty-year-old White police officer on duty that day, responded to the call alone. Officer Schlatt was a Vietnam veteran, a husband, and the father of a nine-year-old girl. He had served on the Atlanta police force for only five years when he arrived at the furniture store that spring afternoon. He parked his patrol car in front of the building and entered the store through the main door. As he was walking down the store's center aisle, someone fired two shots, one of which struck Officer Schlatt in the face, killing him.[6]

Not surprisingly, the murder attracted an enormous amount of public attention. Officer Schlatt was laid to rest a few days later at a funeral service attended by hundreds, including Georgia's governor. Speaking at the funeral, a fellow officer vowed, "We'll find the animals who did this." A manhunt led to McCleskey's arrest in a predawn raid of his house in Marietta on May 30, 1978.[7]

That October, McCleskey was tried for capital murder. During jury selection, the prosecutor used peremptory challenges to remove seven Black people from the jury panel. The resulting jury was made up of one Black and eleven Whites who, like McCleskey, had also likely attended racially segregated schools. The trial was brief, lasting less than a week. McCleskey's accomplices testified against him, identifying him as the shooter, and a man

4   Kirchmeier, *Imprisoned by the Past*, 14–15.
5   Kirchmeier, *Imprisoned by the Past*, 15.
6   McCleskey v. Kemp, 753 F.2d 877, 882 (11th Cir. 1985); Kirchmeier, *Imprisoned by the Past*, 15.
7   Kirchmeier, *Imprisoned by the Past*, 17.

held in a cell next to McCleskey testified that he had confessed while in jail awaiting trial. McCleskey took the witness stand in his own defense and denied being present during the robbery, contradicting a prior confession he had given to the police. The jury deliberated for a little over two hours before finding McCleskey guilty of murder and armed robbery and, after another two hours of deliberations, sentenced him to death on the murder charge. The judge ordered that McCleskey be executed by electrocution, ending his order with the traditional closing line in death penalty cases: "May God have mercy on his soul."[8] The Georgia Supreme Court affirmed McCleskey's conviction and death sentence in 1980, and the US Supreme Court declined to review his case.[9]

McCleskey's conviction and death sentence, however, were playing out against the backdrop of a fierce legal battle in the United States over the constitutionality of the death penalty. The NAACP had been leading this charge against the death penalty because of concerns about the racially tinged history of its use in the American South.[10] In 1972, the US Supreme Court had declared, by a 5–4 vote in the case of *Furman v. Georgia*, that the death penalty in its then-current form was unconstitutionally arbitrary.[11] Four years later, after numerous states amended their death penalty statutes in response to *Furman*, the Supreme Court affirmed the constitutionality of those revised death penalty regimes by a 7–2 vote in *Gregg v. Georgia*.[12]

Following the *Gregg* decision, the NAACP legal team was deeply disappointed but undaunted. In 1981, the organization commissioned a study of the effect of race on death sentences under the newly enacted capital sentencing statutes. John ("Jack") Boger, a young lawyer who also held a divinity degree from Yale, was coordinating this effort on behalf of the NAACP.[13] Boger was the same age as McCleskey and had joined the NAACP in 1978—the same year that McCleskey had murdered Officer Schlatt.

8   McCleskey v. Kemp, 753 F.2d 877, 882 (11th Cir. 1985); Kirchmeier, *Imprisoned by the Past*, 21–27.
9   Notably, the Georgia Supreme Court misspelled McCleskey's last name in its opinion. McClesky v. State, 263 S.E.2d 146 (Ga.), cert. denied, 449 U.S. 891 (1980).
10 For a discussion of that history, see Charles L. Ogletree Jr. and Austin Sarat, eds., *From Lynch Mobs to the Killing State: Race and the Death Penalty in America* (New York: New York University Press, 2006).
11 Furman v. Georgia, 408 U.S. 238 (1972).
12 Gregg v. Georgia, 428 U.S. 153 (1976).
13 Jack Boger later became a law professor at the University of North Carolina School of Law, where he taught for twenty-seven years and ultimately served as the dean. I met him in 1994

To conduct its study, the NAACP retained David Baldus, a law professor at the University of Iowa. Baldus was skeptical of any enduring racial effect on death sentences under the post-*Gregg* sentencing regimes. Nevertheless, he agreed to lead the study, and his arrangement with the NAACP was quite simple. He would conduct a painstaking statistical analysis of the factors affecting death sentences in Georgia. If his research turned up no racial disparity, as he suspected it would, he would be free to publish his findings in an academic journal. If, however, his research uncovered a racial dispar-ity, he would share those results with the NAACP and testify as an expert witness in litigation challenging the constitutionality of the death penalty.[14]

In May 1982, four years after McCleskey had been sentenced to death, Professor Baldus called Boger to report on his findings. Though his results were preliminary, they revealed that, contrary to his expectation, race was still playing a significant role in Georgia's death sentencing system. The raw data Baldus and his team had collected showed that Black defendants received death sentences in 22 percent of cases in which the murder victims were White but only in 1 percent of cases in which the victims were Black. By contrast, only 8 percent of White defendants had been sentenced to death for murders of White victims.[15]

But Baldus had gone well beyond simply analyzing raw data. His research involved a detailed analysis of the case files of a stratified sample of 1,066 murder cases in Georgia, each of which was coded based on more than 230 variables. A statistical regression analysis was then performed to determine whether any of these variables other than race could explain the racially disparate outcomes. The analysis showed that, when the murder victim was White, the likelihood of a death sentence increased 120 percent.[16] "In Baldus's data," Boger later explained, "race never disappeared; no other explanations were ever found."[17] Even more disconcerting, the Baldus study

---

when I enrolled in one of his classes as a law student. We have remained in touch for the nearly thirty years since.

14 John Charles Boger, "*McCleskey v. Kemp*: Field Notes from 1977–1991," *Northwestern University Law Review* 112, no. 6 (2018): 1658, https://scholarlycommons.law.northwestern.edu/nulr /vol112/iss6/13. For a discussion of the study from Professor Baldus's perspective, see David C. Baldus, George G. Woodworth, and Charles A. Pulaski Jr., *Equal Justice and the Death Penalty: A Legal and Empirical Analysis* (Boston: Northeastern University Press, 1990).

15 Boger, "*McCleskey v. Kemp*," 1660.

16 McCleskey v. Kemp, 481 U.S. 279, 326 (1987) (Brennan, J., dissenting).

17 Boger, "*McCleskey v. Kemp*," 1668.

showed that, in a murder of the type committed by McCleskey, "the jury *more likely than not* would have spared McCleskey's life had his victim been black."[18] In short, the statistical study showed that White (victims') lives do matter; indeed, they mattered more.

Based on Baldus's statistical analysis, Boger and the team at the NAACP filed a petition in federal court challenging McCleskey's death sentence as unconstitutional because Georgia's capital sentencing system was infected with racial bias. After a series of legal twists and turns, in July 1986, the US Supreme Court agreed to review McCleskey's case,[19] which squarely presented a question the court had yet to decide: Is a particular death sentence unconstitutional when the justice system as a whole is infected by racial considerations? In other words, is a death sentence meted out by a racially partial justice system constitutional?

The race question was so squarely presented in McCleskey's case because no one seriously contested Professor Baldus's findings. The state of Georgia did not present an expert to rebut Baldus's study, and another expert witness described Baldus's work as "far and away the most complete and thorough analysis of sentencing that's been done. I mean there's nothing even close."[20] Justice Antonin Scalia, who had recently joined the Supreme Court, wrote a private memo to his judicial colleagues acknowledging the force of the Baldus study:

I disagree with the argument that the inferences that can be drawn from the Baldus study are weakened by the fact that each jury and each trial is unique, or by the large number of variables at issue. . . . Since it is my view that the unconscious operation of irrational sympathies and antipathies, including racial, upon jury decisions and (hence) prosecutorial decisions *is real, acknowledged in the decisions of this court, and ineradicable,* I cannot honestly say that all I need is more proof.[21]

18 McCleskey v. Kemp, 481 U.S. 279, 325 (1987) (Brennan, J., dissenting) (empasis in original).
19 McCleskey v. Kemp, 478 U.S. 1019 (1986).
20 Boger, "*McCleskey v. Kemp,*" 1661.
21 Memorandum to the Conference from Justice Antonin Scalia of January 6, 1987, 1, McCleskey v. Kemp, Supreme Court Case Files Collection, Powell Papers, Lewis F. Powell Jr. Archives, Washington & Lee University School of Law, Virginia, accessed November 23, 2021, https:// scholarlycommons.law.wlu.edu/casefiles/249/ (emphasis added). Justice Scalia's memorandum was made available to the public when, after the death of Justice Lewis Powell, his papers were

In other words, Justice Scalia appeared to accept the Baldus study's "inferences" and, indeed, believed that (unconscious) race-based decision-making by prosecutors and juries in criminal cases was "real." The issue was not, in Justice Scalia's view, one in need of "more proof."

Justice Is Blind

While Warren McCleskey's case presented the Supreme Court with the legal question of what the US Constitution requires in the face of such proof, the case poses for the Christian a profound moral question: Is (racially) partial justice biblical justice? If McCleskey got what he had coming as a cop killer, does it really matter that race played a determinative role in securing that outcome? Shouldn't we simply be satisfied that, by whatever means, justice was served in the sense that McCleskey got his due?

To some degree, I can understand that sentiment. If the evidence at McCleskey's trial is to be believed,[22] he committed a heinous crime, gunning down an innocent man in cold blood and deeply affecting many others who loved him, all for a few dollars.[23] McCleskey is not a sympathetic figure, and justice—biblical justice—requires punishment. Even accepting that racial prejudice likely impacted the case, some might think that such prejudice served the salutary purpose of ensuring that McCleskey received his due. What racially biased prosecutors and jurors may have intended for evil, some may see as God using for good.

Loving your neighbor as yourself, however, requires not only that perpetrators receive the punishment they are due but also that the system dispensing those punishments be impartial. To see Scripture's teaching on this point, we turn once again to the parable of the good Samaritan. While

---

made available to the public. Professor Dennis Dorin was the first to report on this memorandum in 1994. Dennis D. Dorin, "Far Right of the Mainstream: Racism, Rights, and Remedies from the Perspective of Justice Antonin Scalia's *McCleskey* Memorandum," *Mercer Law Review* 45, no. 3 (1994): 1035–88.

22 Though he lied during his trial testimony, McCleskey later admitted that he had in fact participated in the robbery. He steadfastly denied, however, that he was the shooter. An eyewitness who testified at trial provided a distinctive description of the shooter that did not match McCleskey. Kirchmeier, *Imprisoned by the Past*, 22–23, 184.

23 A year after the murder, Officer Schlatt's then ten-year-old daughter wrote a heartbreaking poem titled, "Ode to My Dad," about his murder, which no doubt haunted her for years. "Reflections for Police Officer Frank Robert Schlatt," Officer Down Memorial Page, accessed June 15, 2022, https://www.odmp.org.

the legal system was not the context in which Jesus applied the neighbor-love command in his exchange with the lawyer in Luke 10, it *was* the context in which that command was originally delivered in Leviticus 19.[24] There, God directed that his people "do no injustice in court" but rather "love your neighbor as yourself" (Lev. 19:15, 18). Judicial injustice was framed by the Old Testament law as a failure of neighbor love.

Leviticus 19 goes further, calling out one particular form of judicial injustice—partiality. "You shall not be partial to the poor or defer to the great" (Lev. 19:15). The specific type of partiality highlighted in that passage is rendering judgment based on the social status of the litigant rather than based on his or her actions. Yet the broader point is that it is unjust to judge a case based not on what someone *did* (or didn't do) but instead based on who he or she *is*. The apostle Peter much later makes this point expressly, describing God as one "who judges impartially according to each one's deeds" (1 Pet. 1:17; see also Acts 10:34).

The injustice of partiality in judging is a recurring theme in Scripture. In Exodus 23, Moses focuses on partiality based on wealth (Ex. 23:3, 6). Elsewhere, he extends the concept of judicial impartiality to nationality and social status (Deut. 1:16–17). And numerous Old Testament authors speak against bribes, which pervert decision-making by impairing the impartiality of the judge (Ex. 23:8; Deut. 16:19; Prov. 17:23; Eccl. 7:7; Isa. 5:23; Amos 5:12). "In a fallen world," Jonathan Leeman observes, "all of us game the rules and play the people over us in order to slant life's benefits to our advantage."[25] But Scripture admonishes us that loving our neighbors means deciding cases on a neutral application of the law to the facts in question rather than based on a preference for or a bias against those whose conduct is being judged. "Partiality in judging is not good" (Prov. 24:23), Scripture tells us, because partiality is a failure of neighbor love (James 2:8–9).

We see this same principle at play in Jesus's parable of the good Samaritan. The parable is so named because the Samaritan traveler, not the revered Jewish religious figures, stopped to help the man in need. It is hard to overstate how jarring this character casting must have been to Jesus's audience. The hatred between Jews and Samaritans ran deep

---

24 Nicholas Wolterstorff, *Justice in Love* (Grand Rapids, MI: Eerdmans, 2015), 83.

25 Jonathan Leeman, *How the Nations Rage: Rethinking Faith and Politics in a Divided Age* (Nashville: Thomas Nelson, 2018), 25.

in Jesus's day, tracing its roots back hundreds of years to the Assyrians' importation and settlement of foreign peoples in the towns of Samaria to replace the deported Israelites (2 Kings 17:24). The remaining Israelites intermarried with these foreign peoples, resulting in syncretistic religious practices. To the Jewish people of Jesus's day, Samaritans were unclean, untouchable, and "other" because of their mixed ancestry and worship (John 4:9). And the contempt was mutual. Luke recounts how a Samaritan village snubbed Jesus and denied him hospitality because of their religious differences (Luke 9:51–55).[26]

The animosity between Jews and Samaritans was so profound that, when Jesus asked the Jewish lawyer, "Which of these . . . proved to be a neighbor to the man" (Luke 10:36), the lawyer would not even say the word "Samaritan." Instead, he answered curtly, "The one who showed him mercy" (Luke 10:37). So, in Jesus's parable, the Samaritan did more than just love a man in need; he reached across the most divisive cultural boundary of his day to love. He loved based on the *need presented* by the circumstances he encountered rather than based on *whom* he encountered. The point was that the neighbor love Jesus commanded is to be non-preferential.[27]

To say that neighbor love is to be non-preferential is not to deny the idea of moral proximity that we considered in chapter 3. As a Christian, I am called to love everyone, but my finitude means that the *way* in which I love others will not be the same with everyone.[28] The Samaritan helped the crime victim he encountered, not the innumerable other victims about whom he never knew. And the Samaritan rendered the aid he could considering his skills and financial wherewithal. Jesus didn't offer a critique of the Samaritan for a failure to help everyone, but rather commended him for doing what he could. "You go, and do likewise," Jesus said to the lawyer (Luke 10:37). What neighbor love requires of me will depend on my resources and my

---

26 This personal slight renders even more remarkable Christ's casting of the Samaritan as the hero in his parable. Matthew Myer Boulton, "Samaritan Justice: A Theology of 'Mercy' and 'Neighborhood,'" in *Doing Justice to Mercy: Religion, Law, and Criminal Justice*, ed. Jonathan Rothchild, Matthew Myer Boulton, and Kevin Jung (Charlottesville, VA: University of Virginia Press, 2007), 132.

27 Gilbert C. Meilaender, *Friendship: A Study in Theological Ethics* (Notre Dame, IN: Notre Dame University Press, 1981), 54, writes, "Agape, in order to be agape—that is, in order to be faithful love—must, it seems, be nonpreferential and unconcerned with reciprocity." See also Paul Ramsey, *Basic Christian Ethics* (Louisville: Westminster John Knox, 1950), 155–57.

28 Gene Outka, *Agape: An Ethical Analysis* (New Haven, CT: Yale University Press, 1972), 269.

relationship with the person in need of love. Jesus was not suggesting otherwise in his parable.

To say that neighbor love must be non-preferential means that we may not choose *whether* to love those with whom we are in moral proximity based on the person's individual characteristics or conduct.[29] Race, sex, nationality, wealth, social status, position, education, age, and religion have no bearing on whether a person is due our love. Nor does a person's behavior exempt them from our neighbor-love obligation. "Love your enemies," Jesus commanded, including "those who persecute you" (Matt. 5:44).

Each and every person is due our love simply because he or she is a person. We love without respect to who the person is or what they have done because every person with whom we cross paths is an image bearer of God. That universal image-bearing quality, not the person's distinguishing features or individual behavior, determines value. God alone confers worth on our neighbor, and the fact that the God of the universe has created that person to bear the divine image renders him or her of inestimable worth. Our neighbors cannot add to or detract from their value by what they have done, where they have come from, or who their parents were. "The least of these" (Matt. 25:40) are not least but rather of equal worth because they are equally human. And, as discussed in chapter 3, to love another person is to desire and work for that person's good as an end in itself.[30]

Neighbor love, then, seeks the good of others non-preferentially because others, regardless of who they are or what they have done, are all equally image bearers of God. The mandate of Christ's parable is to love those whom the culture has taught us to hate or simply ignore. Even those who have done us wrong or positioned themselves as our enemies remain, for the Christian, our neighbors. As neighbors, we must love them, and to love them requires that we judge their cases impartially. It is this commitment to impartiality—rooted both in our obligation to image the God who is impartial and in our neighbor's inherent worth as an image bearer—that renders Christian love unique. It "discovers the neighbor because it alone

29 According to Outka, *Agape*, 9, "Agape is a regard for the neighbor" that "is for every person qua human existent, to be distinguished from those special traits, actions, etc., which distinguish particular personalities from each other."

30 Wolterstorff, *Justice in Love*, 23; Outka, *Agape*, 8–9 ; Timothy Keller, *Forgive: Why Should I and How Can I?* (New York: Viking, 2022), 107.

begins with neighborly love and not with discriminating between worthy and unworthy people according to the qualities they possess."[31]

A Neighbor Like You

The impartiality of neighbor love is of enormous significance to how Christians should think about criminal justice. When it comes to the justice system, one of the two neighbors—the stereotypical accused or the stereotypical victim—is probably more like you than the other neighbor, and this similarity can lead to partiality.

Each of us brings our own socioeconomic circumstances and life experiences to the discussion about criminal justice. If you live a middle-class suburban life, you probably never think about being a defendant in the criminal justice system. People charged with crimes may seem foreign to you—as "other" as the Samaritans were to the Jews of Christ's day. It's probably easier to envision yourself as a crime victim than as a defendant. If, on the other hand, you live in a heavily policed community, you may worry that you or your children could be falsely accused and convicted of a crime that you or they did not commit. Crime may be of concern to you, but so is being wrongly swept up in the dragnet of criminal justice. Rampant crime in your community and your experiences with law enforcement may leave you conflicted, both worried about crime and wary of the police. Either way, our varied life circumstances and experiences shape our thinking about how the criminal justice system should be structured.

To some degree, this is understandable and even commendable given our moral proximity to family and friends. We *should be* concerned about how the criminal justice system affects those we are obligated to protect. The danger, however, is that we fail to see that our neighborhood of moral proximity extends to those who are not like us as well. I should act on my love for my family differently than I would for another family across my town, my state, or my country, but that does not mean I am absolved of any obligation to love the family on the other side of the tracks. The risk is that our personal circumstances and experiences can open the door to partiality in our views about criminal justice—a preference for those to whom we can most relate at the expense of those to whom we cannot.

---

31 Ramsey, *Basic Christian Ethics*, 93.

I saw this tendency as I interacted with people during the writing of this book. When I raised examples of innocent people who were coerced into guilty pleas (a topic I take up in chap. 11), one response was that "most" or a "large percentage" of those who plead guilty are guilty. That's likely true. But whether "most" or a "large percentage" is good enough for you will likely depend on your socioeconomic circumstances and the resulting risk that *you* could be wrongly swept up in a criminal case and face enormous pressure to plead guilty to a crime you did not commit to avoid a life-wrecking prison sentencing. On the flip side, righteous anger at police and prosecutorial abuses can give rise to a callousness to the important role that law enforcement plays and the very serious risks they face in bringing some measure of justice to real-life humans victimized by crime. In each instance, our experiences can sow seeds of partiality.

We need to be alert to the natural human tendency to protect our own interests at the expense of others. Those fallen, selfish natures shape our instincts concerning criminal justice too. If we most fear being a crime victim and think it unlikely that we could be criminally accused, we may well favor "victim's rights," resent procedural protections for criminal defendants that make convictions more difficult, and support harsh sentences for those convicted. By contrast, if we most fear false conviction, we may hold the opposite views. Such self-interest is not surprising, but it is contrary to loving our neighbors as ourselves. It is, instead, loving ourselves preeminently at the expense of our neighbors. It is preferential love, a "who is my neighbor?" love, which is to say that it is not the love of neighbor Christ commands.

The tribal way of loving based on socioeconomic similarity is understandable in a fallen world. But Christian sanctification involves a different way of thinking, a renewal of the mind (see Rom. 12:2)—a renewal requiring that we look out not only for our own interests but also for the interests of the "other" (see Phil. 2:4). It entails loving the one to whom we do not naturally relate and those whose interests are not aligned in obvious ways with ours. When it comes to criminal justice, this means that we consider the interests of the crime victim as well as the criminally accused and convicted, for they all now live in our neighborhood of obligation. Following Christ includes thinking differently about these neighbors. Going and doing like the good Samaritan means loving neighbors not like us and to

136 A CHRISTIAN ETHIC OF CRIMINAL JUSTICE

whom we cannot relate. They each are due our love, and thus loving them all non-preferentially is what justice demands.

For many of us, loving the criminally accused poses an especially acute challenge. It is not at all uncommon for people to dehumanize violent criminals in ways that can make it difficult to render impartial judgments. The promise at Officer Schlatt's funeral was to find the "animals" who killed him. Prosecutors have invoked similar language in their appeals to juries.[32] In the wake of horrible crimes, it is not uncommon to hear people speak of criminals as "monsters" and their neighborhoods as "jungles." But this sort of talk can distort justice.[33]

It is true that Adam and Eve's original sin involved relinquishing their place of dominion over the animals by submitting themselves to the will of one of those animals (Gen. 1:28; 3:1–4). This idea that we make ourselves like animals when we sin is repeated throughout Scripture (Ps. 32:9; Matt. 7:15; Phil. 3:2; 2 Pet. 2:12). To rape a child, beat an elderly woman, or take the life of an innocent person is monstrous. But not all allusions to the animalistic nature of sin are sanctified ones. Some are dehumanizing and intended as such. Nothing in Scripture condones that, and we are less able to distinguish between righteous anger and degrading rage than we would like to believe. That a person who committed a crime—even a horrific one—failed to treat his or her victim as one made in the image of God does not mean that we are likewise entitled to treat the person who committed the crime as if he or she were not God's image bearer. The criminal, in committing his offense, tells a lie about the victim's dignity. We must not, in anger, respond with a similar lie about the criminal.

32 Darden v. Wainwright, 477 U.S. 168, 180 (1986) (death sentence affirmed in case where prosecutor referred to defendant as an "animal" in closing argument); Lucio v. State, 351 S.W.3d 878, 890 (Tex. Crim. App. 2011) (in closing argument, the prosecutor argued that "this defendant is like a dog"; jury sentenced her to death); State v. Barajas, 177 P.3d 106, 113 (Wash. App. 2007) (affirming conviction where prosecutor referred to defendant in closing argument as a "mangie [sic], mongrel mutt"); State v. Bates, 804 S.W.2d 868, 881 (Tenn. 1991) (affirming death sentence where at trial the prosecutor referred to the defendant as a "rabid dog").
33 Milica Vasiljevic and G. Tendayi Viki, "Dehumanization, Moral Disengagement, and Public Attitudes to Crime and Punishment," in Humanness and Dehumanization, ed. Paul G. Bain, Jeroen Vaes, and Jacques-Philippe Leyens (New York: Psychology, 2013), 129–46. See also Albert Bandura, Bill Underwood, and Michael E. Fromson, "Disinhibition of Aggression through Diffusion of Responsibility and Dehumanization of Victims," Journal of Research in Personality 9, no. 4 (1975): 253–69, https://doi.org/10.1016/0092-6566(75)90001-X.

"It is easy and simple to hate evil men because they are evil," Augustine observed, "but uncommon and dutiful to love them because they are men."[34] And yet that is precisely what we must do—love the accused man or woman simply because he or she is a man or woman. Their worth, their value, their humanity is in no sense diminished because of what they have done. Even those who commit crimes are of inestimable worth in the eyes of the God of the universe whose image they bear. And possessing that worth, they have a right to our love. We owe it to them. To withhold that love, a love they are due, is to treat them unjustly.

In short, we can and often do tend to love the neighbors most like us. We are partial in our judgments; we are not impartial in our love. Rather than being Samaritans who reach across the "v." of criminal justice to love the neighbor unlike us, we instead resemble the priest and Levite who pass by the "other" in need. If we are honest, when it comes to criminal justice, we are all parabolic priests and Levites at times.

Facts Matter

None of this is to suggest that punishing someone based on the crimes he or she commits is unloving. To the contrary, forgoing punishment when the facts demand it can be a failure to love a wrongdoer, not to mention the person or community harmed by the wrongdoer. This is an issue I take up in the next chapter. The point here is simply that committing a crime does not remove someone from the neighborhood of our obligation. Our duty to love does not turn on *whether* someone has committed a wrong.

At the same time, *how* we love will depend on what someone has or has not done. There is a difference between making judgments based on one's actions (justice) and failing to love because of those actions (partiality). We must love even those whose crimes are reprehensible, though how we love that person may differ from how we love his or her victim.[35] To preference one person over the other—to order our love—based on what he or she did or didn't do is to show partiality in our judgment. Identical treatment is

34 Augustine, "Letter 153," in *From Irenaeus to Grotius: A Sourcebook in Christian Political Thought*, ed. Oliver O'Donovan and Joan Lockwood O'Donovan (Grand Rapids, MI: Eerdmans, 1999), 120.
35 Outka, *Agape*, 19–20, 265–66.

not required of offender and victim, but equal regard for the good of them both (impartiality) is a key element of biblical justice.[36]

As we saw earlier, the good of both the perpetrator and the victim is furthered when verdicts are accurate. Impartiality advances the end of accuracy, increasing the likelihood that the case will be judged on the facts rather than on the personalities, and thus that the victim and the actual wrongdoer will receive their due in the form of an accurate verdict and an appropriately measured punishment. Partiality—a preference in our love for one party over the other—can skew how we perceive the facts of the case and thus impair the accuracy of our judgments.

On the one hand, partiality can deny neighbor love to crime victims, treating some victims as less worthy of protection based on who they are. This was the partiality at issue in the Georgia death penalty system that McCleskey faced, a system that treated Black lives as less deserving of protection than Whites. Conversely, partiality can exacerbate the risk of a wrongful conviction if the victim is a person of social status and the defendant is not. In that circumstance, partiality robs the falsely accused of justice while deceiving the victim as well.

But again, passing judgment on an accusation—and, ultimately, on an accused—is not an unloving (and thus unjust) act of partiality. It cannot be, lest we conclude that God himself is unloving. The apostle John tells us that "God is love" (1 John 4:8, 16). God doesn't simply *do* loving things; love *is* his nature. Love is an attribute, not merely an action, of God. At the same time, we are told repeatedly in Scripture that God will judge. The writer to the Hebrews calls him "the judge of all" (Heb. 12:23). Speaking of God, James tells us, "There is only one . . . judge" (James 4:12). The prophets repeatedly warn that the Lord will judge (Ps. 9:8; Isa. 2:4; Mic. 4:3; Joel 3:12). So prevalent in Scripture is this theme of ultimate divine judgment that the Nicene Creed confesses that the Son of God will come again in glory "to judge."[37] The triune God of love will judge, Scripture plainly teaches.

It is not the act of judging that is unloving, but rather the failure to judge impartially. God can *be loving* and at the same time *render judgment* because

---

36 According to Outka, *Agape*, 20, "Equal consideration is not the same as identical treatment. Agape requires the former, but not always the latter."

37 See "The Nicene Creed," in *Creeds, Confessions, and Catechisms: A Reader's Edition*, ed. Chad Van Dixhoorn (Wheaton, IL: Crossway, 2022), 17.

his judgments are impartial. "God shows no partiality" in his judgment, Paul tells us, meaning that God renders judgment on mankind "according to his works" (Rom. 2:6, 11). Peter said the same to Cornelius (Acts 10:34) and then later in his first epistle (1 Pet. 1:17). The Old Testament likewise tells us that there is no partiality with God (Deut. 10:17; 2 Chron. 19:7). Judging impartially is essential to judging with love.

Passing judgment impartially based on what someone has done is precisely what love demands because it is what justice demands. It is what is due both the victim and the wrongdoer. To love does not mean that we do not judge. Rather, love requires that when we judge we do so impartially—that is, we judge each case on its facts, treating like cases alike and dissimilar cases dissimilarly. Impartiality requires an equality of treatment when the circumstances are essentially the same and an inequality of treatment when the circumstances are meaningfully different. As O'Donovan puts it, "We depend on the justice of differentiation."[38]

Impartiality doesn't mean that we don't make judgments but rather means that the facts, not the personalities, are determinative in rendering those judgments. Impartiality means that the events, the circumstances, and the evidence matter. To judge otherwise would be to decide based on whim or bias. Either would be a failure of justice—a failure to accord both the accuser and the accused what they are due, namely, an accurate resolution of the matter—and thus a failure of love. We must love and do justice to both parties to a crime by rendering a verdict based on what they have done (or had done to them) and not who they are.

When it comes to justice, it is no answer to say that some have received their due. Justice requires, according to Augustine, that "everyone" receives their due.[39] If, because of who they are or from where they come, only some receive their due, then the justice rendered can at the same time be an injustice. Partial justice is unjust. Martin Luther King Jr. argues this very point in his "Letter from Birmingham Jail" where he defines an unjust law as one "that a majority inflicts on a minority that is not binding on itself."[40] "Rules for thee but not for me" are not just rules. Though they did not

38 Oliver O'Donovan, *The Ways of Judgment* (Grand Rapids, MI: Eerdmans, 2005), 42.
39 Augustine, *The City of God*, trans. Marcus Dods (Peabody, MA: Hendrickson, 2009), 632 (19.21).
40 Martin Luther King Jr., "Letter from Birmingham Jail," April 16, 1963, The University of Alabama Libraries Special Collections, accessed June 8, 2022, 8, http://purl.lib.ua.edu/181702.

use the term, Augustine and King were both speaking to the injustice of partiality. In effect, they argued that biblical justice requires justice for all without preference for some.

Seeing preferential injustice at times requires stepping back to view the question of justice at a system-wide level. Impartiality is a form of accuracy, both in the individual case and across cases. It is possible for justice to be served in a particular case by the imposition of an appropriate punishment while at the same time for justice to be perverted across cases by the imposition of disparate punishments in factually similar cases. Impartiality is subverted when, in some cases, personalities rather than facts drive judgments. But seeing this type of injustice often requires stepping back and surveying the justice forest, not only its trees. This is precisely what the Baldus study set out to do. Death may have been an appropriate sentence for McCleskey. But, if appropriate, was it imposed universally? Was justice blind—colorblind—in application? The statistical evidence showed that it was not.

Sometimes the law itself fails the test of impartiality by preferencing certain classes of people. The Separate Car Act to which Homey Plessy was subjected because of his race is an example.[41] At other times, partiality is introduced into a case through the application of an otherwise neutral law. It was partiality in application that was at issue in McCleskey's case. No law on the books in 1978 directed that the race of the victim be considered in meting out death sentences, but the statistical evidence showed that actors in the system applied the law in a partial way. McCleskey got his due, and thus in a limited sense justice was served. But McCleskey was subjected to a justice from which others were spared based on race, and in that sense the system, because it was not impartial, was unjust.

A Veil of Ignorance

Scripture's call for us to judge impartially, imaging our heavenly Father who does so, is easier said than done because we are not impartial people. We all have our biases, our favorites, our preferences. We relate to and, thus, tend to prefer those who are more like ourselves. It is here that a variation of John Rawls's thought experiment—known as the "veil of

41 Plessy v. Ferguson, 163 U.S. 537, 541 (1896).

ignorance"—can serve as an instrument for the renewal of our minds that is the beginning of sanctification (Rom. 12:2).

Admittedly, Rawls did not claim to be offering a Christian theory of justice. He wasn't even a Christian. When he wrote his monumental work of political philosophy, *A Theory of Justice*, he was writing as an atheist, and his theory of justice was not the biblical one.[42] Rawls nevertheless offers an insight that can sharpen our thinking as Christians about how to design a system of criminal justice that loves both of our neighbors. We can, as Augustine urges, "plunder the Egyptians" (Ex. 3:22), stealing a nugget of God's truth from a godless philosopher.[43]

In a nutshell, Rawls maintains that the fundamental question a society must answer is not what form of government it should adopt but rather what is just and unjust. If you were to ask someone what is just, they would naturally tend to argue for a definition of justice that benefits them in their current station in life. This isn't justice, however. It's partiality. Recognizing this selfish tendency, Rawls argues that the question of justice must be answered from what he calls the "original position." By this he means that you and I should pretend that we do not know our individual lots in life—a hypothetical situation where "no one knows his place in society, his class position or social status, nor does anyone know his fortune in the

---

42 Rawls rejected the utilitarian theory of justice. John Rawls, *A Theory of Justice*, rev. ed. (Cambridge, MA: Harvard University Press, 1999), 3. His theory of justice as "fairness" nonetheless fell short of the biblical standard. For a discussion of the inconsistencies between Rawls's theory of justice and that of the Bible, see Anthony B. Bradley and Greg Forster, eds., *John Rawls and Christian Social Engagement* (Lanham, MD: Lexington, 2015).

43 "If those who are called philosophers, and especially the Platonists, have said aught that is true and in harmony with our faith, we are not only not to shrink from it, but to claim it for our own use from those who have unlawful possession of it." Augustine, *On Christian Doctrine*, trans. J. F. Shaw (Mineola, NY: Dover, 2009), 75 (2.40.60). John Calvin held a similar view: "Therefore, in reading profane authors, the admirable light of truth displayed in them should remind us, that the human mind, however much fallen and perverted from its original integrity, is still adorned and invested with admirable gifts from its Creator. If we reflect that the Spirit of God is the only fountain of truth, we will be careful, as we would avoid offering insult to him, not to reject or condemn truth wherever it appears. In despising the gifts, we insult the Giver." John Calvin, *Institutes of the Christian Religion*, trans. Henry Beveridge (Peabody, MA: Hendrickson, 2008), 167 (2.2.15). Or as he elsewhere stated it more succinctly, "All truth is from God; and consequently, if wicked men have said anything that is true and just, we ought not to reject it; for it has come from God." John Calvin, *Commentary on Timothy, Titus, Philemon*, trans. William Pringle (Grand Rapids, MI: Christian Classics Ethereal Library, 1999), 246, https://ccel.org/. Christian ethicist Paul Ramsey put it this way: "Christian ethics makes permanent coalition with 'the truth' where it may be found." Ramsey, *Basic Christian Ethics*, 344.

distribution of natural assets and abilities, his intelligence, strength, and the like." Not knowing our life circumstances, we should then and only then answer the question of what is just. In other words, "the principles of justice are chosen behind a veil of ignorance."[44]

When I was young, my father used a Rawlsian approach to disputes with my brother. If we both wanted the remaining slice of pie, my father would require us to share it. One would cut. The other got to pick first. My father put the pie cutter in the "original position." Not knowing which slice you will get, how will you cut the pie? That was essentially Rawls's approach when it came to slicing up the pie of life.

Rawls primarily has distributive (economic) justice in mind in his work, and he argues for what he believes are the principles of justice that would be chosen behind that veil of ignorance. Whether he is right or wrong on those points is not my concern here, nor are matters of distributive justice. Instead, I want to focus on the idea of the veil itself and how it can help us think about criminal justice. Though not framed in Christian terms, what Rawls proposed with his "veil of ignorance" is a way of thinking that can help move us away from tribal affiliation and toward neighborly love in the design of our criminal justice system.

As we saw in earlier chapters, Scripture tells us that justice requires accurate judgments that depend on due process. But as finite creatures in a fallen world of limited resources, we will necessarily have to make judgments about the details of a justice system that Scripture does not address. To take one example, even if we agree that we must use all reasonable means to achieve accurate verdicts, won't our judgment about what means are reasonable necessarily be impacted by our own station in life? If we are more likely to encounter the justice system as a crime victim than as a criminally accused, won't that skew our judgment on questions of what is reasonable? And isn't the converse also true? This is where a modified version of Rawls's thought experiment could prove useful.

Applied to the construction of a system of criminal justice, we ask how we would design the criminal justice system from an original position of ignorance but with love as our goal. How would we design the system if we did not know our lot in life and thus did not know whether we were

44 Rawls, A Theory of Justice, 10–11.

more likely to be a crime victim or a criminal defendant? If we didn't know which neighbor we would be, how would we structure the system to love both neighbors? In other words, how would we frame a justice system if we were impartial?

In this way, a modified version of Rawls's veil of ignorance forces us to go beyond putting ourselves in the criminal justice shoes of someone else and instead asks us to slip into the shoes of two someone elses—what Scripture might call two neighbors. We are forced to ask how we would love—meaning, what would we do to promote the good of each of those neighbors—if we could end up as either of them but didn't know which we would be. In biblical terms, this modified version of Rawls's test is a way of thinking that helps us impartially work out the details of what it means to love our neighbors in the criminal justice system as ourselves (Luke 10:27). Behind the veil of ignorance, what promotes the good of both crime victim and criminal defendant?

It is natural to support easy convictions and harsh punishments if your life's station is such that you relate to crime victims. Conversely, it comes as no surprise that those who worry about being falsely accused would support robust procedural protections for those charged with crimes. But how would you craft and shape the justice system to conform to biblical principles if the chances were fifty-fifty that you would turn out to be either crime victim or a criminal defendant? This is the question that the modified veil of ignorance test poses. It forces us to consider the concerns of the neighbors not like us. By placing ourselves in the hypothetical original position, with its attendant uncertainty as to which neighbor we will be, this thought experiment helps us see what it would mean to love our neighbors—both neighbors—as we would ourselves. The veil of ignorance, it turns out, can help the Christian do justly.

In April 1987, the US Supreme Court handed down its decision in Warren McCleskey's case. In a 5–4 ruling, the court rejected his constitutional claim and affirmed his death sentence. His execution could go forward. As a legal matter, partial justice was justice enough—or at least all the justice the courts would give.

But what of the moral question that McCleskey's case posed? To that question, Reverend Francis Grimké had spoken eighty-eight years earlier in his summer sermon series. In the last of his three sermons that June, he argued from the parable of the good Samaritan for a solution to the dehumanizing theology and resulting partiality that had corrupted America's criminal justice system in his day. Grimké's words to his congregation in 1899 are just as relevant today:

> The neighbor that we are to love as ourselves is not the member of our own family, or nation, or race only; but any and everybody of whatever race or nation—whether white, or black, or red, or brown, makes no difference. . . . [T]he place for this work to begin, is in the church, i.e., among the professed followers of Christ. If there is any class of persons anywhere that we have the right to expect to act upon Christian principles, to treat a fellow being as he ought to be treated, to accord him all his rights, it is those who make up the Christian Church. . . . Here is the church's opportunity of demonstrating the power of Christianity to deal with the most difficult of social problems.[45]

What's the recipe for impartial justice? In a word, love. Love for the neighbor who is *not* like us as we would love ourselves. Love of that sort is the answer to our most difficult of criminal justice problems.

---

45 Francis Grimké, "The Remedy for the Present Strained Relations between the Races in the South," in *Addresses*, vol. 1 of *The Works of Francis Grimké*, ed. Carter G. Woodson (Washington, DC: Associated, 1942), 321, 329, 330.

8

Proportionality

AS DISCUSSED IN CHAPTER 2, a criminal justice system is the actual or threatened application of physical force by the state against those who do what the state forbids or who refuse to do what the state commands. The state's use of physical force begins with an arrest but culminates with a sentence after conviction, especially if the sentence is one of imprisonment or death. And God ordained that such uses of force can be morally permissible. The state may use physical force—may "bear the sword"—to punish those who are, in fact, evildoers (Rom. 13:4).

But to say that the state is divinely authorized to use physical force against wrongdoers does not mean that the state may use an unlimited amount of force. We know intuitively that the death penalty would be an immoral response to, for example, the offense of jaywalking. At the same time, serious punishment of some sort strikes most people as an appropriate response to murder. But even as to murder, people hold a range of views as to what the proper punishment is. Should the murderer be executed? Should *all* murderers be executed? Would life imprisonment with no possibility of parole be a just sentence? Should the possibility of parole be left open? What if the murder was committed by a child? And once we answer all those questions as to the crime of murder, we are then faced with similar questions for numerous other crimes.

For the Christian, the answers to these questions depend on the answer to a more foundational question: How much physical force may the state morally use against someone who has committed a crime? What is Scripture's guiding principle for the punitive use of force against those rightly found guilty of crimes? The simple answer, of course, is that even when punishing, we must love our neighbors—both of them. But even if we agree with that in concept, we then must sort out what it means in practice. Is it even possible to love both neighbors, especially the neighbor who committed a crime and is deserving of punishment? Can the use of punitive force be loving? It's to those questions we now turn.

The God Who Punishes

We live in a day in which many people, even some Christians, are uncomfortable with the idea of punishment. Moral philosophers, theologians, and others have long spilled a great deal of ink on the question of whether punishment is a morally permissible response to wrongdoing. To some extent, the discomfort and debate are understandable. Punishment is the infliction of some sort of suffering, pain, or loss on another person because of a wrong committed by that person. As Hugo Grotius puts it, punishment is "the pain of suffering, which is inflicted for evil actions."[1] It is not hard to see why some Christians struggle with how intentionally causing pain to others can be reconciled with Christ's command to love our neighbors.

No matter how uncomfortable it might make us, though, the Bible teaches that punishment rightly administered is not only just but also loving. We see this first and foremost in what Scripture reveals about both the character and actions of God. He is a God "who practices steadfast love, justice, and righteousness in the earth" (Jer. 9:24). But God does not merely perform loving and just works. As we saw in chapter 7, "the LORD is a God of justice" (Isa. 30:18), *and* "God is love" (1 John 4:8). Love and justice are essential attributes of his character, which means that *all* he does is loving and just. He cannot act otherwise.

Scripture further reveals that God's justice culminates in the punishment of sin. In response to history's first crime—Cain's murder of Abel—God sentenced Cain to a life on the run and of ineffective farming, which Cain described as a "punishment" (Gen. 4:12–13). In Psalm 89, the psalmist opens his song by extolling "the steadfast love of the LORD" (Ps. 89:1) before promising that if God's children forsake his law, then he will "punish" their

---

1   Hugo Grotius, *The Rights of War and Peace*, trans. A. C. Campbell (New York: M. Walter Dunne, 1901), 221 (2.20.1).

sin (Ps. 89:30–32). The prophet Isaiah writes of God's oracle that he "will punish the world for its evil, / and the wicked for their iniquity" (Isa. 13:11). Speaking through Jeremiah, God promises a day when he will "punish" those who are not truly his people (Jer. 9:25). Elsewhere, Jeremiah records that God will "punish . . . according to the fruit of your deeds" (Jer. 21:14). Hosea likewise writes of God's promise to "punish" his people "for their ways" (Hos. 4:9). Jesus himself speaks vividly of that punishment, telling of a coming day when he will command that "all law-breakers" be thrown "into the fiery furnace," a place he describes as one where "there will be weeping and gnashing of teeth" (Matt. 13:41–42). And, as Christ promised, the end of history will culminate with God punishing evil once and for all (Rev. 20:11–15). Over and over, Scripture speaks of God's punishment of sinners for their sin. A deity that fails to punish is quite simply not the biblical God. Whatever our uneasiness with the idea of punishment, the God of the Bible does not share our discomfort.

Given Scripture's revelation both that God punishes *and* that God is just and loving, we are left to conclude that God punishes *because* he is just and *because* (not despite that) he is loving. God punishes, in other words, as an outworking of his character of justice and love. Punishment, rightly understood and rightly administered, is a necessity of justice *and* love. Punishment is not inconsistent with love. It cannot be. For if it were, then God would be only partially loving, able to act in punitive ways that are contrary to love. But because God *is* love, and thus *all* his acts are loving, the only reasonable conclusion is that God's punishment is also loving. His punishment flows from his character as both just and loving. Divine love necessitates divine punishment. In fact, Exodus 34 pairs God's love and punishment, telling us that God is "abounding in love" and at the same time will "not leave the guilty unpunished" (Ex. 34:6–7 NIV). There is, at least in God's mind, no inconsistency between the two.

The difficulty we face in understanding how God could both be loving and cause pain in the form of punishment is another example of what theologians call theodicy, meaning the mystery of how a good and all-powerful God could allow sin in the world. Punishment is only necessary because of sin, and God in his omnipotence could have prevented sin. So why did the loving God allow sin that gives rise to the need for punishment? This is the question that has vexed believers and unbelievers alike for millennia.

Numerous answers have been proposed. None of them are satisfying, in my view. Yet I trust what God has revealed: "The LORD is just in all his actions, / and exhibits love in all he does" (Ps. 145:17 NET). And that loving justice includes punishment.

The important point for us as God's image bearers is not only that we too can punish consistent with love but also that we *must* punish in love if we are to act in accord with the justice and love of God. To fail to punish evil is to fail to embody God's justice and thus his love. But still the question remains: how is punishment—and criminal punishment in particular—an act of love for both neighbors?

Truth Telling

First, punishment can be an act of love by communicating truth. As we've discussed earlier, justice requires accuracy, meaning that only those who have done wrong are punished for that wrong. Just punishment, then, is a response to a wrong and, in particular, a declaration about that wrong. Punishment is, in the words of Oliver O'Donovan, an "expressive act." To punish is to make a statement that the conduct being judged is wrong, and the severity of the punishment imposed is a statement about the seriousness of the wrong.[2]

In a criminal case, the judgment of conviction is entered not after the verdict when the jury declares that the conduct at issue was wrongful (illegal) but rather after the judge imposes a sentence and thereby pronounces how wrongful the conduct was.[3] The judgment of conviction speaks a dual truth about the defendant's moral culpability. This is in accord with biblical justice, which requires that the law rightly differentiate right from wrong in what it criminalizes *and* rightly differentiate between more and less severe wrongs in how it punishes.

For a punishment to be both just and thus loving, the statement made by the punishment must be accurate. This, of course, requires that only the morally guilty are punished. But, even as to the guilty, the severity of the punishment must be true, meaning in line with the reality of the crime to which the punishment is a response. A punishment is just only to the

---

2   Oliver O'Donovan, *The Ways of Judgment* (Grand Rapids, MI: Eerdmans, 2005), 110, 120.
3   Fed. R. Crim. P. 32(k)(1).

extent that it expresses the truth about the extent of the wrong. By imposing a just punishment that tells the truth about the severity of the crime,
we love both the perpetrator, who needs to hear that word of admonition,
and the victim, who needs to hear the community's agreement about the
seriousness of the wrong done to him or her.

We more commonly refer to this truth-telling element of punishment as
proportionality. When we speak of proportional punishment, we mean that
the severity of the harm imposed as punishment is commensurate with the
wrong the defendant committed. There must be a correspondence of some
sort. "To the degree that a person is guilty," Bavinck argues, "to that degree
he or she deserves punishment."[4] It is only when these two degrees align
that proportionality is achieved and the truth is thereby told.

We see this concept of proportionality running throughout Scripture. As
Leviticus 24 makes clear, whether the offense at issue is a property crime
(Lev. 24:18, 21), a violent crime (24:19), or a capital crime (24:17, 21), the
Lord calls for a proportionate response in punishment. In Deuteronomy
25, where Moses ordains corporal punishment in ancient Israel, he is careful to circumscribe it such that it can be inflicted on an offender only "in
proportion to his offense" and not in a manner that serves to degrade him
(Deut. 25:2–3). A punishment that degrades the offender tells a falsehood
about him, suggesting that what he has done has emptied him or her of
humanity. As noted in chapter 7, the offender by his crime tells a lie about
the dignity of his victim, a lie that we cannot repeat in our punishment of
that offender.

It is not surprising, then, that Scripture is likewise careful to describe
divine punishment too as proportionate. The Old Testament is replete with
instances in which God's punishment of humankind is spoken of as being
meted out "according to" the wrong done. King David, for example, calls on
the Lord to, in his justice, give to the wicked "according to the evil of their
deeds" and "according to the work of their hands," describing it as "their
due reward" (Ps. 28:4). The prophet Isaiah tells of how the Lord will "repay"
his enemies "according to their deeds" (Isa. 59:18). Jeremiah cautions that,
though we deceive ourselves about our uprightness, God knows all and will

4   Herman Bavinck, *Sin and Salvation in Christ*, vol. 3 of *Reformed Dogmatics*, ed. John Bolt, trans.
John Vriend (Grand Rapids, MI: Baker Academic, 2006), 166.

"give every man according to his ways, / according to the fruit of his deeds" (Jer. 17:10). God himself warns Judah, "I will punish you according to the fruit of your deeds" (Jer. 21:14). The prophetic examples of this language of correspondence between people's acts and God's punishment are numerous.

In the New Testament, at least three authors repeat this idea of proportionality in God's punishment. Peter writes of God the Father as one who judges "according to each one's deeds" (1 Pet. 1:17). Paul speaks of God's judgment as "rightly" falling on wrongdoers in that he will "render to each one according to his works" (Rom. 2:2, 6). When John later recounts his vision of that day of final judgment, he describes it as one in which God will judge everyone "according to what they had done" (Rev. 20:12–13). The judgment of God will be measured out to match the degree of the wrong. No more than deserved—due—for the evil done.

This idea of proportionality is most vividly captured in the Old Testament phrase "life for life, eye for eye, tooth for tooth, hand for hand, foot for foot, burn for burn, wound for wound, stripe for stripe" (Ex. 21:23–25). In Roman law, this concept came to be known as *lex talionis* (the law of retaliation).[5] As Grotius puts it, "It is undoubtedly one of the first principles of justice to establish an equality between the penalty and the offense."[6] Scripture obviously reflects this "equality" of punishment in its prescribed response to physical injuries. But interestingly, when the Mosaic law sets out the penalties for theft, the proportional response was not dollar-for-dollar equality. Rather, the thief was required to pay five, four, or two times in return, depending on what was stolen (Ex. 22:1–4, 7–9). Nonetheless, even in the case of property offenses, Scripture recognizes that there should be a relationship between the economic harm done and the financial consequence that can be inflicted in return.

The biblical picture of God's justice as proportionate is critical to how we think about earthly justice because we are God's imagers. The authority we possess to work justice in this world is derivative (Rom. 13:1). It is authority God has granted and, thus, must be exercised in accord with

5   "The Twelve Tables," The Avalon Project, Yale Law School, accessed November 7, 2022, https://avalon.law.yale.edu/, which cites Allan Chester Johnson, Paul Robinson Coleman-Norton, and Frank Card Bourne, *Ancient Roman Statutes: A Translation with Introduction, Commentary, Glossary, and Index* (Austin: University of Texas Press, 1961). Table 8.2 reads, "If anyone has broken another's limb there shall be retaliation in kind."
6   Grotius, *The Rights of War and Peace*, 222 (2.20.2).

his character. And when it comes to God, his justice flows from his holiness. His judgment is how his holiness is displayed in response to a fallen
people. This divine justice becomes the model that we who are made
in his image must display in our earthly justice. We are to be holy, and
thus just, as he is holy and just (1 Pet. 1:16). Or as Thomas Aquinas puts
it, "Human justice is conformed to Divine justice."[7] This means, among
other things, that we are to be proportionate in our punishment as he is
proportionate in his. We must punish in a way that tells the truth, God's
truth, about the wrong that has been done.

Restored Order

Punishment can also be an act of love to the extent that it maintains or
restores the moral order of society. Properly understood, punishment is not
an act of retaliation *(talionis)*. It is not the infliction of harm for the sake
of inflicting harm. We do not hurt in return simply because someone has
hurt us. Punishment is not an equalization of injury to somehow rebalance
the cosmic scales of pain. Punishment is not doing harm to another as an
end in itself. Merely repaying evil for evil is precisely what Scripture forbids
(1 Pet. 3:9). Rather, punishment, if it is to be just, must be designed to serve
a loving end, and that end is the peace of society—Augustine's "tranquility
of order" *(tranquilitas ordinis)*.[8]

Punishment can serve this good end of social order by deterring offenders before they do harm, incapacitating them from doing future harm, and
reforming them so that they no longer desire to harm. As Grotius puts it, "All
punishment aims at the common good, and particularly at the preservation
of order and deterrence."[9] Punishment of this sort is an act of love for those

7   Thomas Aquinas, *Summa Theologica*, trans. Fathers of the English Dominican Province (New York: Benzinger Brothers, 1947), 2–2.64.2, https://www.ccel.org. Grotius, quoting Plutarch, likewise writes that "justice is an attribute of God, avenging all transgressions of the divine law; and we apply it as the rule and measure of our dealings with each other." Grotius, *The Rights of War and Peace*, 221 (2.20.1).

8   Augustine, *The City of God*, trans. Marcus Dods (Peabody, MA: Hendrickson, 2009), 624 (19.13). Calvin likewise says that power was given to rulers to maintain "the common tranquility of all." John Calvin, *Institutes of the Christian Religion*, trans. Henry Beveridge (Peabody, MA: Hendrickson, 2008), 977 (4.20.11).

9   Hugo Grotius, "The Satisfaction of Christ," in *From Irenaeus to Grotius: A Sourcebook in Christian Political Thought*, ed. Oliver O'Donovan and Joan Lockwood O'Donovan (Grand Rapids, MI: Eerdmans, 1999), 820 (2.16).

victimized by crime (past and future), those who commit crime, and society at large because it seeks the good of all of them. Punishment, in other words, can and should be an act of social justice.

At a surface level, punishment can maintain or restore social order through deterrence. Wrongdoers at heart forgo further wrongdoing for fear of punishment. This does not alone make wrongdoers righteous.[10] The fear of legal punishment may not change their hearts, but it can stop their evil deeds. That is a good thing, as Dr. King observed, even if not the best thing.[11] Innocent parties are spared from harm, which is an act of love for them. And the would-be wrongdoer is loved by deterrence to the extent that the threat of punishment dissuades him or her from self-destructive and ultimately damnable wrongs.

In the short run, the punitive force of the law may only change actions. But in the long run, it might change hearts by provoking true repentance, maybe even to the saving of souls. "While punishment is inflicted as justice," George Cheever writes, "it may also be turned into a medicine of reclaiming love."[12] Or as the Catechism of the Catholic Church puts it, "Punishment, in addition to preserving public order and the safety of persons, has a medicinal scope: as far as possible it should contribute to the correction of the offender."[13] In either event, the law's punishment is

---

10 Augustine, "Letter 145: Augustine to Anastasius," in *Letters 100–155*, trans. Roland Teske, ed. Boniface Ramsey, in *The Works of Saint Augustine: A Translation for the 21st Century* (Hyde Park, NY: New City, 2003), 313 (4), writes, "He is, then, an enemy of justice if he does not sin out of fear of punishment, but its friend if he does not sin out of love for it. For, then, he will truly fear to sin."

11 Martin Luther King Jr., "Convocation" (Illinois Wesleyan University, Bloomington, IL, February 10, 1966), Illinois Wesleyan University, News and Events, https://www.iwu.edu/mlk/. In this speech, King argues, "It may be true that the law cannot make a man love me, religion and education will have to do that, but it can restrain him from lynching me. And I think that's pretty important also. And so that while legislation may not change the hearts of men, it does change the habits of men."

12 George B. Cheever, *A Defence of Capital Punishment* (New York: Wiley and Putnam, 1846), 194.

13 Catechism of the Catholic Church, part 3, sec. 2, chap. 2, art. 5, I (Respect for Human Life), 2266, accessed November 25, 2022, http://www.vatican.va. See also Compendium of the Social Doctrine of the Church, Pontifical Council for Justice and Peace, part 2, chap. 8, art. 3, e (Inflicting Punishment), 403, accessed November 25, 2022, http://www.vatican.va, which states, "Punishment does not serve merely the purpose of defending the public order and guaranteeing the safety of persons; it becomes as well an instrument for the correction of the offender. . . . There is a twofold purpose here. On the one hand, encouraging the re-insertion of the condemned person into society; on the other, fostering a justice that reconciles, a justice capable of restoring harmony in social relationships disrupted by the criminal act committed."

an act of love for the offended, the offender, and the society in which they both live.

This seeking of the good end of ordered peace is what distinguishes just punishment from cruelty.[14] Recall that biblical love is a desire for the good of another.[15] As people who are called to love our neighbors—all of them—this means that the punishment we dispense through a criminal justice system must be born of a desire for the good of the victim and the perpetrator. The physical force of the criminal justice system must be used as a means to love. Writing about war, Nigel Biggar makes this same point:

> The New Testament does not generate an absolute prohibition of violence, but it does generate an absolute injunction of love. Accordingly, just war doctrine's claim to belong to a *Christian* ethic rests on its conception of the right use of violence as an expression of love for the neighbour. This makes obvious sense when the neighbour in view is the innocent victim of unjust aggression, on whose behalf the just warrior takes up arms. However, the innocent victim is not the only neighbour on site. Since love is an absolute injunction, applying always and everywhere, the just warrior is also bound to love the unjust aggressor. His love—as Jesus made plain—must extend itself to the enemy.[16]

What Biggar says about just war is no less true about criminal justice. It can be just to use punitive force—whether military or judicial—but only if that force is used as an act of love for both the wronged and the wrongdoer. If a punishment is merely the infliction of pain without some good end in view, then that punishment is not the neighbor love that Christ commanded.

14 Augustine, "Letter 153: Augustine to Macedonius," in Ramsey, *Letters 100–155*, 400 (5.19), writes that, when it comes to punishment, "nothing should be done out of the desire to do harm, but everything should be done out of a love to show concern. And let nothing be done cruelly, nothing inhumanely." See also Augustine, "Letter 104: Augustine to Nectarius," in Ramsey, *Letters 100–155*, 47 (2.7).
15 Aquinas, *Summa Theologica*, 1.20.3, writes that "to love a thing is to will it good"; see also Nicholas Wolterstorff, *Justice in Love* (Grand Rapids, MI: Eerdmans, 2015), 23; Gene Outka, *Agape: An Ethical Analysis* (New Haven, CT: Yale University Press, 1972), 8–9.
16 Nigel Biggar, *In Defence of War* (New York: Oxford University Press, 2013), 61. Reproduced with permission of the Licensor through PLSclear.

As biblically conceived, just punishment is a harm imposed on the offender but that has "the good of the offender, or that of the injured party, or of any persons whatsoever in view."[17] We see this in Romans 13:4 where Paul tells us that the governing authorities wield the sword "for your good." They serve to deter us from bad conduct by the threat that they will act against it. Punishment of a scoffer will serve an instructional purpose for others (Prov. 19:25). The wicked are deterred and the innocent are thereby protected. And, ideally, punishment born of love will cause the wrongdoer to repent and change his ways. "We should love those who are bad in order that they might cease to be bad."[18] In these ways, punishment can bring good order to a society for the good of all its members, whether they be good or bad.

Thus, when Paul urges us to pray for those in authority, he has an end in mind, namely that we will live quiet and peaceable lives (1 Tim. 2:1–2). The government's use of authority—including its authority to punish—is a divinely ordained means to bring about domestic order and thus peaceful lives. As Augustine puts it, through punishment "the evil are held in check and the good live more peaceful lives among the evil."[19]

Solomon similarly writes that "when justice is done, it is a joy to the righteous / but terror to evildoers" (Prov. 21:15). The joy that the righteous experience is not a sadistic pleasure in the pain inflicted on and the terror felt by the wicked. Rather the joy is born of order restored and peace reestablished. The terror of punishment serves to bring about the joy of good social order. Peace is preserved by the threat of physical force and, if need be, restored by the infliction of a punishment on the wrongdoer that is intended as a call to repentance and reconciliation both *to* the community at large and *with* the one whom he has harmed.[20] "Severity," as Augustine puts it, is the "means by which our tranquility is also secured."[21]

For this reason, punishment, whether in war or in court, is a "kind harshness" or "benevolent severity."[22] We refer to it as tough love. It is an act of

17 Grotius, *The Rights of War and Peace*, 226 (2.20.6).
18 Augustine, "Letter 153," 397 (5:14).
19 Augustine, "Letter 153," 398 (5:16).
20 Biggar, *In Defence of War*, 61, 68.
21 Augustine, "Letter 153," 399 (5:19).
22 Augustine, "Letter 138: Augustine to Marcellinus," in Ramsey, *Letters 100–155*, 232 (2.14); "Letter CXXXVIII (A.D. 412) to Marcellinus," in *The Confessions and Letters of Augustin, with*

love for the victims, affirming their worth and value. It is an act of love for the community by deterring wrongdoers with the fear of the sword and restraining wrongdoers from doing further harm. And it can also be an act of love for the wrongdoer by seeking to save him from his evil and, ultimately, self-destruction. Punishment of this sort is proportional because it is only as severe as necessary to bring offenders to repentance and reconciliation with both the victim and their community. In this way, justice can be an act of mercy for the offender and the offended (Mic. 6:8). Or as Augustine puts it, "At times mercy punishes."[23]

Fits the Crime

But to say that a punishment should be designed to serve the good ends of deterrence, correction, repentance, and reconciliation does not mean that punishment is just simply because it serves those ends. The biblical theory of justice requires that a punishment be "proportioned both retrospectively to the nature of the wrongdoing and prospectively to the goal of reconciliation or a more just peace."[24] In other words, a just punishment is constrained by a requirement of proportionality *both to the end it serves and to the crime to which it responds*. The severity of the crime limits the severity of the punishment. The maximum punitive authority God has delegated to humankind to serve the good ends of deterrence, correction, repentance, and reconciliation is the authority to punish in a way that corresponds to the seriousness of the crime.

C. S. Lewis argues that purely deterrent and rehabilitative theories of punishment, although perhaps sounding humanitarian, are in fact disguised cruelty and injustice. If the justice of a punishment is defined solely by reference to its deterrent value, then greater punishment is likely better regardless of the proportionality of the penalty imposed. Two eyes for an eye would almost certainly be a more effective deterrent than an eye for an eye. For that matter, the death penalty for an eye might be the greatest deterrent of all. If deterrence is the only measure of just punishment, then there is little if any stopping point between extracting an eye and taking a

---

a Sketch of His Life and Work, vol. 1 of *Nicene and Post-Nicene Fathers*, First Series, ed. Philip Schaff (Peabody, MA: Hendrickson, 1994), 485 (2.14), https://ccel.org.

23 Augustine, "Letter 153," 399 (5:17). See also Augustine, "Letter 138," 232–33 (2.14).

24 Biggar, *In Defence of War*, 72. Reproduced with permission of the Licensor through PLSclear.

life as the proper response to a crime regardless of its severity. The more severity, the more deterrence.[25]

A similar risk of abuse presents itself, Lewis argues, if the goal of punishment is purely rehabilitation. The convict is treated as someone who is sick and in need of a cure, and the treatment will be compulsorily applied and continue until the healing is complete. The problem, of course, is that the time needed to achieve this rehabilitation, during which the defendant is incarcerated, could outlast the proportionate period during which a defendant should be held against his will. But in a system in which a crime is regarded as a sickness to be treated or a flawed character to be reformed, proportion to the severity of the offense carries no sway.[26]

Theories of deterrence or rehabilitation don't ask whether the punishment is the proportional penalty deserved but rather whether the punishment is one that works—that is, whether the punishment deters crime or rehabilitates the offender. "Is the penalty effective?" is the only question. And that answer can, for the same crime, differ from offender to offender. Some defendants are more recalcitrant and thus require more pain to deter. Some offenders have more deep-seated pathologies and thus need more treatment for rehabilitation. This approach to punishment, that focuses exclusively on the deterrent or rehabilitative efficacy of a punishment, is a utilitarian one. "Justice" is defined entirely by the ends achieved rather than according to an objective and stable standard of the right and moral punishment to be inflicted.

These are not the theories of punishment described in Scripture, which instead applies a proportionality constraint to the good goals of deterrence and rehabilitation. A punishment is just, in the biblical view, because it is deserved, and what makes a punishment deserved is its correspondence to the severity of the wrong committed.[27] This is not to say that biblical justice has no concern for deterrence. It plainly does (Rom. 13:3–4). What

---

25 C. S. Lewis, *The Problem of Pain* (San Francisco: HarperCollins, 2001), 91–92; C. S. Lewis, "The Humanitarian Theory of Punishment," in *God in the Dock: Essays on Theology and Ethics*, ed. Walter Hooper (Grand Rapids, MI: Eerdmans, 1970), 287, 291.

26 Lewis, *The Problem of Pain*, 91–92; Lewis, "The Humanitarian Theory of Punishment," 290.

27 According to Bavinck, *Sin and Salvation in Christ*, 162, God "determines the measure of the punishment by the nature of the offense." Furthermore, "punishment . . . is never a matter of expediency but rests in the inviolable ideas of good and evil that are rooted in the holy will of God" (163).

distinguishes a biblical theory of punishment from the deterrence and rehabilitative theories that Lewis condemns is that biblical punishment pursues those ends but is constrained by the severity of the crime. Thus, the biblical approach to punishment treats proportionality as a maximum that may be imposed rather than an absolute that must be imposed. The goal is restoration, which can be pursued through a punishment up to a maximum that corresponds to the severity of the crime but may necessitate less than the maximum punishment that proportionality permits.[28]

In other words, the point of proportional punishment is not only case specific but society wide. A just punishment makes a statement—both to the victim and to the society—about the wrong the offender has done. The hope is that the statement will serve its instructional ends both as to the offender and the broader society so that the offender will change his ways and others will be dissuaded from such conduct, all in anticipation of a more just social order. "The state is armed with the sword," Isaac Backus observes, "to guard the peace, and the civil rights of all persons and societies, and to punish those who violate the same."[29] The tranquility of order—peace—is the goal. Justice is most fully realized when people live together in love, rendering to each his or her due. But when in a fallen world that ideal is not met, justice and mercy demand that the offender receive the proportional punishment he or she is due in hopes of a more peaceful though imperfect future and with a longing for that final day of perfect peace and justice.

Mercy and Forgiveness

Understanding punishment as serving the end of peace helps us resolve some, but not all, of the seeming tension in the command "to act justly and to love mercy" (Mic. 6:8 NIV). One way in which we show mercy is to decline to inflict on people the punishment we have concluded they are due, which seems to be the opposite of justice. It seems as if Scripture tells us both to give people their due punishment and to excuse them of their

---

28 For a further discussion of restorative justice, see Christopher D. Marshall, *Beyond Retribution: A New Testament Vision for Justice, Crime, and Punishment* (Grand Rapids, MI: Eerdmans, 2001); Charles Colson, *Justice That Restores* (Carol Stream, IL: Tyndale, 2001); Howard Zehr, *The Little Book of Restorative Justice*, rev. ed. (New York: Good Books, 2015).

29 Isaac Backus, *An Appeal to the Public for Religious Liberty, against the Oppressions of the Present Day* (Boston: John Boyle, 1773), 13.

due punishment. How do we reconcile the command to do both of what seem like opposites?

There are no easy answers because, as noted earlier, the question is essentially the unresolvable question of theodicy. Niebuhr calls this "the mystery of the relation of forgiveness to punishment."[30] Though I have no tidy solution to this conundrum, I offer four observations.

First, showing mercy to those who deserve punishment is an act of humility on our part. It is an acknowledgement that we are fallible judges. There should be a self-consciousness in our judgment born of a recognition that, at the same time we judge, we are ourselves in need of mercy. We are hypocritical judges. As we pass judgment, we condemn ourselves for violating the same law we enforce (Rom. 2:1). The particular wrongs we commit may be different than those on which we cast judgment, but they are all of a piece of God's perfect law (James 2:10). The law enforcers are themselves law breakers, and this should cause us to flinch in mercy as we administer justice.

Second, we are never more like Jesus than when we forgive. On the cross, Christ absorbed in himself the punishment of God for sins that he did not commit. He suffered harm because of what we have done. When we forgive, we similarly (though differently) absorb the harm caused by another's wrong against us. As those who are forgiven by God, we are to image him in our forgiveness. This is the point of Christ's parable of the unforgiving servant (Matt. 18:32–33). How can we, who have been forgiven so much, not in turn forgive?

Third, the biblical principle of proportionality is one of limitation, not of necessity. While a wrong deserves a proportional punishment, we are permitted to withhold that punishment. Acts of mercy are not necessarily a failure of justice. Though Christ didn't abolish the law—including its principle of proportional punishments—he does call us to forgive wrongs done (Matt. 5:17, 38–42). Here, I think Biggar is on to something in relaxing this tension. If the point of punishment is restoration of a just order, then forgiveness and discontinuation of punishment when someone has repented is not unjust. To the contrary, the punishment and the corresponding forgiveness have together fostered a greater justice of social peace.[31] As pastor

---

30   Reinhold Niebuhr, "What Is Justice?," in *Love and Justice: Selections from the Shorter Writings of Reinhold Niebuhr*, ed. D. B. Robertson (Louisville: Westminster John Knox, 1957), 231.

31   Biggar, *In Defence of War*, 61–72.

Timothy Keller puts it, there is no conflict between justice and forgiveness because each in its own way seeks the good of the offender, the offended, and the community at large.[32]

Fourth, justice and mercy will only be completely reconciled in Christ. We do justice because God is a God of justice who punishes evil (Ex. 34:7). We show mercy because the Lord is rich in mercy (Ex. 34:6). We as his imperfect imagers seek to display all his perfections, the tension in doing so pointing us back to the God in Christ who satisfied justice and secured mercy on our behalf and pointing us ahead to the day when, because of God's mercy to us in Christ, we will experience a world of perfect justice. God is merciful, Isaiah tells us, because he is just (Isa. 30:18). It is only because of God's mercy that we will live forever in a world of just peace. There will be an eternal tranquility of order. Maranatha.

Proportion in Policing

Before concluding this discussion of proportionality, it is worth pausing to consider how these principles apply to arrests. Though policing is not the focus of this book, the principle of proportionality also applies to policing.

As explained in chapter 2, an arrest by a police officer is the actual or threatened application of physical force. Because arrests involve force, they raise questions of biblical justice. With regard to arrests, however, the proportionality question is complicated because the accused has not yet been found guilty of the offense. An allegation has been made, but it has not been proven true. Thus, the force permitted is not the force that would be appropriate to punish an offender once convicted. To the contrary, the biblical justice principle of due process requires that the suspect be afforded a meaningful opportunity to contest those allegations *before* punishment is inflicted.

Once someone is convicted, the proportionality analysis compares the severity of the crime with the severity of the punishment. But the proportionality comparison is different in the context of an arrest. At that point, the question is how much physical force is needed to arrest someone charged with a crime of a given severity. The proportional amount of force for an arrest depends on the danger to the police in making the

---

32 Timothy Keller, *Forgive: Why Should I and How Can I?* (New York: Viking, 2022), 107–8.

arrest and to the public if the arrest is unsuccessful.[33] In other words, an arrest can be thought of as an act taken in defense of another. To the extent that, based on the facts known, the suspect poses an acute and ongoing safety risk to the community, then the amount of force permitted to make the arrest is an amount of force proportional to that risk. And the police must likewise consider what force is proportionate to the risk they face in making the arrest.

So, for example, a significant amount of force, up to and including deadly force, could be morally permissible to arrest a suspected terrorist on the run because that force would be proportional to the risk the fleeing suspect poses. But the same is not true of someone suspected of shoplifting a candy bar. An arrest of the shoplifter might be proper, but use of deadly force to make that arrest would be immoral. If, however, the candy bar shoplifter pulled a gun on the police as they attempted an arrest, the proportional amount of force with which the police could respond would suddenly change in the face of that increased risk to their safety.

Much more could be said of the application of the proportionality principle to policing. My point here is simply to note that proportionality applies not only to punishment but also to uses of physical force earlier in the criminal justice process, including in arrests.

———

Shortly after midnight on January 18, 2015, two bicyclers on their way to a fraternity party spotted a man sexually assaulting a half-naked, unconscious woman behind a dumpster. The man, it turned out, was Brock Turner, a nineteen-year-old Stanford University student and all-American swimmer. After a jury trial, he was convicted of felony sexual assault.[34]

Following his conviction, Turner appeared before Judge Aaron Persky to be sentenced. The victim of the assault, who at the time was known only as "Emily Doe," read a moving statement to the court about the impact of the crime on her life. The judge also heard from Turner and considered written

33 O'Donovan, The Ways of Judgment, 206–7.
34 Michael E. Miller, "All-American Swimmer Found Guilty of Sexually Assaulting Unconscious Woman on Stanford Campus," Washington Post, March 31, 2016, https://www.washingtonpost .com/.

statements from his mother and father. Judge Persky then sentenced Turner to probation and six months in the county jail.[35]

The public backlash to this sentence was intense. News reports filled the airwaves decrying what was widely perceived as an unjustly lenient sentence that failed to account for the seriousness of the horrific crime. The district attorney delivered a public statement lambasting the judge. One of the jurors sent a letter to the judge stating that he was "absolutely shocked and appalled" at the sentence, which, he said, "does not fit the crime."[36] Though the public discussion of the case was not framed in biblical terms, there was a widespread sense that Turner's sentence was not a just one. It was not proportional.

The outrage concerning Judge Persky's sentencing decision did not dissipate. In a matter of days, an online petition demanding that the judge be recalled had gathered over one million signatures. A Stanford Law School professor led the recall effort, and after an intense legal battle, a recall election was set for June 5, 2018. In the weeks leading up to the election, Judge Persky was unapologetic, holding a press conference in which he insisted that, if given the chance to resentence Turner, his ruling would be the same.[37]

Biblical justice demands that due process be observed, that the verdict speak accurately, that justice be impartial, and that the punishment be proportional. Judge Persky believed that justice was served in the case of Brock Turner. The voters disagreed. So they delivered justice of a different sort, holding Judge Persky accountable by stripping him of his seat on the bench. It was the first time in eighty-six years that a California judge had been recalled by the voters.[38]

35 Marina Koren, "Why the Stanford Judge Gave Brock Turner Six Months," *The Atlantic*, June 17, 2016, https://www.theatlantic.com/.
36 Cindy Boren, "'Shame on You': Juror in Stanford Sexual Assault Case Protests Attacker's Sentence," *Washington Post*, June 14, 2016, https://www.washingtonpost.com/.
37 Bridget Read, "Rape Culture Is on the Ballot in California," *Vogue*, May 23, 2018, https://www.vogue.com/; Paul Elias, "Judge in Stanford Rape Case Fights Recall," *Associated Press*, May 18, 2018, https://apnews.com/.
38 Bob Egelko, "Judge Aaron Persky, Who Ruled in Sex Assault Case, Recalled in Santa Clara County," *San Francisco Chronicle*, June 5, 2018, https://www.sfchronicle.com/; "Recall, Superior Court Judge," Statewide Direct Primary Election, Santa Clara County Registrar of Voters, last modified July 9, 2018, https://results.enr.clarityelections.com/CA/Santa_Clara/75369/Web02.207763/#/cid/24. "Emily Doe" later released a book disclosing her true name and recounting her experience: Chanel Miller, *Know My Name: A Memoir* (New York: Viking, 2019).

PART 2

AMERICAN CRIMINAL JUSTICE

9

History

THE FIRST HALF OF THIS BOOK SKETCHED out a Christian ethic of justice. That ethic, rooted in the gospel, provides a framework for evaluating a
criminal justice system. The core of biblical justice is accuracy, due process
is the means to accuracy, impartiality protects accuracy, accountability
punishes inaccuracy, and proportionality ensures accuracy about severity.

The second half of the book consists of chapter-long descriptions of
various features of the American justice system as it exists today. Plea bargaining, jury selection, right to counsel, cross-examination, and the death
penalty are among the topics explained in the chapters that follow. In each
instance, I will pause to compare how a particular feature of the justice
system compares with the principles of biblical justice that were the focus
of the first half of this book.

But before turning to an examination of the way things are, I want to
briefly recount (at least some of) how things came to be this way. The American criminal justice system was not handed down as a unified whole in the
last ten, twenty, or even fifty years. It evolved over an extended period of time.
The justice system we have today is the product of more than two centuries
of choices. Some of those choices were noble. Others were deeply nefarious.
Understanding which is which is a crucial part of a fair evaluation of the
system's justice. As Shakespeare famously wrote, "What's past is prologue."[1]
History sets the stage—for good or for ill—for the scenes that follow.

---

1   William Shakespeare, *The Tempest*, ed. G. Blakemore, Riverside Shakespeare (Boston: Houghton
     Mifflin, 1974), 2.1.253.

A New Nation, Conceived in Liberty

On July 4, 1776, an event of enormous historic and moral significance occurred in Philadelphia, Pennsylvania. A few dozen men convened to declare not only their independence from Britain but also the moral truths that "all men are created equal" and are "endowed by their Creator with certain unalienable Rights." Included in the text of the Declaration of Independence adopted that day was a series of grievances against King George, including his "tyranny" in denying American colonists "the benefits of Trial by Jury."[2] Our nation was birthed, at least in part, over a dispute about the justice system.

A declaration of independence, of course, is not the same as independence itself. American freedom from Great Britain would require a war—the Revolutionary War. Eleven years after independence was declared, the Constitutional Convention convened in Philadelphia with the jury trial again front and center. The Constitution that emerged from the months of convention debates over the summer of 1787 assured that criminal cases would be tried by a jury.[3] The jury trial was viewed not only as an individual right of a criminal defendant but also as an act of democratic citizenship on the part of the jurors who could participate in government through their votes to convict or acquit a criminal defendant.[4]

Four years later, a Bill of Rights was appended to the Constitution.[5] Many of the rights recognized in the ten constitutional amendments that make up the Bill of Rights were directed at restraining the government when it investigated and prosecuted crimes. The Fourth Amendment constrains the government's ability to search your person, property, or residence for evidence of a crime. The Fifth Amendment promises that a criminal defendant will receive "due process," prohibits the government from twice prosecuting a

---

2   "Declaration of Independence: A Transcription" (July 4, 1776), National Archives, accessed September 29, 2022, https://www.archives.gov.

3   U.S. Const. art. III, § 2, cl. 2.

4   Alexis de Tocqueville later observed that the jury was "a political institution," "one form of the sovereignty of the people" that "contribute[s] to the supremacy of the majority." Alexis de Tocqueville, *Democracy in America*, vol. 1, trans. Henry Reeve, ed. Francis Bowen (Cambridge: Sever and Francis, 1863), 362–63. Thomas Jefferson expressed a similar sentiment in his Letter to the Abbé Arnoux, July 19, 1789, in *The Papers of Thomas Jefferson*, vol. 15, ed. Julian P. Boyd (Princeton, NJ: Princeton University Press, 1958), 282–83.

5   For a brief history of the drafting and adoption of the federal Bill of Rights, see "Bill of Rights," History, October 27, 2009, last modified September 15, 2020, https://www.history.com.

defendant for the same crime (double jeopardy), and precludes the prosecution from forcing you to testify against yourself (right to remain silent). The
Sixth Amendment promises a speedy trial on any criminal charges, affords
the right to trial by jury, assures that a criminal defendant can confront accusing witnesses and present evidence of his or her own, and guarantees the
assistance of a defense attorney. The Eighth Amendment prohibits excessive
bail, unreasonable fines, and cruel and unusual punishments for crimes.
But as originally drafted, the Bill of Rights applied only in federal criminal
cases, while the vast majority of crimes were prosecuted by state and local
governments to which those rights did not apply.[6]

Several of the original thirteen colonies (later states) included in their
constitutions some of the same protections for criminal defendants.[7] Most
notable was Virginia's Declaration of Rights, which became the model for
the federal Bill of Rights.[8] Virginia guaranteed a criminal defendant's right
to notice of the charges, to a speedy and impartial trial before a jury "of
twelve men," to confront witnesses and present evidence, and to remain
silent; it also made explicit that a conviction required a unanimous verdict.[9]
The Constitution of Massachusetts, adopted in 1780, contained similar
detailed guarantees.[10] North Carolina's Constitution of 1776 contained a
Declaration of Rights that prohibited excessive bail, guaranteed the right
to confront accusers, and required for conviction "the unanimous verdict
of a jury of good and lawful men."[11]

6   Barron v. Baltimore, 32 U.S. (7 Pet.) 243, 250–51 (1833); Paul Dolan, "Rise of Crime in the Period
    1830–1860," *Journal of Criminal Law and Criminology* 30, no. 6 (1940): 863–64, https://scholarly
    commons.law.northwestern.edu/jclc/vol30/iss6/3. The original federal criminal code was enacted
    in 1790, defining a small number of offenses such as crimes on the high seas or federal property.
    Crimes Act of 1790, ch. 9, 1 Stat. 112, 114 (Apr. 30, 1790). The next major addition to the federal
    criminal code occurred in 1825. Crimes Act of 1825, ch. 65, 4 Stat. 115 (Mar. 3, 1825). The code
    remained mostly unchanged until after the Civil War.
7   For a discussion of how the rights enshrined in state constitutions were the source of the US
    Constitution's Bill of Rights, see Jeffrey S. Sutton, *51 Imperfect Solutions: States and the Making
    of American Constitutional Law* (New York: Oxford University Press, 2018), 10–12.
8   "The Virginia Declaration of Rights," National Archives, accessed September 29, 2022, https://
    www.archives.gov.
9   "The Constitution of Virginia (1776)," Encyclopedia Virginia, accessed August 28, 2022, https://
    encyclopediavirginia.org/. See Bill of Rights, sec. 8.
10 "Constitution of Massachusetts (1780)," National Humanities Institute, accessed August 28,
    2022, http://www.nhinet.org/.
11 "Constitution of North Carolina: December 18, 1776," The Avalon Project, Yale Law School,
    accessed August 28, 2022, https://avalon.law.yale.edu/. See Declaration of Rights, art. IX.

There was, however, one glaring injustice in the text of some states' constitutions: they explicitly treated slaves differently. The jury trial right in North Carolina's Constitution was, by its terms, reserved for a "freeman."[12] South Carolina similarly guaranteed that no "freemen" would be imprisoned except "by the judgment of his peers."[13] Other states simply refused to apply their constitutional protections to slaves. Though Delaware's Constitution of 1792 expressly provided for trial by jury,[14] the state legislature passed a law in 1797 stripping Black slaves of that right when charged with attempted rape of "a white woman or maid."[15] In Louisiana, which became a state in 1812, the supreme court held that the state constitutional right of an "accused" to a jury trial did not extend "to that class of offenders" who were slaves.[16]

The result of this was two systems of criminal justice in antebellum America. In Southern states, criminal cases of enslaved men and women were diverted into separate courts "designed to render quick, rough justice."[17] Until 1850, Georgia law prescribed different procedures for the trial of Black slaves and free White people.[18] Even in Virginia, where its Declaration of

---

12   "The Constitution of North Carolina: December 18, 1776." See Declaration of Rights, arts. VIII, IX, XII, XIII. The North Carolina legislature extended the jury trial to slaves in certain cases in 1793. Rosser H. Taylor, "Humanizing the Slave Code of North Carolina," *The North Carolina Historical Review* 2, no. 3 (1925): 325, https://digital.ncdcr.gov/digital/collection/p16062coll9/id/4199; Ernest James Clark Jr., "Aspects of the North Carolina Slave Code, 1715–1860," *The North Carolina Historical Review* 39, no. 2 (1962): 151, https://www.jstor.org/stable/23517558. However, the jury was to be comprised only of slaveholders, which the chief justice of the North Carolina Supreme Court explained was intended "to protect the property of the owner." State v. Jim, 12 N.C. 142, 144 (1826) (Taylor, C. J.).

13   "South Carolina Constitution of 1790," Carolana.com, accessed August 28, 2022, https://www.carolana.com/. See art. IX, § 2.

14   Del. Const. art. I, § 4 (1792).

15   "An Act concerning Negro and Mulatto Slaves," § 8 (Jan. 18, 1797), in *Laws of the State of Delaware*, vol. 2 (New Castle, DE: Samuel and John Adams, 1797), 1324. That crime would instead be tried before two justices of the peace and "six substantial freeholders," and upon conviction, the defendant would be whipped thirty-nine times and have his ears cropped.

16   State v. Dick, 4 La. Ann. 182, 183 (1849).

17   Randall Kennedy, *Race, Crime, and the Law* (New York: Vintage Books, 1998), 77; see also Alan D. Watson, "North Carolina Slave Courts, 1715–1785," *The North Carolina Historical Review* 60, no. 1 (1983): 24-36, https://www.jstor.org/stable/23534793/; E. Merton Coulter, "Four Slave Trials in Elbert County, Georgia," *The Georgia Historical Quarterly* 41, no. 3 (1957): 237–38, https://www.jstor.org/stable/40577787/; Daniel J. Flanigan, *The Criminal Law of Slavery and Freedom, 1800–1868* (New York: Garland, 1987), 86–101.

18   Anthony v. State, 9 Ga. 266–67 (1851); Daniel J. Flanigan, "Criminal Procedure in Slave Trials in the Antebellum South," *The Journal of Southern History* 40, no. 4 (1974): 545, https://doi.org/10.2307/2206354.

Rights made no distinction between slave and free charged with crimes, the state created separate slave courts.[19] As one Virginia court explained,

Notwithstanding the general terms used in the [state's] Bill of Rights, it is undeniable that it never was contemplated, or considered, to extend to the whole population of the State. Can it be doubted, that it not only was not intended to apply to our slave population, but that the free blacks and mulattoes were also not comprehended in it?[20]

Regardless of the tribunal in which slaves were tried, "no state permitted slaves to testify against whites, but every state allowed slaves to testify against their fellow bondsmen."[21] And the law provided for harsher penalties for slaves convicted of the same crimes as Whites. As Harvard law professor Randall Kennedy has chronicled, it was a crime in some states for slaves to learn to read, assemble for worship outside the supervision of Whites, or defend themselves from an assault. Some states likewise specified disparate punishments for crimes committed by slaves as compared to White people. Slaves could be whipped, castrated, branded, or maimed even when those penalties were forbidden for White criminals, and the death penalty was authorized for a much broader array of crimes when committed by slaves than by Whites.[22] For example, Virginia slaves were subject to death for seventy-three capital crimes as of 1820, only one of which was punishable by death if committed by a White.[23]

While slavery split the country largely along geographic lines in the years before the Civil War,[24] racial bigotry infected the criminal justice systems of

19 Philip J. Schwarz, *Twice Condemned: Slaves and the Criminal Laws of Virginia, 1705–1865* (Baton Rouge, LA: Louisiana University Press, 1988), 25–26.
20 Aldridge v. Commonwealth, 2 Va. Cas. 447, 449 (Gen. Ct. 1824). The court went on to explain that "the numerous restrictions imposed on this class of people [free blacks and mulattoes] in our Statute Book, many of which are inconsistent with the letter and spirit of the Constitution, both of this State and of the United States, as respects the free whites, demonstrate, that, here, those instruments have not been considered to extend equally to both classes of our population" (449).
21 Flanigan, "Criminal Procedure in Slave Trials in the Antebellum South," 556; see also Flanigan, *The Criminal Law of Slavery and Freedom*, 173.
22 Kennedy, *Race, Crime, and the Law*, 76–77.
23 Flanigan, *The Criminal Law of Slavery and Freedom*, 18.
24 The degree to which the Northern states were "free" of slavery is less clear-cut than some may be aware. Four mid-Atlantic colonies (New York, New Jersey, Pennsylvania, and Delaware) all had

the American North and South. In 1798, New Jersey passed a law prohibiting slaves from testifying in criminal trials against anyone other than another slave.[25] Ohio went further in 1807, precluding Black people, slave or free, from testifying in the criminal trial of a White defendant.[26] Laws of this sort made it nearly impossible for Black victims of crime to obtain justice. At the same time, Black people charged with crimes struggled to obtain fair trials. At New York's state constitutional convention in 1846, one participant noted that "it is hardly possible" that Black people in the state "should have an impartial trial. Hated, trodden down, and despised, they had not the means to procure counsel to defend themselves against false and malicious charges, and false witnesses; and too often, an accusation against them was equivalent to conviction."[27] The inability of Black men and women to obtain fair treatment in court was no doubt due, at least in part, to their exclusion from juries both in the North and the South prior to 1860.[28]

small slave populations in the middle of the eighteenth century. By 1780, however, Pennsylvania had begun the "gradual" abolition of slavery, and other mid-Atlantic states soon followed suit. Nevertheless, Pennsylvania, New Jersey, and New York together had approximately 27,000 slaves in 1810, both New York and Pennsylvania listed slaves in their 1840 census returns, and a small number of Black people were held as slaves in New Jersey as late as 1860. Darold D. Wax, "Middle Atlantic States, Slavery in the," in *Dictionary of Afro-American Slavery*, ed. Randall M. Miller and John David Smith (Westport, CT: Praeger, 1997), 471.

25 "An Act Respecting Slaves," § 2 (Mar. 14, 1798), in William Paterson, *Laws of the State of New Jersey; Revised and Published, under the Authority of the Legislature* (Newark, NJ: Matthias Day, 1800), 308.

26 "An Act to Amend the Act, Entitled 'An Act Regulating Black and Mulatto Persons,'" § 4 (Jan. 25, 1807), in *Acts Passed at the First Session of the Fifth General Assembly of the State of Ohio*, vol. 5 (Norwalk, OH: Laning, 1901), 54; Kate Masur, *Until Justice Be Done: America's First Civil Rights Movement, from the Revolution to Reconstruction* (New York: W. W. Norton, 2021), 18.

27 William G. Bishop and William H. Attree, *Report of the Debates and Proceedings of the Convention for the Revision of the Constitution of the State of New York* (Albany, NY: Evening Atlas, 1846), 1030.

28 Albert W. Alschuler and Andrew G. Deiss, "A Brief History of Criminal Jury in the United States," *University of Chicago Law Review* 61, no. 3 (1994): 884, https://doi.org/10.2307/1600170. One eminent historian placed the earliest date of Black people serving on American juries as 1855. C. Vann Woodward, *The Strange Career of Jim Crow: A Commemorative Edition* (New York: Oxford University Press, 2002), 20. Whatever the precise date of the service of America's first Black juror, Black men continued to struggle to achieve jury service for decades afterwards. At the first convention of the Negro Republican Party in 1867, Reverend William F. Butler rallied the crowd with the promise that "soon we will get the jury box." Anne E. Marshall, "'The Rebel Spirit in Kentucky': The Politics of Readjustment in a Border State, 1865–1868," in *The Great Task Remaining before Us: Reconstruction as America's Continuing Civil War*, ed. Paul A. Cimbala and Randall M. Miller (New York: Fordham University Press, 2010), 66.

In the wake of the US Supreme Court's now-infamous decision in *Dred Scott v. Sandford* (1857),[29] the issue of whether Black people were citizens, and thus permitted to serve on juries, took on outsized significance in Illinois's US Senate election of 1858, which pitted incumbent Democratic senator Stephen Douglas against Republican challenger Abraham Lincoln. In the first of their debates, Douglas assured his audience that he was "opposed to negro citizenship in any and every form" and, in an unabashed appeal to racial bigotry, thundered, "If you desire negro citizenship, . . . to make them eligible to office, to serve on juries, and to adjudge your rights, then support Mr. Lincoln and the Black Republican party."[30] For Douglas, Black people had no legitimate role to play in the criminal justice system; that was the domain of White people. On this point, Lincoln agreed. Though he opposed slavery, Lincoln was clear that he was "not in favor of negro citizenship" and, indeed, was "not . . . in favor of bringing about in any way the social and political equality of the white and black races." To put a finer point on it, Lincoln declared in his fourth debate with Douglas that "I am not nor ever have been in favor of making voters or jurors of negroes, nor of qualifying them to hold office."[31]

Lincoln lost the 1858 senate race to Douglas[32] but bested him two years later in the presidential election. The issue of slavery had been roiling the

29 In that case, the US Supreme Court had ruled that "the language used in the Declaration of Independence, show[s] that neither the class of persons who had been imported as slaves nor their descendants, whether they had become free or not, were then acknowledged as a part of the people, nor intended to be included in the general words used in that memorable instrument." Dred Scott v. Sandford, 60 U.S. (19 How.) 393, 407 (1856).

30 "First Debate: Ottawa, Illinois," Lincoln Home National Historic Site, National Park Service, last modified April 10, 2015, https://www.nps.gov.

31 "Fourth Debate: Charleston, Illinois," Lincoln Home National Historic Site, National Park Service, last modified April 10, 2015, https://www.nps.gov. For a discussion of Lincoln's position with regard to Black citizenship (and thus jury service) in the wake of the *Dred Scott* decision, see James Oakes, *The Crooked Path to Abolition: Abraham Lincoln and the Antislavery Constitution* (New York: W. W. Norton, 2021), 99–133.

32 At the time, US senators were appointed by the state legislature rather than elected by the popular vote. Republican candidates for the state legislature in Illinois won a majority of the votes cast in the 1858 election, but that was insufficient to win a majority of the seats in the legislature. Instead, the Democratic party won a majority of the state's legislative seats, and that Democratic-controlled legislature then appointed Douglas as the state's US senator. Allen C. Guelzo, "Houses Divided: Lincoln, Douglas, and the Political Landscape of 1858," *The Journal of American History* 94, no. 2 (2007): 414–16, https://doi.org/10.2307/25094958.

nation for decades.[33] But Lincoln's election as president in November 1860 on a platform that opposed the expansion of slavery brought the dispute to a head, prompting South Carolina to declare its secession from the United States on December 20 of that same year.[34] On January 9, 1861, Mississippi followed South Carolina in seceding from the Union, explaining that "our position is thoroughly identified with the institution of slavery—the greatest material interest in the world" and that "a blow at slavery is a blow at commerce and civilization."[35] Nine other states followed suit in exiting the Union.[36] When the first shots of the Civil War were fired at Fort Sumter on April 12, 1861, nearly four million Black men and women were enslaved in the United States.[37]

A New Birth of Freedom?

The Civil War was still raging when President Lincoln issued the Emancipation Proclamation, freeing the slaves within the rebellious states as of January 1863.[38] That proclamation reached its final outpost in Galveston, Texas, on June 19, 1865, after the Civil War had ended.[39]

From the effective date of the Emancipation Proclamation in 1863 through 1877, Congress sought to rebuild, or reconstruct, the nation and secure for emancipated Black people the rights of citizenship. But even though the Confederate Army surrendered at Appomattox, Virginia, on April 9, 1865, the Southern slaveholders were not about to surrender their way of life and its dependence on slave labor. As a result, the era known as Reconstruction was one of push and pull between the North and the South,

33 Oakes, *The Crooked Path to Abolition*, 9–25.
34 "Declaration of the Immediate Causes Which Induce and Justify the Secession of South Carolina from the Federal Union" (December 24, 1860), The Avalon Project, Yale Law School, accessed May 23, 2022, https://avalon.law.yale.edu/.
35 "A Declaration of the Immediate Causes Which Induce and Justify the Secession of the State of Mississippi from the Federal Union," The Avalon Project, Yale Law School, accessed May 23, 2022, https://avalon.law.yale.edu/.
36 S. Mintz and S. McNeil, "Secession Ordinances of 13 Confederate States," Digital History, accessed November 8, 2022, https://www.digitalhistory.uh.edu/. Four of those states—Virginia, North Carolina, Tennessee, and Arkansas—seceded after the Confederate attack on Fort Sumter.
37 Lincoln Mullen, "These Maps Reveal How Slavery Expanded across the United States," *Smithsonian Magazine*, May 15, 2014, https://www.smithsonianmag.com/.
38 For a discussion of the legal rationale for freeing only rebel state slaves, see Oakes, *The Crooked Path to Abolition*, 134–39.
39 This date has come to be celebrated as a holiday known as Juneteenth.

between Congress on the one hand and state legislatures on the other, and even between Congress and the US presidency.

In describing Reconstruction, it has often been said that while the North won the war, the South won the peace. This Southern victory was accomplished in no small part through those states' criminal justice systems. Politicians in Southern states quickly realized that their justice systems could be turned against the recently emancipated slaves to both keep them in servitude and strip them of political power. Columbia University professor Eric Foner, perhaps the country's preeminent historian of Reconstruction, observes that, by 1866, "the entire complex of . . . criminal laws was enforced by a police apparatus and judicial system in which blacks enjoyed virtually no voice whatever."[40]

In 1865, Congress passed and the states ratified the first of what are known today as the Reconstruction Amendments to the US Constitution. The first of those amendments was the Thirteenth, which banned slavery, with one glaring exception: "Neither slavery nor involuntary servitude, *except as a punishment for crime* whereof the party shall have been duly convicted, shall exist within the United States, or any place subject to their jurisdiction."[41] Seizing on this exception, Southern states promptly enacted "Black Codes" that, among other things, created or revised the crime of "vagrancy."[42] For example, Mississippi passed its Black Code in November 1865, defining that crime:

All rogues and vagabonds, idle and dissipated persons, beggars, jugglers, or persons practicing unlawful games or plays, runaways, common drunkards, common nightwalkers, pilferers, lewd, wanton, or lascivious persons, in speech or behavior, common railers and brawlers, persons who

---

40 Eric Foner, *Reconstruction: America's Unfinished Revolution, 1863–1877*, updated ed. (New York: Perennial, 2014), 203.

41 U.S. Const. amend. XIII, § 1.

42 Foner, *Reconstruction*, 198–200; Allen C. Guelzo, *Reconstruction: A Concise History* (New York: Oxford University Press, 2018), 26; William Cohen, *At Freedom's Edge: Black Mobility and the Southern White Quest for Racial Control, 1861–1915* (Baton Rouge: LSU Press, 1991), 30–33; Douglas A. Blackmon, *Slavery by Another Name: The Re-enslavement of Black Americans from the Civil War to World War II* (New York: Anchor, 2008), 53. For a discussion of how a variety of post-Civil War state laws across the South worked to maintain a system of involuntary servitude, see William Cohen, "Negro Involuntary Servitude in the South, 1865–1940: A Preliminary Analysis," *The Journal of Southern History* 42, no. 1 (1976): 31–60, https://doi.org/10.2307/2205660.

neglect their calling or employment, misspend what they earn, or do not
provide for the support of themselves or their families or dependents, and
all other idle and disorderly persons, including all who neglect all lawful
business, or habitually misspend their time by frequenting houses of ill-
fame, gaming houses, or tippling shops, shall be deemed and considered
vagrants under the provisions of this act; and, on conviction therefore
shall be fined not exceeding $100 . . . and be imprisoned at the discretion
of the court not exceeding ten days.[43]

This law was so open-ended as to effectively allow for conviction at the
discretion of the state.[44] Mississippi's Black Code also defined a number of
crimes applicable only to Black people and carrying mandatory minimum
monetary fines and imprisonment "at the discretion of the court."[45] If any
Black person or freed slave convicted of vagrancy failed to pay his or her
fine within five days of conviction, "such person shall be hired out by the
sheriff . . . to any white person who will pay said fine and all costs and take
such convict for the shortest time."[46]

But the weaponization of criminal justice against Black people in the
South did not end there. By the end of Reconstruction, at least eight Southern states had enacted convict-leasing statutes.[47] As their name suggests,
these statutes allowed the authorities to lease recently emancipated slaves,
upon conviction of manufactured criminal charges, to their former slave
owners. Georgia, for example, legalized convict leasing in 1866, providing

43 *Laws of the State of Mississippi, Passed at a Regular Session of the Mississippi Legislature, Held in the City of Jackson, October, November, December 1865* (Jackson: J. J. Shannon and Co., State Printers, 1866), 90 (An Act to Amend the Vagrant Laws of the State, Section 1 [Nov. 24, 1865]). For further discussion of the Black Codes, see Edward L. Ayers, *Vengeance and Justice: Crime and Punishment in the 19th-Century American South* (New York: Oxford University Press, 1984), 151.
44 It would be more than one hundred years before the US Supreme Court acknowledged this reality and declared such vagrancy laws unconstitutionally vague. Papachristou v. Jacksonville, 405 U.S. 156 (1972).
45 *Laws of the State of Mississippi*, 165 (An Act to Punish Certain Offenses Therein Named, and for Other Purposes, Section 2 [November 29, 1865]).
46 *Laws of the State of Mississippi*, 166–67 (An Act to Punish Certain Offenses Therein Named, and for Other Purposes, Section 5 [November 29, 1865]). For a discussion of convict leasing in Mississippi, see David M. Oshinsky, *"Worse than Slavery": Parchman Farm and the Ordeal of Jim Crow Justice* (New York: Free Press, 1997).
47 Blackmon, *Slavery by Another Name*, 56.

HISTORY 175

that the "Penitentiary ... shall be farmed out to such persons as shall take it on the best terms."[48] In the early 1870s, Nathan Bedford Forrest, the former Confederate general who is believed to have founded the Ku Klux Klan, ran a prison labor camp staffed by enslaved convicts.[49]

Because the slaves in this leasing system were rentals, the business owners who made use of them had little incentive to invest in their long-term well-being. "One dies, get another," the saying went.[50] As historians at the Southern Baptist Theological Seminary observe, "The legal system entrapped thousands of black men, often on trumped up charges and without any due process protections, and earned money for sheriffs and state treasuries by selling their labor. It was worse than slavery."[51]

The Southern criminal justice system, then, was a mechanism by which White people could enslave Black people to staff the very plantations from which they had been freed by a bloody war. Black criminal defendants were subjected to these state criminal justice systems without the protections that the US Constitution provided to defendants in federal criminal cases. It would be nearly one hundred years before the US Supreme Court ruled that the Reconstruction Amendments extended the protections of the Bill of Rights to defendants in state criminal cases.[52]

In the meantime, this situation in the South did not go unnoticed by Congress. After Southern state legislatures enacted Black Codes and convict leasing regimes, Congress passed a series of Reconstruction Acts and two

48 A. Elizabeth Taylor, "The Origin and Development of the Convict Lease System in Georgia," *The Georgia Historical Quarterly* 26, no. 2 (1942): 113, https://www.jstor.org/stable/40576830.
49 Blackmon, *Slavery by Another Name*, 55; Jack Hurst, *Nathan Bedford Forrest: A Biography* (New York: Vintage Books, 1994), 371.
50 Matthew J. Mancini, *One Dies, Get Another: Convict Leasing in the American South, 1866–1928* (Columbia: University of South Carolina Press, 1996). For another helpful and nuanced discussion of convict leasing following the Civil War, see Ayers, *Vengeance and Justice*, 185–222.
51 *Report on Racism and Slavery in the History of the Southern Baptist Theological Seminary* (The Southern Baptist Theological Seminary, December 12, 2018), 7, https://sbts-wordpress-uploads.s3.amazonaws.com/sbts/uploads/2018/12/Racism-and-the-Legacy-of-Slavery-Report-v4.pdf. Southern Baptist Theological Seminary's most important benefactor and chairman of its board of trustees from 1880 to 1894 was Joseph E. Brown. He had previously served as Georgia's governor, US senator, and chief justice of the Supreme Court of Georgia; he made a fortune in coal mines and iron furnaces worked by convicts leased from the state of Georgia. It was observed regarding Brown's coal operation that "if there is a hell on earth, it is [his] coal mines" (33, 35).
52 Gideon v. Wainwright, 372 U.S. 335, 341 (1963), holding that "those guarantees of the Bill of Rights which are fundamental safeguards of liberty immune from federal abridgment are equally protected against state invasion by the Due Process Clause of the Fourteenth Amendment."

additional Reconstruction Amendments to the US Constitution. The Fourteenth Amendment, ratified by the states in 1868, declared that all Americans were entitled to "due process" and the "equal protection of the laws" of their respective state governments. The US Senator who introduced the Fourteenth Amendment explained that it was, at least in part, directed at Southern criminal justice systems, its purpose being to "prohibi[t] the hanging of a black man for a crime for which the white man is not to be hanged."[53] Ratified in 1870, the Fifteenth Amendment prohibited any state from denying the right to vote based on race or prior servitude.[54]

The Civil Rights Act of 1866, passed over President Andrew Johnson's veto, invalidated the Black Codes to the extent that they contained explicitly race-based provisions.[55] But laws that were racially neutral on their face could be disparately applied to Blacks and Whites, whether by prosecutors, judges, or juries. The result, as one observer of Southern justice in 1867 quipped, was that "the verdicts are always for the white man and against the colored man."[56]

Congress sought to address this inequality in the application of state law with the passage of the Civil Rights Act of 1875, which among other things prohibited states from excluding Black Americans from jury service on account of race.[57] Armed with both this statute and the Fourteenth

---

53 Cong. Globe, 39th Cong., 1st Sess. 2766 (1866) (statement of Senator Jacob Howard of Michigan). For a fascinating discussion of the original public meaning of the Fourteenth Amendment, see Randy E. Barnett and Evan D. Bernick, *The Original Meaning of the 14th Amendment: Its Letter and Spirit* (Cambridge, MA: Belknap, 2021).

54 This constitutional provision was not ratified until 1870 because immediately after the Civil War ended in 1865 there was no political appetite for guaranteeing Black men the right to vote. Andrew Kull, *The Color-Blind Constitution* (Cambridge, MA: Harvard University Press, 1992), 70.

55 Civil Rights Act of 1866, 14 Stat. 27, § 1 (Apr. 9, 1866), providing that "citizens, of every race and color, without regard to any previous condition of slavery or involuntary servitude, . . . shall be subject to like punishment, pains, and penalties, and to none other, any law, statute, ordinance, regulation, or custom, to the contrary notwithstanding"; Guelzo, *Reconstruction*, 31–39 (discussing Johnson's veto). The purpose of the Civil Rights Bill of 1866 was, in the words of one congressman, "to destroy all these discriminations" like those found in the Mississippi Black Code. Foner, *Reconstruction*, 244.

56 Foner, *Reconstruction*, 198–200.

57 Civil Rights Act of 1875, 18 Stat. 335, § 4 (Mar. 1, 1875), providing that "no citizen possessing all other qualifications which are or may be prescribed by law shall be disqualified for service as grand or petit juror in any court of the United States, or of any State, on account of race, color, or previous condition of servitude."

Amendment, the Supreme Court ruled in 1879 and again in 1880 that it was unlawful to exclude Black people from jury service, either by means of a state law limiting jury service to White people or by means of a judicial official who, on his own initiative, intentionally excluded legally qualified Black citizens from jury lists due to their race.[58] Despite these rulings, however, the exclusion of Black Americans from jury service was common for decades to come, and "the effects of this exclusion were devastating, especially for black victims of crime," given the widespread violence they were facing.[59]

Redemption

Reconstruction, and whatever modest advances it had achieved for the Black population in the South, came to a screeching halt in the aftermath of the US presidential election of 1876. Incumbent president Ulysses S. Grant, a Republican and Northern Civil War hero, had declined to run for a third term. Ohio Governor Rutherford B. Hayes was selected as the Republican nominee, facing off against Samuel J. Tilden, a Democrat who had previously served as governor of New York.

The election was marred by voter fraud, and the results were hotly disputed. Congress was in turmoil over who to certify as the election victor. After intense negotiations and with inauguration day approaching, the two sides reached what is now known as the Compromise of 1877. Democrats agreed to accept that Hayes had won the election, but in return they secured from Republicans an agreement to withdraw federal troops from the Southern states.[60] This concession by Republicans in effect marked the end of Reconstruction and began what Southerners hailed as Redemption.

---

58 Strauder v. West Virginia, 100 U.S. 303, 310 (1880), concluding that it violates the Fourteenth Amendment's guarantee of equal protection of the laws to try a criminal defendant before a jury from which Black men were categorically excluded by law because of their race; Ex parte Virginia, 100 U.S. 339, 344, 349 (1879), holding that Congress possessed the authority, under the Fourteenth Amendment, to enact Section 4 of the Civil Rights Act of 1875 criminalizing the exclusion of Black men from state juries.

59 James Forman Jr., "Juries and Race in the Nineteenth Century," *Yale Law Journal* 113, no. 4 (2003): 931, https://doi.org/10.2307/4135685. For a brief discussion of the violence to which Black men and women were subjected during Reconstruction, see Douglas Egerton, "Terrorized African-Americans Found Their Champion in Civil War Hero Robert Smalls," *Smithsonian Magazine*, September 2018, https://www.smithsonianmag.com/.

60 "Compromise of 1877," History, March 17, 2011, last modified November 27, 2019, https://www.history.com.

What the North had achieved in the war the South took back in the peace. Historian W. E. B. Du Bois famously described this turn of events: "The slave went free; stood a brief moment in the sun; then moved back again toward slavery."[61]

What followed the demise of Reconstruction was a series of laws enacted across the South that legally mandated racial segregation (known as "Jim Crow laws"[62]), giving rise to a supposedly "separate but equal" social system that the Supreme Court blessed in *Plessy v. Ferguson* as consistent with the Fourteenth Amendment.[63] At the same time, convict leasing continued to spread across the South. By 1898, 73 percent of Alabama's state government revenue was derived from convict leasing.[64] And while the Supreme Court had ruled unconstitutional those state statutes that expressly limited jury service to White men, the court was, at least for a time, unwilling to do much to protect Black defendants from all-White juries selected by less overtly discriminatory means.[65]

The exclusion of Black people from criminal juries facilitated what is the most enduring attack on their equality by means of the criminal justice system: felon disenfranchisement.[66] While the Fifteenth Amendment held out the promise that the right to vote would not be denied on account of race or prior enslavement, it provided no hedge against stripping felons of the right to vote. Thus, as a unanimous Supreme Court later observed, "a movement . . . swept the post-Reconstruction South to disenfranchise blacks" by enacting laws denying felons the right to vote.[67]

These disenfranchisement laws used race-neutral ("color-blind") language, but the state legislatures offered little pretense to conceal their actual motivations. In the summer of 1890, Mississippi held a state constitutional convention at which the delegates adopted poll taxes and "reconfigured"

---

61 W. E. B. Du Bois, *Black Reconstruction in America* (New York: Free, 1998), 30.
62 The term "Jim Crow law" seems to have originated in the late 1800s to describe laws that imposed racial segregation on Black people in the United States. Woodward, *The Strange Career of Jim Crow*, 7; "Louisiana's 'Jim Crow' Law Valid," *New York Times*, December 21, 1892, 1. Jim Crow segregation originated in the Northern states. Woodward, *The Strange Career of Jim Crow*, 17.
63 Plessy v. Ferguson, 163 U.S. 537, 544 (1896).
64 Mancini, *One Dies, Get Another*, 112.
65 Virginia v. Rives, 100 U.S. 313, 321–22 (1880).
66 Technically, the disenfranchisement of those convicted of crimes was not always limited to felons and sometimes extended to misdemeanants.
67 Hunter v. Underwood, 471 U.S. 222, 229 (1985).

the state's constitution "to eliminate voter disenfranchisement for crimes thought to be 'white crimes' and by adding crimes thought to be 'black crimes.'"[68] These voting qualifications likewise applied to jury service, with the additional requirement that any juror be able to read and write. Though these provisions made no mention of race in their text, they were all designed to exclude Black people both from voting and from jury service in the state, thereby reestablishing White supremacy after the collapse of Reconstruction.[69]

In the fall of 1895, South Carolina too called a constitutional convention for "a revision of the suffrage laws as would make any appeal to the negro or any chance of negro domination an impossibility." In the words of one observer, the state was hoping to adopt "the Mississippi plan or something better."[70] And, in fact, the South Carolina requirements, both for voting and jury service, essentially mirrored those of Mississippi.[71] By imposing requirements that voters (and thus jurors) be able to read, write, and have paid taxes on at least $300 worth of property, the amended South Carolina constitution was designed to "put negro control of the State beyond possibility and still preserve the suffrage for the illiterate whites of the present generation."[72]

In May 1898, the state of Louisiana held a convention to revise its constitution as well. During that convention, speakers repeatedly affirmed its purpose to "perpetuate the supremacy of the Anglo-Saxon race" and "establish the supremacy of the white race."[73] The amended state constitution placed limits on the rights of Black Louisianans to vote, including through the use of poll

---

68 Harness v. Watson, 47 F.4th 296, 300 (5th Cir. 2022) (en banc; per curiam). As the Mississippi Supreme Court acknowledged only a few years later, because the delegates were "restrained by the federal constitution from discriminating against the negro race, the convention discriminated against its characteristics and the offenses to which its weaker members were prone." Ratliff v. Beale, 20 So. 865, 868 (Miss. 1896).

69 "The Mississippi Constitution of 1890 as Originally Adopted," art. 12 (secs. 241, 242, 244), art. 14 (sec. 264), Mississippi History Now, accessed May 24, 2022, https://www.mshistorynow .mdah.ms.gov; John W. Winkle III, s.v. "Constitution of 1890," Mississippi Encyclopedia, July 10, 2017, last modified June 8, 2018, https://mississippiencyclopedia.org.

70 D. D. Wallace, "The South Carolina Convention of 1895," *The Sewanee Review* 4, no. 3 (1896): 354–55, https://www.jstor.org/stable/27527896.

71 S.C. Const. of 1895, art. II, § 4; art. V, § 22.

72 Wallace, "The South Carolina Convention of 1895," 355.

73 *Official Journal of the Proceedings of the Constitutional Convention of the State of Louisiana* (New Orleans: H. J. Hearsay, 1898), 375, 381.

taxes.[74] The new state constitution that emerged from that convention also disenfranchised those convicted of any "crime punishable by imprisonment in the penitentiary."[75] And in the same document, the state's constitution for the first time allowed for non-unanimous jury verdicts in criminal cases,[76] a tactic that the US Supreme Court finally acknowledged in 2020 was designed to "ensure that African-American juror service would be meaningless."[77]

The president of Alabama's Constitutional Convention in 1901 delivered an opening speech in which he explicitly stated the convention's purpose: "to establish white supremacy in this State."[78] Those gathered at the convention sought to accomplish that goal by, among other things, vastly expanding the list of crimes for which one could be disenfranchised upon conviction to any crime "involving moral turpitude," including some misdemeanors.[79]

Slowly, over time, the US Supreme Court declared the racially discriminatory Jim Crow laws unconstitutional, a welcome step in cleansing the stain of *Plessy*. But one thing the Supreme Court still allowed was discrimination against felons. It would be more than seven decades until the US Supreme Court concluded that Alabama's felon disenfranchisement was unconstitutional because statements at the 1901 constitutional convention made clear that, at least in that instance, it was "enacted with the intent of disenfranchising blacks."[80] But as long as states were more circumspect than Alabama had been in expressing their motives when passing a felon disenfranchisement

74 *Constitution of the State of Louisiana: Adopted in Convention at the City of New Orleans, May 12, 1898* (New Orleans: H. J. Hearsay, 1898), art. 197, 198.

75 *Constitution of the State of Louisiana*, art. 159.

76 *Constitution of the State of Louisiana*, art. 116. Previously, Louisiana had required that criminal jury verdicts be unanimous. State v. Reddick, No. 2021-KP-01893, slip op. at 7–8 (La. Oct. 21, 2022).

77 Ramos v. Louisiana, 140 S. Ct. 1390, 1394 (2020). Justice Neil Gorsuch subsequently observed that, "during the Jim Crow era, some states restricted the size of juries and abandoned the demand for a unanimous verdict as part of a deliberate and systematic effort to suppress minority voices in public affairs." Khorrami v. Arizona, 143 S. Ct. 22, 27 (2002) (Gorsuch, J., dissenting from denial of certiorari).

78 *Official Proceedings of the Constitutional Convention of the State of Alabama: May 21st, 1901, to September 3rd, 1901*, 4 vols. (Wetumpka, AL: Wetumpka Printing, 1940), 1:8.

79 *Official Proceedings of the Constitutional Convention of the State of Alabama*, 4:5020 (Section 182 of the Constitution of the State of Alabama).

80 Hunter v. Underwood, 471 U.S. 222, 229 (1985). "While laws disfranchising certain classes of convicted criminals have long been part of the Anglo-European law, in the decades after the Civil War white southern Democrats found ways to use them to disproportionately affect African Americans." Pippa Holloway, *Living in Infamy: Felon Disfranchisement and the History of American Citizenship* (New York: Oxford University Press, 2014), 1.

law, the Supreme Court permitted states to deny felons the right to vote for life.[81] Felons could likewise be stripped of other privileges consistent with the Constitution. In a culture in which racism was deeply ingrained, the ability to lawfully deny felons a variety of civil rights created a powerful incentive to employ the criminal justice system to achieve indirectly what the Reconstruction Amendments had sought to forbid.

At the Hands of Persons Unknown

The exclusion of Black Americans from juries did far more, however, than simply facilitate their criminal conviction and resulting disenfranchisement. It left them exposed to brutal physical violence. The Fourteenth Amendment's promise of the "equal protection of the law" was meant to ensure, among other things, that Blacks and Whites alike would be protected from criminal violence.[82] The reality following the Civil War, and especially after Reconstruction, was much different.

Sheriffs and other local officials were "extremely reluctant to prosecute whites accused of crimes against blacks."[83] In the rare instance when those crimes were prosecuted, all-White juries frequently refused to convict the White defendants no matter how strong the evidence.[84] For example, "in the years 1865 and 1866, all-white juries in Texas decided a total of 500

81 Richardson v. Ramirez, 418 U.S. 24, 74 (1974). One leading rationale advanced in support of felon disenfranchisement is based on social contract theory. In Green v. Board of Elections, 380 F.2d 445, 451 (2d Cir. 1967), the court wrote, "The early exclusion of felons from the franchise by many states could well have rested on Locke's concept, so influential at the time, that by entering into society every man 'authorizes the society . . . to make laws for him as the public good of the society shall require, to the execution whereof his own assistance (as to his own decrees) is due.' A man who breaks the laws he has authorized his agent to make for his own governance could fairly have been thought to have abandoned the right to participate in further administering the compact. On a less theoretical plane, it can scarcely be deemed unreasonable for a state to decide that perpetrators of serious crimes shall not take part in electing the legislators who make the laws, the executives who enforce these, the prosecutors who must try them for further violations, or the judges who are to consider their cases."
82 Forman, "Juries and Race in the Nineteenth Century," 917 and n117.
83 Foner, Reconstruction, 204.
84 Forman, "Juries and Race in the Nineteenth Century," 909–10, 921–22. For a discussion of the law's failure to protect Black people from violence during the Jim Crow era, see Margaret A. Burnham, By Hands Now Known: Jim Crow's Legal Executioners (New York: W. W. Norton, 2022). For a discussion of how, in particular, the ritualized rape of Black women by White men went unprosecuted during the Jim Crow era, see Danielle L. McGuire, At the Dark End of the Street: Black Women, Rape, and Resistance—a New History of the Civil Rights Movement from Rosa Parks to the Rise of Black Power (New York: Alfred A. Knopf, 2010).

prosecutions of white defendants for killing African-Americans. All 500 were acquitted."[85] At the same time, all-White juries were likely to convict Black defendants without regard to their actual guilt. As if to emphasize that there was no justice to be had for Black people in that day, many a courthouse across the South was adorned with monuments celebrating the Confederacy. "To enter a courthouse to stand trial in a case that they were all but certain to lose, survivors of slavery had to pass statues of Confederate soldiers looking down from literal pedestals."[86] The scenario brings to mind the words of the biblical preacher: "In the place of justice, even there was wickedness" (Eccl. 3:16).

If juries hearing charges against Black defendants refused to convict, lynch mobs stood ready outside the courthouse to impose "justice" of their own on the Black defendant. From 1877 through 1950, more than 4,080 Black men and women were lynched in twelve Southern states—an average of more than one lynching per week.[87] But lynching was not an exclusively Southern phenomenon. The social and legal oppression that Black people in the South faced in the early twentieth century prompted what is known as the Great Migration, in which six million Black Americans from the rural South moved to the West, Midwest, and Northeast between 1915 and 1970.[88] These Black refugees were not, however, welcomed with open arms in the new cities where they settled. While conditions in their new homes were certainly better relatively speaking, they still faced widespread discrimination in various forms and were lynched in nearly every state in the nation.[89]

The brutality of these lynchings is hard to overstate. The rope noose is commonly associated with lynching, which can leave the misperception

---

85 Pena-Rodriguez v. Colorado, 137 S. Ct. 855, 867 (2017).
86 Isabel Wilkerson, *Caste: The Origins of Our Discontents* (New York: Random House, 2020), 336.
87 *Lynching in America: Confronting the Legacy of Racial Terror*, 3rd ed. (Montgomery, AL: Equal Justice Initiative, 2017), 4.
88 Isabel Wilkerson, *The Warmth of Other Sons: The Epic Story of America's Great Migration* (New York: Random House, 2010), 9. John Perkins tells the story of his move in 1947 from Mississippi to California in John M. Perkins, *Let Justice Roll Down* (Grand Rapids, MI: Baker, 2014).
89 Douglas O. Linder, "Lynchings: By State and Race, 1882–1968," University of Missouri-Kansas City School of Law, accessed May 24, 2022, https://famous-trials.com; *Lynching in America*, 44–47. For a discussion of some lynchings outside the American South, see Michael J. Pfeifer, ed., *Lynching beyond Dixie: American Mob Violence outside the South* (Champaign, IL: University of Illinois Press, 2013); Philip Dray, *A Lynching at Port Jervis: Race and Reckoning in the Gilded Age* (New York: Farrar, Straus and Giroux, 2022).

that a lynching was "merely" a hanging. In fact, lynching was often a tor-turous affair. It was common for the victim's fingers and toes to be cut off while the person was still alive and then later sold as mementos. In one instance, a pregnant woman was sliced open with knives and her unborn child removed and stomped to death. Lynching victims often were burned alive after being doused with gasoline. Other times, the bodies of those who were hung were then burned as they swung from a tree branch. Families were lynched, with parents forced to watch the lynching of their children and husbands forced to watch the lynching of their wives, all before they themselves were lynched. Photographers would capture these events, selling picture post cards for the participants to preserve the memory. Hundreds, if not thousands, of photographs of lynchings are still in existence today.[90]

Lynchings were carried out openly and notoriously, often taking the form of community events attended by men, women, and children. Newspapers would report in advance of a lynching to occur on a date and time and at a specified location.[91] People would travel from miles around to view the spectacle in a carnival-like atmosphere that included vendors on site selling food. Local train companies ran special routes to accommodate the flood of passengers hoping to attend. After the fact, the same newspapers would report on a lynching committed "at the hands of persons unknown."[92] Rarely, if ever, did a criminal prosecution, much less a conviction, follow. In Georgia alone, 589 Black people were lynched between 1877 and 1950; not a single White person was convicted for any of these crimes.[93]

---

90 *Lynching in America*, 27–28, 33, 35; Christopher Waldrep, ed., *Lynching in America: A History in Documents* (New York: New York University Press, 2006), 197-98; Philip Dray, *At the Hands of Persons Unknown: The Lynching of Black America* (New York: Modern Library, 2003), 82, 246; Walter F. White, "The Work of a Mob," *The Crisis* 16, no. 5 (September 1918): 222; James Allen, *Without Sanctuary: Lynching Photography in America*, 15th ed. (Santa Fe, NM: Twin Palms, 2021).

91 For a discussion of the role that newspapers played in inciting lynchings, see "Printing Hate," The Howard Center for Investigative Journalism, accessed May 30, 2022, https://lynching.cns maryland.org.

92 *Lynching in America*, 33–34; Dray, *At the Hands of Persons Unknown*, 14, 78; Waldrep, *Lynching in America*, 23.

93 *Lynching in America*, 48, adding that "of all lynchings committed after 1900, only 1 percent resulted in a lyncher being convicted of a criminal offense"; see also p. 40 (Table 1: African-American Lynching Victims by Southern State, 1877–1950); Manfred Berg, *Popular Justice: A History of Lynching in America* (Lanham, MD: Ivan R. Dee, 2011), 153; Blackmon, *Slavery*

The criminal justice system was co-opted to, in effect, reverse the outcome of the Civil War. Black people were over-prosecuted (to facilitate convict leasing and felon disenfranchisement) and White people were under-prosecuted (to facilitate White terrorization of Black citizens). "The courts of law [we]re employed," a leading historian concluded, "to reenslave the colored race."[94] As Pulitzer Prize-winning journalist Douglas Blackmon summed it up, "By 1900, the South's judicial system had been wholly reconfigured to make one of its primary purposes the coercion of African Americans to comply with the social customs and labor demands of whites."[95] Through the 1960s, Martin Luther King Jr. was still speaking out against the abuses of the criminal justice system—what he called "the long and desolate night of our court injustice."[96] The weapon of criminal "justice" was lethal to civil rights.

———

The events of the past present questions, frame opportunities, and pose challenges for the days that follow. When it comes to criminal justice,

———

by *Another Name*, 364, identifying the only white man convicted in Georgia for murdering a Black man between 1877 and 1966. For more about that lone conviction of John Williams, who killed Black laborers on his plantation, see Pete Daniel, "We Are Going to Do Away with These Boys," *American Heritage*, April 1972, https://www.americanheritage.com/.

94 Foner, *Reconstruction*, 594.

95 Blackmon, *Slavery by Another Name*, 7.

96 Martin Luther King Jr., "Statement Delivered at the Prayer Pilgrimage Protesting the Electrocution of Jeremiah Reeves" (Dexter Avenue Baptist Church, Montgomery, AL, April 6, 1958), Stanford University, The Martin Luther King, Jr. Research and Education Institute, https://kinginstitute.stanford.edu/. "It is obvious, then, that what is needed is a reforming of the racist legal system of the South in such a way as to effectuate substantive justice within the procedural framework of the instrumentalities of law and order." Martin Luther King Jr., "When a Negro Faces Southern Justice," *New York Amsterdam News*, April 16, 1966, 31. "'The police are little more than 'enforcers' of the present system of exploitation and often demonstrate particular contempt for poor Negroes so that they are deprived of any sense of human dignity and the status of citizenship in order that they may be controlled and 'kept in line.'" Martin Luther King Jr., "Why We Are in Chicago," *New York Amsterdam News*, March 12, 1966, 21. "The double standard of justice is equally applicable to lesser crimes [than rape] as well." Martin Luther King Jr., "The Verdict," *New York Amsterdam News*, November 20, 1965, 16. "The segregated character of southern justice runs all the way through the judicial system, extending from the lowest municipal courts all the way up to the federal bench." Martin Luther King Jr., "New Harassment," *New York Amsterdam News*, June 23, 1962, 11. See also Martin Luther King Jr., "The Complexion of Southern Justice," *New York Amsterdam News*, December 4, 1965, 33.

embedded in American history are both revolutionary advances and disturbing abuses. "History could make a stone weep," the novelist Marilynne Robinson writes.[97] That is certainly true of the American history of criminal justice well into the second half of the twentieth century. The question is whether that history served as a prologue to better days or to more bitter tears. If better, how much better? And what remains to be corrected? Those questions linger in the background of the chapters that follow.

97 Marilynne Robinson, *Gilead: A Novel* (New York: Picador, 2004), 190.

10

Crime

TO STATE THE OBVIOUS, you only end up as a defendant in the criminal justice system if you are accused of a crime. Seems indisputable, even natural. But underlying this simple reality are choices, not only by the accused but also by the society in which the accusation arises. You and I decide how we will behave. A given society chooses to deem certain behavior criminal and other behavior not.

The choices a society makes about what it calls criminal aren't necessarily the result of some law of nature. Bound up in the choices about how to define "crime" are value judgments, biases, power plays, and acts of self-preservation. Many of those choices—whether to prohibit murder, to take one example—are relatively consistent across cultures and time. But others are not. Different societies, even within the same country, take different approaches to the same conduct—for example, marijuana usage or prostitution. Some states or countries decriminalize conduct entirely; others reduce the criminality of particular misconduct from a felony to a misdemeanor. These are all choices made by people other than the individual who is ultimately charged with a crime.

These societal choices determine whether there ever even is a "crime." We tend to think that a criminal case begins in a courtroom. Or maybe the criminal case begins when the police arrest a suspect. Or, perhaps we think, the case originates at the scene of the crime where the murder, rape, or robbery is perpetrated. But in a very real sense, a criminal case begins in the state capital when the legislature designates behavior criminal. Without this legal declaration that it is a crime to commit certain acts, there will be no crime scene, no arrest, no trial, and no imprisonment. In a sense, then, whether someone in a given society commits a "crime" is as much the society's choice as the individual's. For the Christian, the question is whether those choices to label certain conduct "criminal" and other conduct not align with God's moral law.

Breaking the Law

That "crime" is the result of societal choices may not be immediately obvious because we tend to think of crime as a relatively straightforward concept. We have a vision in our minds of "criminals" and "crimes." Murder, rape, robbery, assault, theft. And drugs. Criminals carry guns. Criminals are violent. Other people commit crimes. Certainly not you and me.

But even if you've never committed a crime, you likely *have* violated the law. When we refer to someone "breaking the law," we probably have in mind committing a crime. However, you and I commit innumerable acts that "break the law" if by that we simply mean doing something the law prohibits or failing to do something the law requires. We violate the law, probably with some regularity. But not every violation of the law is a "crime." Breaking the law isn't always criminal. The fact that some legal violations are not crimes is the result of choices—societal choices whether to label particular violations of the law as "crimes."

To take a simple example, you speed. You likely do that every week. One mile per hour over the speed limit is breaking the law. But in my home state of Virginia, speeding is only a "crime" if I exceed the speed limit by more than twenty miles per hour. Nineteen miles per hour over the speed limit is an "infraction." Twenty miles per hour over the speed limit is a crime for which you can be sentenced to a year in jail.[1] The legislature chose to draw a line of criminality. There may be good reasons for drawing that line where it is drawn. But that line is certainly not a matter of moral imperative in any religious tradition. It is a choice undoubtedly influenced by a variety of considerations, some noble and others less so.

Speeding is what the law calls *malum prohibitum*, rather than *malum in se*. An act that is *malum in se* (meaning, wrong in itself) is inherently immoral and thus prohibited by law because of its immorality. But a society

---

1   Va. Code Ann. §§ 18.2-11(a), 46.2-862, 46.2-868.

may choose not to criminalize some acts that are *malum in se*. Or a society may criminalize behavior that is not at all immoral. An act that is *malum prohibitum* (meaning, wrong because prohibited) is not inherently immoral but is wrong, if at all, only because the law has declared it to be so. Speeding at least twenty miles over the speed limit is *malum prohibitum* in Virginia. So whether I commit that crime is a combination of my choices and the state's. I choose how far over the speed limit to drive. The legislature chose to prohibit that conduct and to call it a crime. But the legislature's choice to criminalize my speeding does not change the fact that speeding twenty or more miles per hour over the limit is not *malum in se*. It is not inherently, morally wrong.

Let's consider another example: violation of the law prohibiting discrimination in employment based on race. In a literal sense, one breaks the law if he or she engages in race-based discrimination in hiring or firing decisions. Racial discrimination in employment is also *malum in se*—it is morally wrong. This type of bigotry could have catastrophic financial, not to mention emotional and psychological, consequences for an individual and his or her family victimized by it. But racial discrimination in employment is not a crime. In only one state (Idaho) in the United States is either refusing to hire or firing someone from a job because of their race a crime.[2] If you engage in that conduct, you will never be arrested, prosecuted, go to jail, or have a criminal record. And this is true no matter how severe the economic impact of the discrimination on the job applicant or employee.

Why isn't race-based employment discrimination a crime? At a moral level, is it less reprehensible to deny someone employment, and thereby oppress them economically, for an immoral reason such as racial bias than it is to, say, shoplift a pair of tennis shoes? Both are *malum in se*. Yet the legislature of every state in America has declared that the latter is a crime while the former is almost always not. This is the choice that our society has made. Both acts break the law. Both acts are immoral. Only one of the acts is a "crime." And the one that is a crime is the less morally culpable of the two. Whether someone is a "criminal," then, is as much our choice as theirs.

---

2   Iris Hentze and Rebecca Tyus, "Discrimination and Harassment in the Workplace," National Conference of State Legislatures, August 12, 2021, https://www.ncsl.org; Idaho Code § 18-7303.

Civil and Criminal Law

When it comes to a society's choices about criminalizing conduct, you might think that the most relevant distinction in the law is the choice to label something a "felony" as opposed to a "misdemeanor." Both are crimes. But we tend to think of felonies as the really bad acts while misdemeanors are much less so. This is certainly true to some extent. Murder is a felony; speeding by more than twenty miles per hour is (in Virginia) a misdemeanor. Accordingly, felonies are generally punished much more severely than misdemeanors.

But the far more meaningful distinction legislatures make when it comes to violations of the law is the distinction between criminal violations and civil ones. The criminal-civil distinction has far more dramatic consequences than the felony-misdemeanor distinction. As a general rule, a crime is an act that the law punishes with imprisonment or, in some instances, death. A civil violation, by contrast, is an act that is unlawful but is usually only punishable with a fine. Misdemeanors are less serious than felonies, but misdemeanors are still crimes and will leave you with a criminal record. And misdemeanors can earn you jail time. Civil law violations never will.

Someone accused of a misdemeanor is likely to experience an arrest by the police. The US Supreme Court has said that an arrest is a "reasonable," and thus constitutional, action by the police even for criminal offenses for which jail time is not an available punishment.[3] A misdemeanor criminal charge authorizing such an arrest is merely an accusation, nothing more. But that mere accusation combined with an arrest will result in a criminal record with potentially life-altering consequences.[4] Additional consequences are legally mandated upon conviction of a misdemeanor. In South Carolina, people convicted of misdemeanors cannot vote while in jail.[5] In California, a misdemeanant is subject to loss of his or her license to work as a home

---

3   Atwater v. City of Lago Vista, 532 U.S. 318 (2001).
4   In almost every state it is lawful for an employer to deny you a job or fire you from your job if you have been merely accused, even if never convicted, of a misdemeanor. Hentze and Tyus, "Discrimination and Harassment in the Workplace." You may be familiar with the movement to "ban the box," which is an effort to limit the ways in which employers can take a job applicant's criminal history into account in the hiring process.
5   S.C. Code § 17-5-120(B)(2).

care aid.[6] In Massachusetts, some misdemeanor convictions render a person ineligible to purchase self-defense spray.[7]

By contrast, a civil law violation will not result in an arrest or criminal record of any sort. None. A jury trial verdict that you engaged in race-based employment discrimination even dozens of times is reprehensible, but it does not make you a "criminal" in the United States. Failing to live up to the promises in a contract you signed could put you at risk of a lawsuit, but it is not a crime even though the Westminster Catechism says that it violates the ninth commandment.[8] Price-gouging generally is not a crime; it is typically only a civil violation of the law even though it is widely regarded as deeply immoral.[9]

These are just a few examples of the ways in which our societal choices, as much as someone else's conduct, determine whether that person is a "criminal" in the eyes of the law. And in our society today, the "criminal" label is not necessarily tied to moral culpability. The tennis shoes shoplifter and the lead-foot speeder are criminals. The contract breacher and the race-based discriminating employer are not. A resident of my home state decides how fast to drive, whether to shoplift tennis shoes, if he or she will honor a contract, and whether to discriminate in employment. We the people choose whether or not to label such conduct "criminal."[10]

Line Drawing

The important point in all of this for the Christian is that we are not free to choose to apply the label of "criminal" to any act we wish. Why not? Because of love. The biblical justice principles of accuracy, impartiality, and proportionality bear on the questions of what actions we can justly categorize as criminal and whether we can thereby subject a fellow image bearer to all the ramifications such a categorization entails.

---

6   Cal. Health & Safety Code § 1796.25(a)(1).

7   Mass. Gen. Law ch. 140, § 122D.

8   Westminster Larger Catechism, question 145. See also Ps. 15:4, which describes a true follower of God as one "who swears to his own hurt and does not change."

9   Heather Morton, "Price Gouging State Statutes," National Conference of State Legislatures, March 10, 2022, https://www.ncsl.org.

10 For a more extended examination of this phenomenon, see Alec Karakatsanis, "The Punishment Bureaucracy: How to Think about 'Criminal Justice Reform,'" *Yale Law Journal Forum* 128 (March 28, 2019): 848–935, https://www.yalelawjournal.org/forum/the-punishment-bureaucracy.

As we saw in chapter 2, calling something a crime is an authorization for the state to use physical force in response to that conduct. But as we also saw in chapter 4, the principle of accuracy means that the government can, as a moral matter, only use physical force against Romans 13 "wrong-doers"—that is, people who have done evil. There is no divinely granted authority for the government to use physical violence against those who have committed no moral wrong.

Thus, we cannot label something a crime—and thereby authorize the government to use or threaten physical force to compel compliance or punish noncompliance—simply because doing so would be effective at deterring that conduct. It is likely that criminalizing a particular act will serve as a more effective deterrent than simply making that conduct a civil violation. If we as a society really want to deter certain conduct, criminalizing it will be most effective. But making something criminal simply because doing so will be an effective deterrent is a utilitarian way of thinking, not a Christian one.

The relevant issue for the Christian is what authority God has granted to government. All human authority is derivative (Rom. 13:1). If the authority to use punitive force exists, it does so only because God has conferred it. And God has conferred on human authorities the authority to use physical force only in response to conduct that is evil (Rom. 13:4). Otherwise, there is no biblical warrant to criminalize conduct and then punish it with physical force, and this is true no matter how effective that criminalization might be at deterring the conduct. As Baptist minister John Leland (1754–1841) puts it, "Every state crime is a moral evil or sin, (provided the laws of state are legitimate)."[11] Isaac Backus similarly observed that the crimes which fall within the magistrate's "jurisdiction to punish," according to Romans 13, "are only such as work ill to our neighbor."[12]

Someone whose conduct is *malum in se*—that is, inherently immoral—is necessarily a Romans 13 wrongdoer. But what about someone whose conduct is merely *malum prohibitum*? In that case, the analysis is more

11 John Leland, "On Sabbatical Laws," in *The Writings of the Late Elder John Leland*, ed. L. F. Greene (New York: G. W. Wood, 1845), 441.

12 Isaac Backus, *An Appeal to the Public for Religious Liberty, against the Oppressions of the Present Day* (Boston: John Boyle, 1773), 11–12.

complicated. It is certainly possible that some conduct that is *malum prohibitum* could, in a particular social context, be morally blameworthy. It is not inherently wrong, for example, to drive on the left side of the road. But once the organizing principle in a particular society is that people drive on the right side of the road, to then drive on the left side of the road against traffic on a crowded street creates physical danger to others. Given that social context, the conduct covered by a *malum prohibitum* offense could be morally blameworthy.

But other *malum prohibitum* offenses outlaw conduct that is disfavored for some policy reason unrelated to moral culpability. For example, until very recently, it was a federal crime to make unauthorized use of Smokey the Bear, to transport water hyacinth plants, and to affix a theft-prevention decal to a car without authorization.[13] There may be good reasons to prohibit these actions. But none of these activities are inherently evil. No one who commits these acts is a Romans 13 wrongdoer. Thus, it was immoral for the federal government to criminalize these acts and thereby authorize physical force to be used against those who do them. The use of punitive force against people who commit these acts is contrary to the biblical principles of accuracy (calling conduct evil when it is not) and proportionality (imposing a punishment that is not commensurate to a wrong).

While these particular acts are no longer crimes as of December 2020,[14] numerous other federal criminal laws apply to conduct that is not Romans 13 wrongdoing. In fact, there is a Twitter feed devoted to highlighting the many activities that the federal government criminalizes. A recent tweet explains that it is a federal crime "to sell 'sliced' canned peaches unless the peaches are cut into wedge-shaped sectors."[15] Perhaps the wedge shape is critical for reasons that elude me. But selling as "sliced" peaches that are cut in something other than a wedge shape certainly isn't immoral. The US Constitution may allow Congress to criminalize the sale of "sliced" peaches that aren't wedge-shaped, but there is no moral authority for the federal government to employ the punitive physical force

---

13 18 U.S.C. § 711 (2020); 18 U.S.C. § 46 (2020); 18 U.S.C. § 511A (2020).
14 Consolidated Appropriations Act, 2021, Pub. L. 116–260, 134 Stat. 2155, div. O, title X, § 1002 (December 27, 2020).
15 A Crime a Day (@CrimeADay), Twitter, November 28, 2021, https://twitter.com/CrimeADay /status/1464957670981578753, citing 21 U.S.C. § 333, 21 C.F.R. § 145.170(a)(2)(iii)(e).

of the criminal law against those who sell as "sliced" peaches that are not wedge-shaped. Criminalizing this conduct is itself immoral. The law is unjust. And those who passed this unjust law are themselves Romans 13 wrongdoers.

It is doubtful, however, that many legislators recognize the moral limit on their power to criminalize conduct. In the United States, there are few legal restrictions on what conduct the government can call a crime. The text of the Constitution makes it (generally) illegal to criminalize speech or religion. The US Supreme Court invented limits on the ability of governments to criminalize a few other categories of conduct. But for the most part, the state and federal governments are free to criminalize whatever they wish, however foolish or unethical the decision to do so might be.

Conversely, legislatures exclude some immoral conduct from the reach of the criminal law and instead make it only a civil violation. When conduct is only a civil violation, certain punishments (including prison) are unavailable. To take an example mentioned above, breach of contract is *malum in se* and could have devastating financial consequences to its victim. But because breach of contract isn't a crime, punishment by physical force is legally unavailable for those who fail to keep their contractual promises. Similarly, race-based employment discrimination isn't criminal, and thus the state's ability to punish wrongdoers who engage in this conduct is narrow. We are protecting people from non-wedge-shaped "sliced" peaches with the force of the federal criminal law, while those subject to race-based employment discrimination and breach of contract have only the more limited civil remedies available to them.

Which brings me back to the point with which I started this chapter. Someone made a choice as to what conduct will be deemed criminal and what conduct will be treated only as a civil violation. These choices force us to grapple with one last biblical principle of justice: impartiality. *Why* have we chosen to designate only certain conduct criminal? And this is where the questions get really uncomfortable. Are we choosing the way we are choosing because the choices we are making about what to criminalize favor certain groups and disfavor our society's "others"? Given the gross immorality and severe financial consequences of race-based employment discrimination, why isn't it criminalized anywhere in the United States outside of Idaho? Why has our society refused to bear the sword against that conduct even though it is *malum in se*? The question almost answers itself.[16]

Which Immoralities?

At the same time, the *mere* fact that conduct is immoral does not entitle the state to use the punitive force of the criminal law against a person who engages in that conduct. As Leland puts it, "Every sin is not a crime to be punished by law,"[17] and "penal laws should be few."[18] Determining when the state should enforce by law principles that find their root in Christian morality is a complicated issue that has, in recent years, attracted a great deal of attention among conservative evangelicals and others, often under the heading of "Christian Nationalism." I don't intend to take up the topic in detail here other than to identify four principles that guide my thinking on the question of what conduct the state may appropriately criminalize.

First, the fact that my views about morality have a religious basis does not preclude me from seeking to criminalize conduct I think immoral. In a democracy, we all bring beliefs about what is right or wrong to the so-called "public square" to debate with our fellow citizens what justice demands that we criminalize. It is implausible that religious people would exclude their faith commitments from their assessments of what is just. I wouldn't even know how to debate a criminal justice policy in an honest way other than through reference to my religious conception of justice. That a citizen's beliefs about what conduct is immoral have a religious basis

16 Christopher D. Marshall, *Beyond Retribution: A New Testament Vision for Justice, Crime, and Punishment* (Grand Rapids, MI: Eerdmans, 2001), 118.

17 Leland, "On Sabbatical Laws," 441.

18 John Leland, "The Result of Observation," in Greene, *The Writings of the Late Elder John Leland*, 595. Aquinas similarly observes that "human laws do not forbid all vices, from which the virtuous abstain, but only the more grievous vices, from which it is possible for the majority to abstain; and chiefly those that are to the hurt of others, without the prohibition of which society could not be maintained: thus human law prohibits murder, theft and such like." Thomas Aquinas, *Summa Theologica*, trans. Fathers of the English Dominican Province (New York: Benzinger Brothers, 1947), 1–2.96.2, https://www.ccel.org. For a modern articulation of this view by a Roman Catholic intellectual, see John Courtney Murray, *We Hold These Truths: Catholic Reflections on the American Proposition* (Lanham, MD: Rowman and Littlefield, 2005), 158, who writes, "Law seeks to establish and maintain only that minimum of actualized morality that is necessary for the healthy functioning of the social order. . . . Beyond this, society must look to other institutions for the elevation and maintenance of its moral standards."

does not preclude that person from participating in the public debate.[19] Consequently, the propriety of criminalizing conduct is not negated by the fact that a citizen who argues for that criminalization does so based on a religious belief about the conduct's immorality.

Second, the state may not enforce religious adherence through the criminal law. In chapter 1, we saw that Augustine defined a just society as one that lives out love of "God as God ought to be loved, and his neighbor as himself."[20] A failure to love God is an injustice because it fails to render to God his due, but it does not follow that the state is entitled to criminally punish those who do not love the Lord as he should be loved. In the Baptist tradition, there has historically been a commitment to the notion that true faith in and worship of God cannot be, and thus should not be, compelled by the sword.[21] For example, Leland, who was a driving force behind the First Amendment's religion clauses,[22] argued that "the notion of a Christian commonwealth should be exploded forever"[23] and that it is not "possible for man to give greater evidence that he is ignorant of the precepts of Christianity, and destitute of the spirit of it, th[a]n he does when he makes use of the arm of the law to force others to believe as he does."[24] More recently, Baptist seminary professor Andrew Walker put it this way: "The gospel advances in only convicted, not coerced, consciences."[25]

19 Richard John Neuhaus, *The Naked Public Square: Religion and Democracy in America*, 2nd ed. (Grand Rapids, MI: Eerdmans, 1986). Yale sociology professor Philip Gorski, *American Covenant: A History of Civil Religion from the Puritans to the Present* (Princeton, NJ: Princeton University Press, 2017), 17, writes that "radical secularists insist that public life can and should be a 'neutral' realm. What they really mean by this is that the public square must be made religion-free. This is neither possible nor fair. It is not possible because religious convictions have political implications. It is not fair because it requires that religious citizens translate their arguments into the secularists' language, but not the other way around."

20 Augustine, *The City of God against the Pagans*, ed. and trans. R. W. Dyson (New York: Cambridge University Press, 2002), 959 (19.23).

21 Admittedly, this has not always been the view of Christians of all traditions across the ages.

22 Eric C. Smith, *John Leland: A Jeffersonian Baptist in Early America* (New York: Oxford University Press, 2022), 5.

23 John Leland, "The Virginia Chronicle," in Greene, *The Writings of the Late Elder John Leland*, 107.

24 John Leland, "Letter to the Rev. O. B. Brown," in Greene, *The Writings of the Late Elder John Leland*, 609.

25 Andrew T. Walker, *Liberty for All: Defending Everyone's Religious Freedom in a Pluralistic Age* (Grand Rapids, MI: Brazos, 2021), 162.

Third, freedom of religion would be of limited significance unless it also included some, but not an unlimited, degree of freedom to act on one's religious convictions. Leland appears to have recognized as much because he argued both that "a man has a civil right to do that which is morally wrong"[26] and that religious conviction does not protect a man from the "civil sword" to punish his "overt acts of violence" committed from "religious phrenzy."[27] In other words, Leland seems to have been of the view that the government's punitive jurisdiction is limited to immoral conduct that causes some sort of direct harm to others. Or as Augustine at one point puts it, "The law of the people deals with acts it must punish in order to keep the peace among ignorant men, insofar as deeds can be governed by man," while "other sins have other suitable punishments."[28] More recently, Baptist political theologian Jonathan Leeman has made a similar argument.[29] In the absence of this harm limitation, it is hard to draw another line that would preclude the government from criminalizing acts such as blasphemy, ritual sacrifice, or idolatry.[30]

Fourth, the state's use of punitive force is limited by the principle of proportionality. Prison may be a disproportionate response to some undeniably immoral acts that result in harm to others—for example, shoplifting a pack of bubble gum. The punishment doesn't fit the crime, as we say. Even

---

26 Leland, "The Result of Observation," 588.

27 John Leland, "The Rights of Conscience," in Greene, *The Writings of the Late Elder John Leland*, 184. Leland went on to say that "there are many things that Jesus and the apostles taught, that men ought to obey, which yet the civil law has no concern in" (187). Yet he also wrote that "if any, under a pretence of religion, commit overt acts, punish them for their crimes." Leland, "Letter to the Rev. O. B. Brown," 610. By "overt acts," Leland means to "assault the life, liberty or property of any man." Leland, "On Sabbatical Laws," 444.

28 Augustine, "On Free Choice of the Will, Book 1," in *From Irenaeus to Grotius: A Sourcebook in Christian Political Thought*, ed. Oliver O'Donovan and Joan Lockwood O'Donovan (Grand Rapids, MI: Eerdmans, 1999), 114. Augustine wrote this passage in *On Free Choice of the Will* around AD 388. It appears that he subsequently changed his view as reflected in a letter he wrote around AD 407. Augustine, "Letter 93: Augustine to Vincent," in *Letters 1–99*, trans. Roland Teske, ed. John E. Rotelle, in *The Works of Saint Augustine: A Translation for the 21st Century* (Hyde Park, NY: New City, 2001), 387 (5.17).

29 Jonathan Leeman, *How the Nations Rage: Rethinking Faith and Politics in a Divided Age* (Nashville: Thomas Nelson, 2018), 120–22; Jonathan Leeman, *Political Church: The Local Assembly as the Embassy of Christ's Rule* (Downers Grove, IL: IVP Academic, 2016), 198–204.

30 This was the mistake of John Calvin's theology, which called for the use of civil authority to punish idolatry, blasphemy, and "other offenses to religion." John Calvin, *Institutes of the Christian Religion*, trans. Henry Beveridge (Peabody, MA: Hendrickson, 2008), 971 (4.20.3).

if probation rather than imprisonment is the punishment for the offense, a criminal conviction has numerous collateral consequences, including exclusion from some employment, education, housing, credit, and other opportunities. The cascading consequences to someone's life as the result of labeling conduct "criminal" may not align with the severity of the wrong committed and harm caused.

When evaluating the proportionality of a criminal law enforcement response to a wrongful act, it is important to keep in mind that government is not the only institution God has ordained to restrain wrongdoing. Families instruct, churches discipline, schools educate, social circles shame, and employers incentivize. Each of these is a means of deterring and restraining sinful acts. Government has a role in responding to immoral activity but not a totalizing role. The sword of the state is often a disproportionate response to a wrong.

Prosecutorial Discretion

One last topic we must consider when defining a "crime" is the topic of prosecutorial discretion. The number of criminal laws and thus the number of crimes committed in the United States vastly outstrips the resources of police and prosecutors to address those crimes. Choices must be made. Priorities must be set. In a very real sense, what is a "crime" depends as much on what the police officer or prosecutor chooses to enforce as it does on what the legislature chooses to legislate against.

To take a simple, everyday example of this, we all know that in practice the speed limit is not really the number on the roadside sign but rather some number five to ten miles above that posted number. We recognize that as a technical matter we could be ticketed for driving twenty-six miles per hour in a twenty-five miles-per-hour zone. We also know that's effectively never going to happen.[31]

My focus here, though, isn't on speed limits. Police and prosecutors make many far more consequential decisions every day about what and what not to prosecute criminally. In the wake of the Civil War, state legislatures passed laws that were colorblind on their face but that were

---

31 But see United States v. Fuehrer, No. CR15-1016 (N.D. Iowa Aug. 20, 2015), upholding traffic stop when car was "traveling 66 miles per hour in a 65 mile-per-hour zone."

enforced in racially discriminatory ways by prosecutors, judges, and juries. Vagrancy became the catchall crime that was used to ensnare the Black man. In the late nineteenth century, the Supreme Court declared that discriminatory enforcement of a race-neutral law runs afoul of the US Constitution:

> Though the law itself be fair on its face and impartial in appearance, yet, if it is applied and administered by public authority with an evil eye and an unequal hand, so as practically to make unjust and illegal discriminations between persons in similar circumstances . . . the denial of equal justice is still within the prohibition of the Constitution.[32]

One hundred years later, the court reached a different conclusion in Warren McCleskey's capital murder case.[33]

Similar concerns about disparate enforcement of the criminal law persist today, particularly with regard to drug crimes. The difference in approach to the crack cocaine epidemic of the 1990s (which largely impacted urban Blacks) and the opioid epidemic of the 2000s (which largely impacts rural Whites) is stark. So too with marijuana. In 2022, the Mississippi Supreme Court affirmed the life sentence of Allen Russell, a 38-year-old Black man, for possession of 1.55 ounces of marijuana.[34] That same year, Colin Landforce, a 34-year-old White man from Oregon was boasting on Twitter about his marijuana business that was publicly traded and had $40 million in sales in 2020.[35] It is easy to brush aside disparities like this with simplistic references to their geographic locations, one in Mississippi and the other in Oregon. But marijuana possession and distribution are still federal crimes nationwide as of the publication of

---

32 Yick Wo v. Hopkins, 118 U.S. 356, 373–74 (1886).

33 McCleskey v. Kemp, 481 U.S. 279 (1987).

34 Russell v. State, No. 2019-CT-01670-SCT (Miss. June 16, 2022). Russell had previously been convicted of burglary and illegal gun possession, for which he had served eight years and two years in prison, respectively. He had completed the latter of those two sentences more than a year before his arrest on the marijuana possession charge. Russell was sentenced under a habitual offender statute, an issue I take up in chap. 17.

35 Colin Landforce (@landforce), Twitter, December 27, 2021, https://twitter.com/landforce/status /1475508173599481858?s=20&t=N2dVQM266JjDWZumIAO16g. For details and numbers regarding his business, see the entire tweet thread.

this book, and yet the US Department of Justice exercises its discretion not to prosecute these offenses.[36]

The danger of disparate enforcement of the law is compounded when the number of crimes increases while the resources to investigate and prosecute those crimes does not increase accordingly. When the US Department of Justice was asked to report to Congress on how many federal crimes there are, it was unable to produce a precise number.[37] In 2008, a think tank in Washington, DC, estimated the number of federal crimes at around 4,400, not to mention the numerous state and local criminal statutes.[38] Given the proliferation of criminal laws, we live in a society where far too many people commit crimes daily, often without even knowing it.[39] In that situation, the need for prosecutorial discretion is at its highest, and the law becomes what is enforced rather than what is written. This creates a danger that the law will not be applied impartially, that those who will be prosecuted will be the most disfavored in society rather than the most morally culpable.

————

The very definition of a crime—whether that definition comes through legislation or application—raises profound moral questions for the Christian. Is the law accurately defining what should and should not be a crime? Is the criminalization of conduct being done impartially and proportionally? Is the law, in a word, just? People decide whether they will engage in immoral conduct. We as a society choose whether we will justly or unjustly call that conduct criminal. How we choose determines, at least in part, whether a "crime" ever occurs.

36 21 U.S.C. §§ 841, 844. In October 2022, President Biden pardoned thousands of men and women convicted of federal marijuana offenses. "A Proclamation on Granting Pardon for the Offense of Simple Possession of Marijuana," The White House, October 6, 2022, https://www .whitehouse.gov/. This pardon does not reach people like Allen Russell, who was convicted under state law.

37 Gary Fields and John R. Emshwiller, "Many Failed Efforts to Count the Nation's Federal Criminal Laws," Wall Street Journal, July 23, 2011.

38 John S. Baker, Revisiting the Explosive Growth of Federal Crime (Washington, DC: The Heritage Foundation, June 16, 2008), https://www.heritage.org.

39 Harvey Silverglate, Three Felonies a Day: How the Feds Target the Innocent (New York: Encounter, 2011).

11

Plea Bargaining

WHY WOULD SOMEONE PLEAD GUILTY to a crime? Criminal defendants in the United States are entitled to a jury trial, a right that was central to the American founding and the only one that appears twice in the US Constitution.[1] Given those jury trial guarantees, why would anyone, even if he or she had committed the crime, give up the right and plead guilty?

And yet criminal defendants do plead guilty. In fact, guilty pleas, rather than jury trials, are the norm in the American justice system. As the US Supreme Court observed, "The reality [is] that criminal justice today is for the most part a system of pleas, not a system of trials."[2] Roughly 95 percent of criminal cases are resolved through guilty pleas.[3] And this isn't a regional phenomenon. It's as true in New York, Michigan, and California as it is in Florida, Missouri, and Texas.[4] In 2021, 100 percent of federal criminal defendants pled guilty in Rhode Island.[5] A 2018 study found that ten of North Carolina's one hundred counties reported no jury trials over the three-year period examined.[6]

---

1 U.S. Const. art. III, § 2; U.S. Const. amend. VI.
2 Lafler v. Cooper, 566 U.S. 156, 170 (2012).
3 Missouri v. Frye, 566 U.S. 134, 143 (2012).
4 In 2021, the percentage of felony cases resolved by trial was 0.6 percent (New York), 0.6 percent (Michigan), 1.6 percent (California), 0.9 percent (Florida), 0.5 percent (Missouri), and 1.9 percent (Texas). S. Gibson, B. Harris, N. Waters, K. Genthon, M. Hamilton, and D. Robinson, eds., "Trial Court Caseload Overview," CSP STAT Criminal, Court Statistics Project, last modified July 8, 2022, https://www.courtstatistics.org.
5 *2021 Annual Report and Sourcebook of Federal Sentencing Statistics* (United States Sentencing Commission, 2021), 56, table 11, https://www.ussc.gov/.
6 "The clerks in 10 of the 100 counties reported that *no jury trials at all* occurred in their counties between 2011 and 2013." Ronald F. Wright, Kami Chavis, and Gregory S. Parks, "The Jury

How could this be? Why wouldn't every criminal defendant—or at least the estimated 80 percent of defendants who have court appointed counsel for which they aren't paying[7]—take a shot at acquittal by the jury? It's their right after all. What's to lose?

To understand how we got to the point where nearly all criminal defendants plead guilty rather than go to trial, we need to back up and consider two constitutional amendments that bear on the issue and how the US Supreme Court has interpreted each of those provisions in a way that turned our criminal justice system into, as professor and criminal law expert Carissa Byrne Hessick has explained, "a system of pressure and pleas, not truth and trials." The reason that innocent people plead guilty is that, as our system is currently structured, "*everyone* is pressured into pleading guilty."[8]

Bail

As a general rule, criminal proceedings against an individual begin with an arrest. The police can arrest someone either because an officer has probable cause or because a grand jury, after an investigation, has returned an indictment based on a finding of probable cause that a particular person committed a crime.[9]

After the suspect is arrested, whether for a misdemeanor or a felony, a hearing to determine bail is held before some type of judicial officer. These hearings can occur within hours of the arrest for minor offenses prosecuted in state court.[10] In federal criminal cases, bail hearings typically occur within three to five business days of the arrest.[11]

Sunshine Project: Jury Selection Data as a Political Issue," *University of Illinois Law Review* 2018, no. 4 (2018): 1421, https://www.illinoislawreview.org/wp-content/uploads/2018/10/Wright.pdf (emphasis in original).

7   Tony Messenger, *Profit and Punishment: How America Criminalizes the Poor in the Name of Justice* (New York: St. Martin's, 2021), xi.

8   Carissa Byrne Hessick, *Punishment without Trial: Why Plea Bargaining Is a Bad Deal* (New York: Abrams, 2021), 5 (emphasis in original).

9   Not every state has grand juries, and the US Supreme Court has ruled that they are not a constitutional necessity. Hurtado v. California, 110 U.S. 516 (1884). In those states without grand juries, the initiation of a case will vary somewhat in ways not relevant here. For a discussion of variations and similarities in the criminal process, see Ronald J. Allen, Richard B. Kuhns, and William J. Stuntz, *Constitutional Criminal Procedure*, 3rd ed. (New York: Little Brown, 1995), 4–13.

10 For example, in Virginia, a statute provides that the arresting officer must bring the arrested person before a judicial officer "without unnecessary delay" and the judicial officer must "immediately conduct a bail hearing." Va. Code Ann. § 19.2-80.

11 18 U.S.C. § 3142(f).

Originally, the idea behind bail was to ensure that the defendant would appear for his or her trial. The judge sets conditions of the defendant's release prior to trial, and those conditions can include a requirement that the defendant deposit a sum of money with the court that will be forfeited if he or she does not return to court for trial.[12] The US Bill of Rights prohibits courts from setting bail at an "excessive" amount,[13] which the Supreme Court had until 1987 interpreted to mean "a figure higher than an amount reasonably calculated" to ensure that, if the defendant were released before trial, he or she would show up for trial.[14] In other words, bail amounts cannot be used as a means to punish the defendant before conviction,[15] but if the defendant cannot pay a properly set bail amount, he or she can be held in jail until trial.[16]

In 1984, Congress passed the Bail Reform Act, which allowed judges to deny federal criminal defendants bail and hold them in custody before trial based on a finding that they were dangerous to the community, meaning likely to commit some future crime.[17] This was a sea change in the purpose of bail. But, in 1987, the Supreme Court held that it was constitutional, concluding that protecting the safety of the community by jailing a defendant before trial served a legitimate "regulatory" purpose and was not preconviction punishment. The result of this ruling was that someone charged with a crime can be denied bail entirely and jailed prior to trial because, even though not yet convicted and thus presumed innocent, he or she is viewed as a threat to commit future crimes.[18]

Whether bail is granted and in what amount can determine whether the defendant spends months, or even years, in jail awaiting trial. Despite

---

12 Ex parte Milburn, 34 U.S. 704, 710 (1835).

13 U.S. Const. amend. VIII.

14 Stack v. Boyle, 342 U.S. 1, 5 (1951). "The statutes of the United States have been framed upon the theory that a person accused of a crime shall not, until he has been finally adjudged guilty in the court of last resort, be absolutely compelled to undergo imprisonment or punishment, but may be admitted to bail not only after arrest and before trial, but after conviction and pending a writ of error." Hudson v. Parker, 156 U.S. 277, 285 (1895).

15 "Due process requires that a pretrial detainee not be punished." Bell v. Wolfish, 441 U.S. 520, 535 n.16 (1979).

16 But see In re Humphrey, 482 P.3d 1008, 1012 (Cal. 2021), holding that "the common practice of conditioning freedom solely on whether an arrestee can afford bail is unconstitutional."

17 18 U.S.C. § 3142(e).

18 United States v. Salerno, 481 U.S. 739, 755 (1987).

the importance of this bail decision, there is no right under the US Constitution to the assistance of an attorney at the bail hearing. "The majority of states does not provide counsel to indigent defendants at their initial appearance,"[19] and the Supreme Court has never held that a defendant too poor to pay for an attorney must be provided with one at a bail hearing. Thus, a criminal defendant in state court who is unable to pay for counsel may be, and often is, forced to navigate the bail hearing on his or her own without an attorney to help.[20]

If, at the conclusion of the bail hearing, the judicial officer sets bail for the defendant, that doesn't necessarily mean the defendant will be released from jail. Those defendants who are granted bail in even modest amounts may be entirely unable to meet it because of their limited financial means. According to the Federal Reserve, the median amount of financial assets of Americans aged thirty-five and younger (the age bracket that commits the vast majority of crimes[21]) is about $8,500.[22] By contrast, the median bail amount in the United States is estimated as approximately $10,000.[23]

The result is that nearly 500,000 people, though they have been convicted of *nothing*, are in jail every day in the United States prior to the trial on the charges against them.[24] The vast majority (approximately three quarters) of

---

19 John P. Gross, "The Right to Counsel but Not the Presence of Counsel: A Survey of State Criminal Procedures for Pre-Trial Release," *Florida Law Review* 69, no. 3 (2017): 833, https://scholarship.law.ufl.edu/flr/vol69/iss3/4.

20 Douglas L. Colbert, "Prosecution without Representation," *Buffalo Law Review* 59, no. 2 (2011): 333–453, https://digitalcommons.law.buffalo.edu/buffalolawreview/vol59/iss2/2.

21 Studies show that people tend to "age out" of crime after age forty. Rachel Elise Barkow, *Prisoners of Politics: Breaking the Cycle of Mass Incarceration* (Cambridge, MA: Harvard University Press, 2019), 44–45.

22 "Survey of Consumer Finances, 1989–2019," Board of Governors of the Federal Reserve System, last modified November 4, 2021, https://www.federalreserve.gov/econres/scf/dataviz/scf/chart/#series:Financial_Assets;demographic:agecl;population:1,2,3,4,5,6;units:median.

23 *The Civil Rights Implications of Cash Bail* (US Commission on Civil Rights, January 2022), 32, https://www.usccr.gov/.

24 John F. Pfaff, *Locked In: The True Causes of Mass Incarceration and How to Achieve Real Reform* (New York: Basic Books, 2017), 2. In numerous jurisdictions, criminal defendants who are jailed prior to trial are charged a daily fee for their time in jail. These fees can run to thousands of dollars in total, but the criminal defendants charged these fees are frequently indigent. Thus, after a defendant has served a prison sentence, he or she can be saddled with thousands of dollars in debt to the state for the cost of being jailed prior to conviction. Messenger, *Profit and Punishment*, 73–87.

those being held face relatively minor charges—traffic violations, property crimes, or drug possession.[25] The Supreme Court, however, got comfortable with this setup because any pretrial detention will supposedly be brief given the right to a speedy trial.[26]

Speedy Trial

This arrangement might be tolerable if defendants were brought promptly to trial. After all, the Sixth Amendment to the US Constitution, which is one of two constitutional provisions guaranteeing a jury trial, also guarantees that the trial will be "speedy."[27]

But what exactly does "speedy" mean? The Supreme Court was presented with that question in a case involving a more-than-five-*year* delay between the defendant's arrest and his trial. Though the justices thought it a "close" case, they unanimously concluded that the defendant's speedy trial right was not violated, taking some comfort in the fact that he was free on bail for all but ten months of the pretrial delay.[28]

It should come as no surprise, then, that lower courts regularly find that lengthy delays in getting to trial do not violate the speedy trial right, and it is very common for criminal defendants to sit in jail for years awaiting trial. In 2013, the *Houston Chronicle* reported on the cases of dozens of defendants who had languished in the local jail for years—in some instances, nearly eight years—awaiting trial. Among the cases cited were those of Donald Jones (six years and four months in jail awaiting trial for injury to a child), James Beattie (four years and three months in jail awaiting trial for assault on a peace officer), Antonio Ward (four years and two months in jail awaiting trial for robbery), and Aaron Smith (three years and eleven months in jail awaiting trial for injury to child).[29] These are all serious charges, but each

---

25 Christopher Ingraham, "Why We Spend Billions to Keep Half a Million Unconvicted People behind Bars," *Washington Post*, June 11, 2015, https://www.washingtonpost.com/.
26 United States v. Salerno, 481 U.S. 739, 747 (1987).
27 "In all criminal prosecutions, the accused shall enjoy the right to a speedy and public trial." U.S. Const. amend. VI. As originally enacted, the Sixth Amendment applied only to federal criminal prosecutions. West v. Louisiana, 194 U.S. 258, 264 (1904). But the Sixth Amendment's speedy trial guarantee was extended to state criminal trials as an element of due process under the Fourteenth Amendment. Klopfer v. North Carolina, 386 U.S. 213, 223 (1967).
28 Barker v. Wingo, 407 U.S. 514, 534–35 (1972).
29 "Stuck in Jail," *Houston Chronicle*, August 23, 2013, https://www.chron.com/.

of these defendants spent years in prison *before* they had an opportunity to contest the charges at trial. Even defendants charged with very low-level crimes often languish in jail for well over a year awaiting trial in Houston.[30]

This phenomenon of lengthy pretrial detention is not unique to Texas. In 2005, the Mississippi Supreme Court ruled that a four-year delay in bringing a defendant's case to trial following his indictment and arrest did not violate his speedy trial right because the court "does not recognize . . . as prejudice" the "negative emotional, social, and economic impacts on [the defendant's] life" resulting from pretrial detention.[31] In 2011, the Mississippi Supreme Court rejected a speedy trial claim where the defendant's trial was delayed nearly two years because of the trial court's "overcrowded docket." The court refused to "indulge in an assumption" that the defendant "experienced anxiety and concern from his [pretrial] incarceration."[32] As recently as 2015, the Mississippi Supreme Court held that an eighteen-month delay during which the defendant was jailed was not a speedy trial violation, faulting the defendant for failing to offer "a scintilla of evidence" that he "experienced anxiety and concern from his incarceration" while awaiting trial.[33] In November 2021, a Mississippi man who had been jailed for *six years* prior to trial was found not guilty when he finally got his day in court.[34]

When I first shared with others that this practice of jailing unconvicted people was occurring, the immediate response was to dismiss it as an outlier practice of "backward" southern states. But that isn't the case. In fact, it is widespread and common across the country. In 2013, a California appellate court ruled that it did not violate the speedy trial guarantee for a defendant to be jailed for *seven years* prior to trial despite the "oppressive nature of pretrial incarceration and the anxiety it produces."[35] In 2020, a Massachusetts appellate court was presented with the case of a defendant who was held in jail for nearly five years pretrial because of his inability to make bail, during which time he lost

30 Lise Olsen, "Thousands Languish in Crowded Harris County Jail," *Houston Chronicle*, August 22, 2009, https://www.chron.com/.
31 Manix v. State, 885 So.2d 167, 177 (Miss. 2005).
32 Johnson v. State, 68 So.3d 1239, 1242, 1245 (Miss. 2011).
33 Taylor v. State, 162 So.3d 780, 787 (Miss. 2015).
34 Jerry Mitchell, "'Dead Zone' Leads Innocent Mississippi Man to Spend Six Years behind Bars for Murder," *Clarion-Ledger*, January 18, 2022, https://www.clarionledger.com/.
35 People v. Williams, 315 P.3d 1, 40 (Cal. 2013).

his job and was away from his children. Nonetheless, the court concluded that this did not violate the speedy trial guarantee.[36] In 2019, a man in Washington state was acquitted at trial after spending more than eight years in jail, unable to make bail.[37] In 2014, a New York appellate court ruled that a seventeen-month trial delay during which the defendant was jailed did not violate the speedy trial clause of the Sixth Amendment.[38] As a federal appeals court in Chicago summed it up, "Significant pretrial incarceration . . . does not alone make out a deprivation of the right to a speedy trial."[39]

Pressure to Plead

It isn't hard to see how this combination of pretrial detention and a trial date a year or more away can exert incredible pressure on a defendant, particularly one who is financially vulnerable. While the defendant is in jail, he or she is unable to earn an income. The defendant will likely lose his or her job. Rent or mortgages go unpaid, resulting in eviction or foreclosure. Children may be farmed out to relatives or social services.

At the same time, confinement in the local jail is a harrowing experience. Facilities are overcrowded and unsanitary, health care is substandard, and the risk of sexual assault is ever present. Recent press reports about the conditions at Rikers Island in New York City, which holds in excess of ten thousand prisoners on any given day, include photos and accounts of twenty-six men held in a single cell and forced to relieve themselves in plastic bags because of a lack of toilets.[40] Confinement in these conditions can drag on for months or years, all the while taking a physical, emotional, financial, and psychological toll on a person who has yet to be convicted of anything.

When someone is detained in such deplorable conditions, the prosecutor has an enormous amount of leverage to secure a guilty plea. A defendant

36 Commonwealth v. McNair, 158 N.E.3d 507, 517 (Mass. App. 2020).
37 Sara Jean Green, "After Nearly 11 Years and Two Trials, Killing of Redmond Woman Who Had Been 'Living Her Dream' Remains Unsolved," *Seattle Times*, June 14, 2019, last modified June 15, 2019, https://www.seattletimes.com/; Hannah Murphy Winter, "He Spent Eight Years in Jail without a Conviction. Now, He's Suing Everyone Who Kept Him There," *Rolling Stone*, April 1, 2022, https://www.rollingstone.com/.
38 People v. Anderson, 114 A.D.3d 811, 981 N.Y.S.2d 200 (2014).
39 United States v. White, 443 F.3d 582, 591 (7th Cir. 2006).
40 Gabrielle Fonrouge, "Photos inside Rikers Island Expose Deadly, Hellish Conditions," *New York Post*, October 21, 2021, https://nypost.com/.

sitting in jail has the right to a trial, but it will likely be many months, maybe even years, before that trial will occur. It is not uncommon for a defendant who cannot make bail to wait a month or more just to meet his or her court-appointed attorney for the first time. But what if, when the attorney makes that first visit with the client at the jail, he or she has a plea offer from the prosecutor? What if the prosecutor offered that the defendant could plead guilty and receive a sentence of time served, meaning that the prison sentence accompanying the guilty plea will be only the time the defendant has already been sitting in jail waiting for trial? What if the offense is a relatively minor one and pleading guilty, even if the defendant is actually innocent, means he or she would be released from jail the next day? What if choosing instead to prove one's innocence means sitting in a hellhole like Rikers Island for another year or two awaiting trial?

If you are a person of some means, you likely will never face this impossible choice. If you were charged with a relatively minor offense, even a felony, you would almost certainly be granted bail in an amount that you could scrape together the funds to cover. You would still have to face the charges, but you could do so while living at home and, if you are lucky, continuing to work and support your family. But if you are poor and cannot pay even a small bail amount while waiting for your court-appointed lawyer who may be unable to see you for a month, the situation is far grimmer. You lose your job. You're evicted from your apartment. Your children are sent to foster care. You can't see a doctor for your chronic health condition. You may be raped in jail. Your options are much less appealing. In fact, your so-called options may not really be options at all. You swallow your pride, take the deal, and admit to something regardless of whether you actually did it.

Lest you think any of this is hyperbolic or exaggerated, let me assure you that it is not. It is the reality that thousands of Americans face every day. To be sure, they aren't all innocent. In fact, many (or even most) of them may not be. But we don't know. We don't know because so many guilty pleas are coerced under any normal definition of coercion. And that's the problem. Guilty pleas, because they are so often coerced, are not a reliable indicator of guilt, and they short-circuit the Constitution's trial process at which the evidence against the accused could be tested. Too many defendants can't wait that long. They can't afford to sit in jail. The cost to their family, finances, safety, and health wouldn't allow it. And so they take the plea deal and are home the next night.

Trial Penalty

But maybe you would be that unusually determined criminal defendant who, facing financial wreckage, sexual assault, and family trauma, is willing to toil away for another year or two in jail awaiting your trial to prove your innocence. If that's you, you will soon learn that the system has even more pressure that it will bring to bear on you to take the plea deal. You will be threatened with a longer prison sentence if you exercise your constitutional right to a trial and lose.

In the federal justice system, the threat of more jail time is written explicitly into the law. Under the federal sentencing guidelines, your sentencing level will be two or three levels higher if you are convicted after trial on a charge than if you plead guilty to that same charge. That increase of two or three levels could save you ninety-eight months (more than eight years) of prison time at the high end of the scale or be the difference in avoiding prison entirely at the low end of the scale.[41]

But the pressure the system will put on you to waive your trial right and plead guilty will be much greater than a few months or even years of prison time. If you refuse to plead guilty, prosecutors may add charges with mandatory minimum sentences that even the judge cannot override if you are convicted at trial. Or the prosecutor will bring more charges that by law must be added together (what the law calls, "running consecutively") when imposing your sentence.

In one recent example of this tactic that attracted a great deal of publicity, Rogel Aguilera-Mederos, a 23-year-old truck driver, caused a traffic accident in Colorado that resulted in the death of four people. The evidence at trial was that he made a series of reckless decisions that caused a multi-car pileup on the interstate. Prior to trial, the prosecutors made the defendant what they deemed a reasonable plea offer. He opted instead for the jury trial that the Constitution guarantees him. Because the prosecutors stacked multiple charges against him after Aguilera-Mederos was convicted at trial, the judge had no option under the law but to run the sentences for

41 U.S.S.G. § 3E1.1; U.S.S.G. Ch.5, Pt.A.

each charge consecutively, resulting in a total prison sentence of 110 years. When public backlash over the sentence ensued, the prosecutor sought to justify what many saw as a disproportionate sentence by arguing that the result, if it was unfair, was the defendant's fault for turning down the plea offer. In the prosecutor's view, if you want a reasonable and just sentence, then you must waive your right to a trial and plead guilty. Trials and the chance to prove your innocence come with a penalty, and that penalty is a disproportionate sentence that not even the prosecutor was willing to defend in the face of public scrutiny.[42]

A few months later, Pamela Moses's case attracted similar attention when she was sentenced to six years in prison for attempting to improperly register to vote in Tennessee in the 2020 election. When a public outcry arose that this sentence was wildly disproportionate to the crime, the district attorney offered this response: "I gave her a chance to plead to a misdemeanor with no prison time. She requested a jury trial instead. She set this unfortunate result in motion and a jury of her peers heard the evidence and convicted her."[43] The unjust sentence was the fault, not of the prosecutor who sought it or the judge who imposed it, but the defendant who received it after exercising her right to a trial.

These aren't one-off examples. These are simply instances where the prosecutor admitted what was going on. But the practice seen in those cases isn't rare. In fact, it is so common that it has a name: the "trial penalty." A recent study found that defendants who go to trial received sentences that are on average three times longer than the sentences of defendants who plead guilty.[44] The result of this trial penalty is further pressure on criminal defendants to plead guilty. That's the whole point of the trial penalty.

42 Shelly Bradbury, "Trucker's 100-Year Sentence in Fatal I-70 Crash Spotlights Colorado Sentencing Laws, Prosecutors' Charging Decisions," *The Denver Post*, December 16, 2021, https://www.denverpost.com/. When this case came to the public attention, an online petition circulated asking the governor to grant clemency. Facing this torrent of criticism, the prosecutors vowed to return to court and seek a reduction of the prison sentence to twenty to thirty years. Days before Christmas 2021, the Colorado governor intervened and granted clemency, reducing the sentence to ten years in prison. Elise Schmelzer, "Colorado Governor Reduces I-70 Truck Driver Rogel Aguilera Mederos' Sentence to 10 Years," *The Denver Post*, December 30, 2021, https://www.denverpost.com/.

43 Sybil C. Mitchell, "As Voter-Fraud Sentence Goes National, DA Weirich Doubles Down on Her Support for It," *Tri-State Defender*, February 12, 2022, https://tri-statedefender.com/.

44 Hessick, *Punishment without Trial*, 45.

To make sure that judges don't impose lenient sentences, legislators pass criminal laws that attach mandatory minimum terms of imprisonment to certain crimes. In other words, these crimes have not only a maximum sentence that a defendant can receive but also a minimum sentence that must be imposed—often five, ten, or fifteen years in prison. The judge cannot sentence the defendant, if convicted of that crime, to less than the mandatory minimum. This gives prosecutors enormous leverage to extract a plea because, while the judge cannot reduce the sentence to something reasonable, the prosecutor can agree to drop the charge that carries the mandatory minimum if the defendant pleads guilty. But if the defendant goes to trial, the prosecutor has a guarantee that a trial penalty, in the form of a mandatory minimum sentence, will be imposed by the judge if the defendant is convicted.[45]

In fact, the Supreme Court has ruled that it is constitutional for a prosecutor to threaten these enhanced penalties if the defendant refuses to plead guilty. In *Bordenkircher v. Hayes*, the defendant had been charged with passing a forged check in the amount of $88.30. The prosecutor offered the defendant, who had two prior convictions, a plea bargain with a five-year prison sentence "to save the court the inconvenience and necessity of a trial." However, if the defendant did not accept the plea bargain, the prosecutor threatened that he would add a charge under the state's "three strikes" statute, which mandated life imprisonment for the same crime. When the defendant refused the plea offer, the prosecutor added the "three strikes" charge as promised. The defendant was convicted of the enhanced charge at trial and sentenced to life in prison.

On appeal, the Supreme Court concluded that this raised no constitutional concerns. The enhanced charge was available to the prosecutor under the law, and it was not, in the court's view, unconstitutional to threaten it to extract a guilty plea. The court distinguished between bad faith overcharging (in which defendants are charged with crimes the government cannot prove) and legal overcharging (in which defendants are charged with offenses that carry excessive sentences to coerce plea bargains).[46] The former is prohibited by the Constitution while the latter is not.

45 For a further discussion of the relationship between mandatory minimum sentences and plea bargaining, see George Fisher, *Plea Bargaining's Triumph: A History of Plea Bargaining in America* (Stanford, CA: Stanford University Press, 2003), 166–70.

46 Bordenkircher v. Hayes, 434 U.S. 357, 364 (1978). See also Michael Tonry, "Prosecutors and Politics in Comparative Perspective," *Crime and Justice* 41, no. 1 (2012): 22–23, https://doi.org /10.1086/666975. US Supreme Court Justice Ketanji Brown Jackson wrote about the coercive

Since these mandatory minimum sentences give prosecutors enormous plea-bargaining leverage, it should come as no surprise that prosecutors lobby legislatures for them. In 2015, the head of the National Association of Assistant United States Attorneys, an organization that represents federal prosecutors, expressed his opposition to a reduction of certain mandatory minimum sentences because, as he put it, "the leverage, the hammer we have comes in those penalties."[47]

What a Bargain

It is widely accepted among the American public that plea bargaining is an entirely normal, even expected, part of the criminal justice process. So entrenched is plea bargaining today that it may never even have occurred to you that it is either morally or legally questionable. You may not have stopped to consider why justice in a given case is up for negotiation[48] or where the government derives its authority to condition a sentencing outcome on your waiver of your due process right to present your defense in a trial before a neutral decisionmaker.[49]

There was a time, however, when it was not at all clear that plea bargaining was permissible under the US Constitution. In 1962, the Supreme Court seemed to suggest that a guilty plea induced by a prosecutor's promise of a more lenient sentence was constitutionally suspect.[50] Six years later, the Supreme Court held that a statute that allowed for the death penalty if the defendant went to trial but not if he pled guilty was unconstitutional because it "penalizes the assertion of a constitutional right" to a jury trial. The court went on to explain that "the evil" in the "statute is not that it necessarily

---

aspect of plea bargaining in her undergraduate senior thesis. Ketanji Onyika Brown, "'The Hand of Oppression': Plea Bargaining Processes and the Coercion of Criminal Defendants" (senior thesis, Harvard College, 1992).

47 Ann E. Marimow, "Softening Sentences, Losing Leverage," *Washington Post*, October 31, 2015, https://www.washingtonpost.com/.

48 In the mid-1800s, some questioned whether plea bargaining was malpractice by prosecutors. Fisher, *Plea Bargaining's Triumph*, 30.

49 By comparison, the Supreme Court has held that, while you do not have a right to government employment, a state cannot condition your government employment on the waiver of your constitutional right to, for example, practice your religion. Lane v. Franks, 573 U.S. 228, 236 (2014): "This Court has cautioned time and again that public employers may not condition employment on the relinquishment of constitutional rights."

50 "A guilty plea, if induced by promises or threats which deprive it of the character of a voluntary act, is void." Machibroda v. United States, 368 U.S. 487, 493 (1962).

coerces guilty pleas and jury waivers, but simply that it needlessly *encourages* them." In other words, the court's view as of 1968 was that even encouraging a defendant to plead guilty "impose[s] an impermissible burden upon the assertion of a constitutional right" to a jury trial.[51] If the Supreme Court had really meant this, it would have been the end of plea bargaining since there is no doubt that plea bargaining at least encourages the waiver of the trial right by allowing for a longer sentence if the defendant insists on a trial.

But only two years later, in 1970, the Supreme Court began to backtrack, holding that a guilty plea was not "involuntary" even though it was induced by a threat that the defendant could receive the death penalty if, but only if, he went to trial.[52] A guilty plea is not involuntary, the court explained, merely because the prosecutor "extend[s] a benefit to a defendant" in the form of a reduced sentence if he or she pleads guilty. While it is impermissible for a prosecutor to "produce" a guilty "plea by actual or threatened physical harm or by mental coercion," the justices ruled that it is permissible for the state to "encourage a guilty plea by opportunity or promise of leniency."[53] Lost on the court was the fact that a threat of extra jail time—not to mention the death penalty—*is* a threat of physical harm, as we saw in chapter 2.

The court expressed confidence that "the encouragement of guilty pleas by offers of leniency" would not "substantially [increase] the likelihood that defendants . . . would falsely condemn themselves." The only evidence the court cited for this confidence was its expectation that judges would, when accepting guilty pleas, "satisfy themselves" that there is no reason "to question the accuracy and reliability of the defendants' admissions that they committed the crimes with which they are charged."[54]

At the same time, the Supreme Court said that a judge could accept the guilty plea merely on the defendant's admission that he committed the crime even if he did not admit that "he committed the particular acts claimed to constitute the crime." In fact, the court went a step further and ruled that a defendant could plead guilty to a crime even if, while pleading guilty, he *denied* that he committed the acts that constituted the crime. In the Supreme Court's view, there is no reason a defendant cannot "consent

51   United States v. Jackson, 390 U.S. 570, 583 (1968).
52   Parker v. North Carolina, 397 U.S. 790 , 795 (1970).
53   Brady v. United States, 397 U.S. 742, 750, 753 (1970).
54   Brady v. United States, 397 U.S. 742, 758 (1970).

to the imposition of a prison sentence even if he is unwilling or unable to admit his participation in the acts constituting the crime."[55]

The next year, the Supreme Court put to rest all doubt about the constitutionality of plea bargaining in *Santobello v. New York*, in which the court extolled the virtues of the practice. Only a year after blessing the practice of plea bargaining as constitutional, the court was calling it "an essential component of the administration of justice." If plea bargaining were not permitted and trials required in every case, the court fretted that the government "would need to multiply by many times the number of judges and court facilities." Thus, the court saw plea bargaining to be not only a practical necessity but also something "desirable" and "to be encouraged." It ensures "prompt" and "final" resolution of cases while avoiding "enforced idleness during pretrial confinement." And, again, the court took comfort from its belief that judges would ensure that there was a "factual basis" for the plea.[56]

This brief legal history of plea bargaining is not intended to suggest that the practice didn't exist prior to the early 1960s. It most certainly did.[57] Nor is my point to critique the soundness of the court's constitutional reasoning. My point is that, while we accept plea bargaining as a normal and natural part of the criminal justice system today, only in my lifetime has its constitutionality been settled. In that sense, it is a relatively recent legal phenomenon.[58] It is by no means a given, and even today plea bargaining is not the practice in many nations around the world.[59]

Biblical Justice?

So what is a Christian to make of all this? Plea bargaining is widely accepted in both American society and its legal system today. But legality is not determinative for the Christian. The question for the follower of Jesus Christ is not whether judges are comfortable with the practice or whether

---

55 North Carolina v. Alford, 400 U.S. 25, 32, 37 (1970).

56 Santobello v. New York, 404 U.S. 257, 260–61 (1971).

57 Stephanos Bibas, *The Machinery of Criminal Justice* (Oxford: Oxford University Press, 2012), 11–34; Fisher, *Plea Bargaining's Triumph*.

58 The ability to extract guilty pleas vastly increases the prosecutor's ability to bring more cases, and one commentator has argued that this increase in the number of cases brought has more than anything else contributed to the exorbitant incarceration rates in the United States. Pfaff, *Locked In*, 7.

59 Stephen C. Thaman, ed., *World Plea Bargaining: Consensual Procedures and the Avoidance of the Full Criminal Trial* (Durham, NC: Carolina Academic Press, 2010), 344, 363–66.

a nation's constitution permits it. The proper question is whether it is just—that is, biblically just. Does it demonstrate love for our neighbors—both the accused and the victim—as ourselves? To answer that question, we need to examine this plea-bargaining system in light of the biblical components of justice that we considered in chapters 4–8.

Accuracy. As we saw in chapter 4, a biblically just legal system must be committed to accuracy. Before reading this chapter, you might have been inclined to believe that plea bargains increase the accuracy in the criminal justice system. If a defendant admits under oath in court that he committed the crime, doesn't that give us reason to have confidence that he is in fact guilty? Absent the coercion to plead guilty, this might be a reasonable conclusion. But the plea-bargaining system, especially when combined with the bail process and detestable jail conditions, is enormously coercive. We know as a fact that innocent people plead guilty. I recounted some examples at the beginning of this chapter. Statistics from the National Registry of Exonerations reveal that, since 1989, 24 percent of defendants who have been exonerated after conviction of crimes they did not commit were convicted by their own guilty pleas.[60] Subsequently discovered evidence, such as DNA, proved that they did not commit the crime to which they had pled guilty.[61]

Why would an innocent person plead guilty? One answer is because of the trial penalty, particularly when combined with a lack of confidence that the truth would prevail at trial (future chapters will discuss the basis for this lack of confidence). And the pressure to plead guilty despite innocence is especially worrisome in misdemeanor cases where incarceration prior to trial likely means the defendant has already served whatever sentence he or she would likely receive after trial if convicted. Recent research seems to confirm this concern.[62]

60 "Exonerations by State," The National Registry of Exonerations, University of Michigan, accessed April 8, 2023, https://www.law.umich.edu/special/exoneration/Pages/Exonerations-in-the-United-States-Map.aspx.
61 Of the first 250 people exonerated by DNA evidence, sixteen had pled guilty. Brandon L. Garrett, *Convicting the Innocent: Where Criminal Prosecutions Go Wrong* (Cambridge, MA: Harvard University Press, 2011), 7, 26–27, 150–53.
62 "Almost eighty percent of the misdemeanor exonerations we know about are from convictions based on guilty pleas." Samuel R. Gross, "Errors in Misdemeanor Adjudication," *Boston University Law Review* 98, no. 3 (2018): 1009, https://www.bu.edu/bulawreview/files/2018/06/GROSS.pdf. A large-scale study in Harris County, Texas, showed that conviction rates, particularly through

Maybe you are nonetheless confident that the vast majority of those who plead guilty are guilty. But "vast majority" is not the appropriate standard of justice, at least not for the Christian. The proper test is whether the system uses "all reasonable means" to avoid false convictions. And therein lies the problem. The plea-bargaining system does not just pressure the *guilty* to accept the plea deal. The pressure to plead guilty is brought to bear on *everyone* who is charged, the guilty and the innocent alike, because the prosecutor thinks that everyone he or she charged is guilty. That is presumably why the prosecutor charged them all in the first place. (We would have another problem entirely if the prosecutor is charging people he or she does not think are guilty.) But even if a prosecutor sincerely believes in the charges brought, prosecutors are not infallible. As we discussed in chapter 5, accuracy depends on process. The American process for testing the truth of the prosecutor's allegations to sort out the mistaken charges against the innocent is the jury trial. The biblically required process is likewise some version of a trial (Prov. 18:17).

Prosecutors, however, are pressuring everyone who is charged to cut their losses, waive their right to a trial, and plead guilty to some lesser charge with a shorter sentence. If these were uncoerced decisions, we might be able to rely on the accuracy of the resulting guilty pleas. But the pressure to plead—whether the economic impact of pretrial detention or threats of stiffer sentences after trial—creates an enormous risk that the innocent among those charged, even if it is only a few of them, will be coerced into pleading guilty as well. If you think I must be exaggerating, then don't take my word for it. Justice Antonin Scalia, after twenty-five years on the Supreme Court, observed that the American system of plea bargaining "presents grave risk of prosecutorial overcharging that effectively compels an innocent defendant to avoid massive risk by pleading guilty to a lesser offense."[63]

There is another sense in which plea bargaining distorts accuracy. By allowing a guilty defendant the benefit of a plea bargain to a lesser charge, the system misrepresents the seriousness of what the defendant actually did to the victim. We see this most egregiously in the case of sex crimes

---

guilty pleas, decreased significantly after the county revised its bail practices to allow for greater pretrial release. Paul Heaton, *The Effects of Misdemeanor Bail Reform* (Quattrone Center for the Fair Administration of Justice, August 16, 2022), 20, https://www.law.upenn.edu/.

63 Lafler v. Cooper, 566 U.S. 156, 185 (2012) (Scalia, J., dissenting).

and domestic violence. Sexual abuse of children results in a plea bargain to "child endangerment." Domestic violence against a spouse is disposed of through a guilty plea to "disorderly conduct." It is understandable at times why these cases are resolved as they are, given the trauma the victims face if they are needed to testify at trial. But these plea deals violate the biblical principles of accuracy. They tell a lie to society about what really happened, the trauma actually inflicted, and the damage often irreparably imposed.

Due Process. The pretrial detention system also raises questions of due process and, as a result, affects accuracy. The Supreme Court has justified pretrial detention on the fiction that it is regulatory rather than punitive.[64] The truth, as we saw in chapter 2, is that jailing someone is an act of actual or threatened physical force, and this is no less true because of the legal label applied to that force.

The biblical justice issue this raises is that the pretrial jailing—the physical force—generally occurs without any meaningful process. The defendant has no constitutional right to an attorney to assist him or her at the bail hearing. None of the witnesses making the accusation testify at and are subject to cross-examination at the bail hearing. And there is no requirement of proof beyond a reasonable doubt at the bail hearing. In short, something far less than "all reasonable means" is being used to ensure that we are not locking up someone—who may be innocent—for months or years on end.

At the same time, there is a very real issue in some cases that releasing the defendant prior to trial will endanger public safety. In those instances, it may be proper to think about pretrial detention more as an act of self-defense or defense of another, and there is a long history of Christian thought to guide us here. But the use of physical force even in defense of another is a narrow exception to the biblical condemnation of physical violence, and even then it is one of last resort.[65] There is no serious argument, much less empirical evidence, that locking up hundreds of thousands of people prior to trial for drug possession, property crimes, and traffic violations comes

<hr />

64 The fact that time spent in pretrial detention is treated as punishment under a "time served" plea agreement puts the lie to the notion that the pretrial detention was only "regulatory." Hessick, *Punishment without Trial*, 84.
65 Paul Ramsey, *War and the Christian Conscience: How Shall Modern War Be Conducted Justly?* (Durham, NC: Duke University Press, 1961), 40–45.

218 AMERICAN CRIMINAL JUSTICE

anywhere near meeting the biblical standard for the use of force in self-defense or defense of another.[66]

Proportionality. But there is a more fundamental justice issue with plea bargaining that should make everyone oppose it. As practiced in the United States today, plea bargaining is premised on disproportionate, and thus unjust, sentences. It thrives on either actual or threatened injustice in sentencing.

Take the case of Pamela Moses, who was sentenced to six years in prison as the result of a jury trial on a charge of voter fraud after she turned down a no-jail misdemeanor plea bargain. It simply cannot be the case that both no jail time and six years in prison are just—meaning, proportionate—sentences for her offense. Those are mutually exclusive sentencing options. If six years in prison were the just sentence, then a no-jail plea bargain was unjust even if the defendant was willing to plead guilty. If instead a misdemeanor conviction with no jail time were the just sentence, then it should have been the sentence regardless of whether the conviction was rendered by guilty plea or jury trial. Either the plea bargain offer was unduly lenient, or the post-trial sentence was unduly harsh. But both outcomes, given how widely different they are, cannot be just ones.

In other words, plea bargains create injustice even in those cases where the defendant is guilty, and they risk injustice when the defendant is not guilty. Either the plea agreement results in a disproportionately lenient sentence being imposed or, if the sentence under the plea agreement was justly proportionate, the guilty plea was extracted with a threat of an unjustly severe sentence. The former outcome is unjust on its own terms because it is a disproportionate sentence. As Justice Scalia explains, "For guilty defendants [plea bargaining] often—perhaps usually—results in a sentence well below what the law prescribes for the actual crime." The latter outcome creates a risk that, as Justice Scalia describes it, "effectively compels" the defendant to plead guilty without regard to guilt to avoid an even more unjust outcome.[67] In either case, this plea-bargaining process is not morally defensible, at least not if the moral standard is one of biblical justice.

---

66 To the contrary, a large-scale study of recidivism rates after Harris County, Texas, revised its pretrial bail policy concluded that recidivism went down when bail practices were reformed to increase the pretrial release rate. Heaton, *The Effects of Misdemeanor Bail Reform*, 22–24.

67 Lafler v. Cooper, 566 U.S. 156, 185 (2012) (Scalia, J., dissenting).

Impartiality. Underlying both the accuracy and proportionality critiques of the plea-bargaining system is the issue of wealth. Those mired in poverty do not have attorneys to represent them at their bail hearings. The poor in society cannot make bail and are, as a result, detained prior to trial. The impoverished cannot hire an attorney and instead wait months in jail to meet with a public defender only to be told that a trial will be even months later. The already destitute suffer life-wrecking financial consequences from pretrial detention. Thus, the poor feel enormous financial pressure to take the plea bargain, guilty or not, and move on with life, all the while unaware that the guilty plea they signed up for will result in a conviction that compounds their financial struggles for the rest of their lives as they are denied jobs, public assistance, educational opportunities, and housing because of a criminal record. It is factually undeniable that there are two systems of justice in America, one for the poor and another for the rich. Lady Justice is not blind, and her scales are not even.

———

The American system of plea bargaining is unjust. It is designed to coerce people out of their right to trial, and it does so through disproportionate sentences and inordinate financial pressure on the poor. Unsurprisingly, the result is that innocent people plead guilty to crimes they didn't commit. In short, the system fails every element of biblical justice: accuracy, due process, impartiality, and proportionality. And for operating this system of injustice, no government official is held accountable when the innocent are convicted.

This isn't to suggest that plea bargaining as a concept is categorically unjust. But our society and our legal system have come to accept a particular form of plea bargaining that, while perhaps efficient, does not measure up to the biblical standards of justice. That is a system Christians should reject. In fact, it's a system that Christians should, in the pursuit of justice, press to reform. By highlighting the flaws in the American system of bail and plea bargaining, I have attempted to point the way toward needed reform. But the precise contours of those reforms are matters of prudence over which Christians of good faith can and will disagree. Scripture dictates the standard of justice but not the specifics of its practice. Those are left to us to work out in our day, in our context, and in love of our neighbors.

12

Jury Selection

EVEN WITH ALL THE GUILTY PLEAS, thousands of criminal defendants across the United States still go to trial every year. The US Constitution guarantees that, at least in serious criminal cases, those trials will be "public," before an "impartial jury," and in the locality where the crime was committed.[1] This is what we commonly refer to as the right to a trial before a jury of your peers.[2]

Not every country affords a criminal defendant the right to a trial by jury. Even many modern, industrial countries do not have jury trials. In some, judges hear the evidence and deliver the verdict in criminal cases. In the United States, a judge presides over the courtroom, rendering rulings on objections to evidence and on the law about which the jury will be instructed. The decision as to whether the defendant committed the crime, however, is the jury's alone to make.

The theory behind the jury trial, at least in the United States, is one of both democratic participation and restraint on government overreach. As noted in chapter 9, jury service allows citizens to participate in government through their deliberation and voting on a verdict. At the same time, the right to trial by jury was, in Thomas Jefferson's view, "the only anchor ever yet imagined by man, by which a government can be held to the principles of

---

1 U.S. Const. art. III, § 2; U.S. Const. amend. IV; Duncan v. Louisiana, 391 U.S. 145, 156 (1968) (jury trial right applies to state criminal cases); Baldwin v. New York, 399 U.S. 66, 69 (1970) (plurality) (the right to jury trial applies in any case where the charged offense could result in a sentence of more than six months imprisonment).

2 It was not until 1975 that the Supreme Court held that these "peers" included women. Taylor v. Louisiana, 419 U.S. 522, 531 (1975).

its constitution."[3] A legislature can pass an unconstitutional law, a prosecutor can charge you with violating that unconstitutional law, and a judge can hold a trial on the charge that you violated the unconstitutional law—but none of that will result in your conviction if a jury of your peers refuses to return a guilty verdict. Jurors are the Constitution's backstop. Or as the US Supreme Court would later say, "Providing an accused with the right to be tried by a jury of his peers gave him an inestimable safeguard against the corrupt or overzealous prosecutor and against the compliant, biased, or eccentric judge."[4]

But a jury does more than protect against lawlessness. The jury serves as a check against callousness. The jury trial system removes the decision to pass judgment from the hands of professionals who could easily become jaded by their constant interaction with the criminally accused. The English writer G. K. Chesterton (1874–1936) explains the danger of a professional class enforcing the criminal law this way:

> It is a terrible business to mark a man out for the vengeance of men. But it is a thing to which a man can grow accustomed, as he can to other terrible things. . . . And the horrible thing about all legal officials, even the best, about all judges, magistrates, barristers, detectives, and policemen, is not that they are wicked (some of them are good), not that they are stupid (several of them are quite intelligent), it is simply that they have got used to it. Strictly they do not see the prisoner in the dock; all they see is the usual man in the usual place. They do not see the awful court of judgment; they only see their own workshop.[5]

Thus, to avoid the danger of familiarity, Chesterton argues, juries are better suited to decide criminal cases than are legal professionals. What the judge has become accustomed to, a jury of average and untrained citizens sees with fresh eyes. "Our civilisation has decided, and very justly decided, that determining the guilt or innocence of men is a thing too important to be

3   Letter from Thomas Jefferson to Thomas Paine, July 11, 1789, in *The Writings of Thomas Jefferson*, vol. 7, ed. Albert Ellery Bergh (Washington, DC: Thomas Jefferson Memorial Association, 1904), 408.

4   Duncan v. Louisiana, 391 U.S. 145, 156 (1968).

5   G. K. Chesterton, "The Twelve Men," in *Tremendous Trifles* (New York: Dodd, Mead and Company, 1920), 85–86.

trusted to trained men. . . . [W]hen it wishes anything done which is really serious, it collects twelve of the ordinary men standing around."[6]

The Mechanics

While juries are composed of ordinary citizens, juries are not simply selected randomly from those passing by on the streets in front of the courthouse. We don't, in fact, just collect twelve ordinary people standing around.

The selection of a jury in the United States is an elaborate process that begins with the calling of a panel of jurors to appear at the courthouse for jury service. Perhaps you have received in the mail a summons advising you of the day and time when you are to appear. Each state has different rules governing who is eligible for jury service. In my home state of Virginia, a group of commissioners creates a list of eligible jurors by compiling names from voter registration rolls, driver's license records, and property tax rolls. Virginia excludes from these lists those who have been convicted of felonies.[7] Some number of those whose names are included on this list receive a summons in the mail directing that they appear at the courthouse on a certain day. This does not mean that those who receive a summons will serve on a jury, only that they are eligible to be selected. The group of people summoned to the courthouse for possible jury service is known as a jury venire.

Once the jury venire assembles at the courthouse, the jurors will be divided into various groups and sent to different courtrooms, each where a trial is scheduled to occur. The prospective jurors will typically file into the pews in the back of the courtroom where the public sits to watch court proceedings. A clerk will then typically call the names of twelve[8] randomly selected prospective jurors to sit in the jury box.

At that point, either the judge or the lawyers will ask the prospective jurors questions. The potential jurors may have been asked to complete a written questionnaire in advance. The judge may have additional questions. Some judges let the lawyers, both the prosecutor and defense counsel,

---

6   Chesterton, "The Twelve Men," 86–87.
7   Va. Code Ann. §§ 8.01-338, 8.01-345.
8   The Supreme Court has held that a jury as small as six members is constitutional. Williams v. Florida, 399 U.S. 78, 103 (1970). Recently, Justice Gorsuch has called the ruling in *Williams* into question. Khorrami v. Arizona, 143 S. Ct. 22 (2022) (Gorsuch, J., dissenting from denial of certiorari).

ask questions directly of the jurors. These written and oral questions are designed to determine whether these prospective jurors have biases that disqualify them from serving as jurors in that particular case. Maybe they know one of the parties or witnesses. Maybe they know one of the lawyers or the police officer involved. Maybe they know the victim. Maybe they were themselves a victim of a similar crime such that it would be hard to view the evidence objectively. Whatever the issue, the judge and the lawyers are trying to sort out whether there is "cause" for excluding some of the potential jurors from serving in that case.

If any of the twelve prospective jurors in the jury box is excluded for cause, he or she will be excused and replaced in the jury box by another member of the jury venire sitting in the courtroom pews. The new prospective juror will then be questioned to determine if he or she should be excused for cause.

Once the jury box is filled with twelve jurors with no cause to excuse them, the lawyers for both the prosecution and the defense typically have some number of "peremptory" challenges they can use as to those jurors. Peremptory challenges are different than cause challenges in that no reason needs to be offered for using a peremptory challenge against a prospective juror. Maybe the prospective juror was wearing a pro-law enforcement T-shirt. That's not cause for excusing the juror if he convinced the judge he could be fair, but the defendant might not want that person serving as a juror. So defense counsel could use a peremptory challenge against that prospective juror and remove him from the jury. Another prospective juror might have mentioned that she had a boyfriend who was mistreated by the police one time. But she too promised she could set that aside and be fair in this case so that the judge could decline to remove her for cause. The prosecutor, however, might be unconvinced and so could use a peremptory challenge to remove that potential juror.

The jurors against whom peremptory challenges are used would then be replaced with another member of the venire patiently waiting in the pews. The process would then repeat itself until both sides use all their peremptory challenges and a jury is selected. At that point, the remaining members of the jury venire would be sent home, and the lucky twelve jurors in the jury box would be sworn in. This select group of jurors is known as a petit jury, and they are the ones who will render a verdict in the case.

History of Exclusion

This process of randomly selecting a jury venire and then, from that venire, selecting petit jurors who could be impartial is intended to, as Jefferson and Chesterton noted, protect the accused from the government. But that purpose can be frustrated if the juror selection process is corrupted by the government. "By compromising the representative quality of the jury," the US Supreme Court would later acknowledge, "discriminatory selection procedures make juries ready weapons for officials to oppress those accused individuals who by chance are numbered among unpopular or inarticulate minorities."[9]

American history following the Civil War proved this to be true. As we saw in chapter 9, Southern states weaponized all-White juries to facilitate the over-prosecution of Black people and the under-prosecution of White people. If Black citizens could be categorically excluded from juries, if the jury venire was not fully representative of the community, if it was something less than a jury of the defendant's peers, then outcomes in cases could be skewed.

In 1880, the US Supreme Court ruled that a West Virginia state law that by its terms limited jury service to White men was an unconstitutional violation of the Fourteenth Amendment's equal protection guarantee.[10] That same year the court also ruled in a case from Delaware that, even if state law allowed for the service of Black men on juries, it would violate the equal protection guarantee if state officials compiling lists of prospective jurors excluded Black men from those lists because of their race.[11]

States officials still wishing to exclude Black men from jury service quickly devised ways to evade the Supreme Court's decisions. As discussed in chapter 9, a series of state constitutional conventions across the South around the turn of the twentieth century resulted in amendments to those states' constitutions that banned felons not only from voting in elections but also from serving on juries. The practical effect of this was that racist prosecutors were incentivized to use their prosecutorial discretion to target Black people when deciding who to charge with crimes, knowing that each Black man convicted would be excluded from future

9   Batson v. Kentucky, 476 U.S. 79, 86n8 (1986).
10 Strauder v. West Virginia, 100 U.S. 303, 308 (1880).
11 Neal v. Delaware, 103 U.S. 370, 394 (1880).

jury service, making it that much easier to secure a Whiter jury in the next trial. Each successive trial and conviction made it more likely that the jury in the next trial would be more White and thus more likely to convict the next Black defendant.

But the exclusion of felons from jury service was not the only means by which Black Americans were being excluded from jury service. Even when state juror qualification laws made no reference to race, state officials responsible for selecting jurors continued their practice of systematically excluding Black men from lists of prospective jurors. In case after case in the late nineteenth and early twentieth centuries, the US Supreme Court was required to intervene and address this noxious practice.

For example, Alabama passed a statute providing that the roll of prospective jurors was to be composed of "all male citizens of the county who are generally reputed to be honest and intelligent men." When the preliminary list of qualified jurors was prepared based on voter registration rolls and property tax records, the notation "col." (colored) was placed next to the name of each man who was Black. A final jury roll was then prepared from that list. As a result of this process and even though Black residents made up about 18 percent of the population of one particular county, "within the memory of witnesses long resident there, no negro had ever served on a jury in that county or had been called for such service." The jury commissioner testified that this result was not because of racial discrimination but rather because he was unaware of any Black residents in his county who had a qualifying reputation. The Supreme Court rejected this excuse. The year was 1935—fifty-five years after the court had declared unconstitutional the practice of excluding prospective jurors on the basis of race.[12]

In the decades that followed, the Supreme Court was repeatedly called on to review and reverse criminal cases involving racial discrimination in jury selection, including a 1938 case from Kentucky, a 1939 case from Louisiana, a 1940 case from Texas, a 1942 case from Texas, a 1947 case from Mississippi, a 1950 case from Texas, a 1953 case from Georgia, a 1954

---

12 Norris v. Alabama, 294 U.S. 587, 590, 594–99 (1935). The defendant in this case, Clarence Norris, was one of the nine Black men charged with the rape of a White woman on a train in Alabama. The case has since become famous as the case of "the Scottsboro boys." James Goodman, *Stories of Scottsboro* (New York: Vintage Books, 1995).

case from Texas, two 1955 cases from Georgia, a 1958 case from Louisiana, a 1962 conviction in California, and a 1964 case from North Carolina.[13] In one of those cases, the jury commissioners responsible for compiling juror lists maintained that they did not discriminate based on race but rather chose prospective jurors "with whom they were personally acquainted," and they claimed they didn't know any qualified Black people. The Supreme Court rejected this argument, explaining that it was the commissioners' "duty to familiarize themselves fairly with the qualifications of the eligible jurors of the county without regard to race or color."[14] In another of the cases, the names of White jurors were written on white slips of paper and the names of Black jurors written on yellow slips of paper, all of which were placed together in a box. The judge then randomly selected slips from the box to compile a list of prospective jurors. Remarkably, this "random" process resulted in the selection of sixty white slips and no yellow slips.[15] In case after case, the Supreme Court found violations of the Fourteenth Amendment's equal protection guarantee based on racial discrimination against jurors.

In 1967, the Supreme Court took up the case of *Whitus v. Georgia* in which, in the court's exasperated words, it "once again" was "confronted with the question of racial discrimination in the selection of" criminal juries. The defendants in that case had been convicted of murder in a trial before an all-White jury. The six jury commissioners compiled lists of prospective jurors using a county tax digest that was "in one volume, but was segregated into two sections—one for white and the other for Negro taxpayers." The commissioners insisted that they did not take race into account when selecting jurors eligible for the venire, but other witnesses testified that no Black man "had ever served on juries within the memory of witnesses" despite that 45 percent of the county population was Black. The commissioners explained that they

13 Hale v. Kentucky, 303 U.S. 613 (1938); Pierre v. Louisiana, 306 U.S. 354 (1939); Smith v. Texas, 311 U.S. 128 (1940); Hill v. Texas, 316 U.S. 400 (1942); Patton v. Mississippi, 332 U.S. 463 (1947); Cassell v. Texas, 339 U.S. 282 (1950); Avery v. Georgia, 345 U.S. 559 (1953); Hernandez v. Texas, 347 U.S. 475 (1954); Williams v. Georgia, 349 U.S. 375 (1955); Reece v. Georgia, 350 U.S. 85 (1955); Eubanks v. Louisiana, 356 U.S. 584 (1958); Vasquez v. Hillery, 474 U.S. 254 (1986); Arnold v. North Carolina, 376 U.S. 773 (1964).
14 Cassell v. Texas, 339 U.S. 282, 287–89 (1950) (plurality).
15 Avery v. Georgia, 345 U.S. 559, 560–61 (1953).

had simply compiled a list of "those persons whom they knew personally from their respective communities." In Whitus's case, ninety jurors had been selected for the venire, of which only seven were Black and none of whom were selected for the trial jury. Given this evidence of racial discrimination, the court once again found an Equal Protection Clause violation and reversed the convictions.[16]

Try, Try Again

Faced with this string of Supreme Court precedents overturning state efforts to exclude Black citizens from juries, prosecutors devised yet another way to do so—the race-based peremptory challenge. The court was confronted with this practice in a 1965 case from Alabama in which Robert Swain, a nineteen-year-old Black man, was sentenced to death by an all-White jury for the rape of a White teenager.[17] The court acknowledged that peremptory challenges were "frequently exercised" based on race but declined to "hold that the striking of Negroes in a particular case is a denial of equal protection of the laws." As the court saw it, "in the quest for an impartial and qualified jury, Negro and white, Protestant and Catholic, are alike subject to being challenged without cause."[18]

This reasoning was, of course, nonsense. Black people across the South were still struggling even to make it on to jury venires in small numbers, much less in numbers proportionate to their representation in the population at large. A prosecutor, armed with even a few peremptory challenges could easily remove from the petit jury those few Black people on the jury venire. In fact, as of 1965, no Black person had, since 1950, served on a criminal jury in Talladega County, Alabama, where Robert Swain was tried.[19] There was no comparable risk that all Protestant or White people would be uniformly stricken from all petit juries.

Not surprisingly, prosecutors seized on this work-around, and "the practice of peremptorily eliminating blacks from petit juries in cases with black

16 Whitus v. Georgia, 385 U.S. 545, 546, 548–50 (1967).
17 Swain v. State, 156 So.2d 368 (Ala. 1963); Swain v. Alabama, 380 U.S. 202, 231 (1965) (Goldberg, J., dissenting).
18 Swain v. Alabama, 380 U.S. 202, 220–21 (1965). After years of litigation, including another return to the US Supreme Court, Swain's death sentence was converted to a sentence of life imprisonment. Swain v. State, 274 So.2d 305, 306 (Ala. 1973).
19 Swain v. Alabama, 380 U.S. 202, 205, 226 (1965).

defendants remain[ed] widespread" for the next twenty years.[20] But in 1986, the Supreme Court revisited the issue in the case of *Batson v. Kentucky*. James Batson, a Black man, had been charged with burglary and receipt of stolen goods; he was tried in a Jefferson County (Louisville) court. Four Black citizens were on the jury venire in his case, but the prosecutor struck them all using his peremptory challenges. After a short trial, Batson was convicted by the all-White jury. He appealed, arguing that the prosecutor's elimination of all the Black veniremen in his case violated his right to equal protection of the law.[21]

This time, the Supreme Court agreed. The court acknowledged that the "exclusion of black citizens from service as jurors constitutes a primary example of the evil the Fourteenth Amendment was designed to cure." Though no states had laws in 1986 precluding Black men and women from serving on juries, ensuring the equal protection of laws requires more than just reading statutory language. It also requires that judges "look beyond the face of the statute" at the juror selection "practices." A state may not, the court concluded, "draw up its jury lists by neutral procedures but then resort to discrimination at other stages in the selection process."[22]

Accordingly, the court ruled—one hundred and twenty-one years after the Civil War ended—that "the Equal Protection Clause forbids the prosecutor to challenge potential jurors solely on account of their race or on the assumption that black jurors as a group will be unable impartially to consider the State's case against a black defendant."[23] Two justices dissented.[24] The court, however, tempered its ruling by holding that peremptory challenges to Black jurors were still permissible so long as some race-neutral reason could be offered for striking the juror,[25] an exception that Justice Thurgood Marshall predicted would swallow the rule.[26]

---

20 Batson v. Kentucky, 476 U.S. 79, 101 (1986) (White, J., concurring).
21 Though the *Batson* case was not a federal one, the US Department of Justice filed a brief in the case given that the Supreme Court's decision would inevitably apply to federal prosecutors as well. Remarkably, the Department argued that race-based peremptory challenges by a prosecutor in a single trial are not unconstitutional. Brief of the United States as Amicus Curiae Supporting Affirmance, Batson v. Kentucky, No. 84-6263 (October Term, 1985), 4–5.
22 Batson v. Kentucky, 476 U.S. 79, 85, 88 (1986).
23 Batson v. Kentucky, 476 U.S. 79, 89 (1986).
24 Batson v. Kentucky, 476 U.S. 79, 112 (1986) (Burger, C.J., dissenting); 134 (Rehnquist, J., dissenting).
25 Batson v. Kentucky, 476 U.S. 79, 98 (1986).
26 Batson v. Kentucky, 476 U.S. 79, 106 (1986) (Marshall, J., concurring).

Although the *Batson* decision settled the question whether prosecutors could strike Black jurors to facilitate the conviction of Black defendants, it left open the question whether White defendants could, through their attorneys, strike Black jurors to facilitate the acquittal of White defendants, particularly in cases of White-on-Black crime. In *Georgia v. McCollum*, a case in which several White defendants were charged with physically assaulting a Black man and woman, the Supreme Court finally ruled that defense attorneys were likewise precluded from striking jurors based on their race. The year was 1992. Still, two justices dissented.[27]

Not Just History

The ruling in *McCollum* was handed down by the Supreme Court when I was a college student, three days after I turned twenty years old. It is disturbing enough that not until my adult years did Black men and women in the United States finally secure the right to serve on criminal juries without regard to their race. More troubling is the fact that prosecutors continue to ignore these Supreme Court rulings.

Another study by Professor David Baldus (of *McCleskey v. Kemp* fame) showed that, after the *Batson* decision, prosecutors in Philadelphia struck 51 percent of Black prospective jurors as compared to 26 percent of non-Black jurors.[28] In 1997, a video surfaced of a training session for new prosecutors in Philadelphia in which, after *Batson*, an assistant district attorney told the recruits, "Let's face it, the blacks from the low income areas are less likely to convict. I understand it. There's a resentment for law enforcement. There's a resentment for authority. And as a result, you don't want those people on your jury."[29] In 2018, a Pennsylvania appellate court reversed a 2015 murder conviction from Philadelphia on the ground that the prosecution "struck at least one juror with discriminatory intent."[30] Studies of jury se-

27 Georgia v. McCollum, 505 U.S. 42, 59 (1992); 62 (O'Connor, J., dissenting); 69 (Scalia, J., dissenting).

28 David C. Baldus, George Woodworth, David Zuckerman, Neil Alan Weiner, Barbara Broffitt, "The Use of Peremptory Challenges in Capital Murder Trials: A Legal and Empirical Analysis," *University of Pennsylvania Journal of Constitutional Law* 3, no. 1 (2001): 53, https://scholarship .law.upenn.edu/jcl/vol3/iss1/2/.

29 Barry Siegel, "Storm Still Lingers over Defense Attorney's Training Video," *Los Angeles Times*, April 29, 1997, https://www.latimes.com/. To watch the entire training video, see "Jury Selection with Jack McMahon," YouTube video, April 6, 2015, https://www.youtube.com/.

30 Commonwealth v. Edwards, 177 A.3d 963, 967 (Pa. Sup. Ct. 2018).

lection in other states—including Louisiana, North Carolina, California, Arizona, and New York—have shown similar discrimination.[31] One study from Alabama showed that, between 2005 and 2009, prosecutors "used peremptory strikes to remove 80% of the African Americans from jury service" in death penalty cases.[32]

In recent years, the US Supreme Court has repeatedly overturned death sentences after state supreme courts ignored obvious *Batson* violations by state prosecutors.[33] One of those cases in particular shows the lengths to which prosecutors still go to remove Black jurors. In 1996, Curtis Flowers, a Black man, was charged with murdering four people in a furniture store in Winona, Mississippi. The state sought the death penalty for these crimes, and the case went to trial in October 1997. During jury selection, the prosecutor struck all five of the prospective Black jurors, and Flowers was tried by an all-White jury.[34] After a five-day trial, the jury found him guilty and sentenced him to death.[35] On appeal, the Mississippi Supreme Court reversed the conviction and sentence, finding that the prosecutor had engaged in "numerous instances of prosecutorial misconduct" during the trial. Because the court reversed on that ground, it did not address Flowers's claim that the prosecutor had engaged in *Batson* violations during jury selection.[36]

Flowers was retried in March 1999, with the State represented by the same prosecutor who had engaged in misconduct at the first trial.[37] The prosecutor again used his peremptory challenges against all five of the Black jurors on the new jury venire, but the judge ruled that one of

31 Ronald F. Wright, Kami Chavis, and Gregory S. Parks, "The Jury Sunshine Project: Jury Selection Data as a Political Issue," *University of Illinois Law Review* 2018, no. 4 (2018): 1425, https://www.illinoislawreview.org/wp-content/uploads/2018/10/Wright.pdf; Catherine M. Grosso and Barbara O'Brien, "A Stubborn Legacy: The Overwhelming Importance of Race in Jury Selection in 173 Post-*Batson* North Carolina Capital Trials," *Iowa Law Review* 97, no. 5 (2012): 1533, http://dx.doi.org/10.17613/hnk1-1687; Anna Offit, "Race-Conscious Jury Selection," *Ohio State Law Journal* 82, no. 2 (2021): 239–40, https://ssrn.com/abstract=3587892.

32 *Illegal Racial Discrimination in Jury Selection: A Continuing Legacy* (Montgomery, AL: Equal Justice Initiative, 2010), 14, https://eji.org.

33 Flowers v. Mississippi, 139 S. Ct. 2228 (2019); Foster v. Chatman, 136 S. Ct. 1737 (2016); Snyder v. Louisiana, 552 U.S. 472 (2008).

34 Flowers v. Mississippi, 139 S. Ct. 2228, 2236 (2019).

35 Flowers v. State, 773 So.2d 309, 313–15 (Miss. 2000).

36 Flowers v. State, 773 So.2d 309, 317, 327 (Miss. 2000).

37 Flowers v. State, 842 So.2d 531, 535 (Miss. 2003).

those strikes was racially motivated and sat that Black juror on the petit jury.[38] Flowers was again convicted and sentenced to death at his second trial, but the Mississippi Supreme Court reversed the conviction on the ground that the same prosecutor had engaged in misconduct during that trial. Again, the court declined to rule on Flowers's *Batson* claim.[39]

Flowers was tried for a third time in February 2006. Fifteen Black men and women were among the members of the jury venire. The same prosecutor struck fifteen of the sixteen prospective Black jurors using his peremptory challenges, and Flowers was once again tried by a nearly all-White jury and was once again convicted and sentenced to death. The Mississippi Supreme Court again reversed the conviction and sentence, this time ruling that the prosecutor had violated *Batson* in striking the prospective Black jurors. In fact, the court stated that the evidence of racial discrimination by the prosecutor was "as strong . . . as we have ever seen in the context of a *Batson* challenge."[40]

Flowers was tried yet again in 2007, with the case ending in a mistrial because the jury was unable to reach a verdict. The jury also hung in Flowers's fifth trial in 2008. In the fourth trial, the prosecutor used his peremptory challenges against eleven Black prospective jurors, but five Black jurors were seated on the petit jury for that trial. Three Black jurors were seated on the petit jury for the fifth trial.[41]

A sixth trial of Flowers was held in June 2010. The same prosecutor yet again used his peremptory challenges to strike five of the six prospective Black jurors. Flowers was convicted and yet again sentenced to death. This time, however, the Mississippi Supreme Court upheld Flowers's conviction and death sentence by a 5–4 vote.[42]

At this point, the US Supreme Court took up Flowers's case and, in an opinion written by Justice Brett Kavanaugh in June 2019, the court over-

---

38 Flowers v. Mississippi, 139 S. Ct. 2228, 2236 (2019).

39 Flowers v. State, 842 So.2d 531, 538 (Miss. 2003).

40 Flowers v. State, 947 So.2d 910, 916, 935 (Miss. 2007); Flowers v. Mississippi, 139 S. Ct. 2228, 2237 (2019).

41 Flowers v. Mississippi, 139 S. Ct. 2228, 2237 (2019); Alissa Zhu, "Curtis Flowers: How a Mississippi Man Was Tried Six Times for the Same Murders," *Clarion-Ledger*, March 18, 2019, https://www.clarionledger.com/.

42 Flowers v. State, 240 So.3d 1082, 1092, 1122 (Miss. 2017); Flowers v. Mississippi, 139 S. Ct. 2228, 2237-38 (2019).

turned Flowers's conviction and sentence on the ground that the prosecutor had once again used his peremptory challenges to strike Black jurors based on their race. As the court noted, across six trials the prosecutor had used his peremptory challenges to strike forty-one of the forty-two Black prospective jurors eligible to be stricken.[43] The Supreme Court sent the case back to the trial court, at which point the State dropped the case entirely. Flowers was released from death row at the age of fifty after having spent twenty-three years in prison.[44] The prosecutor who engaged in the misconduct in Flowers's six trials was reelected to an eighth term as district attorney a few months later in November 2019.[45]

Despite this extraordinary intervention by the US Supreme Court, the practice of race-based jury selection continues. In 2022, at least five convictions—from Rhode Island, Illinois, Colorado, North Carolina, and Oregon—were reversed because prosecutors struck jurors based on their race.[46] Even today, Black people face a continuing struggle to participate in our democratic system of government through jury service, and Black defendants still must fight to have their cases decided by a jury drawn from their peers of all races.[47]

Biblical Justice?

You likely know at a visceral level that the exclusion of Black jurors based on their race is improper. What Scripture provides is a framework that we can use to put words to our instinct. This practice, past and present, of racially biased jury selection implicates all five of the biblical components of justice.

Impartiality. Most obviously, racial bias in jury selection raises questions about whether impartial justice is being distributed. Historically, at least,

---

43 Flowers v. Mississippi, 139 S. Ct. 2228, 2251 (2019).

44 Nicholas Bogel-Burroughs, "After 6 Murder Trials and Nearly 24 Years, Charges Dropped Against Curtis Flowers," *New York Times*, September 4, 2020, https://www.nytimes.com/.

45 Parker Yesko, "Will Doug Evans Face Accountability?," *American Public Media*, October 14, 2020, https://www.apmreports.org/.

46 Porter v. Coyne-Fague, 35 F.4th 68 (1st Cir. 2022); People v. Martin, No. 1-12-3561, slip. op. at 11 (Ill. App. Ct. May 24, 2022); People v. Johnson, 523 P.3d 992, 1004 (Colo. App. 2022); State v. Clegg, 867 S.E.2d 885 (N.C. 2022); State v. McWoods, 514 P.3d 1151 (Or. Ct. App. 2022).

47 For a comprehensive discussion of the history of racial discrimination in jury selection and how it continues even today, see *Race and the Jury: Illegal Discrimination in Jury Selection* (Montgomery, AL: Equal Justice Initiative, 2021), https://eji.org.

234 AMERICAN CRIMINAL JUSTICE

the practice of excluding Black people from criminal jury service was a means to subvert justice. Innocent Black people were over-prosecuted, and guilty White people were under-prosecuted. This history gives reason for concern that what is being sought by prosecutors and defense attorneys who engage in race-based jury strikes is something less than impartial justice.

Accuracy. Concerns about impartiality are, at bottom, concerns about accuracy. As the Philadelphia prosecutor said in the infamous training video, it's "ridiculous" for a prosecutor to select a "fair and impartial jury"; instead, he wanted jurors who will be "unfair and more likely to convict."[48] But "justice" that is not impartial is not just because it is not accurate—or at least is at severe risk of being inaccurate. Justice that is not impartial grants a preference to one side or the other that the facts do not warrant. In fact, the prosecutor in the training video fretted that smart, impartial jurors "will analyze the hell out of your case" and "take those words 'reasonable doubt,' and they actually try to think about them."[49] The concern, born out by American history, is that racially skewed juries deliver verdicts reflecting something less than the truth of what happened.

Due Process. Also bound up with the issue of accuracy is that of due process. An innocent defendant, faced with a trial penalty, may accept a plea bargain if he or she doubts that a fair trial process is available. As the Supreme Court acknowledged in *Batson*, jury "selection procedures that purposefully exclude black persons from juries undermine public confidence in the fairness of our system of justice."[50] And this perceived unfairness only serves to exacerbate the pressure to accept a plea bargain.

Proportionality. Even in those instances where the defendant is guilty, a jury selected in a racially biased way may be willing to deliver a sentence that is too harsh or too lenient depending on the race of either the defendant or the victim. We will consider this issue in chapter 18 in the context of the death penalty. But suffice it to say that there is abundant statistical evidence to confirm that racial considerations impact the imposition of death sentences. Taking race into account in the selection of juries raises concerns that the juries will likewise take race into account in the selection of an appropriate sentence.

---

48 "Jury Selection with Jack McMahon," YouTube video, April 6, 2015, https://www.youtube.com/.
49 "Jury Selection with Jack McMahon," YouTube video.
50 Batson v. Kentucky, 476 U.S. 79, 87 (1986).

Accountability. That race-based jury selection practices have continued in the years since the *Batson* decision also raises questions of accountability. The law, as interpreted by the US Supreme Court, provides prosecutors who engage in this conduct with absolute immunity from federal civil rights lawsuits for money damages.[51] Other means of accountability are still available but go unused. Why, for example, is a prosecutor who on multiple occasions engaged in race-based jury selection not disciplined by the state bar that licenses lawyers?[52] Why is such a prosecutor reelected to office? And, given that such conduct is a federal crime,[53] why is he or she not prosecuted criminally?

———

In May 2020, Archie Williams appeared on an episode of the television reality show *America's Got Talent.* In January 1983, Archie, then age twenty-two, was arrested and charged with raping a White woman in her home. He was tried, convicted, and sentenced to life in prison without the possibility of parole. He spent nearly thirty-seven years in prison for that crime.

And he was innocent. In 2019, fingerprint evidence proved that Archie had been wrongly convicted for what he rightly described as "somebody else's crime."[54] The day Archie was exonerated, the district attorney stated in court, "As a representative of the state, I apologize."[55]

---

51 Imbler v. Pachtman, 424 U.S. 409 (1976) (absolute prosecutorial immunity).

52 I located one example of a trial judge personally sanctioning prosecutors who engaged in such conduct in a criminal trial. Brian Rogers, "DA Lykos Says Two Were Wrong to Deny Black Jurors," *Houston Chronicle,* March 26, 2009, https://www.chron.com. However, I was unable to locate a single instance of a prosecutor being professionally disciplined by a state bar association for a *Batson* violation. Parker Yesko, "Why Don't Prosecutors Get Disciplined?," *American Public Media,* September 18, 2018, https://www.apmreports.org/. In 1998, the New Jersey Advisory Committee on Professional Ethics advised that *Batson* violations would not be deemed a basis for professional discipline. Opinion 658, *The Use of Peremptory Challenges to Exclude Minorities from Sitting on Jury,* 154 N.J.L.J. 434 (November 9, 1998). In January 2022, the Advisory Committee withdrew that opinion. Withdrawing Opinion 685 and Requesting Comments on Potential New Opinion (January 7, 2022), https://www.njcourts.gov/.

53 18 U.S.C. § 243.

54 You can watch Archie tell his story at "Archie Williams Free after 37 Years Wrongly-Imprisoned for Murder Rape—Sings for Justice!," YouTube video, May 22, 2020, https://www.youtube.com.

55 Thomas Fuller, "He Spent 36 Years behind Bars. A Fingerprint Database Cleared Him in Hours," *New York Times,* March 21, 2019, https://www.nytimes.com/.

Apologies are commendable. But how did this miscarriage of justice happen? Well, Archie is Black. At his trial in April 1983, the prosecutor used all thirteen of his peremptory challenges to strike prospective Black jurors, a practice the court allowed because Archie's case was tried three years before the Supreme Court's decision in *Batson*. The entirety of the evidence against Archie at trial was the testimony of the White victim identifying him as the rapist. She was mistaken.[56]

Thirty-seven years after his wrongful conviction, in his appearance on *America's Got Talent*, Archie sang. He explained to the show's judges that he would "pray and sing" during the dark times in prison. The song he chose for his appearance on the show that evening was Elton John's "Don't Let the Sun Go Down on Me." The lyrics Archie sang were haunting: "Losin' everything is like the sun goin' down on me."[57]

Would a different jury have reached a different result in Archie's case? Might the sun not have gone down on thirty-seven years of Archie's life? Tragically, we will never know.

---

56 State v. Williams, 458 So.2d 1315, 1324–25, 1331 (La. App. 1st Cir. 1984). As will be discussed in chap. 16, cross-racial eyewitness identification is notoriously unreliable.

57 "Don't Let the Sun Go Down on Me" by Elton John and Bernie Taupin, track 9 on *Caribou*, MCA Records, 1974. Reprinted by permission of Hal Leonard LLC.

13

Judges

NINA MORRISON GRADUATED FROM one of the nation's top law schools in 1998, and in 2002 she joined the Innocence Project to represent men and women convicted of heinous crimes they may not have committed. During her twenty-year career at the Innocence Project, Ms. Morrison helped free nearly thirty wrongly convicted people. Later in her career, while still working at the Innocence Project, Ms. Morrison advised newly elected district attorneys on their creation of conviction integrity units within their offices to review old cases for accuracy.

After more than twenty years as a practicing lawyer, Ms. Morrison was nominated to be a federal district court judge in New York City and, as with all nominees for federal judgeships, her nomination had to be considered and ultimately confirmed by the US Senate before she could take her seat on the bench. During Ms. Morrison's Senate confirmation hearing, her experience at the Innocence Project became a central focus of attention. One senator charged that rising crime rates in the United States were "the direct result of the policies you have spent your entire lifetime advocating." That senator went on to describe her as "yet another judge who will let more violent criminals go," while another senator attacked her for "encouraging defiance" by a convicted killer and asked her if she "knew better" than the prosecutor. Still another senator declared that he would not support judicial nominees who are "soft on crime and soft on criminals."[1]

1   "'Is Philadelphia More Safe or Less Safe?': Ted Cruz Grills Nominee on the Results of Philadelphia
    D.A.," YouTube video, February 16, 2022, https://www.youtube.com; "Senator Cotton Q&A
    During Senate Judiciary Committee Hearing," YouTube video, February 16, 2022, https://www

Rhetoric of this sort, while perhaps not surprising in our partisan moment, raises important questions about how we select judges and whether that process serves the ends of justice. Are we selecting judges in a way that will afford biblical justice to the criminally accused and the crime victim alike? Or are we instead stacking the deck before the trial ever begins?

Judicial Independence

Juries are not the only decision-makers in criminal cases. While jurors make the final decision as to guilt or innocence in most criminal cases, judges make numerous legal rulings along the way that affect the jury's verdict. Many of those decisions are ones in which the judge can choose any number of different approaches that are all lawful. Judges decide what evidence will be admitted, what arguments the lawyers can make to jurors, how long the parties will have to present their cases, and how the legal instructions to the jury will be phrased. Those discretionary decisions can make or break a case at times.

It is critical, then, that judges make those decisions without bias or favoritism. In particular, judges must make their decisions free from control by or the influence of the other branches of government. This is what political scientists refer to as an "independent judiciary."[2] In a similar vein, judges must be controlled by the law in rendering their decisions, something we refer to as the "rule of law." What "rules" in a court case is not the personality or preferences of the judge, nor the relationship the parties might have to the judge or others in positions of power. What rules, what governs, is the law. Legal disputes are decided by legal principles, not personalities. In the United States, ours is, in the words of founding father John Adams, "a government of laws and not of men."[3]

In the federal judicial system, one of the ways in which we attempt to ensure that judges rule without bias, favoritism, or influence is by provid-

---

.youtube.com; "'For That Reason Alone, I Cannot Support Your Nomination': Hawley Flat Out Rejects Biden Nominee," YouTube video, February 22, 2022, https://www.youtube.com.

2   Judicial independence was the topic of *Federalist*, no. 78 (Hamilton), accessed June 15, 2022, https://guides.loc.gov/.

3   Mass. Const. part 1, art. XXX. As Chief Justice John Marshall would later put it, "The Government of the United States has been emphatically termed a government of laws, and not of men." Marbury v. Madison, 5 U.S. (1 Cranch) 137, 163 (1803). For a discussion of the natural law (and Christian) roots of the rule of law, see Kody W. Cooper and Justin Buckley Dyer, *The Classical and Christian Origins of American Politics: Political Theology, Natural Law, and the American Founding* (New York: Cambridge University Press, 2022), 7–15.

ing them with a lifetime appointment. According to the US Constitution, federal judges, once appointed, serve in that role for life. They have no tenure, do not stand for reelection or reappointment, and have no mandatory retirement age. A judge can, of course, resign if he or she wishes. But federal judges cannot be removed from office except by impeachment for misconduct of some sort.[4] This life tenure protects the judge from fear that he or she will be removed from the bench for ruling in an unpopular way as the law requires. Life tenure protects the independence of the judiciary and, thus hopefully, the rule of law.

The US Constitution also provides federal judges with an additional guarantee to ensure their independence. Their pay cannot be reduced while they are in office. Life tenure would be little protection for judges if Congress could simply starve them out of the job by refusing to pay them. To avoid this type of financial pressure that could skew judicial decisions to politicians' liking, the Constitution protects both the tenure and the pay of federal judges.

Most state court judges, however, have no such protections. This is an important distinction because more than 97 percent of felony criminal cases in the United States are brought in state, not federal, courts.[5] In only three states do judges receive something approximating a lifetime appointment. In Rhode Island, the judges are appointed by the governor for a life term, while in Massachusetts and New Hampshire the judges are appointed for a term lasting until the mandatory retirement age of seventy. In every other state, judges are subject to some sort of removal that can put pressure on the evenhandedness of their rulings.[6]

Judicial Elections

Another important distinction between state and federal judges is that state court judges are frequently elected, not appointed. At the federal

4   U.S. Const. art. III.
5   State courts dispose of roughly two million felony cases each year, while federal courts handle about sixty thousand felony cases. "Trial Court Caseload Overview: Caseload Detail—Total Felony," CSP STAT Criminal, Court Statistics Project, accessed January 17, 2023, https://www .courtstatistics.org; *Fiscal Year 2021 Overview of Federal Criminal Cases* (US Sentencing Commission, April 2022), 3, https://www.ussc.gov/.
6   "Judicial Selection: An Interactive Map," Brennan Center for Justice, accessed March 1, 2022, http://judicialselectionmap.brennancenter.org.

level, judges are nominated by the president and then must be confirmed by the Senate. This is true not only of US Supreme Court justices, but also of judges on the federal appellate courts and district (trial) courts where most federal cases are decided. While the few dozen cases that make their way to the US Supreme Court each year attract outsized attention by lawyers and the public at large, the lower federal courts hear thousands of cases every year. And these judges too are protected with life tenure and against pay reductions.

The selection of judges by the president with confirmation by the Senate does not eliminate all concerns about independence. At times, concerns have arisen about unduly close relationships between the president and his nominee.[7] Lawyers nominated for federal judgeships are frequently pressed during confirmation hearings for their views on legal positions, which could impair their independence by committing them to positions before they actually hear cases. But these pressures are easily addressed. Judicial nominees, for example, regularly decline to state their positions on legal issues that may come before them, and this refusal has not hampered their confirmations.

In the state judicial system, however, the public pressure that can be brought to bear on judges is much greater, particularly in those states where judges are elected or, even if appointed, do not have lifetime appointments. State judicial candidates may, for instance, be pressured to reveal during the election how they would rule on legal issues they could confront in future cases, and it may not be a viable campaign strategy to evade such questions. Even if the campaign rhetoric does not rise to the level of forecasting legal rulings, there are abundant examples of judges running on "tough on crime" platforms,[8] which seems antithetical to the judicial obligation to treat the parties as equals and apply the law as written, rather than with an eye to a particular outcome.

---

7   Senator Leahy raised concerns about the judicial independence of President George W. Bush's nominee to the Supreme Court, Harriet Miers, who had served as White House Counsel. Similar questions about judicial independence were raised about a nominee by President Trump to serve on the United States Court of Appeals for the DC Circuit because he had worked in the White House Counsel's Office. President Lyndon Johnson and his Supreme Court nominee, Abe Fortas, were also accused of being too close to maintain independence.

8   Kate Berry, *How Judicial Elections Impact Criminal Cases* (Brennan Center for Justice, 2015), https://www.brennancenter.org/.

More concerning is the risk that a judge already on the bench might be influenced in his or her rulings out of fear that a ruling one way or the other will be used in an upcoming election. What judge running for reelection wants to defend a ruling in favor of a violent criminal defendant even if the law demanded that result? A variety of academic studies suggest that these sorts of concerns skew judicial decision-making.[9]

At a commonsense level, ask yourself the modified version of John Rawls's veil of ignorance question test that I proposed in chapter 7: If you might be on trial for your life, would you be comfortable having your case, especially a high-profile one, tried before a judge who was standing for election in a few months? Or how about before a judge who had announced during the election campaign that he or she would be "tough on crime"? It is under-standable why, if you were a crime victim, you would prefer that judge. But what if you didn't know in advance what your lot in life would be, whether victim or accused? From what Rawls called the original position, would you design a system of picking judges through elections with campaigns of this sort? And, if not, are we loving our neighbors as ourselves when we subject others to a system of justice administered by judges selected in this way?

In an effort to address the pressure that elections place on judicial rulings, some states passed rules that precluded prospective judges from announcing during a campaign their views on disputed legal issues. The US Supreme Court, however, concluded that rules of this sort are unconstitutional in that they restrict a candidate's free speech rights.[10] This creates a conundrum. The election gives judicial candidates a right to speak about the issues on which voters will vote. But what effect does this campaign speech have on the ability of criminal defendants to get a fair hearing unaffected by electoral concerns?

It's also important to see how judicial elections interact with felon disenfranchisement. As I explained in chapter 9, the United States has a long and racially tinged history of stripping convicted felons of the right to vote. The practice of felon disenfranchisement, whatever the motive

9 Joanna Shepherd and Michael S. Kang, "Skewed Justice: *Citizens United*, Television Advertis-ing and State Supreme Court Justices' Decisions in Criminal Cases" (American Constitution Society, 2014), https://www.acslaw.org; Travis N. Taylor, "Judicial Elections, Public Opinion, and Their Impact on State Criminal Justice Policy" (PhD diss., University of Kentucky, 2020), https://doi.org/10.13023/etd.2020.327.
10 Republican Party of Minnesota v. White, 536 U.S. 765, 788 (2002).

behind it today, continues in nearly every state. When states elect judges but also deny the right to vote to those who have firsthand experience with the justice system as criminal defendants, the inevitable result is an electorate that tilts against defendants more than it would if everyone were allowed to vote. This facilitates the candidacies of those with a "tough on crime" platform.

One last issue to consider when it comes to judicial elections is their financing. Judicial campaigns cost money. In recent years, special interests, usually business interests, have paid increasing attention to judicial elections. The US Supreme Court has recognized that this creates due process concerns for parties that appear before judges whose campaigns are financed by opposing parties.[11] Lawyers are the most likely contributors to judicial campaigns, and this opens the door for lawyers to curry favor with the judges before whom they appear to the disadvantage of their opponent and at the expense of impartiality. Campaign contributions can infect judicial impartiality in other ways too. For example, one recent empirical study has uncovered a relationship between which lawyers contribute to a judicial campaign and which lawyers are appointed to represent indigent defendants. Worse yet, the study showed that those appointed attorneys achieved, on average, less favorable results for their clients.[12]

A Recent Example

It is, of course, impossible to know whether a ruling in any particular case is influenced by either a judge's campaign platform or the prospect of an upcoming judicial election. But there is reason to be concerned, and a recent case from Texas provides a ready example of why.

The highest court in Texas that hears criminal cases is the Texas Court of Criminal Appeals,[13] and all nine of its judges are elected.[14] That court's presiding (chief) judge, when she originally ran for office, campaigned as a "prosecution-oriented person," which she described as meaning that she sees "legal issues from the perspective of the state instead of the perspective of the

11 Caperton v. A. T. Massey Coal Co., 556 U.S. 868 (2009).
12 Neel U. Sukhatme and Jay Jenkins, "Pay to Play? Campaign Finance and the Incentive Gap in the Sixth Amendment's Right to Counsel," *Duke Law Journal* 70, no. 4 (2021): 782–83, https://scholarship.law.duke.edu/dlj/vol70/iss4/2.
13 Texas has separate appellate courts for criminal and civil cases.
14 Tex. Const. art. 5, §§ 1, 4(a).

defense."[15] Another of the judges, during her campaign, touted endorsements by several law enforcement organizations.[16] Seven of the nine judges on the court were formerly prosecutors.[17] How might all of this impact whether justice is served in that court?

Consider the case of Terence Andrus who was convicted and sentenced to death in Texas for the murder of a man and a woman while attempting a carjacking in a grocery store parking lot. In his subsequent appeals, Andrus argued that his defense attorney had not provided the minimally competent representation to which he was constitutionally entitled because the attorney failed to conduct virtually any investigation of a potential defense to the death penalty. During an extended court hearing at which the defense attorney testified, he offered no explanation for his failure to investigate. At the close of that hearing, the trial court issued a twenty-page opinion recommending that Andrus's death sentence be reversed and he be retried. But the Texas Court of Criminal Appeals rejected Andrus's argument unanimously in a single sentence.[18]

Andrus then took his case to the US Supreme Court, which reversed the ruling of the Texas Court of Criminal Appeals by a 6–3 vote, concluding that "the record makes clear that Andrus has demonstrated counsel's deficient performance." After cataloging the defense attorney's many failures, the Supreme Court concluded that this "is hardly the work of reasonable counsel."[19] Two of the court's most conservative justices (including Justice Brett Kavanaugh), all of whom have life tenure, joined this ruling. Not a single judge on the elected Texas Court of Criminal Appeals thought the

15 Jennifer Lenhart, "Texas Court of Criminal Appeals," *Houston Chronicle*, October 30, 1994, 16; Bruce Nichols, "Allegations Stir Up Appeals Court Races," *Dallas Morning News*, October 9, 1994, 45A.

16 Lauren McGaughy, "Candidates Cite Politics as Key to Criminal Court Race," *Houston Chronicle*, January 31, 2016, https://www.houstonchronicle.com/.

17 See "Judges," About the Court, Court of Criminal Appeals, Texas Judicial Branch, accessed March 2, 2022, https://www.txcourts.gov/cca/about-the-court/judges.

18 Ex parte Andrus, No. WR-84,348-01, 2019 WL 622783, at *5–6 (Tex. Crim. App. Feb. 13, 2019) (per curiam).

19 Andrus v. Texas, 140 S. Ct. 1875 (2020). Having concluded that the defense provided by Andrus's counsel fell below minimally competent standards, the US Supreme Court sent the case back to the Texas Court of Criminal Appeals to determine whether that deficient performance impacted the outcome of the case. The Court of Criminal appeals ruled 5–4 that it did not, and the US Supreme Court declined to reverse that decision. Andrus v. Texas, 142 S. Ct. 1866 (2022).

deficient performance of Andrus's defense counsel warranted more than a sentence of discussion.

Does the use of judicial elections for one court and lifetime appointments for the other explain the different rulings by the Texas Court of Criminal Appeals and the US Supreme Court? We don't know. But we can and should ask ourselves whether elections are the method of selecting criminal judges that we would fashion if we did not know whether our lot in life would be as a criminal defendant or a crime victim? To put it in more explicitly Christian terms, do judicial elections promote love for both neighbors—the victim and the accused—as we would want to be loved?

Judicial Qualifications

The method by which judges are selected is not the only thing that can influence case outcomes. Whom we select to serve as judges also has an impact. Judges are humans too, as I often tell young lawyers, meaning judges are not robots mechanically applying laws and rules. Cases present judges with facts that often point in both directions and laws that are ambiguous. So they must decide; they must judge. We would like to think that their decisions are unbiased. But we would be naïve to think that judges' life experiences do not affect their rulings.

If you doubt that, consider this example. Imagine that you are a criminal defense attorney in your hometown, and I am called for jury duty in a case that you are defending. Further imagine that I had spent my entire career as a prosecutor. (In fact, my career is about equally divided between my time as a prosecutor and as a defense attorney.) During jury selection, you must decide whether to keep me on the jury.[20]

Now answer this question honestly: Are you going to allow me to stay on the jury? Of course you aren't. And neither would I if I were in your shoes. Why? Because if my entire career had been as a prosecutor, I would likely be more sympathetic to the government in my review of your case. I would have been conditioned to that mindset by my daily job responsibilities. It isn't that I would, as a juror, set out to be unfair. I might even think myself fair. But it is inconceivable that my life's work would not play a part in my

20 I am grateful to attorney Clark Neily for this hypothetical. Clark Neily, "Are a Disproportionate Number of Federal Judges Former Government Advocates?," Cato Institute, May 27, 2021, https://www.cato.org.

thinking as a juror. Now ask yourself this additional question: Do you think judges are immune from that same conditioning? If you think they are, would you be willing to bet your life on it?

This isn't to suggest that judicial bias of this sort could run only in one direction. If I had spent my entire career as a criminal defense attorney, you would have similar concerns if you were the prosecutor in my hypothetical. The problem our justice system presents, however, is that its judges are overwhelmingly former prosecutors rather than defense attorneys. On the federal bench, the ratio of former prosecutors to former public defenders is five to one (as of early 2021).[21] On state supreme courts, the ratio is more than five to one.[22] Of the 159 active judges on the federal courts of appeals that hear criminal cases, fifty-two were formerly federal or state criminal prosecutors while only eleven were formerly public defenders.[23]

Biblical Justice?

We claim to have "a government of laws and not of men" that rests on the "rule of law." But does our judiciary, and the way in which we select it, bear that out? If it is truly the case that judges are only neutrally applying the statutes and rules as written, then why the seeming preference for former prosecutors and aversion to former defense attorneys on the bench? Why does the personality matter? What relevance does prior experience have if the law truly rules?

The reason the personality matters is that we know deep down that judging is not as simple as "calling balls and strikes."[24] Laws are ambiguous at times. Facts can cut both ways. We know that even the most well-intentioned

---

21 Neily, "Are a Disproportionate Number of Federal Judges Former Government Advocates?"

22 Janna Adelstein and Alicia Bannon, "State Supreme Court Diversity—April 2021 Update," Brennan Center for Justice, April 20, 2021, last modified May 25, 2022, https://www.brennan center.org/.

23 "Biographical Directory of Article III Federal Judges, 1789–Present," Federal Judicial Center, accessed October 22, 2022, https://www.fjc.gov/. Colleen M. Berryessa, Itiel E. Dror, and Bridget McCormack, "Prosecuting from the Bench? Examining Sources of Pro-Prosecution Bias in Judges," *Legal and Criminological Psychology* 28, No. 1 (2023): 3, https://doi.org/10.1111 /lcrp.12226, write, "The idea that judges, like all humans, can show biases because of prior life experiences is now well-established in research."

24 This was the claim famously made by now-Chief Justice John Roberts in his confirmation hearing in 2005. "Chief Justice Roberts Statement—Nomination Process," United States Courts, accessed October 22, 2022, https://www.uscourts.gov/.

judge will bring his or her life experiences to bear on a case. Pitchers and batters see the strike zone differently. And we know that judges can and do make the law, not just interpret it. Given whom we elect as judges, it appears that our society wants prosecutors, not defense attorneys, making that law. And this can raise issues of biblical justice.

Impartiality. The most obvious concern raised by whom we appoint and how we appoint judges is the issue of impartiality. When the Supreme Court ruled that it was unconstitutional to preclude judges from stating their view of the law during a judicial election, the court reasoned that doing so did not present a risk of judicial partiality because, in the Supreme Court's view, partiality is bias against parties to the case, not bias in favor of one approach to the law.[25] Maybe that's correct. But what about a candidate who describes himself or herself as "prosecution oriented"? Statements of that sort are not just statements about the law. Those are literally expressions of bias in favor of one party and against another. An approach to judging that reads the law in a way that is influenced by who is making the argument is the definition of partiality, which Scripture forbids.

Accuracy. Partiality in turn raises concerns about accuracy because partiality causes cases to be decided on something other than their merits. Partiality preferences people over the particulars of the case, the faces of those who appear in court over the facts proven in court. That approach to decision-making is rife with risk of error.

———

Here is one final hypothetical to end this chapter. Imagine that you are a US Senator who has been asked by the president to confirm a judicial nominee. The candidate whom you are considering defended an accused axe murderer in a recent murder trial in your county.

Knowing only that, what is your feeling about the judicial nominee? Do you fear that he or she will be "soft on crime"? Why? Do you truly believe that the nominee is pro-axe murderer? Is anyone pro-axe murderer? Or is your concern that the nominee will be more protective—maybe too protective, in your view—of the procedural rights of criminal defendants? Is

25 Republican Party of Minnesota v. White, 536 U.S. 765, 775–77 (2002).

that a specific concern or simply a general one? Is there some procedural right this nominee favors that you think is unwarranted? Or are you just assuming that, as a defense attorney, the nominee would support rights for criminal defendants that are unjust?

Now flip the hypothetical. What if the judicial nominee were the prosecutor of the alleged axe murder? Would you have the same concerns? Would you fear that the candidate might be too little concerned with the procedural rights of criminal defendants when the alleged crime is a revolting one? If not, why not? What is the basis for your confidence that life experiences would influence one nominee but not the other?

Because judges—all judges—are humans too.

14

Assistance of Counsel

CLARENCE EARL GIDEON DIED in Fort Lauderdale, Florida, in 1972, the same year as my birth. Born in 1910 in Hannibal, Missouri, Gideon and his parents were members of Calvary Baptist Church in that small town on the bank of the Mississippi River. Following eighth grade, Gideon dropped out of school and ran away from home, becoming a drifter and committing a string of theft offenses across several states over the ensuing years, serving prison terms for each of them.[1]

Gideon was married four times, fathered three children with his fourth wife, and worked a variety of odd jobs, including as tugboat cook, security guard, bartender, and mechanic. In 1957, he moved his family to Panama City, Florida, where, in 1959, they began attending Cedar Grove Baptist Church. He chose that church, he later explained, because he had been a Baptist as a child and "the Christian religion . . . is based on love."[2]

On June 3, 1961, somebody stole five dollars in change and a few bottles of beer and soda from a pool hall in Panama City. A young man who lived nearby claimed that he saw Gideon leave the establishment with the money and drinks in hand and hail a cab. As a result, Gideon was charged with breaking and entering.[3]

Gideon's trial on that felony charge was held on Friday, August 4, 1961, in the Bay County courthouse before Judge Robert McCrary. When Gideon's case was called, he explained to the judge that he wasn't ready for trial

---

1 Anthony Lewis, *Gideon's Trumpet* (New York: Random House, 1964), 68–69.
2 Lewis, *Gideon's Trumpet*, 69–74.
3 Lewis, *Gideon's Trumpet*, 60.

because he didn't have an attorney. He couldn't afford one, he explained, so he asked that the judge appoint a lawyer to defend him. "I am sorry," the judge replied, "but I will have to deny your request." Florida law only allowed for the appointment of counsel in capital cases.[4]

A jury of six men was then seated to hear Gideon's case. The state's primary witness against Gideon was the young man who claimed to have seen Gideon leave the scene of the robbery. A police officer called by Gideon to testify revealed that the young man had himself been found by the officer outside the pool hall at 5:30 a.m. on the morning of the robbery. This fact was not explored further, and the trial ended as quickly as it started. Gideon gave an eleven-minute closing argument on his own behalf; the prosecutor took only nine minutes to deliver his jury address. The jurors promptly convicted Gideon the same day, and the judge sentenced him to the maximum—five years in state prison.[5]

On January 8, 1962, the US Supreme Court received Gideon's handwritten petition asking the court to review his case and, in particular, his claim that the US Constitution guaranteed him the right to an attorney at trial even if he could not afford one. It was a long-shot argument. The court had already ruled in 1942 that indigent criminal defendants were not necessarily guaranteed the right to defense counsel in state criminal cases.[6] Gideon was unaware of that decision, but his petition was in effect asking the court to overturn its prior ruling. He claimed that without an attorney to assist him he was denied due process.[7] To his surprise, the court agreed to hear his case, and in an ironic twist, an attorney was appointed to represent him before the Supreme Court.[8]

In the spring of 1963, the Supreme Court ruled in Gideon's case that the Fourteenth Amendment's guarantee of due process in state court proceedings included a right to counsel. The court explained its rationale:

In our adversary system of criminal justice, any person haled into court, who is too poor to hire a lawyer, cannot be assured a fair trial unless counsel

4   Lewis, *Gideon's Trumpet*, 9–10.
5   Lewis, *Gideon's Trumpet*, 60–64.
6   Betts v. Brady, 316 U.S. 455, 471 (1942).
7   Lewis, *Gideon's Trumpet*, 1–11.
8   Gideon v. Wainwright, 372 U.S. 335, 337 (1963). Before the Supreme Court, Gideon was represented by Abe Fortas, who later became a justice on that court. Lewis, *Gideon's Trumpet*, 46–51.

is provided to him. This seems to us to be an obvious truth. Governments, both state and federal, quite properly spend vast sums of money to establish machinery to try defendants accused of crime. Lawyers to prosecute are everywhere deemed essential to protect the public's interest in an orderly society. Similarly, there are few defendants charged with crime, few indeed, who fail to hire the best lawyers they can to prepare and present their defenses. That government hires lawyers to prosecute and defendants who have money hire lawyers to defend are the strongest indications of the widespread belief that lawyers in criminal courts are necessities, not luxuries. . . . The right to be heard would be, in many cases, of little avail if it did not comprehend the right to be heard by counsel. Even the intelligent and educated layman has small and sometimes no skill in the science of law. . . . He is unfamiliar with the rules of evidence. . . . He lacks both the skill and knowledge adequately to prepare his defense, even though he have a perfect one. He requires the guiding hand of counsel at every step in the proceedings against him. Without it, though he be not guilty, he faces the danger of conviction because he does not know how to establish his innocence.[9]

And with that, Clarence Gideon's conviction was reversed.

The Road to *Gideon*

It might surprise you to learn that, as of 1962, there was no universal right to appointed counsel in state criminal prosecutions like Gideon's. Every television crime drama involves a scene in which a suspect is "read his rights." "You have the right to an attorney," the suspect is told. "If you cannot afford an attorney, one will be appointed for you."[10] And the Sixth Amendment says that "in all criminal prosecutions, the accused shall enjoy the right . . . to have the Assistance of Counsel for his defence." But prior to its decision in *Gideon*, the Supreme Court had concluded that the Sixth Amendment was originally intended to apply only to federal criminal cases and not to state ones.[11] And it is state criminal prosecutions that make up the overwhelming proportion of criminal cases in the United States.

9   Gideon v. Wainwright, 372 U.S. 335, 344–45 (1963).
10 That language derives from the Supreme Court's decision in Miranda v. Arizona, 384 U.S. 436, 473 (1966).
11 Betts v. Brady, 316 U.S. 455, 461 (1942); Johnson v. Zerbst, 304 U.S. 458, 463 (1938).

Over the years, each state decided whether, as a matter of state law, it would provide indigent defendants with appointed counsel and, if so, in what types of criminal cases. In some states, the right to appointed counsel applied only in capital cases. In other states the right extended to some, but not all, felony cases.[12] But at least as of 1930, the US Supreme Court had not recognized a federal constitutional right to have defense counsel appointed in *every* state criminal case if the accused could not afford an attorney. As a result, poor men and women caught up in the American justice system were routinely being forced to trial in state court on criminal charges without *any* attorney to assist them. But the Supreme Court had begun to acknowledge the injustice of this.

In 1931, eight Black teenagers were convicted of raping two White girls on a train near Scottsboro, Alabama. Their trials were held six days after the defendants were indicted and arraigned on the capital rape charge, and it was not until the morning of their trials that the young men were provided with attorneys, none of whom had spent any time preparing a defense. Their trials were all completed the same day, and the juries sentenced all the defendants to death.[13]

Those young men—known today as the "Scottsboro boys"—took their cases to the US Supreme Court, arguing that they were convicted without due process of law given that they were not provided with counsel in time to prepare a meaningful defense. The justices agreed, but the court did not rule that defendants in every criminal case were entitled to appointed lawyers to defend them. Instead, the court concluded that, "under the circumstances" of that case—meaning, "in a capital case, where the defendant is unable to employ counsel and is incapable adequately of making his own defense because of ignorance, feeblemindedness, illiteracy, or the like"—due process required that the trial judge assign counsel for the defendants. Agreeing

12 William M. Beaney, *A Right to Counsel in American Courts* (Ann Arbor, MI: University of Michigan Press, 1955), 238–39.

13 Powell v. Alabama, 287 U.S. 45, 50–51 (1932). Nine young men were charged with the rape, and they were tried in four separate trials held on the same day. The last defendant tried, Roy Wright, was found not guilty. Powell v. Alabama, 287 U.S. at 74 (Butler, J., dissenting). On appeal, the Alabama Supreme Court reversed the conviction of one of the eight defendants because he was not yet sixteen years old and thus his case should have been tried in juvenile court. Powell v. State, 141 So. 201 (Ala. 1932) (reversing conviction of Eugene Williams). The remaining seven defendants took their cases to the US Supreme Court.

with the young men that appointing lawyers on the morning of trial is the equivalent of having no lawyer at all, the court reversed their convictions and sent their cases back to Alabama for retrial.[14]

A decade later, the Supreme Court explained in the case of *Betts v. Brady* that its ruling in the case of the Scottsboro boys only required a state to appoint a lawyer for a criminal defendant in "special circumstances." A death penalty case satisfied that test, obviously, but the court did not specify what other types of cases might require counsel, instead framing the question as whether conviction and incarceration without counsel would be "offensive to the common and fundamental ideas of fairness and right."[15] This test was not, to put it mildly, a model of clarity. But it was nonetheless the test that lower courts were required to apply for the next two decades until the Supreme Court's decision in *Gideon* put an end to the case-by-case determination and ruled that every criminal defendant facing imprisonment had a right to counsel.[16]

In the years after *Betts* and leading up to the *Gideon* decision, more and more states had been expanding the right to appointed counsel as a matter of state law. By 1955, twenty-two states legally guaranteed all criminal defendants, including those charged with misdemeanors, the right to counsel. But eight states—including Florida, Massachusetts, and Pennsylvania—afforded a right to counsel only in capital cases, meaning the state could prosecute an indigent defendant and sentence him or her to life in prison without any defense attorney involvement. Only thirty-six states had a right to counsel in all felony cases.[17]

In those jurisdictions that provided defense attorneys to the poor prior to the decision in *Gideon*, there were at least three ways in which they did so. In some states (for example, New Jersey), private attorneys were appointed without compensation on a rotating basis. In other states (such as New

14 Powell v. Alabama, 287 U.S. 45, 71 (1932). This would not be the last time that the Supreme Court would hear from the Scottsboro boys. The defendants were retried before an all-White jury and again convicted and sentenced to death. The young men again brought their case to the Supreme Court, this time challenging the exclusion of Black men from the jury. Norris v. Alabama, 294 U.S. 587 (1935).

15 Betts v. Brady, 316 U.S. 455, 473 (1942); see also Bute v. Illinois, 333 U.S. 640, 677 (1948).

16 As a technical matter, the Supreme Court later clarified that counsel need only be provided in a case where the defendant was sentenced to prison upon conviction. Scott v. Illinois, 440 U.S. 367, 373–74 (1979).

17 Beaney, *A Right to Counsel in American Courts*, 238–39.

York), charitable Legal Aid Societies or Voluntary Defender organizations were funded by private donations and staffed largely with attorneys who volunteered a portion of their time to represent defendants unable to pay. Societies and organizations of this sort were founded even in some states that did not provide a legal right to counsel. Western and midwestern states (like California and Illinois) took a different approach, establishing public defender offices funded by the government. The first public defender office in the United States opened in Los Angeles in 1914. By 1930, Chicago and San Francisco had followed suit.[18] But as of the time *Gideon* was decided in 1963, thirteen states still did not legally guarantee the right to counsel in all felony cases.[19]

The Unfulfilled Promise of *Gideon*

In the years since *Gideon*, America's commitment to funding an adequate defense for the poor has been something short of stellar. In accord with the ruling in *Gideon*, every state in the nation has some mechanism for providing an indigent criminal defendant with an attorney of some sort. But in some instances, the provision of counsel has been little more than nominal.

After *Gideon*, it was not immediately clear that the public defender model would be the one that states would choose to fulfill their obligations to provide defense counsel to the poor. Some were concerned that a model in which the defense attorney was employed by the government would not allow that attorney to work independently and entirely in the defendant's interests. This concern was not unfounded, as the public defender model was at times pitched to the public on the ground that it would facilitate guilty pleas.[20] Over the next decade, however, public defender offices sprang up across the country and, by 1973, nearly two-thirds of Americans lived in jurisdictions with an organized defender. Other jurisdictions contracted out the indigent defense function to private

18 Beaney, *A Right to Counsel in American Courts*, 233; Sara Mayeux, "What *Gideon* Did," *Columbia Law Review* 116, no. 1 (2016): 30, 55–73, https://scholarship.law.vanderbilt.edu/faculty-publications/748/.

19 Yale Kamisar, "The Right to Counsel and the Fourteenth Amendment: A Dialogue on 'the Most Pervasive Right' of an Accused," *University of Chicago Law Review* 30, no. 1 (1962): 18, https://chicagounbound.uchicago.edu/uclrev/vol30/iss1/2.

20 George Fisher, *Plea Bargaining's Triumph: A History of Plea Bargaining in America* (Stanford, CA: Stanford University Press, 2003), 194–97.

attorneys through a competitive bidding process. But most every jurisdiction also continued to use private attorneys paid by the government
and appointed (usually by a judge) to represent indigent defendants in
some circumstances.[21]

Unfortunately, it quickly became clear that there was little political will to
fund indigent defense, regardless of how it was provided, at a level needed
to secure meaningful representation. This is not surprising since there is
no electoral advantage for a politician to run a campaign on a platform of
helping "criminals." The result has been chronic underfunding of the public
defense function, which has manifested itself in two ways.

As an initial matter, public defenders are generally paid less than their
counterparts in the local prosecutor's office. To take the example of a county
in northern Virginia near where I live, in 2020 an entry-level prosecutor
made $65,000 while an entry-level public defender made $59,500. In that
same county, attorneys with three years of experience in the prosecutor's
office made $86,800; public defenders with the same experience made
$67,300. The deputy prosecutor made $126,100 compared to $93,700 for
the deputy public defender.[22] As another example from my home state,
in 2019, all but two public defenders for the city of Richmond, Virginia,
made less than the highest paid secretary in the office of the city's prosecutor.[23] This pattern repeats itself in county after county and city after city
across the country. In 2019 in Denver, Colorado, the average entry-level
prosecutor in the district attorney's office made $82,600, while the average
entry-level public defender made $67,700. Mid-career prosecutors (with
approximately eleven years of experience) made $126,700; the average

---

21 Private attorneys were needed even in states that had private defender organizations because
   a single law office cannot defend clients with conflicting interests. So, for example, if a crime
   was committed as part of a conspiracy of two or more individuals, the defender organization
   cannot represent both of those individuals because there is a conflict of interest. Each of the
   coconspirators could seek to reduce his or her sentence by cooperating with the government
   and testifying against the other, and the same attorney cannot advise one client to cooperate
   with the government against another client.

22 Letter from Chief Public Defender Lori E. O'Donnell to Loudoun County Board of Supervisors, February 25, 2020, https://loudoun.granicus.com/MetaViewer.php?view_id=77&clip_
   id=6269&meta_id=175340 (see fifth page of the digital file).

23 Ned Oliver, "Most Public Defenders in Richmond Make Less Than a Secretary in the Prosecutor's Office. They Want a Raise," *Virginia Mercury*, September 30, 2019, https://www.virginia
   mercury.com/.

public defender at the same experience level was paid $105,800.[24] The pay disparity in Minneapolis was so bad that, in March 2022, the city's public defenders threatened to strike.[25]

Of equal concern is the pay for private attorneys appointed to defend indigent defendants. In 2018, the Wisconsin Supreme Court acknowledged that the state's compensation rate of $40 per hour for appointed counsel was "abysmally low"—the lowest in the entire nation—with the result being that "most attorneys will not accept . . . appointments because they literally lose money if they take these cases." As the court observed, "Forty dollars an hour does not even cover a lawyer's overhead expenses." The result in one rural Wisconsin county was that it would at times require contacting more than 250 lawyers before one could be found to take a case. In another rural county, it took an average of twenty-four days to locate a lawyer willing to accept an appointment. In one instance, a defendant was detained prior to trial for six months before an attorney was secured. The court took some measure of comfort that "this funding crisis is not unique to Wisconsin." Pointing to class action litigation in Massachusetts, Michigan, New York, Texas, California, Pennsylvania, and Idaho, the court observed that "across the nation, inadequate funding for indigent criminal defense has compromised the constitutional rights of individuals, as well as the ability of the justice system to function properly."[26]

But the concern is not merely with the hourly rate paid to appointed counsel. States also put caps on the total amount a lawyer will be reimbursed for representing an indigent defendant. As of 2022, the rate paid by the state of Alabama to an attorney appointed to represent an indigent criminal defendant charged with a felony (other than a charge with a potential sentence of death or life in prison without parole) is $70 per hour with an unalterable reimbursement maximum of $4,000. In cases where the charged crime carries a maximum sentence of up to ten years in prison, the attorney's fee cap is $2,000.[27] In other words, Alabama will reimburse

---

24 "2019 Budget/Salary Comparison," Office of State Public Defender Trial Offices and District Attorney Trial Offices, March 2020, 7, https://www.coloradodefenders.us/.

25 Rochelle Olson, "Minnesota Public Defense Attorneys, Support Staff Authorize First Ever Strike," *Star Tribune*, March 10, 2022, https://www.startribune.com/.

26 In re the Petition to Amend SCR 81.02, No. 17-06, slip op. at 2–3, 6–11 (June 27, 2018), https://www.wicourts.gov.

27 Ala. Code §§ 15-12-21(d), 13A-5-6(a).

defense counsel for spending no more than twenty-eight hours of time defending someone facing ten years in prison. Illinois has a compensation cap of $1,250 that can be exceeded "in extraordinary circumstances." However, Illinois's hourly rate for appointed counsel is only $40.[28] Even in a high cost of living state like New York, the reimbursement rate as of 2022 was barely higher than Alabama's—$75 per hour with a cap of $4,400 that can only be waived by the court in "extraordinary circumstances" no matter how serious the felony.[29]

Worse yet, several states use flat-rate contracts with appointed counsel,[30] which create perverse incentives for defense counsel to encourage guilty pleas rather than time-consuming trials. In 2016, the New Mexico Supreme Court considered a constitutional challenge to the state's flat-fee model for appointed counsel under which appointed attorneys are paid $700 for the most serious felonies (other than first-degree murder) and $180 for misdemeanors. An appointed attorney challenged the flat fee in a case requiring so much of his time that he was effectively being paid $3 per hour. The state's supreme court ruled that this did not violate the requirement of *Gideon* because, despite the below-minimum-wage rate of pay, the court "assume[d] that attorneys represent their clients honorably."[31]

Of far greater concern than the pay of an individual defense attorney is the consistent failure of states to provide funds for *enough attorneys* to handle the flood of cases. Over the last decade, the American Bar Association has been sponsoring state-by-state studies of the work loads of public defenders. Using a technique developed by researchers at the Rand Corporation, the studies develop estimates of the time needed for lawyers to provide reasonably competent representation for various criminal charges. These estimates are then applied to the state's unique caseload to develop an estimate of the number of hours of defense attorney time needed to represent the state's indigent population. In January 2022, the study of Oregon's public

28 725 Illinois Compiled Statutes § 5/113-3(c).
29 N.Y. Consolidated Law § 722-b.
30 *2021 Annual Report* (Virginia Defenders Indigent Defense Commission, 2021), Appendix B, https://rga.lis.virginia.gov/.
31 Kerr v. Parsons, 378 P.3d 1, 8 (N.M. 2016); Lorelei Laird, "Flat Fees for Contract Public Defenders Are Not Unconstitutional, New Mexico Supreme Court Says," *ABA Journal*, June 6, 2016, https://www.abajournal.com/.

defense system concluded that 1,888 defense attorneys were needed for the state's caseload, but only 592 were funded.[32] The report on New Mexico was issued that same month and similarly concluded that three times the number of current public defense attorneys were needed.[33] Rhode Island's study published in November 2017 concluded that between 136 and 145 full-time public defenders were needed to address the state's caseload. The State had 49 such attorneys.[34]

The state of Louisiana is perhaps the most extreme example of this underfunding of defense counsel for the poor. In 1993, that state's supreme court warned that the caseloads for public defenders were reaching a level such that indigent defendants "are generally not provided with the effective assistance of counsel the constitution requires." For example, one public defender in Orleans Parish had, in a seven-month period in 1991, represented 418 defendants and "had at least one serious case set for trial for every trial date during that period." As the Louisiana Supreme Court observed, "No attorney can prepare for one felony trial per day, . . . not even a lawyer with an S on his chest."[35]

The situation in Louisiana has not meaningfully improved since 1993. As recently as 2015 "in New Orleans, public defenders assigned to misdemeanor courts each had upward of 19,000 cases per year, affording them an average of seven minutes for every client."[36] In January 2017, a federal judge in Louisiana concluded, "It is clear that the Louisiana legislature is failing miserably at upholding its obligations under *Gideon*."[37] In February 2017, the American Bar Association released its report on Louisiana's public defense system, concluding based on its study that the state's caseload required 1,769 public defenders to handle the cases; the state had 363 public defenders as of

---

32 *The Oregon Project: An Analysis of the Oregon Public Defense System and Attorney Workload Standards* (American Bar Association Standing Committee on Legal Aid and Indigent Defendants, January 2022), 27, https://www.americanbar.org/.

33 *The New Mexico Project: An Analysis of the New Mexico Public Defense System and Attorney Workload Standards* (American Bar Association Standing Committee on Legal Aid and Indigent Defendants, January 2022), 5, https://www.americanbar.org/.

34 *The Rhode Island Project: A Study of the Rhode Island Public Defender System and Attorney Workload Standards* (American Bar Association Standing Committee on Legal Aid and Indigent Defendants, November 2017), 26, https://www.americanbar.org/.

35 State v. Peart, 621 So.2d 780, 784, 789, 790 (La. 1993).

36 Dylan Walsh, "On the Defensive," *The Atlantic*, June 2, 2016, https://www.theatlantic.com.

37 Yarls v. Bunton, 231 F. Supp. 3d 128, 137 (M.D. La. 2017).

October 2016.[38] In 2019, a newspaper profiled a public defender in Lafayette, Louisiana, who had 194 felony cases at a single time—a caseload that would require 10,000 hours to handle competently.[39] In a December 2020 ruling, a justice of the Louisiana Supreme Court observed that "the excessive workloads and chronic lack of resources consistently and regularly encountered by public defenders, and brought to light [during the litigation in 1993], continue."[40]

This chronic underfunding and the resulting inadequacy of time devoted to a client's case have effectively denied the poor a lawyer who can meaningfully defend them. As the US Supreme Court recognized, the Constitution's right to counsel entails more than that "a person who happens to be a lawyer is present at trial alongside" you while the state prosecutes you.[41] *Gideon's* promise to the poor is not satisfied by the "mere formal appointment" of a lawyer; they are entitled to "a reasonably competent attorney" who provides professionally reasonable advice and assistance in their cases.[42] Our constitution may not guarantee you the right to F. Lee Bailey in your defense, but it does protect you against the Three Stooges. And whether you get as your attorney a stooge or a capable advocate can turn, in part, on whether that lawyer is fairly compensated.

On any objective review of the data, the unavoidable conclusion is that the poor are regularly and egregiously shortchanged when it comes to the appointment of counsel. In 2013, fifty years after *Gideon* was decided, Yale Law School held a symposium to lament the then sad state of affairs in indigent representation.[43] *Gideon's* sixtieth anniversary is no more encouraging.[44]

Biblical Justice?

These facts about the current state of the indigent defense system in the United States raise the question whether a biblical system of justice requires

---

38 *The Louisiana Project: A Study of the Louisiana Public Defender System and Attorney Workload Standards* (American Bar Association Standing Committee on Legal Aid and Indigent Defendants, February 2017), 2, https://www.americanbar.org/.

39 Richard A. Oppel Jr. and Jugal K. Patel, "One Lawyer, 194 Felony Cases, and No Time," *New York Times*, January 31, 2019, https://www.nytimes.com.

40 State v. Covington, 318 So.3d 21, 29 (La. 2020) (Weimer, J., concurring).

41 Strickland v. Washington, 466 U.S. 668, 685 (1984).

42 United States v. Cronic, 466 U.S. 648, 655 (1984).

43 "The *Gideon* Effect: Rights, Justice, and Lawyers Fifty Years after *Gideon v. Wainwright*," Symposium Issue, *Yale Law Journal* 122, no. 8 (June 2013), https://www.jstor.org/stable/i23527836.

44 For a recent discussion of the unfulfilled promise of *Gideon*, see Jake Tapper, "This Is Not Justice," *The Atlantic*, October 12, 2022, https://www.theatlantic.com/.

that everyone accused of a crime have an attorney. In short, I don't think so, at least not if one is asking whether appointed counsel is a necessary requirement of *every* just legal system. But the facts recounted in this chapter also raise the question whether biblical justice requires that attorneys be provided to the poor when the criminal justice process is governed by intricate rules of evidence and procedure and the prosecution is represented by counsel trained in those rules. I believe it does. Under those circumstances, the assistance of defense counsel is critical to achieving the biblical justice principles of accuracy, due process, impartiality, and accountability.

Accuracy. The Supreme Court's reasoning in *Gideon v. Wainwright*— a case now considered a landmark one in American history[45]—draws heavily on the principle of accuracy. For obvious reasons, the court never cited Scripture in support of its conclusion; it's a secular court, and almost certainly did not have the Bible in mind when it rendered its decision. But the court recognized, as did Reverend Parker nearly a century earlier (see chap. 5), that process is the key to accurate outcomes, and the process can misfire without the assistance of counsel. In a sophisticated legal system, the failure to provide defense counsel to those who cannot afford it poses a serious risk of convicting the innocent.

Due process. The reason a competent defense attorney is critical to an accurate verdict is that criminal trials in the United States operate according to a variety of rules, including detailed rules that dictate what type of evidence is admissible and how it is admitted. For the most part these rules serve a good and important purpose—they are designed to ensure the reliability of the evidence the jury considers. But the rules for offering evidence in a criminal case are complicated, and even experienced attorneys are often confused by them. And therein lies the rub. A defendant is due, as a matter of biblical justice, the right to present his or her evidence and challenge that of the prosecution. At the same time, it is inconceivable that a defendant could do so effectively without legal assistance. To deny a defendant the right to counsel, then, is in effect to deny the defendant the process to which he or she is due as a matter of biblical justice.

---

45 The story of this case was made into a 1980 television movie titled *Gideon's Trumpet* (directed by Robert Collins), in which Henry Fonda played Clarence Gideon.

Impartiality. Also underlying the Supreme Court's reasoning in *Gideon* was a strong dose of concern for impartiality. The court contrasted the prosecution, itself well-funded and represented by counsel, with the plight of the impoverished defendant left to fend for himself. The court also noted how the wealthy defendant can hire the best of attorneys, as compared to Clarence Gideon and others like him who sat at trial alone and unaided. This extreme imbalance was, in effect, partiality—a preference for the interests of the state over the interests of its poor citizens and a different form of justice for the wealthy defendant than for the indigent.[46]

Accountability. The right to counsel is also a necessity to hold the government accountable, as biblical justice requires. We would all like to believe that every police officer, prosecutor, and judge will always act ethically. The Christian doctrine of human sinfulness, not to mention the testimony of history, tells us that this is wishful thinking. The next chapter will explain one type of prosecutorial and police conduct that is all too common. It is hard enough for experienced lawyers to ferret this out. There is little chance that an untrained layman could do so, especially if he or she is trying to do so from pretrial detention. And, yet, uncovering official misconduct, even if it is a rare occurrence, is the first step in holding a corrupt official accountable. Defense counsel functions, in a sense, to police the police and prosecutors. To deny the accused the right to counsel is, thus, to further insulate government actors from accountability when they go astray.

After the Supreme Court reversed Clarence Gideon's conviction in March 1963, his case was sent back to Florida for a new trial, this time with counsel to represent him. That retrial, like the original trial, lasted only a day and was held on Monday, August 5, 1963, again before Judge McCrary. The

---

46 Impartiality concerns are amplified when appointed counsel for the poor fail to take reasonable steps to ensure that the jury is not racially biased against the defendant. In October 2022, the US Supreme Court was presented with a case where a defendant's appointed counsel failed to object to the seating of three jurors who "expressed firm opposition to interracial marriage and procreation." The defendant, who is Black, was then sentenced to death by that jury for killing his White wife. Thomas v. Lumpkin, 143 S. Ct. 4 (2022) (Sotomayor, J., dissenting from the denial of certiorari).

judge opened court that day with a short prayer, asking that God would "help us to do impartial justice, for Christ's sake. Amen."

Once again, the state's case relied largely on the testimony of an eyewitness who had supposedly seen Gideon that morning. This time, however, Gideon's newly appointed lawyer conducted a devastating cross-examination of the witness, suggesting that his presence at the scene of the crime was likely due to his serving as a lookout for the real perpetrators of the break-in. Gideon's defense counsel also called as a witness the cab driver who had picked up Gideon that morning, and he testified that Gideon was not carrying any bottles of soda or beer.

At the close of the trial, the jury quickly acquitted Gideon after only an hour of deliberation.[47] Fair process, including representation by defense counsel, is critical to accurate outcomes.

47 Lewis, *Gideon's Trumpet*, 234–50.

15

Exculpatory Evidence

ON THE EVENING OF SEPTEMBER 24, 1983, an eleven-year-old girl went missing in Red Springs, North Carolina, a small town of less than four thousand residents in the southeastern corner of the state. Two days later, her half-naked body was found lying in a soybean field. The little girl had been raped and an item of her clothing jammed down her throat with a stick. She died of suffocation.

Based on a neighborhood rumor relayed by a local high school student, the police quickly focused their attention on a nineteen-year-old Black man, Henry McCollum. Two days after the young girl's body was discovered, McCollum was interrogated by the police for more than four hours and, at two o'clock in the morning, finally confessed, signing a written statement implicating himself, his fifteen-year-old brother Leon Brown, and two other men. Brown too confessed in writing that same night. Both McCollum and Brown suffered from severe intellectual disabilities, Henry having an IQ of 56 and Leon having an IQ in the mid-50s.[1]

McCollum and Brown (but not the two other men whom McCollum named) were each charged with first-degree murder and rape and went on trial in October 1984. The prosecutor was Joe Freeman Britt, known as the deadliest prosecutor in America because of his record of securing death sentences.[2] McCollum and Brown both testified at trial, protesting their

1   Gilliam v. Sealey, 932 F.3d 216, 222–23 (4th Cir. 2019).
2   For a discussion of prosecutor Britt's record of death penalty prosecutions, see Seth Kotch, *Lethal State: A History of the Death Penalty in North Carolina* (Chapel Hill, NC: University of North Carolina Press, 2019), 153, 184–85.

innocence. Both were convicted and sentenced to death. But on appeal, the North Carolina Supreme Court reversed the convictions due to an error in the judge's instructions to the jury, and a new trial was ordered.[3]

This time, separate trials were held for the two men. McCollum's trial was held first in November 1991, now more than eight years after the crime. During jury selection, the trial judge found that the prosecution was striking jurors based on race in violation of *Batson*, requiring that jury selection begin anew.[4] Once a jury was seated and the trial began, McCollum's attorney argued, with his client's consent, that McCollum was present at the little girl's murder but urged the jury to convict him only of second-degree murder. The jury rejected this plea, convicted McCollum of first-degree murder and rape, and again sentenced him to death. Brown's trial followed in June 1992, but he was convicted only of the rape and sentenced to life in prison.[5]

On appeal to the North Carolina Supreme Court for a second time, that court affirmed both McCollum's and Brown's convictions.[6] McCollum then asked the US Supreme Court to take up his case. Though the Court declined to do so, several justices took an interest in the case. Justice Harry Blackmun dissented from the court's decision not to review the case, expressing his recent conclusion that "the death penalty, as currently administered, is unconstitutional."[7] Justice Scalia had a very different view. He believed that McCollum's "quiet death by lethal injection" was "enviable" compared with the death suffered by the victim of his crimes, and if the people of North Carolina believed "that justice requires such brutal deaths be avenged by capital punishment," the court "should not prevent them."[8] Given the horrific nature of the crimes against that young girl, the sentiment was understandable.

Except for the fact that McCollum and Brown were innocent. During McCollum's decades on death row, he watched forty-two of his fellow inmates make the final walk to the execution chamber, all the time wondering whether he—an innocent man—would be next.[9] But, finally, twenty

---

3   State v. McCollum, 364 S.E.2d 112, 114 (N.C. 1988).
4   State v. McCollum, 433 S.E.2d 144, 159 (N.C. 1993).
5   Gilliam v. Sealey, 932 F.3d 216, 224–25 (4th Cir. 2019).
6   State v. McCollum, 433 S.E.2d 144 (N.C. 1993); State v. Brown, 453 S.E.2d 165 (N.C. 1995).
7   McCollum v. North Carolina, 512 U.S. 1254, 1255 (1994) (Blackmun, J., dissenting).
8   Callins v. Collins, 510 U.S. 1141, 1143 (1994) (Scalia, J., concurring).
9   "Exonerated North Carolina Men Freed from Prison," *CBS News*, September 3, 2014, https://www.cbsnews.com/.

years after the US Supreme Court refused to hear McCollum's case, DNA evidence showed that neither he nor Brown had committed the crimes. All the while, the police had evidence in their files suggesting who the actual killer and rapist was, evidence that was concealed from the defendants at the time of their trials.[10] Thirty-one years after they had been arrested for crimes they did not commit, Henry McCollum and Leon Brown walked out of prison on September 2, 2014.[11]

Duty to Disclose

Henry McCollum's decades-long journey through the justice system shows how that system can misfire in tragic ways. Appellate judges rely on and defer to juries to determine guilt or innocence. Juries decide cases based on the evidence presented by the prosecutor and defense attorneys. Defense attorneys present the evidence to which they have access. If the prosecution conceals evidence collected during the investigation, that evidence may never be available for the jury's consideration. And without the jury's review of all the evidence, the entire system can—and, in McCollum's case, did—malfunction. The consequences can be fatal.

The nearly fatal malfunction in McCollum's case demonstrates why it is crucial that the state share with the defense *all* the evidence collected during the criminal investigation, not just the evidence suggesting guilt. The government enjoys an enormous advantage in its ability to investigate a case and gather evidence prior to trial. While in theory a crime suspect is permitted to hire an attorney to investigate on his behalf prior to indictment, the suspect might not know he is a suspect, might not have the funds to hire an attorney, and is unlikely to be able to secure the cooperation of the public.

The police and prosecutor, however, have unique and early access to the crime scene. The state typically has a crime lab to assess forensic evidence. Citizens are often willing to cooperate with the police. If a potential witness refuses to speak with the police, the grand jury can usually subpoena the person and compel him or her to testify in the investigation. All of this gives the government a tremendous evidentiary advantage in the early days of a criminal investigation. But that advantage isn't, or at least shouldn't be,

---

10 Gilliam v. Sealey, 932 F.3d 216, 228 (4th Cir. 2019).
11 Jonathan M. Katz and Erik Eckholm, "DNA Evidence Clears Two Men in 1983 Murder," *New York Times*, September 2, 2014, https://www.nytimes.com/.

a tactical one. The government's evidence gathering powers are meant to advance truth-seeking. The point of justice is accuracy.

Using its full array of investigative powers and privileges, the police may ultimately reach the conclusion that they have enough evidence to charge someone with the crime. At that point, the police will present that evidence to a prosecutor who must decide whether to charge the suspect whom the police have identified. In making that decision, the prosecutor will have to consider not only the strength of the evidence of the suspect's guilt but also the evidence collected during the investigation that cuts against the suspect's guilt. The prosecutor will weigh that evidence and decide whether and with what crimes to charge.

If used correctly, the government's investigative powers and prosecutorial discretion can serve to increase the accuracy of the charges the state brings. But even the most well-intentioned police officer or prosecutor is not infallible. They may mistakenly discount the importance of a piece of evidence that suggests the defendant's innocence. They may misbelieve a witness who is telling a lie, fail to believe a witness who is telling the truth, or be entirely unaware of a witness who could provide a defense. But more importantly, the police and the prosecutor are not the final arbiters of the facts. The jury is. Which means the jury needs the evidence, the good and the bad.

In 1963, in the case of *Brady v. Maryland*, the Supreme Court ruled that the prosecution violates due process if it doesn't provide the defendant with evidence the government collected during its investigation that is "favorable" to the defendant and "material" to his or her guilt or punishment.[12] In other words, the government is obligated, as a matter of constitutional law, to provide the defendant with evidence in the government's files that may tend to show he or she is not guilty or deserves a lesser sentence.

This obligation to produce what is known as "exculpatory" evidence arises from the prosecutor's obligation to seek the truth. As the Supreme Court explained in *Brady*, due process is not satisfied if the prosecution "contrived a conviction through the pretense of a trial which in truth is but used as a means of depriving a defendant of liberty through a deliberate deception of

12 Brady v. Maryland, 373 U.S. 83, 87 (1963).

court and jury."[13] In other words, in order for a trial to be meaningful, the jury needs to see the evidence that might suggest the defendant is innocent, which means that evidence of innocence the government collected must be provided to defense counsel so that he or she can evaluate how, if at all, to use that evidence at trial.

In the years after the *Brady* decision, the Supreme Court explained that the government's obligation to hand over exculpatory evidence to the defense applies whether or not the defense requests it.[14] Due process is not a matter of hide-and-go-seek requiring that defense counsel ask the right question of the prosecutor in order to gain access to evidence of innocence. Instead, the government's disclosure obligation is rooted in the ideal of truth-seeking and turns on whether the suppressed evidence "undermines confidence in the outcome of the trial." And the prosecutor cannot sit back and rely on the fact that he or she is unaware of evidence the police collected that is material to the defendant's innocence. The prosecution's obligation to disclose requires that the prosecutor search the police files for exculpatory evidence.[15]

There are numerous types of evidence that might qualify as what is now called "*Brady* material." For example, if the police interviewed a witness who identified someone other than the defendant as the perpetrator of the crime, that would be an obvious example of *Brady* material that should be disclosed. Other examples might include DNA or fingerprint evidence that does not match the defendant, or a store surveillance camera recording that shows the robber to be of a different height, weight, sex, or race from the person charged. The examples of *Brady* material that must be shared with the defendant are innumerable.

One subset of *Brady* material is evidence that tends to undermine the credibility of the government's witnesses at trial—what is known as "impeachment evidence."[16] In other words, *Brady* material includes not only evidence that directly contradicts the prosecution's case but also evidence that tends to undermine the reliability of the witnesses on whom the

13 Brady v. Maryland, 373 U.S. 83, 86 (1963) (quoting Mooney v. Holohan, 294 U.S. 103, 112 [1935]).
14 United States v. Agurs, 427 U.S. 97, 107 (1976); Kyles v. Whitley, 514 U.S. 419, 433 (1995).
15 Kyles v. Whitley, 514 U.S. 419, 434 (1995).
16 Giglio v. United States, 405 U.S. 150, 154 (1972); United States v. Bagley, 473 U.S. 667, 676–77 (1985).

government is relying to prove its case. A witness whom the police interviewed during their investigation and who could provide the defendant with an alibi would be an example of exculpatory evidence at the core of *Brady*. Evidence that the government's star witness is unreliable is impeachment evidence also covered by *Brady*. For example, if a witness who will testify for the government at trial to identify the defendant as the person who committed the crime previously gave a statement to the police that he or she did not see the perpetrator or offered a description of the perpetrator that did not match the defendant, then that would be impeachment evidence the prosecution is obligated to disclose to the defense.

Epidemic of Concealment

One would think the *Brady* obligation to be both straightforward and noncontroversial. After all, who would want to conceal evidence of the defendant's innocence? But sixty years after the Supreme Court's decision in *Brady*, prosecutors still frequently ignore their obligations under that decision. In 2013, a federal court of appeals judge appointed by President Reagan sounded the alarm: "There is an epidemic of *Brady* violations abroad in the land," he warned in a court opinion. "Only judges can put a stop to it."[17]

To take one example, let's return to the saga of Pamela Moses, the woman who was convicted of committing voter fraud in the 2020 election in Tennessee and sentenced to six years in prison after rejecting a no-jail misdemeanor plea deal (see chap. 11). The central issue in that case was whether Moses knew she was ineligible to vote when she attempted to register. After a trial in November 2021, Moses was convicted and her bail was revoked, meaning she was jailed while awaiting sentencing. But shortly after her sentencing in January 2022, a newspaper reporter uncovered a document from the Tennessee Department of Corrections showing that the Department had concluded, after an investigation, that a probation officer had mistakenly signed a certificate that Moses's probation from a prior conviction was complete, meaning she was authorized to vote.[18]

17 United States v. Olsen, 737 F.3d 625, 626 (9th Cir. 2013) (Kozinski, J., dissenting from denial of rehearing en banc).
18 Sam Levine, "New Evidence Undermines Case against Black US Woman Jailed for Voting Error," *The Guardian*, February 24, 2022, https://www.theguardian.com/.

Obviously, this document was highly relevant to whether Moses knew she was ineligible to vote when she attempted to register, but the state had not disclosed the document to the defense at the time of Moses's trial. When the document came to light, Moses filed a motion for a new trial in February 2022, which the judge immediately granted. But by that point, Moses had already spent eighty-two days in jail. The state then dropped the case because, as the prosecutor put it, the time Moses had spent in jail was "sufficient."[19] Sufficient? Moses spent eighty-two days in jail based on a conviction secured only because exculpatory evidence was not disclosed, resulting in the conviction being overturned. The eighty-two days in jail wasn't sufficient; it was an injustice.

Unfortunately, Moses's case is not a rarity. A study by *Chicago Tribune* reporters of eleven thousand cases of prosecutorial misconduct between 1963 (when *Brady* was decided) and 1999 found 381 homicide convictions overturned because of *Brady* violations, 67 of which had resulted in death sentences.[20] A study by a *Pittsburgh Post-Gazette* reporter of 1,500 federal criminal cases found similarly disturbing results.[21] Over the past fifteen years alone, dozens of convictions have been overturned because of *Brady* violations. With little effort, I located eight convictions for crimes such as murder, robbery, and kidnapping overturned in 2021 alone due to *Brady* violations. In May 2021, for example, a federal conviction in my home state was thrown out after it came to light that the government had failed to disclose evidence undermining the defendant's guilt, marking the third time in five years that convictions obtained by that same prosecutor's office were overturned after *Brady* issues were discovered.[22]

19 Sam Levine, "Prosecutor Drops All Charges against Pamela Moses, Jailed over Voting Error," *The Guardian*, April 22, 2022, https://www.theguardian.com/. The prosecutor claims that the failure to disclose the exculpatory evidence was the fault of the Department of Corrections, not the prosecutor's office.

20 Ken Armstrong and Maurice Possley, "The Verdict: Dishonor," *Chicago Tribune*, January 11, 1999, https://www.chicagotribune.com/.

21 Bill Moushey, "Win at All Costs," *Pittsburgh Post-Gazette*, November 22, 1998, http://www.usa-the-republic.com/.

22 Laurence Hammack, "Woman Sees Federal Conviction Thrown Out after Prosecutors Failed to Turn Over Evidence," *Roanoke Times*, May 18, 2021, https://roanoke.com/. In one of the three cases, the conviction was overturned on other grounds, but undisclosed exculpatory evidence led the government to elect not to retry the defendant.

Nor is the prevalence of *Brady* violations a regional phenomenon. In 2020, a federal court of appeals unanimously overturned the murder convictions and life sentences of two people in Arkansas, concluding that the state prosecutor (who by that time was a justice on the state's supreme court) and police "worked together to intentionally conceal" evidence from the defense.[23] In another case that same year, a New York appellate court vacated a man's murder conviction, concluding that the prosecution had failed to disclose material impeachment evidence concerning a trial witness.[24] The Tennessee Supreme Court reversed a woman's murder conviction based on the prosecution's failure to produce an earlier witness statement that was in the "physical possession" of the prosecution during that trial and that undermined the testimony of a star prosecution witness.[25] Also in 2020, a California appellate court reversed a man's conviction for child rape after the prosecution failed to produce impeachment evidence in its files with regard to one of the state's witnesses.[26] These are just a few of what is a remarkable track record of prosecutorial misconduct, particularly given the difficulty defendants face in ever discovering that the state has concealed evidence bearing on their guilt.

Especially disturbing is the prevalence of *Brady* violations in the highest of high stakes cases—death penalty prosecutions. In Henry McCollum's case, the police had identified another suspect who lived less than a hundred yards from where the young girl's body was discovered and who had confessed to committing a remarkably similar murder and rape in the same area around the same time. A witness had informed the police that she had seen that man, not McCollum and Brown, attack the young girl. None of this was disclosed to the defense team. Only after McCollum had spent decades on death row was this evidence uncovered by his attorneys, and DNA evidence recovered at the crime scene was finally tested and found to match that other suspect.[27]

But McCollum's case would be neither the first nor the last time a *Brady* violation occurred in a death penalty case. On numerous occasions, state and federal appellate courts have reversed death sentences because of the

23 Jimerson v. Payne, 957 F.3d 916, 930 (8th Cir. 2020).
24 People v. Rodriguez, 186 A.D.3d 1724, 1725–26 (N.Y. App. Div., 2d Dept. 2020).
25 State v. Jackson, 444 S.W.3d 554, 593–98 (Tenn. 2014).
26 People v. Stewart, 55 Cal. App. 5th 755, 759 (2020).
27 Gilliam v. Sealey, 932 F.3d 216, 225, 228 (4th Cir. 2019).

prosecution's failure to disclose exculpatory or impeachment evidence. And on several occasions in recent years, the US Supreme Court has intervened to overturn death sentences because of the state's failure to comply with *Brady*.

In 1995, the US Supreme Court overturned the death sentence of Curtis Lee Kyles due to the state's failure to disclose impeachment evidence in violation of *Brady*. Kyles was charged with the murder of a sixty-year-old woman during a robbery outside a New Orleans grocery store. His first trial ended in a hung jury. At his second trial, the state's case relied primarily on the testimony of two eyewitnesses who identified Kyles as the killer. What the prosecution failed to disclose was that one of those witnesses—whom the state described as its "best"—had previously told the police that the shooter was five feet four inches and medium build, while Kyles was six feet tall and thin. The second supposed eyewitness who testified at trial that he saw the shooting had given a different statement to police immediately after the incident. None of this was disclosed to the defense, and the Supreme Court concluded that the prosecution's failure to disclose "destroy[ed] confidence" in the trial's result.[28] The Supreme Court sent Kyles's case back to the state court to be retried. In three consecutive retrials, the juries hung. In 1998, after the fifth trial, the prosecution dropped the charges against him.[29]

In 2004, the US Supreme Court overturned the death sentence handed down in Texas against Delma Banks. Prior to trial, the prosecutors had promised Banks's attorneys that they would provide the defense with all *Brady* material. Despite this promise, the prosecution concealed evidence that one of the key witnesses at trial was a paid informant and another had been "intensively coached by prosecutors and law enforcement officers."[30]

In 2012, the Supreme Court reversed Juan Smith's five first-degree murder convictions because of a *Brady* violation by the state of Louisiana. The only evidence at trial connecting Smith to the crime was the testimony of an eyewitness who survived the incident. But the prosecution failed to disclose that when that witness was interviewed on the night of the murders, he told the

28 Kyles v. Whitley, 514 U.S. 419, 441–43 (1995).
29 Jed Horne, *Desire Street: A True Story of Death and Deliverance in New Orleans* (New York: Farrar, Strauss and Giroux, 2005). Kyles was later charged with and convicted of a 2010 murder and is serving a life sentence for that murder. Andrea Shaw, "Curtis Kyles, Ex-Death Row Inmate, Convicted of Killing Metairie Woman," *Nola.com*, September 23, 2015, https://www.nola.com/.
30 Banks v. Dretke, 540 U.S. 668, 675 (2004).

police that he "could not . . . supply a description of the perpetrators other th[a]n they were black males." Nor was the defense told that the witness, in a follow-up interview five days later, reiterated that he "could not ID anyone because [he] couldn't see faces" and "would not know them if [he] saw them."[31]

In 2016, the Supreme Court reversed the conviction and death sentence of Michael Wearry for a brutal murder in Louisiana. The court described the state's case as "resemble[ing] a house of cards" depending on the testimony of a single witness. The prosecution, however, had failed to disclose (a) a statement by the witness that he was trying to settle a score with Wearry and (b) medical evidence showing that the witness's description of the events was a physical impossibility.[32] Shortly before Wearry's case was set to be retried in early 2019, the prosecutor offered him a plea bargain to a manslaughter charge carrying a twenty-five-year prison sentence, which Wearry accepted. Afterwards, the prosecutor commented that "when you put the devil on trial, you have to go to hell to get your witnesses,"[33] missing entirely the point of *Brady*: when you go to hell to find your witnesses, you must disclose the inferno where you found them. With credit for time already served, Wearry is expected to be released in 2023.[34]

The *Kyles*, *Banks*, *Smith*, and *Wearry* cases are only the death sentences that the US Supreme Court has itself overturned in the last two decades for *Brady* violations. Since 1989, dozens of men and women on death row have been exonerated after convictions facilitated at least in part by *Brady* violations. There is, indeed, an epidemic of *Brady* violations abroad in the land.

Plea Bargaining *Brady* Waivers

The prevalence of *Brady* violations in cases where defendants were convicted at trial is disturbing. But as we saw in chapter 11, most criminal cases never make it to trial because of plea bargaining. This raises the question whether

---

31 Smith v. Cain, 565 U.S. 73, 75 (2012). On the first day of his retrial, Juan Smith pled guilty to two counts of manslaughter in a plea deal with the state. Helen Freund, "Juan Smith Pleads Guilty to Manslaughter in 1995 Quintuple Shooting, Gets 80 Years," *Nola.com*, May 20, 2014, https://www.nola.com/.

32 Wearry v. Cain, 577 U.S. 385, 389–93 (2016).

33 Caroline Grueskin, "Freedom Closer for Man in Killing of Albany Pizza Boy; DA's Personal Opinion: Man 'Rots in Hell,'" *The Advocate*, December 26, 2018, https://www.theadvocate.com/.

34 Trey Schmaltz, "Killer in 20-Year Murder Saga Likely Won't Be Released Anytime Soon," *WBRZ2 ABC*, December 27, 2018, https://www.wbrz.com/.

prosecutors are obliged to disclose *Brady* material in cases that are resolved through guilty pleas.

The US Supreme Court has not yet addressed that question in its entirety. The court has ruled that prosecutors do *not* have a constitutional obligation to disclose one type of *Brady* material (impeachment evidence) to a defendant during the plea-bargaining process.[35] But the court has yet to decide whether, as a constitutional matter, prosecutors must disclose core *Brady* material—meaning, information directly bearing on the defendant's innocence—during the plea-bargaining process.

Several lower courts have ruled on the issue and the trend is to hold that the Constitution does require disclosure of *Brady* material during plea bargaining. Those courts that have concluded that there is a duty to disclose have reasoned that a defendant's guilty plea is not knowing and voluntary if it is entered without knowledge of evidence bearing on his or her innocence.[36] But some courts have ruled the other way, concluding that "*Brady* focuses on the integrity of trials and does not reach pretrial guilty pleas."[37]

It isn't hard to imagine how the suppression of exculpatory evidence during plea bargaining could work an injustice. In fact, we don't have to imagine. In August 1992, Troy Mansfield was indicted by a Texas grand jury on three counts of sexual misconduct with a child. In response to a defense motion, the trial judge in the case ordered the state to produce all *Brady* material. The very next day, the prosecutor interviewed the victim and wrote in the case file that "she does not remember what happened" and "at one point, told me nothing happened, then says little boy might have done it." These statements were never produced to the defense. Instead, four days before trial the prosecutors told the defense attorney that "the victim would be a strong witness at trial and that they had a doctor's statement and physical evidence corroborating the victim's identification of Mansfield." None of this was true. Faced with a seemingly insurmountable case, Mansfield pled guilty to a lesser charge and was sentenced to 120 days in the county jail. More than a decade later, he learned of the

---

35 United States v. Ruiz, 536 U.S. 622, 633 (2002).
36 United States v. Ohiri, 133 F. App'x 555, 562 (10th Cir. 2005); Buffey v. Ballard, 782 S.E.2d 204, 216 (W.Va. 2015); Hyman v. State, 723 S.E.2d 375, 380 (S.C. 2012); State v. Huebler, 275 P.3d 91, 93 (Nev. 2012); Medel v. State, 184 P.3d 1226, 1233 (Utah 2008).
37 Mansfield v. Williamson County, 30 F.4th 276, 280 (5th Cir. 2022).

prosecutors' false statements and persuaded a Texas state court to vacate his conviction. But when Mansfield tried to sue the prosecutors for violating *Brady*, a federal court of appeals ruled that he could not bring such a lawsuit because the obligation to disclose exculpatory evidence does not apply to plea bargaining.[38]

Because the Supreme Court has not yet resolved whether *Brady* applies prior to trial, prosecutors seek to moot the issue by requiring defendants to waive their right to *Brady* material as part of their plea bargain. In other words, prosecutors routinely insist that plea agreements include a provision stating that the defendant waives his right to receive *Brady* material, which precludes the defendant from challenging his guilty plea if he later discovers that the prosecution was in possession of exculpatory evidence.

It is important to see how these waivers work together with the other pressures on defendants to accept plea offers. Setting aside considerations of justice for a moment, a rational criminal defendant deciding whether to accept a plea bargain would naturally want to evaluate not only whether he is innocent but also whether he is likely to be able to establish his innocence at trial. Even if entirely innocent, it would be understandable why a defendant would accept a guilty plea to a reduced sentence if he or she was highly likely to be wrongly convicted at trial. In fact, we know that innocent defendants make that very judgment, as many of them have pled guilty and then subsequently been exonerated.[39] On the other hand, an innocent defendant might be more willing to risk a lengthy prison sentence if he or she were aware of evidence in the government's files tending to show his or her innocence.

By requiring *Brady* waivers as a condition of plea bargaining, the government is in effect forcing an innocent defendant into a high stakes game of blind man's bluff. The government can give a defendant (through his or her attorney) a preview of the evidence that suggests guilt in an attempt to induce a plea bargain, all without showing the defendant any evidence

---

38 Mansfield v. Williamson County, 30 F.4th 276, 278, 280 (5th Cir. 2022). To read more about Troy Mansfield's ordeal, see Tony Plohetski, "'Wept Like Babies That Day': Man Recalls Family's Reaction after Child Sex Abuse Conviction Overturned," *KVUE*, November 15, 2019, https://www.kvue.com/.

39 "Exonerations by State," The National Registry of Exonerations, University of Michigan, accessed April 8, 2023, https://www.law.umich.edu/special/exoneration/Pages/Exonerations-in-the-United-States-Map.aspx (filtered for cases involving guilty pleas).

the government might hold that suggests innocence. The defendant then must decide: accept the plea bargain, or proceed to trial and hope there is *Brady* material demonstrating his or her innocence that the government will produce later. Some prosecutor's offices take this gamesmanship to the next level, conditioning a plea bargain on the defendant's waiver of his right to see *any* of the government's investigative file. The result is that a defendant is subject to enormous pressure to plead guilty, as discussed earlier, but must make the decision without knowing about evidence the police have collected that might show his innocence.

These types of tactics certainly promote efficiency, meaning the speedy resolution of cases with the least effort by the prosecution. But do they promote justice—biblical justice, that is?

Lack of Judicial Oversight

One explanation for the epidemic of *Brady* violations is the lack of judicial oversight of the disclosure process. In theory, the prosecutor's obligation to disclose *Brady* material is supervised by the court presiding over a defendant's case. In reality, whether information gets disclosed depends almost entirely on the prosecutor's good faith. The trial judge presiding over a criminal case lacks the resources to review police investigative files to make disclosure determinations. Defense counsel is not authorized to personally peruse police files in a search for *Brady* material. Nor is defense counsel entitled to interrogate the police officer in advance of trial as to what exculpatory evidence might exist. Instead, the duty falls on the prosecutor to review the police investigative files and produce any material that must be disclosed under *Brady*, and defense attorneys are left to rely on the prosecutor's representations that he or she has done so.

A simplified example might serve to illustrate why this process is fraught with risk of nondisclosure. Imagine that a police officer interviews a witness to a bank robbery. The witness is asked if she can describe the robber. The witness pauses, searching her memory. She then tells the officer that the suspect was wearing black jeans. But after some more thought, the witness changes her description a few minutes later. The suspect was wearing black sweatpants, the witness now says. The officer writes in his notes, "Black sweatpants." No mention is made in the notes of the witness's original statement that the defendant was wearing black jeans.

276 AMERICAN CRIMINAL JUSTICE

A few blocks away, another officer arrests a suspect in the robbery. He is wearing black sweatpants. If the witness who gave the statement to the police is called to testify at trial that the robber was wearing sweatpants, the witness's equivocation in her initial description to the police officer could be *Brady* (impeachment) material that tends to cast doubt on the accuracy of her testimony. She was, at least at the time of the crime, uncertain. Critical to evaluating a witness's truthfulness at trial is comparing the witness's trial testimony against prior versions of the events the witness has provided. That the witness changed her description is information known to the government and is thus impeachment material *regardless of whether the police officer writes it down*. But if the witness's change in description is not recorded in the police officer's notes, then it might never be known to the prosecutor and thus never produced to the defense as *Brady* material.

In this example, the risk that *Brady* material will be lost (because not written down) arises from the way police officers record witness interviews: handwritten notes. All the twists and turns in the witness's story could be captured if the interview were audio recorded. But as a general rule, the police do not audio record witness interviews. For example, the FBI's official policy even today is to take handwritten notes of a witness interview rather than audio record it. Inevitably, notes are not verbatim recitations of what the witness said during the interview, and the notes can easily omit the hedging and evolution of a witness's statements during an interview that could be used to cross-examine the witness at trial. This is no small thing given the extensive body of studies concluding that eyewitness identification is highly unreliable (as will be discussed in chap. 16).

By not audio recording witness interviews, the police officer or FBI agent can, even unintentionally, omit from interview notes inconsistent statements, instead including only a summary of the statements made by the witness that are helpful to the prosecution. In a day and age when everyone has an audio recorder in his or her pocket in the form of a smartphone, this approach to witness interviews is hard to explain. And the failure to audio record witness statements can have dramatic consequences in terms of whether *Brady* material is even captured in the investigative files, much less disclosed to the defense.

But even assuming evidence is written down, disclosure depends on the prosecutor's thoroughness in collecting it and good faith in disclosing it. Did the prosecutor gather the interview notes of everyone interviewed by the police? Does the prosecutor even know the identities of all those who were interviewed? Did the prosecutor attempt to collect information from every law enforcement agency involved in the investigation? Does the prosecutor know what to ask about the types of evidence the police gathered? Did the prosecutor ask about all forensic testing? Does the prosecutor know whether fingerprints or DNA evidence was collected? Sorting out what evidence is available, determining where it is located, and systematically collecting it are no small tasks, and it is not hard to see how even a well-intentioned but overworked prosecutor may leave some stones unturned. Not all *Brady* violations are intentional. Some are the result of negligence or oversight. But the lack of meaningful supervision by the court and the dependence on the prosecutor to ensure his or her own compliance are a recipe for disaster. Or, you might say, an environment conducive to an epidemic.

Lack of Discipline

Despite the prevalence of *Brady* violations even today, prosecutors are rarely subject to sanctions of any sort for violating their disclosure obligations. In April 1871, Congress passed a law allowing people whose federal constitutional rights were violated to bring a lawsuit in federal court (before unelected judges) against the state or local government employee who violated those rights.[40] That law, known today as Section 1983, would seem to allow innocent criminal defendants convicted because of a prosecutor's *Brady* violation to sue the prosecutor for money damages.

But in 1976, the Supreme Court invented an exception to Section 1983 that is found nowhere in the statute's text. The court ruled that individual prosecutors have "absolute immunity" from any lawsuits seeking money damages based on their prosecutorial activities.[41] The Supreme Court later made up another exception to the statute, holding that a district attorney's

---

40 Ku Klux Klan Act, Pub. L. 42-22, 17 Stat. 13, ch. 22, § 1 (April 20, 1871), https://govtrackus.s3 .amazonaws.com/legislink/pdf/stat/17/STATUTE-17-Pg13.pdf.
41 Imbler v. Pachtman, 424 U.S. 409, 427 (1976).

office is not liable under Section 1983 for the actions of its district attorneys, including those attorneys' *Brady* violations.[42]

In ruling that defendants cannot sue prosecutors under Section 1983 for *Brady* violations, the Supreme Court acknowledged that it was "leav[ing] the genuinely wronged defendant without civil redress against a prosecutor whose malicious or dishonest action deprives him of liberty." But the court concluded that this was necessary to ensure "the vigorous and fearless performance of the prosecutor's duty." The court took comfort that prosecutors are subject to criminal prosecution, or at least professional discipline by their states' bar associations, if they violate their disclosure obligations under *Brady*.[43]

This reasoning was Pollyannaish in the extreme as time has proved. A 1987 study found that professional discipline of prosecutors for *Brady* violations was, as of that date, virtually nonexistent.[44] A follow-up study ten years later found a similar dearth of disciplinary actions against prosecutors who violate *Brady*.[45] Court opinions that conclude *Brady* violations have occurred typically omit the name of the offending prosecutor so as not to damage his or her career.[46] In two known instances in which prosecutors were criminally prosecuted for *Brady* violations, they were charged with misdemeanors and paid $500 fines.[47] Only one prosecutor has ever gone to jail for a *Brady* violation. His sentence was ten days (of which he served five); the defendant he wrongly convicted of murder had spent nearly twenty-five years in prison.[48] Prosecutors face essentially no ramifications for their *Brady* violations, no matter how severe the damage they cause.

---

42 Monell v. New York City Dept. of Social Servs., 436 U.S. 658, 691(1978); Connick v. Thompson, 563 U.S. 51, 60 (2011).

43 Imbler v. Pachtman, 424 U.S. 409, 427, 429 (1976).

44 Richard A. Rosen, "Disciplinary Sanctions against Prosecutors for *Brady* Violations: A Paper Tiger," *North Carolina Law Review* 65, no. 4 (1987): 730–71, https://scholarship.law.unc.edu /nclr/vol65/iss4/2/.

45 Joseph R. Weeks, "No Wrong without a Remedy: The Effective Enforcement of the Duty to Disclose Exculpatory Information," *Oklahoma City University Law Review* 22, no. 3 (1997): 833–934.

46 Adam M. Gershowitz, "Prosecutorial Shaming: Naming Attorneys to Reduce Prosecutorial Misconduct," *University of California-Davis Law Review* 42, no. 4 (2009): 1067–68, https://law review.law.ucdavis.edu/issues/42/4/articles/42-4_gershowitz.pdf.

47 Armstrong and Possley, "The Verdict: Dishonor," 13.

48 Alexa Ura, "Anderson to Serve 9 Days in Jail, Give Up Law License as Part of Deal," *Texas Tribune*, November 8, 2013, https://www.texastribune.org/; Claire Osborn, "How Ken Anderson

Biblical Justice?

When it comes to the disclosure of exculpatory evidence to criminal defendants, is the American criminal justice system a biblically just one? If you answer that question by looking only at the law as it appears in the *Brady* decision, you might be tempted to conclude that it is just. But the justice "system" is more than one court decision. The "system" includes not only the rule on the books but also the methods by which the rule is carried out (or not) and compliance is enforced (or not). And viewed as a "system," there is reason to be concerned.

Accuracy. As the Supreme Court itself explained in the *Brady* opinion, the rule laid down in that case was designed to serve the interest of accuracy. This is something that Christians should celebrate. "Keep far from a false charge," the Old Testament warns (Ex. 23:7). Discerning a false charge from a true one depends, of course, on evidence. There is no other way for finite humankind to sift the true from the false. Given that, one important way to keep our distance from wrongful convictions is demanding that evidence calling the prosecution's case into question be shared with the defense so that, if appropriate, it can be considered by the jury. Absent that, juries are left to make decisions based on half the story, a recipe for hit-or-miss justice. Dozens, if not hundreds, of exonerations in recent years bear testimony to this. *Brady* is designed to ensure that the full story sees the light of day, that all the facts inform the jury's decision-making. As Christians, we should see this as a moral good, a biblical act of social justice.

Due Process. The *Brady* decision seeks to promote accuracy by ensuring that the trial process is meaningful rather than a sham. Again, Christians should see in this an element of biblical justice. Testing the government's case, whether by cross-examining its witnesses or presenting contrary evidence, is recognized in Scripture as a means of reaching wise and sound verdicts (Prov. 18:17). But these biblically rooted tools are only as powerful as the factual fuel that powers them. If evidence is suppressed, it cannot be presented in rebuttal. If impeachment material is concealed, it cannot be deployed on cross-examination. Process can be rendered hollow without the facts that procedures are used to introduce. The *Brady* decision sought to ensure that the

---

Was Released after Only Five Days in Jail," *Austin American-Statesman*, November 15, 2013, https://www.statesman.com/.

procedures afforded criminal defendants are meaningful ones. By requiring disclosure, the law, in its design at least, seeks to facilitate more accurate verdicts. We cannot on the one hand profess a commitment to accuracy without also insisting on the process—the disclosure—that is needed to ensure that accuracy. True verdicts, we are again reminded, depend on fair process, and *Brady* is meant to ensure a fair process that yields reliable results.

Accountability. Though *Brady* was a significant step forward in the quest for justice, its impact has been eroded in large part due to the failure to hold accountable those prosecutors who violate it. The rule that *Brady* laid down is a good and just one, but courts have not surrounded that decision with the legal apparatus needed to ensure that, in practice, the disclosure obligation functions in a just way. Courts simply trust that prosecutors will diligently comply despite decades of evidence to the contrary. And when noncompliance is detected, the consequences for the prosecutor are essentially nonexistent. The conviction may be overturned (decades too late), but no one on the prosecution team is called to account for their failure to live up to the law of the land and the law of love.

In the absence of personal and professional ramifications for the prosecutor who fails to comply with *Brady*'s mandate, the law fails to incentivize prosecutors to act diligently to comply and fails to punish them for their injustices when they do not. The boomerang of justice never turns back on the prosecutor who, because of concealed evidence, unjustly wielded the sword of the state.[49] Prosecutors can and do act, in Irenaeus's words, "to the subversion of justice" without any fear that they will "perish"—or even lose their job—as a result.[50] And so injustice, rather than justice, rolls down like a mighty river as the steady stream of *Brady* violations continues to flow year after year.

———

September 2, 2014, was a hard day for the family of that young girl from Red Springs, North Carolina. After believing for thirty years that her killers

---

49 Jonathan Leeman, *How the Nations Rage: Rethinking Faith and Politics in a Divided Age* (Nashville: Thomas Nelson, 2018), 111.

50 Irenaeus, *Against Heresies* 5.24, in *From Irenaeus to Grotius: A Sourcebook in Christian Political Thought*, ed. Oliver O'Donovan and Joan Lockwood O'Donovan (Grand Rapids, MI: Eerdmans, 1999), 17.

had been brought to justice, they learned that they had been fooled—by the state. One relative described it as "hell" to know that "the killers are running around loose," and the family was mystified as to how the investigative file was managed so poorly. They feared that the girl they still see as the eleven-year-old from 1983, would simply be forgotten. "Who's going to pay for this?" they wondered.[51]

Even today, nearly forty years after the crime, the man who raped and killed that little girl and left her body in a soybean field has never been prosecuted, much less convicted. That the perpetrator has not been called to account is an agonizing reality for her family. Accurate outcomes—for the accused *and* the victims—depend on due process. And a government's defiance of the process, when it causes inaccurate results, cries out for accountability. We owe it to the accused who are wrongly convicted and the crime victims who are cruelly deceived.

51 "Sabrina Buie Family: 'It Feels Like Hell,'" *ABC11 News*, September 3, 2014, https://abc11.com/.

16

Witnesses

EACH TIME I MEET WITH WITNESSES to prepare for a trial, I explain to them what it will be like in a real courtroom when they testify. People have conceptions of trials based on what they have seen in television shows or movies, but I want to prepare witnesses for what will happen at an actual trial. As I put it, "Real trials are sort of like what you see on television, but not really."

As on television, the judge in a real trial is seated above the fray on what we call a "bench." The jury is located to one side or the other of the judge in the "jury box." The witness sits in the "witness stand," which is usually a chair surrounded on three sides by a short wall connected to but lower than the judge's bench. The trial usually begins with the prosecutor and then the defense attorney presenting an opening statement to the jury— a short roadmap of what the case is about and what each lawyer expects the evidence at trial will prove. At the end of the trial, the lawyers then address the jury again, making arguments about what evidence should be believed, what evidence should be distrusted, and how the facts proven apply to the law on which the judge instructs the jury.

In between these speeches to the jury is the heart of the case: the evidence. Most of the evidence in a trial is introduced, in one way or another, by witnesses. Either the witness testifies as to what he or she saw, or the witness testifies as to why some tangible thing—a gun, some documents, a bloody T-shirt, or a store surveillance video, for example—should be part of the evidence in the case. The defendant, perhaps, sent the email to the witness. The police officer called to testify found the gun when he searched the defendant's house. Or the store owner explains how the recording came from a surveillance camera in the parking lot. Even physical evidence of this sort typically requires the testimony of a witness to connect it to the case.

Procedural rules govern whether this evidence is admissible and how its reliability can be tested. This means that the accuracy—and, thus, justice—of our trials depends in significant part on the rules for admitting and excluding evidence. True verdicts require a fair process. In this chapter, we'll explore the process for admitting evidence in American criminal trials.

Call Your First Witness

Once the parties have made their opening statements to the jury, the prosecution bears the burden of proving the charges and thus goes first in calling its witnesses to testify. The Sixth Amendment to the US Constitution guarantees that a person charged with a crime will have a chance to cross-examine the prosecution's witnesses and then, after the prosecution rests its case, call witnesses of his or her own.[1]

What types of witnesses are called by the prosecution and defense and what lines of cross-examination are used with those witnesses differ from trial to trial. But only occasionally is the testimony or cross-examination at a real trial nearly as dramatic as is depicted on television. In a complicated case, especially, the presentation of evidence can be a mostly plodding affair with the witnesses recounting what they saw and the defense picking away at certain points here and there. Rarely does the witness break down in a "*Perry Mason* moment," confessing that he or she has in fact been fabricating the whole story. That's why I tell prospective witnesses that trials are like what they see on television, but not really.

The type of witness with which most people are familiar is the eyewitness. A bank teller might describe how the robber was dressed. A bystander may have seen the getaway car. The defendant's coworker perhaps recalls a particular remark he made. A relative of the accused can recount how he flaunted a wad of cash in the days after the robbery. There are innumerable things that eyewitnesses may have seen or heard.

No single witness needs to have seen the whole crime or even any of the crime. The key requirement for a witness's testimony to be admissible is

---

1   U.S. Const. amend. VI.

that he or she personally saw, heard, smelled, or touched something that is relevant to the case. The party (the prosecution or the defense) calling the witness asks the witness to testify to the jury about what he or she witnessed—that is, perceived through one of the senses. The witness can testify to what he saw John do. But, as a general rule, the witness cannot testify about what Sally told him that John did. That would be what the law calls "hearsay." Witnesses generally can only testify about their own personal knowledge of what happened. The prosecutor will ask the witness open-ended questions—who, what, where, when, or how—to allow the witness to tell the story in his or her own words. This is called the "direct" examination of the witness.

Here's the thing you may not realize about eyewitnesses: there are serious questions about their reliability. This isn't to suggest that all, or even many, witnesses are intentionally lying. They almost certainly aren't. In most instances, eyewitnesses sincerely believe what they are testifying to. But sincerity doesn't ensure accuracy. An extensive body of scientific research has demonstrated that even well-intentioned eyewitnesses are frequently mistaken. In particular, the research demonstrates that (a) eyewitnesses are very poor at identifying the perpetrator of the crime when that person is a stranger, and (b) memory about the details of events can be contaminated in various ways.[2] Human memory is not the video recorder we tend to think it is.[3] You don't remember "exactly what happened."

Since the development of DNA technology, hundreds of criminal defendants who were convicted based on eyewitness testimony have been exonerated. Of the first 250 people exonerated by DNA evidence, 76 percent had been convicted based on eyewitness testimony; 36 percent were identified at trial by multiple eyewitnesses.[4] In fact, "mistaken eyewitness

2 National Research Council, *Identifying the Culprit: Assessing Eyewitness Identification* (Washington, DC: The National Academies Press, 2014), https://doi.org/10.17226/18891; Gary L. Wells, "Eyewitness Testimony," in *The Encyclopedia of Crime and Punishment* (Great Barrington, MA: Berkshire, 2002), 663; Gary L. Wells et al., "Eyewitness Identification Procedures: Recommendations for Lineups and Photospreads," *Law and Human Behavior* 22, no. 6 (1998): 605, https://doi.org/10.1023/A:1025750605807.

3 Donna J. Bridge and Joel L. Voss, "Hippocampal Binding of Novel Information with Dominant Memory Traces Can Support Both Memory Stability and Change," *Journal of Neuroscience* 34, no. 6 (February 5, 2014): 2203–13, https://doi.org/10.1523/JNEUROSCI.3819-13.2014.

4 Brandon L. Garrett, *Convicting the Innocent: Where Criminal Prosecutions Go Wrong* (Cambridge, MA: Harvard University Press, 2011), 48, 50.

identification is responsible for more . . . wrongful convictions than all other causes combined."[5] These exonerations and other research have led experts to conclude that "eyewitness identification evidence is among the least reliable forms of evidence."[6] Especially fraught with risk of error is the eyewitness who makes a cross-racial identification, meaning that the witness testifies as to the identity of a perpetrator who is of a different race than the witness. Study after study shows that people do a remarkably poor job of correctly distinguishing among people of a different race; this is particularly true of White people trying to identify Black people.[7]

Juries, however, tend to place great reliance on eyewitness testimony.[8] Convinced that there was no reasonable doubt as to a defendant's guilt, jurors have returned verdicts against criminal defendants based on the testimony of a single eyewitness, going so far as to sentence a defendant to death on that meager evidence alone. In 1981, for example, Gary Graham was convicted of murder and sentenced to death by a Texas jury. The murder occurred at 9:30 p.m. in a grocery store parking lot in Houston when a young man shot the fifty-three-year-old victim in the chest and stole less than one hundred dollars from him. No physical evidence tied Graham to the crime. He was in possession of a gun when he was arrested, but ballistics testing determined that it was not the murder weapon. The entirety of the evidence linking him to the murder was the testimony of a woman who observed the crime from her car from about thirty feet away, admitting that she saw the perpetrator's face for about ninety seconds. Based on this testimony, Gary Graham was convicted in a one-day trial.[9]

---

5   Wells et al., "Eyewitness Identification Procedures," 605.

6   Wells et al., "Eyewitness Identification Procedures," 605.

7 · Christian A. Meisner and John C. Brigham, "Thirty Years of Investigating the Own-Race Bias in Memory for Faces: A Meta-Analytic Analysis," *Psychology, Public Policy, and Law* 7, no. 1 (2000): 3–35, https://doi.org/10.1037/1076-8971.7.1.3 ; John Paul Wilson, Kurt Hugenberg, and Michael J. Bernstein, "The Cross-Race Effect and Eyewitness Identification: How to Improve Recognition and Reduce Decision Errors in Eyewitness Situations," *Social Issues and Policy Review* 7, no. 1 (2013): 84–85, https://doi.org/10.1111/j.1751-2409.2012.01044.x.

8   Katherine Puddifoot, "Re-evaluating the Credibility of Eyewitness Testimony: The Misinformation Effect and the Overcritical Juror," *Episteme* 17, no. 2 (June 2020): 255–79, https://doi.org /10.1017/epi.2018.42; John C. Brigham and Robert K. Bothwell, "The Ability of Prospective Jurors to Estimate the Accuracy of Eyewitness Identifications," *Law and Human Behavior* 7, no. 1 (1983): 19–30, https://doi.org/10.1007/BF01045284.

9   Graham v. Johnson, 94 F.3d 958, 960 (5th Cir. 1996) (per curiam): "Skillern was the only trial witness to identify Graham as the shooter."

After exhausting his appeals, he was executed by lethal injection on June 23, 2000.[10]

Was Gary Graham the murderer? I don't know. Given the sparse evidence, I couldn't know beyond a reasonable doubt. And here's the haunting truth: neither could the jury. Eyewitness identifications just aren't that reliable.

Cooperating Witnesses

If even well-intentioned and disinterested eyewitness are of questionable reliability, how much more so when the witness is being offered some benefit in return for his or her testimony? Given the risk that witnesses will skew their testimony if not outright lie, the law has long forbidden attorneys from paying witnesses for their testimony. In every state in America, the rules governing attorney conduct prohibit them from offering witnesses money or other things of value in return for even truthful testimony. In fact, it is a federal felony to offer a witness "anything of value" for testimony, truthful or not.[11]

Prosecutors, however, play by different rules. Courts have held that the government can literally pay witnesses money for their testimony.[12] But far more commonly, prosecutors offer witnesses something much more valuable than cash in return for testimony. Prosecutors offer freedom. If two or more people were involved in a crime, one of the defendants can agree to "cooperate" with the prosecution and testify against a codefendant in return for a reduction in his or her criminal charges or sentence. This practice has taken different forms over the years, but the US Supreme Court has condoned it in part based on its long history.[13] So ingrained in the criminal justice system is the concept of "flipping" one defendant on another that virtually nobody gives it a second thought.

That is, until some enterprising defense attorneys challenged the practice in the late 1990s on the ground that it violated the federal statute criminalizing witness bribery. As those defense lawyers argued,

10 Claudia Kolker and Megan Garvey, "Texas Executes Convicted Murderer in Case Surrounded by Controversy," *Los Angeles Times*, June 23, 2000, https://www.latimes.com/.
11 18 U.S.C. § 201(c)(2).
12 United States v. Levinite, 277 F.3d 454, 464 (4th Cir. 2002), upholding conviction where the FBI paid a witness one hundred thousand dollars for his testimony.
13 Hoffa v. United States, 385 U.S. 293, 310–11 (1966); United States v. Ford (Whiskey Cases), 99 U.S. 594, 599 (1878).

physical freedom from prison certainly fits the definition of "anything of value," and thus the prosecutorial practice of offering witnesses leniency in their own criminal cases in return for testifying in another criminal defendant's trial was unlawful witness bribery. To everyone's surprise, the argument worked. A three-judge panel of a federal court of appeals in Colorado agreed and precluded the government from "bribing" witnesses in this way.[14]

The defense victory, however, was short-lived. The US Department of Justice immediately appealed the ruling to the full court of appeals, arguing that the inability to offer leniency in return for testimony had caused "chaos" in the justice system and "crippled" law enforcement.[15] In a ruling seven months later, the full court of appeals reversed the panel's decision. As the majority explained, there was "a longstanding practice sanctioning the testimony of accomplices against their confederates in exchange for leniency," and the court was unwilling to read the federal bribery statute as upsetting that established practice.[16]

But this ruling by the full appellate court was not unanimous. Three judges dissented, concluding that the prosecution's conduct violated the federal bribery statute and raised serious concerns about witnesses providing false testimony against their alleged coconspirators in return for reduced sentences. As the dissenting judges explained, while leniency is "in theory" offered only in exchange for truthful testimony, "common sense" suggests that such a witness "has a greater interest in lying in favor of the prosecution rather than against it" and to assume that the witness will not lie "to obtain favors from the prosecution for themselves is indeed to clothe the criminal class with more nobility than one might expect to find in the public at large."[17] This dissenting perspective, however, did not catch on with the courts,[18] and cooperating witnesses who testify against their codefendants in expectation of leniency are a mainstay of criminal prosecutions.

---

14   United States v. Singleton, 144 F.3d 1343 (10th Cir. 1998).

15   Supplemental Brief of the United States, United States v. Singleton, Case No. 97-3178 (July 1998), The United States Department of Justice Archives, last modified January 22, 2020, https://www.justice.gov/.

16   United States v. Singleton, 165 F.3d 1297, 1301 (10th Cir. 1999) (en banc).

17   United States v. Singleton, 165 F.3d 1297, 1309 (10th Cir. 1999) (Kelly, J., dissenting).

18   E.g., United States v. Anty, 203 F.3d 305 (4th Cir. 2000).

One subset of cooperating witnesses is the so-called "jailhouse snitch." This type of witness is himself facing criminal charges and is seeking leniency from the prosecution based on his cooperation, but the crimes with which he is charged are entirely unrelated to those of the defendant against whom he cooperates. The jailhouse snitch doesn't testify against a coconspirator in a common crime. Instead, the jailhouse snitch testifies against someone with whom he is jailed awaiting trial. The snitch approaches the prosecutor claiming that his cellmate confessed while they were housed together in a cell. In return for testifying about this supposed confession, the snitch is offered a reduction in his own criminal charges or sentence.

Prosecutors will typically argue that the snitch is reliable because, to the extent that he or she knows details of another defendant's crime, it must be because the defendant shared those details. This might be a reasonable inference if the snitch had no other means of learning those details. But the snitch may have learned the details by reading his cellmate's legal papers stored in their shared cell. Or the details may have been shared with the snitch by a relative who read about the crime in the newspaper. Or, worst of all, the details may have been fed to the snitch by the police or the prosecutors. What we know is that at least 8 percent of all exonerations between 1989 and 2015 (and 15 percent of all exonerations in murder cases) were of people convicted in part based on the testimony of jailhouse snitches.[19]

Confessions

One witness whom the prosecution cannot call to prove its case is the defendant. In the United States, a criminal defendant cannot be compelled to be a witness against himself, meaning that the prosecution cannot force the defendant to be a witness in his or her own trial. The Constitution's Fifth Amendment guarantees this right to criminal defendants—which is why refusing to testify is often called "pleading the Fifth."[20]

19 "Snitch Watch," The National Registry of Exonerations, University of Michigan, May 13, 2015, http://www.law.umich.edu. For a discussion of how the use of jailhouse informants contributed to the wrongful convictions of those later cleared by DNA evidence, see Garrett, *Convicting the Innocent*, 118–44.

20 The Fifth Amendment right not to testify against oneself was originally applicable only in federal criminal cases but was later extended to state criminal prosecutions as an element of due process under the Fourteenth Amendment. Malloy v. Hogan, 378 U.S. 1, 8–10 (1964).

If a defendant elects not to testify at trial, the prosecutor cannot argue to the jury that the defendant's silence is evidence of guilt.[21] Nor can the prosecutor comment on the defendant's refusal to speak with the police after his or her arrest.[22] The theory underlying these prohibitions is that allowing prosecutorial comment on a defendant's silence is a "penalty" imposed on the exercise of the right; it, in effect, "cuts down on the privilege by making its assertion costly."[23]

That the prosecutor cannot compel the defendant to testify at trial or comment on the defendant's silence does not mean that the prosecution cannot offer at trial statements the defendant made earlier. The government can introduce statements the defendant made either during the crime, to friends or relatives after the crime, or while being interrogated by the police during the investigation of the crime.

When the police are investigating a crime, they may attempt to interview one or more suspects. A person who is a suspect in a criminal investigation has a right to remain silent and refuse to speak with the police. But a suspect can waive that right and choose to answer questions, and any statements the suspect makes will be admissible at trial so long as they were voluntary.[24] The US Supreme Court has ruled that, if a police officer is questioning someone after an arrest, the officer is required to advise the suspect of his rights (what we commonly refer to as "reading him his rights")—in particular, his right to remain silent—before questioning so that the suspect can make an informed and voluntary decision whether to waive those rights and speak with the police.[25]

During an interrogation, the police are constitutionally permitted to lie to the suspect in an effort to elicit a confession. For example, the officer

21 Griffin v. California, 380 U.S. 609, 615 (1965).
22 Wainwright v. Greenfield, 474 U.S. 284, 291 (1986). The prohibition against prosecutorial use of a defendant's silence following arrest is not as absolute as it is regarding silence at trial. For example, if a defendant chooses to testify, the prosecution may try to persuade the jury that his story is fabricated because he did not provide it to the police earlier. Jenkins v. Anderson, 447 U.S. 231, 238–39 (1980). However, the prosecution cannot make this argument based on the defendant's choice to remain silent after receiving his *Miranda* warnings. Doyle v. Ohio, 426 U.S. 610, 611 (1976).
23 Griffin v. California, 380 U.S. 609, 614 (1965).
24 Bram v. United States, 168 U.S. 532, 557–58 (1897). The Supreme Court has extended the voluntariness requirement to state criminal prosecutions as an element of due process. Brown v. Mississippi, 297 U.S. 278, 286 (1936); Ashcraft v. Tennessee, 322 U.S. 143, 154–55 (1944).
25 Miranda v. Arizona, 384 U.S. 435, 469 (1966).

might tell one suspect that his friend was questioned in another room and admitted that the two friends committed the crime together.[26] Or the officer might tell the suspect that they found his DNA on the murder weapon.[27] In fact, the police are sometimes permitted to go so far as to suggest that the suspect will receive leniency if he confesses.[28]

A suspect being questioned by the police might make a full-blown confession or make an incriminating statement of some sort (for example, admitting being at the victim's house the night of the murder) but not confess entirely. In either instance, the prosecution can call the police officer to testify at trial about the statement the defendant made prior to trial.

In some instances, police record the interrogation so that there is no doubt at trial about what the defendant said. You may have seen a recording of this type on a real-crime television show. But some law enforcement agencies (including, until 2014, the Federal Bureau of Investigation[29]) have a policy against recording the interrogation, instead relying on the officer who did the questioning to testify truthfully and accurately from memory as to what was said. The trend, however, is toward requiring that interrogations of suspects be recorded, with numerous states passing laws requiring such.[30]

There is a substantial body of evidence demonstrating that confessions are not entirely reliable. Psychologists have studied the factors that lead people to confess to even horrendous crimes they did not commit. As Professor Saul Kassim of the John Jay College of Criminal Justice observes,

It is hard to imagine any aspect of human behavior more counterintuitive than the proposition that an innocent person, as a function of social pressure, would knowingly confess to a heinous crime that he or she did

26 Frazier v. Cupp, 394 U.S. 731, 737–39 (1969).
27 Rachel Weiner, "Virginia Beach Police Used Forged Forensic Documents in Interrogations," *Washington Post*, January 12, 2022, https://www.washingtonpost.com/.
28 United States v. Villalpando, 588 F.3d 1124, 1128 (7th Cir. 2009).
29 "Attorney General Holder Announces Significant Policy Shift Concerning Electronic Recording of Statements," The United States Department of Justice, May 22, 2014, last modified September 15, 2014, https://www.justice.gov.
30 "Dep't of Justice, New Department Policy Concerning Electronic Recording of Statements," *Harvard Law Review* 128, no. 5 (March 2015): 1552–59, https://harvardlawreview.org/2015/03/dept-of-justice-new-department-policy-concerning-electronic-recording-of-statements/.

292 AMERICAN CRIMINAL JUSTICE

not commit—an act that can cost the confessor liberty, and sometimes even his or her life. Yet false confessions occur with some regularity.[31]

Henry McCollum and his brother Leon Brown, whose case was discussed in the previous chapter, both confessed and were sentenced to death for a brutal murder and rape they did not commit. And they are not alone. Of the first 250 people exonerated in the United States by DNA evidence, 16 percent had falsely confessed to crimes they did not commit,[32] and 12 percent of all exonerations since 1989 involved false confessions.[33]

Forensic Evidence

In recent years, television shows like *CSI: Crime Scene Investigation* have popularized the use of forensic evidence in criminal investigations and trials.[34] Forensic evidence is evidence based on scientific methods and is usually introduced at trial by a witness who has been recognized by the judge as an expert of some sort. Examples of forensic analysis include fingerprint comparison, hair fiber analysis, ballistics, bite mark examination, bloodstain analysis, drug testing, and handwriting identification.

In both the federal and state court systems, rules of evidence control when expert testimony is admissible at trial. Generally speaking, courts have adopted one of two different tests governing the admissibility of forensic evidence. One test, known as the *Frye* test, allows for the admission of forensic evidence at trial only if the scientific method used by the expert witness has gained "general acceptance in the particular field"

---

31 Saul M. Kassin, "The Social Psychology of False Confessions," *Social Issues and Policy Review* 9, no. 1 (2015): 26, https://doi.org/10.1111/sipr.12009.

32 Garrett, *Convicting the Innocent*, 18.

33 "Exonerations by State," The National Registry of Exonerations, University of Michigan, accessed April 8, 2023, https://www.law.umich.edu/special/exoneration/Pages/Exonerations-in-the-United-States-Map.aspx (filtered for cases involving false confessions).

34 Prosecutors, defense attorneys, and judges have referred to the "*CSI* effect," meaning the degree to which jurors familiar with television shows of that sort have acquitted defendants because of unrealistic demands about the scientific evidence the prosecution will be able to offer in support of its case. At least one study sponsored by the US Department of Justice concluded that, while jurors who watch shows like *CSI* do have higher expectations as to the amount and types of forensic evidence that will be offered by the prosecution at trial, they are not more likely to acquit when that proof is not offered. Donald E. Shelton, "The '*CSI* Effect': Does It Really Exist?," *National Institute of Justice Journal* 259 (2008): 1–6, https://nij.ojp.gov/topics/articles/csi-effect-does-it-really-exist.

at issue.[35] The theory underlying the *Frye* test is that court is a place for expert evidence that is based on established scientific approaches, not on novel theories.

For decades, the *Frye* test was the predominant rule in both federal and state courts when it came to the admissibility of forensic evidence. That all changed with the US Supreme Court's 1993 decision in a case known as *Daubert*, in which the court concluded that scientific evidence is admissible if it is "reliable" even though it may involve scientific methods that are not generally accepted in the relevant scientific field. This rule made trial judges gatekeepers, forced to determine whether novel scientific methods are sufficiently trustworthy as to be admissible.[36] The decision in *Daubert*, however, applies only in federal courts, leaving each state court system free to adopt its own rule of evidence. State courts have divided between the *Frye* and *Daubert* standards.[37]

In November 2005, Congress directed the National Academy of Sciences (NAS) to conduct a study of the forensic science used in criminal cases to assess the strengths and shortcomings of that evidence. In response, a committee comprised of distinguished scientific experts and a federal appellate judge was formed, and hearings were held over several years with testimony provided by an array of experts in various forensic fields. The result of this effort was a three-hundred-page report issued by the committee in February 2009. The findings were devastating.

The report noted that, contrary to the theory underlying the *Daubert* decision, the judicial process "is not suited to the task of finding 'scientific truth.'" The shortcomings of the judicial system were exacerbated by the lack of uniform standards governing forensic disciplines, which raised "serious questions and concerns about the validity and reliability of some forensic methods and techniques and how forensic evidence is reported to juries and courts." Focusing specifically on forensic evidence purporting to identify a

---

35 Frye v. United States, 293 F. 1013, 1014 (D.C. Cir. 1923).
36 Daubert v. Merrell Dow Pharmaceuticals, Inc., 509 U.S. 579, 597 (1993).
37 Christine Funk, "Daubert Versus Frye: A National Look at Expert Evidentiary Standards," Expert Institute, last modified April 11, 2022, https://www.expertinstitute.com. Some studies have concluded that a court's choice between the two tests does not affect the admissibility of expert testimony in criminal cases. Jennifer L. Groscup et al., "The Effects of *Daubert* on the Admissibility of Expert Testimony in State and Federal Criminal Cases," *Psychology, Public Policy, and Law* 8, no. 4 (2002): 339–72, https://doi.org/10.1037/1076-8971.8.4.339.

particular person, the report concluded that, "with the exception of nuclear DNA analysis, . . . no forensic method has been vigorously shown to have the capacity to consistently, and with a high degree of certainty, demonstrate a connection between evidence and a specific individual or source."[38] Citing the NAS's report, Justice Antonin Scalia later observed that "forensic evidence is not uniquely immune from the risk of manipulation."[39] Forensic science, in other words, is only as good as the scientists and their methods.

In 2019, ten years after the NAS report was issued, the federal appellate judge who served as cochair of the committee that led the study observed that "we are still facing serious problems in the forensic science community" and "are still struggling with the inability of courts to assess the efficacy of forensic evidence." The judge described the situation as "unacceptable," noting that "we are not talking about good science merely for its own sake. We are talking about the need for good science in order to serve justice."[40]

This use of so-called "junk science" in criminal prosecutions has, as you would imagine, real-world consequences for defendants. To take one example, in 1985, Charles McCrory was convicted of killing his wife based on testimony by Dr. Richard Souviron, a supposed bite mark expert who claimed that he could link teeth marks on the victim's body to McCrory. Bite mark identification evidence has long since been debunked as entirely unreliable, and Souviron has admitted under oath that, "as a forensic odontologist I no longer believe the individualized teeth marks comparison testimony I offered in [McCrory's] case was reliable or proper." And, yet, to this day, Charles McCrory, now age sixty-two, sits in prison having been convicted based on evidence that was not scientifically valid.[41]

---

38 Committee on Identifying Needs of the Forensic Science Community (National Research Council), *Strengthening Forensic Science in the United States: A Path Forward* (Washington, DC: The National Academies Press, 2009), 6, 7, 12, 39, www.nationalacademies.org.

39 Melendez-Diaz v. Massachusetts, 557 U.S. 305, 318 (2009).

40 Harry T. Edwards, "Ten Years after the National Academy of Sciences' Landmark Report on Strengthening Forensic Science in the United States: A Path Forward—Where Are We?," NYU School of Law, Public Law Research Paper No. 19–23, April 12, 2019, last modified June 29, 2019, 2–3, http://dx.doi.org/10.2139/ssrn.3379373.

41 Liliana Segura and Jordan Smith, "Duty to Correct," *The Intercept*, March 12, 2022, https://theintercept.com. The state of Alabama has offered to release McCrory from prison if he will simply admit that he committed the murder. He refuses to do so and instead continues to fight to prove his innocence.

Confrontation

Once a witness called by the prosecution has testified on direct examination, the defense attorney is provided with a chance to cross-examine the witness. (Likewise, the prosecution is entitled to cross-examine defense witnesses after they complete their direct examination.) Cross-examination isn't just allowed as a matter of judicial grace. The Sixth Amendment to the US Constitution guarantees a criminal defendant the right "to be confronted with the witnesses against him"—a right that has been interpreted to require not only that the witness testify in the defendant's physical presence, but also that the defendant (through his or her attorney) be afforded an opportunity to cross-examine the prosecution witness.[42]

Broadly speaking, there are two types of cross-examination. One type seeks to elicit from the witness additional facts that give context to his testimony provided on direct examination. Maybe the defendant did say the words that the witness testified that he heard, but there is more that the witness said that gives a different meaning to those words. Or maybe the witness did in fact see the defendant punch the victim, but there was aggression by the victim toward the defendant that led to the punch that was not discussed on direct examination. Cross-examination can be used to draw out such details. Context can matter, and cross-examination can be used to elicit testimony about that context.

A second type of cross-examination seeks to impeach the witness. Impeachment is an effort to prove that the witness's testimony should not be believed, and there are several well-established grounds for impeaching a witness:

- Perception—the witness did not observe what he or she claims.
- Recollection—the witness did observe the events but does not clearly recall them.
- Bias—the witness may have an axe to grind with the defendant or may have a financial interest in the outcome of the case.
- Character—the witness may be someone whose character demonstrates that he or she should not be believed.

---

42 Pointer v. Texas, 380 U.S. 400, 401 (1965). In *Pointer*, the Court ruled that the right to confront one's accusers was included with the guarantee to due process that applies in state criminal cases (405).

- Prior inconsistent statements—the witness previously spoke about the events and said something different.[43]

One reason courts have gotten comfortable with the idea of cooperating witnesses is that they are subject to cross-examination, particularly regarding their bias but also concerning their character and prior inconsistent statements.[44] As discussed in the previous chapter, the prosecution's duty to disclose *Brady* material includes the duty to disclose impeachment evidence, which includes evidence about a cooperating witness's bias, criminal record, prior criminal acts, and statements made to the government that contradict his or her trial testimony.[45] The prosecution's duty to disclose evidence of a cooperator's bias requires the disclosure of any promises made or other benefits provided to the witness by the government.

Defense Witnesses

So far I have focused on the prosecution's witnesses, but a defendant is also entitled to call witnesses and present physical evidence at trial. The Sixth Amendment guarantees a criminal defendant the right to "compulsory process for obtaining witnesses in his favor," which "is in plain terms the right to present a defense, the right to present the defendant's version of the facts as well as the prosecution's to the jury, so it may decide where the truth lies."[46]

The Sixth Amendment was included in the US Constitution in reaction to the long-established rule under English law that a criminal defendant "was not allowed to introduce witnesses in his defense at all." Initially, however, the Sixth Amendment right to present witnesses, like the rights guaranteed to criminal defendants in the Bill of Rights, applied only in federal criminal cases. Thus, until well into the twentieth century, some states had laws prohibiting a coconspirator from testifying in favor of the defendant even though the prosecution could call that same coconspirator to testify against the defendant under a cooperation agreement.[47]

---

43 Irving Younger, *The Art of Cross-Examination* (Chicago: American Bar Association, 1976), 5–15.
44 United States v. Singleton, 165 F.3d 1297, 1309 (10th Cir. 1999) (Kelly, J., dissenting).
45 Giglio v. United States, 405 U.S. 150, 154 (1972); United States v. Bagley, 473 U.S. 667, 676–77 (1985).
46 Washington v. Texas, 388 U.S. 14, 18–19 (1967).
47 Washington v. Texas, 388 U.S. 14, 19–20 (1967).

Shockingly, every state precluded defendants from testifying in their defense until 1864, when Maine changed its law in this respect and other states began doing the same. The theory behind barring a defendant from testifying was that he was an "interested" (biased) witness and thus unreliable. Though most states abandoned this reasoning in the late 1800s, the state of Georgia continued to preclude an accused from testifying in his defense until, in 1961, the US Supreme Court ruled that prohibition unconstitutional.[48]

Even today, however, an accused's ability to gather evidence in his or her defense does not equal that of the government. Most states have grand juries that can subpoena witnesses and physical evidence in the investigation of crimes. This allows the prosecution to learn prior to trial what witnesses will say under oath. And through cooperation agreements or otherwise, the prosecution can induce witnesses to meet prior to trial and ultimately to testify. The defense, by contrast, has no ability in most states to compel or even incentivize witnesses to speak prior to trial. Witnesses generally have no obligation to cooperate with defense counsel. And it's unlawful for a defense attorney to offer witnesses something of value in return for testifying. This often leaves the defense in the position of not knowing prior to trial what a witness will say, whether helpful or hurtful.

And the government has one tool it can use even today to prevent a defendant from calling favorable witnesses: the threat of prosecution. Remember, everyone has a Fifth Amendment right to remain silent, including a right not to testify at trial. This right applies not only in your own criminal trial but also in someone else's trial. If testifying in another person's criminal case would require you to testify on topics that could incriminate you, then you can decline to answer certain questions during your testimony in that trial. This allows the prosecution to threaten prospective defense witnesses with prosecution themselves if they testify in favor of a defendant. The predictable response to these threats is that the witness will invoke his or her Fifth Amendment right and refuse to

48 Ferguson v. Georgia, 365 U.S. 570, 574–77, 596 (1961). For a discussion of how repeal of laws prohibiting defendants from testifying impacted plea bargaining, see George Fisher, *Plea Bargaining's Triumph: A History of Plea Bargaining in America* (Stanford, CA: Stanford University Press, 2003), 104–10.

testify for the defense. And prosecutors do level these threats—often in veiled form—scaring off defense witnesses.[49]

Biblical Justice?

From the perspective of biblical justice, there is much to admire in the American approach to witness testimony, yet there is reason for concern as well.

Accuracy. The point of witnesses and other evidence is to provide the jury with a basis to reach a verdict. Not just any verdict, of course, but an accurate verdict. And accuracy requires attention not only to the trial processes but also to the types of evidence admitted and the way in which that evidence is obtained.

Even before the first witness testifies, justice requires that we confront questions about what type of tactics will be permitted to secure the testimony of an accusing witness. Can witnesses be paid for their testimony? Will reduced prison sentences be offered in return for cooperation? What degree of scientific reliability will be required for expert testimony to be admissible? Can confessions be elicited by deception? One empirical study of people who were convicted but later exonerated through DNA evidence reveals the four most common types of trial evidence leading to wrongful convictions: eyewitness identification, forensic evidence, informant testimony, and false confessions.[50] This means that the ways in which investigators conduct a lineup, perform a scientific test, incentivize a cooperator, and elicit a confession are pressing questions of biblical justice because they bear on the accuracy of the verdict that evidence will yield.

Scripture doesn't codify the permissible investigative techniques to be used in a twenty-first century justice system. Instead, we are left to call on the wisdom of men and women, believers and unbelievers, whose research has discovered circumstances under which the evidence yielded by various investigative methods is unreliable. Armed with that knowledge, our elected officials and law enforcement leaders can fashion investigative guidelines

49   Courts have acknowledged that these threats can go too far and violate due process. E.g., Earp v. Ornoski, 431 F.3d 1158, 1170–71 (9th Cir. 2005).
50   Brandon L. Garrett, "Judging Innocence," *Columbia Law Review* 108, no. 1 (2008): 55–142, http://www.jstor.org/stable/40041767.

that lead to reliable evidence.[51] In recent years, for instance, legislators in a few states have passed laws prohibiting the police from lying to minors to secure their confessions. These laws were prompted by social science research about the susceptibility of children to making false confessions under those circumstances.[52] Similarly, research on the way police lineups are conducted has revealed that certain practices lead to inaccurate eyewitness identifications. In response, some police departments have altered the manner in which they conduct lineups to avoid false identifications.[53] This application of social science research to investigative techniques and evidentiary rules is the work of biblical justice.

Due process. Just as Scripture does not mandate particular investigative techniques, it also does not codify a singular process for receiving and testing evidence. Biblical justice does, however, require some process for challenging the accusations leveled (Prov. 18:17), and that process must include all reasonable means needed to avoid false convictions. The American constitutional process—which affords the accused a chance both to cross-examine the state's witnesses and offer witnesses of his or her own—is one such method, and a good one at that. Regardless of whether the American founders had Scripture in mind when they adopted the Sixth Amendment guarantees, those provisions nonetheless serve the ends of biblical justice.

Northwestern University philosophy professor Jennifer Lackey, who specializes in epistemology, has written about "testimonial injustice," which she defines as both disbelieving testimony that should be believed and believing testimony (including confessions) that should not be believed.[54] Testing evidence by cross-examination is a means to avoiding testimonial injustice

---

51 For an example of proposed reforms to interrogation practices based on what social science has revealed about false confessions, see Brandon L. Garrett, "The Substance of False Confessions," *Stanford Law Review* 62, no. 4 (2010): 1051–1118, https://www.jstor.org/stable/40649624.

52 Allison D. Redlich and Gail S. Goodman, "Taking Responsibility for an Act Not Committed: The Influence of Age and Suggestibility," *Law and Human Behavior* 27, no. 2 (2003): 141–56, https://doi.org/10.1023/A:1022543012851, finding that children are three times as likely as adults to give false confessions. As a result, two states (Illinois and Oregon) have passed laws barring police from lying to children during interrogations. Two additional states—New York and Colorado—are currently considering similar measures.

53 Michael Ollove, "Police Are Changing Lineups to Avoid False IDs," *Stateline*, July 13, 2018, https://www.pewtrusts.org.

54 Jennifer Lackey, "False Confessions and Testimonial Injustice," *The Journal of Criminal Law and Criminology* 110, no. 1 (2020): 43–68, https://www.jstor.org/stable/48572214.

and, ultimately, an inaccurate verdict. This means that, as Christians, we should not begrudge a defendant whose lawyer conducts withering cross-examination of the state's witnesses, nor should we resent a prosecutor who presents the testimony of accusing witnesses or tests the memory of defense witnesses. There is no reason to cheer for a witness to perform well on direct examination or hold up to tough questioning on cross-examination. If a witness's story collapses on cross-examination, this may be a moment of justice, not reason for disappointment.

The accusation leveled by an indictment and repeated by a prosecution witness on direct examination may be true. Or it may not be. Until the evidence is presented and tested, we have no basis to know whose version of events is the right one. Accuracy turns not on the accusation but on the process to test it. A just process reveals the truth. Part of that process is the accusation. But another part of a just process, Scripture tells us, is the testing of the evidence. Accusations and probing questions about the accusation are, together, the God-ordained means to ferret out the truth (Prov. 18:17).

Impartiality. The evidentiary decisions we make in designing a criminal justice system also implicate the principle of impartiality. We know that the use of jailhouse snitches contributes to inaccurate verdicts, and those detained prior to trial face the risk of an opportunistic cellmate providing false testimony against them. Merely by their inability to meet bail, the poor are subjected to this threat of injustice that the well-heeled criminal defendant does not face. This partiality in our justice system provides an additional reason for those concerned about biblical justice to reconsider current bail practices.

Accountability. As noted above, the most common types of evidence leading to wrongful convictions are eyewitness identification, forensic evidence, informant testimony, and false confessions. When an eyewitness incorrectly identifies the perpetrator of a crime, it is often because of an unduly suggestive police lineup. When faulty forensic evidence is introduced at trial, it is typically because a forensic scientist used an unreliable technique or misperformed a reliable one. When a cooperator falsely accuses a codefendant or cellmate, it is almost always after the prosecutor incentivized him to do so with promises of leniency or other favorable treatment. When a suspect falsely confesses, it is typically because of psychological pressure brought to bear during the police interrogation. And all this faulty evidence gets before a jury only because a prosecutor decides to present it, perhaps with insufficient probing of its reliability before doing so.

Police and prosecutorial conduct of this sort raises the moral question whether the government actors responsible in some respect for the false evidence and resulting wrongful conviction took all reasonable means to avoid that result. At times, they certainly did not. And if they did not, biblical justice demands that they be punished themselves for their role in a miscarriage of justice. The reality, however, is that justice of this sort is rarely, if ever, realized.

———

Once all the evidence has been offered, the prosecution and defense deliver their closing arguments to the jury, and the judge instructs the jurors on the law they should apply in rendering their verdicts. At that point, all that the parties can do is wait. There is nothing more agonizing. Time seems to stand still. Occasionally, the jury sends out a question asking for a clarification on this or that point of law. The lawyers huddle, strategizing about how they should urge the judge to answer the question while also attempting to gather clues about the jury's deliberations from the question posed.

Finally, there is a knock on the door of the jury room. The bailiff sticks his head in the door for a moment. He then turns to announce that the jury has a verdict. The room turns electric. Hearts begin to race. Palms begin to sweat. Who will "win"? Will justice be done? Will both victim and accused be loved?

We'll know in a minute.

17

Sentencing

FOR THE NEARLY EIGHT YEARS I SERVED as a federal prosecutor, I found sentencing hearings to be deeply unsettling. My discomfort with sentencing was not born of fear that the defendant was innocent but from the knowledge that he or she was guilty. That guilt, I knew, deserved punishment. I wanted justice, but I knew that justice would involve the use of physical force against the perpetrator.

Sentencing was the moment when I requested that the judge order that force be applied to the defendant in the form of imprisonment. How could I without a moment's hesitation want that seeming harm to be inflicted on another human being? More troubling still was the pain and damage that, I knew, sentencing a defendant would inflict on his or her family. I found the whole exercise agonizing at the same time I thought it was just. As I left the house on those mornings when I had a sentencing hearing to attend that day, I said the same thing to my wife each time: "I hate sentencings."

Looking back, I believe that my uneasiness with sentencing was healthy. The day that you as a prosecutor don't hate sentencing—the day you can without a moment's hesitation call for the application of physical force to a fellow image bearer, the day you can sit through a victim's emotional pleas for justice without shedding a tear of your own, the day you have lost your sense of the humanity of *both* players in the criminal drama—is the day you should resign. Oliver O'Donovan rightly observes that "anyone who decides to send a man to prison must feel a pang, however right the decision may be, or else he has been brutalized."[1] I always felt that pang, so I hated sentencings.

---

1   Oliver O'Donovan, *In Pursuit of a Christian View of War* (Bramcote, UK: Grove, 1977), 5.

To impose any sentence is difficult. Difficult emotionally, to be sure. But more than that, it's difficult at times to determine what the just sentence should be. To sentence rightly—that is, true to the wrong done and the person who did it—is to grapple with issues that are myriad and complex. In this chapter, I will explain how sentencing works, how sentences are determined, and what a sentence of prison entails in the American justice system. I will end with some reflections on how the biblical principles of justice inform how we think about some of these sentencing issues. I don't have all the answers. I still feel the pang.

Sentencing Guidelines

In the United States, each crime carries with it a maximum sentence that can be imposed—what criminal lawyers call the "statutory maximum." This is true of both federal and state law crimes. The federal bank robbery statute, for example, provides that someone convicted of that offense can be "fined . . . or imprisoned not more than twenty years, or both."[2] But this maximum sentence is not necessarily, and not even likely, the sentence the defendant will receive if convicted. This isn't because of unwarranted leniency by judges, but because not every crime deserves the maximum sentence. Not every bank robbery is the same, so even if bank robbery carries a statutory maximum sentence of twenty years, robbing a bank of $1,000 is not the same as robbing it of $1,000,000. Once the defendant is convicted of a crime, someone must determine what sentence is appropriate given the facts of the case.

In most states, sentencing is a matter for the judge, though in some states the jury that heard the evidence and returned the guilty verdict also imposes a sentence.[3] In states where the jury determines the sentence, the defendant can typically introduce evidence relevant to punishment and the lawyers then make arguments to the jurors, much like the closing argument at the guilt stage, about what sentence is appropriate.[4] The jury can impose a sentence up to (but not higher than) the statutory maximum or can impose a sentence lower (even much lower) than the maximum if the facts warrant it. In states where the judge sentences, he or she too

---

2   18 U.S.C. § 2113(a).
3   E.g., Texas Code Crim. Proc. art. 37.07, § 2(b).
4   E.g., Texas Code Crim. Proc. art. 37.07, § 3.

can impose a sentence anywhere up to the statutory maximum based on the facts of the case.

In the early 1900s, the preferred approach to sentencing was what is known as "indeterminate sentencing," meaning that the judge (or jury) would impose a sentence stated as a wide range (for example, five to ten years), with the actual sentence the defendant served depending on his or her progress toward rehabilitation while in prison. Parole boards would monitor that progress and order the defendant's release when he or she was deemed ready to return to society.

In the mid-1970s, there was a backlash, driven by rising crime rates, against the "early" release of offenders from prison. At the same time, there was a sense that some judges were being unduly lenient in their sentencing, with the sentence handed down for the same crime differing dramatically based on the judge. As a result, liberals (like US Senator Ted Kennedy) and conservatives (like US Senator Strom Thurmond) came together in support of what became known as "truth in sentencing," meaning that the sentence imposed was (close to) the sentence the defendant served.[5]

The federal Sentencing Reform Act of 1984 created the US Sentencing Commission with the mandate to adopt "sentencing guidelines" that would, as their name suggests, guide the discretion of federal judges when imposing sentences for federal crimes. In the words of the statute, the guidelines were to "provide certainty and fairness in meeting the purposes of sentencing, avoiding unwarranted sentencing disparities among defendants."[6] Numerous states have likewise implemented sentencing guidelines, beginning with Minnesota in 1980.[7]

---

5 The concept of sentencing guidelines is attributed to federal district court judge Marvin Frankel, who gave a speech on the topic in 1971 and subsequently wrote a book about the issue. Marvin E. Frankel, "Lawlessness in Sentencing," *University of Cincinnati Law Review* 41, no. 1 (1972): 1–54; Marvin E. Frankel, *Criminal Sentences: Law without Order* (New York: Hill and Wang, 1972). US Senator Ted Kennedy introduced the first sentencing guidelines legislation in 1975. Michael Tonry, "Federal Sentencing 'Reform' since 1984: The Awful as Enemy of the Good," *Crime and Justice* 44, no. 1 (September 2015): 100, https://doi.org/10.1086/681666.
6 Comprehensive Crime Control Act of 1984, Pub. L. 98-473, 98 Stat. 1837, Title II, § 217(a) (October 12, 1984) (18 U.S.C. § 991(b)(1)(B)), https://www.govinfo.gov.
7 Kelly Lyn Mitchell, "State Sentencing Guidelines: A Garden Full of Variety," *Federal Probation* 81, no. 2 (September 2017): 28, https://www.uscourts.gov; Neal B. Kauder and Brian J. Ostrum, *State Sentencing Guidelines: Profiles and Continuum* (National Center for State Courts, July 2008), https://www.ncsc.org/.

In the federal court system and in states with sentencing guidelines, sentencing first involves a calculation of the guideline sentence. In the federal system, points are assigned based on various features of the crime (e.g., dollar amount involved, number of victims, use of a firearm, etc.), and these points are totaled to determine an "offense level." Each offense level has an associated range of months imprisonment that increases depending on the defendant's criminal history. For example, a defendant with an offense level of 25 but no prior criminal convictions would fall into a sentencing range of 57–71 months imprisonment. The same offense level for a person with a higher "criminal history category" could yield a sentencing range of 110–137 months in prison.[8]

The idea behind the sentencing guidelines was that, once the applicable sentencing range is identified, the judge was required to sentence the defendant to a particular term of months that falls within that range. So, for example, if the applicable range is 57–71 months, the judge must select a term of months within that range as the defendant's sentence. In the federal system, parole has been abolished, with the result being that the defendant will then serve at least 85 percent of the sentence imposed, with the reduction of 15 percent achievable based on the defendant's good behavior while in prison.[9]

As enacted, the sentencing guidelines were for all intents and purposes mandatory, meaning that the judge could only in the rarest of circumstances deviate above or below the guidelines sentencing range.[10] In theory, at least, this would result in defendants with the same criminal history who committed similar offenses receiving essentially the same sentence, thus reducing sentencing disparities attributable to the idiosyncrasies of the judge who handed down the sentence. But what the sentencing guidelines achieved in uniformity was, in the minds of many, at the expense of fairness. People familiar with the guidelines, including numerous judges, often concluded that this chart-based approach to sentencing was yielding sentences that were unduly harsh compared to the actual seriousness of the offense.[11]

8   U.S.S.G. Ch.5, Pt.A.
9   18 U.S.C. § 3624(b)(1), providing that the defendant can earn up to 54 days of credit toward his or her sentence each year based on satisfactory behavior.
10   Koon v. United States, 518 U.S. 81, 92 (1996).
11   The reaction of federal district court judges to the federal sentencing guidelines was not favorable, with more than 200 (of the 541) judges declaring all or part of the guidelines unconsti-

Then, in 2005, the US Supreme Court ruled that the federal sentencing guidelines, to the extent that they were mandatory and did not allow a trial judge discretion to deviate from the recommended range, were unconstitutional. In essence, the guidelines were mandating that a sentence be imposed based on factual findings made by the judge (e.g., dollar amount of loss, number of victims, use of a firearm, etc.), while the Sixth Amendment right to a jury trial requires that facts mandating a particular sentence be found by the jury.

The result of this ruling was not to invalidate the sentencing guidelines in their entirety but rather to render the sentencing range "advisory." Judges were no longer required to sentence within the sentencing range resulting from the guidelines calculation. Now judges are still required to calculate the sentencing range, but they can deviate above or below the range as long as they explain their reasons for doing so.[12] Ultimately, federal law requires that judges impose a sentence to "reflect the seriousness of the offense," "afford adequate deterrence," "protect the public from future crimes," and provide the defendant with needed rehabilitation.[13]

Acquitted Conduct

One especially troubling feature of the federal sentencing guidelines is that they allow defendants to be sentenced to prison for conduct for which they were never charged or for which they were charged and found not guilty. (Yes, you read that right.) Under the guidelines, a sentencing range is calculated based not only on the crime for which the defendant was convicted by the jury but also based on what is referred to under the sentencing guidelines as "relevant conduct."

Whether relevant conduct occurred isn't necessarily an issue to be decided by a jury. The judge makes that decision based on a process far less rigorous than a jury trial. The relevant conduct might be conduct that was never even charged by indictment and tried to a jury. Instead, after the defendant is convicted of one or more crimes with which he was charged, the prosecutors can then ask the judge to make a finding that additional

---

tutional. Tonry, "Federal Sentencing 'Reform' since 1984," 111. The US Supreme Court settled the issue, finding the guidelines constitutional. Mistretta v. United States, 488 U.S. 361 (1989).

12   United States v. Booker, 543 U.S. 220, 259–60 (2005).

13   18 U.S.C. § 3553(a)(2).

uncharged relevant conduct occurred. Or, the prosecutors can ask the judge to determine that "relevant conduct" occurred even though the jury found the defendant not guilty of that conduct[14]—what lawyers came to refer to as "acquitted conduct."

Here's an example of how this acquitted conduct sentencing might work. Imagine that a defendant is charged with one count of possession of drugs in a hotel room on a particular day (let's call that day, hypothetically, September 18, 2018) and a second and third count of possession of more drugs and a firearm in a car on another day (let's call the second day September 27, 2018). Now, further imagine that the defendant goes to trial, is found not guilty of the charge of drug possession on September 18, not guilty of possessing a firearm on September 27, but guilty of possessing drugs on September 27. Following the verdict, the case then proceeds to sentencing. The statutory maximum sentence on the first drug possession charge was 20 years in prison, but, if the defendant was sentenced based only on the September 27 drug possession for which he was convicted, his sentence under the guidelines would be 24–30 months.

But under the sentencing guidelines, the judge is not limited to sentencing the defendant based only on the conduct for which he was convicted. The judge can calculate the defendant's sentence based on the quantity of drugs possessed on September 27 *and* on the quantity from September 18. The judge can also calculate the sentencing range as if the defendant possessed a firearm even though the jury found him not guilty of possessing a firearm. If the sentence is calculated based on the conduct for which the defendant was convicted *and* acquitted, the sentencing range would be 87–108 months. And the judge can impose that much higher guideline sentence (as long as it is less than the 20-year statutory maximum for the one crime of which he was convicted). In fact, the judge did. None of this is hypothetical, as you might have guessed.[15]

It is not hard to see how this "acquitted conduct" sentencing increases the pressure on prospective defendants to plead guilty. Even if a defendant is innocent of the most serious charge the prosecution is threatening, and even if the defendant believes he can convince the jury that he is not guilty,

14 U.S.S.G. § 1B1.3(a)(2).
15 United States v. Osby, 832 F. App'x 230 (4th Cir. 2020).

and even if the defendant does convince the jury that he is not guilty of that charge, the judge can conclude otherwise and sentence the defendant based on that conduct underlying that charge of which the defendant was acquitted. This only adds to the pressure on a defendant to accept a guilty plea, knowing that if he goes to trial and wins on the most serious charge, the prosecution will, in effect, get a second bite at the apple—a chance to convince the judge during sentencing that the defendant is actually guilty of the conduct for which he was found not guilty by the jury. This risk is especially acute because the judge need only find that acquitted conduct by a preponderance of the evidence, not the beyond-a-reasonable-doubt standard that the jury applies.

If all of this sounds bizarre—un-American, even—it is. And yet somehow it has become the norm in the federal judicial system. The only constraint on this ability to sentence for acquitted conduct is the statutory maximum penalty for the charge(s) on which the defendant was convicted.[16]

Mandatory Minimums

Most criminal statutes specify only a maximum penalty, but since the earliest days of the United States some criminal statutes also set a minimum sentence to be imposed on anyone convicted of the offense. When a defendant is convicted of one of these crimes with what is now called a "mandatory minimum," the judge has no discretion to deviate below the statutory minimum sentence, though in most cases the judge can impose a higher sentence.

The prevalence of mandatory minimums has waxed and waned over time, but in the mid-1980s their usage increased dramatically, as did their severity.[17] In the same congressional bill that created the federal sentencing guidelines in 1984, Congress also substantially expanded the use of mandatory minimum sentences for federal crimes. For example, Section 924(c) of the federal criminal code was amended to provide that if someone commits an armed bank robbery (which carried a 25-year maximum sentence),

---

16 Several US Supreme Court justices have suggested that this acquitted conduct sentencing is unconstitutional, but the court has not yet taken up the issue. Jones v. United States, 574 U.S. 948 (2014) (Scalia, J., joined by Thomas and Ginsburg, J.J., dissenting from denial of certiorari).

17 *2011 Report to the Congress: Mandatory Minimum Penalties in the Federal Criminal Justice System* (US Sentencing Commission, 2011), 7–36, https://www.ussc.gov.

then they must be sentenced to a prison term of 5 years in addition to any sentence for the armed bank robbery. The statute further provided that a "second or subsequent" conviction under Section 924(c) carried another mandatory minimum prison term of 10 years.[18]

A bank robbery example might help to illustrate how the sentencing guidelines interact with a mandatory minimum. A common type of bank robbery is what is known as a "note job" where the robber never displays a firearm but instead slides a note across the counter to the teller demanding money and stating that he has a firearm. Let's assume for simplicity that the robber obtains $5,000 in a note job bank robbery in which he has a firearm in his jacket but never displays it. As I mentioned earlier, bank robbery has a 20-year statutory maximum, while armed bank robbery carries a 25-year statutory maximum prison term.[19] But assuming the robber has no criminal history, his guideline sentencing range will be well below those maximums. The guideline offense level for a bank robbery of less than $20,000 is 22, which has a sentencing range of 41–51 months in prison. The possession of the firearm adds 5 levels to the sentencing level, bringing it to 27, which has a sentencing range of 70–87 months.[20]

But that sentencing range is before the mandatory minimum is applied. If the prosecutor charges the defendant under Section 924(c) in addition to charging him with armed bank robbery, then the defendant's sentencing range would remain at 41–51 months (rather than 70–87 months) in prison, but he would receive an additional 5-year mandatory prison sentence on top of that guideline sentence. In other words, the mandatory minimum for the firearm possession more than doubles the sentence whether or not the firearm is used or even displayed during the robbery. The result is that a robbery of $5,000 in which no one is harmed would yield a prison sentence of at least 101 months (41 months plus 60 months, for a total of 8 ½ years) in prison.

Now imagine that the defendant commits two "note job" bank robberies in a single afternoon and in total gets $5,000. The defendant would again be

18 Comprehensive Crime Control Act of 1984, Pub. L. 98-473, 98 Stat. 1837, Title II, § 1005(a) (October 12, 1984), https://www.govinfo.gov/. Section 924(c) has since been amended to provide that a first offense carries a 5-year mandatory minimum term of imprisonment and a subsequent violation of Section 924(c) that occurs after the first conviction carries a mandatory minimum term of imprisonment of 25 years.

19 18 U.S.C. § 2113.

20 U.S.S.G. § 2B3.1; U.S.S.G. Ch.5, Pt.A.

subject to the 41–51 month sentencing range for the armed robbery. But the prosecutor could charge two Section 924(c) offenses, one for each bank robbery. Under the law as passed in 1984, the first Section 924(c) charge carried a 5-year mandatory minimum. The second Section 924(c) charge carried an additional 10-year mandatory minimum, for a total of a 15-year mandatory minimum on top of the 41–51 months sentence. Even if the judge sentenced the defendant at the lower end of that range (41 months), the judge would have no choice but to sentence the defendant to 15 years in addition to the 41 months (just short of 19 years in total) for two bank robberies on a single afternoon in which no one was harmed and the defendant obtained $5,000.

Three Strikes

One variation on mandatory minimum sentences is what has become known as "three strikes laws." Recidivism or "habitual offender" laws, as they were originally known, have been on the books in the United States for more than two hundred years, and the US Supreme Court has repeatedly rejected constitutional challenges of all types to these laws.[21]

In the mid-1900s, several states took an even more harsh approach to recidivism, mandating life in prison for a third consecutive felony conviction. Texas, for example, enacted a law in 1952 requiring that a defendant be sentenced to life in prison if convicted three times of any felony.[22] Several other states followed suit.[23] In 1980, the US Supreme Court upheld the constitutionality of a life prison sentence for a Texas man who committed three nonviolent property crimes (fraudulent use of a credit card, passing a forged check, and obtaining property by false pretenses) that in total caused $229.11 in losses.[24]

The rise of these so-called "three strikes laws," however, is usually tied to Washington state when, after a woman was murdered by a convicted

21 Moore v. Missouri, 159 U.S. 673 (1895); McDonald v. Massachusetts, 180 U.S. 311 (1901); Graham v. West Virginia, 224 U.S. 616 (1912).
22 Texas Pen. Code Ann. art. 63 (1952): "Whoever shall have been three times convicted of a felony less than capital shall on such third conviction be imprisoned for life in the penitentiary." The US Supreme Court held that introduction at trial of evidence of those prior convictions was not unfairly prejudicial so as to violate due process. Spencer v. Texas, 385 U.S. 554 (1967).
23 "Recidivism: The Treatment of the Habitual Offender," *University of Richmond Law Review* 7, no. 3 (1973): 525–37, https://scholarship.richmond.edu/lawreview/vol7/iss3/9.
24 Rummel v. Estelle, 445 U.S. 263 (1980).

rapist following his release from prison, a 1993 ballot initiative called for a mandatory sentence of life without parole upon conviction of a third violent offense.[25] The next year, a similar measure passed in California after a twelve-year-old girl was murdered by a man who was on parole after a life of crime.[26] That same year, President Clinton endorsed "three strikes and you're out" as federal sentencing policy during his State of the Union address, and by 1997 twenty-four states had adopted a version of this policy.[27]

Under California's three strikes law as enacted in 1994, only certain "serious" or "violent" crimes counted as the first two strikes, but any felony could serve as the third strike. The result of this arrangement was extraordinarily harsh sentencing for third strike crimes that at times bordered on the trivial. For example, in November 1995, Leandro Andrade shoplifted nine children's videotapes worth $153.54 from two Kmart stores. He was caught on surveillance camera and charged under California's three-strikes statute because of his prior criminal record. A drug addict, Andrade had committed a variety of nonviolent crimes over the years, including three residential burglaries and transportation of marijuana. As a result, Andrade's shoplifting convictions mandated two consecutive sentences of twenty-five years to life in prison.[28]

Gary Ewing faced a similarly harsh sentence for an only slightly more serious third strike. Ewing had been committing mostly small-grade crimes since he was twenty-two years old, escalating to three burglaries and a robbery at an apartment complex in December 1993, for which he was sentenced to nine years in prison. Ten months after he was released from prison, Ewing shoplifted three golf clubs worth $1,197 from a pro shop

25 James Austin, John Clark, Patricia Hardyman, and Alan Henry, *"Three Strikes and You're Out"*: *The Implementation and Impact of Strike Laws* (US Department of Justice: National Institute of Justice, 1999), 1, https://www.ojp.gov/.
26 Sara Sun Beale, "The Story of *Ewing*: Three Strikes Laws and the Limits of the Eighth Amendment Proportionality Review," in *Criminal Law Stories*, ed. Donna Coker and Robert Weisberg (New York: Foundation, 2012), 432.
27 "Address before a Joint Session of the Congress on the State of the Union, January 25, 1994," in *Public Papers of the Presidents of the United States: William J. Clinton (1994, Book I)* (Washington, DC: Federal Register), 133; John Clark, James Austin, and D. Alan Henry, "'Three Strikes and You're Out': A Review of State Legislation," *National Institute of Justice: Research in Brief* (September 1997): 1–14, https://www.ojp.gov/.
28 Lockyer v. Andrade, 538 U.S. 63, 66–68 (2003).

in El Segundo, California, and was charged with felony theft of property worth more than $400. For that shoplifting charge, Ewing was sentenced to twenty-five years to life in prison.[29]

Both Andrade and Ewing took their cases to the US Supreme Court in the fall of 2002, arguing that their sentences violated the Eighth Amendment's prohibition against cruel and unusual punishments.[30] In each case, the Supreme Court rejected their arguments. While the court agreed that the Eighth Amendment requires that sentences be proportionate to the crime, the court concluded that California's goals of "deterring," "segregating," and "incapacitating" career criminals with admittedly severe sentences was a "rational legislative judgment" and not "grossly disproportionate" to the crimes.[31] For stealing video tapes and golf clubs, the people of California could constitutionally condemn Leandro Andrade and Gary Ewing to, in all likelihood, die in prison if they so wished. The Supreme Court would not stand in the way.

Juvenile Sentencing

In contrast to the "lock them up and throw away the key" approach to career criminals like Andrade and Ewing, most states approach juvenile sentencing with an eye toward rehabilitation. Nevertheless, the United States stands alone in the severity with which it punishes juvenile offenders.

As a general rule, juvenile delinquency is handled outside the normal criminal justice process. In almost every state, juvenile courts have jurisdiction over children through age seventeen, though three states (Texas, Georgia, and Wisconsin) draw the limit at sixteen, and three states (Vermont, Michigan, and New York) extend juvenile jurisdiction to age eighteen.[32] Prior to the adjudication of their cases, children are held in juvenile detention. If, after conviction, a child is sentenced to a period of confinement, it will typically be served in a juvenile correctional center, though roughly 650

---

29 Ewing v. California, 538 U.S. 11, 18–20 (2003) (plurality).
30 U.S. Const. amend. XIII. The US Supreme Court had years earlier ruled that the Eighth Amendment applies to state criminal cases. Robinson v. California, 370 U.S. 660, 667 (1962).
31 Ewing v. California, 538 U.S. 11, 25, 29–30 (2003) (plurality); Lockyer v. Andrade, 538 U.S. 63, 74 (2003).
32 Anne Teigen, "Juvenile Age of Jurisdiction and Transfer to Adult Court Laws," National Conference of State Legislatures, April 8, 2021, https://www.ncsl.org; "Age Boundaries in Juvenile Justice Systems," National Governors Association, August 12, 2021, https://www.nga.org.

children are held in adult jails and prisons.[33] In recent years, the number of children confined has dropped dramatically, mirroring a similarly steep decline in youth arrests.[34] Even then, an estimated 48,000 youth are being held in some form of confinement on any given day in the United States.[35]

Every state provides for the possibility that children can be prosecuted and punished as adults in especially serious cases. As of January 2022, the most common minimum age set by states for prosecution of a child as an adult is fourteen years old, though four states (Indiana, Missouri, Montana, Washington) set it at twelve, six states (Georgia, Mississippi, New York, Nevada, North Carolina, Oklahoma) set it at thirteen, and some states have no minimum age.[36] In recent years, no state has prosecuted more children as adults than Florida.[37]

The United States is the only country in the world that sentences juveniles to life in prison without the possibility of parole,[38] although the practice differs by state. Twenty-five states have banned life without parole sentences for children, and another nine states that allow it by law have no one serving such a sentence for a crime committed as a child. As of January 2020, there were 1,465 people in the United States serving a sentence of life without parole for a juvenile crime, with Pennsylvania leading the nation with more than 400 "juvenile lifers."[39] Another 8,600 people are serving life sentences with the possibility of parole for crimes committed as children.[40]

33 *The State of America's Children 2021* (Washington, DC: Children's Defense Fund, 2021), 69 (Table 32: Children in Adult Prisons, Select Years), https://www.childrensdefense.org/.
34 *Youth Incarceration in the United States* (The Annie C. Casey Foundation, December 2021), https://www.aecf.org/, showing youth confinement rates down 70 percent from 1995 to 2019.
35 Wendy Sawyer, "Youth Confinement: The Whole Pie 2019," Prison Policy Initiative, December 19, 2019, https://www.prisonpolicy.org.
36 "Age Matrix," Interstate Commission for Juveniles, accessed April 9, 2022, last modified January 20, 2022, https://www.juvenilecompact.org.
37 Tachana Joseph-Marc, "Florida Leads the Nation in Prosecuting Children as Adults. What's Being Done about It?," Florida Policy Institute, March 8, 2019, https://www.floridapolicy.org.
38 Since 1990, eight countries are known to have executed children. "Executions of Juveniles outside the U.S.," Death Penalty Information Center, accessed January 13, 2023, https://death penaltyinfo.org/.
39 Josh Rovner, *Juvenile Life without Parole: An Overview* (The Sentencing Project, May 24, 2021), https://www.sentencingproject.org/; "Juvenile Lifers Information," Pennsylvania Department of Corrections, December 31, 2022, https://www.cor.pa.gov. To read the story of one of those children sentenced to life without parole but later freed as a result of the work of Bryan Stevenson and the Equal Justice Initiative, see Ian Manuel, *My Time Will Come: A Memoir of Crime, Punishment, Hope, and Redemption* (New York: Pantheon, 2021).
40 Ashley Nellis, *No End in Sight: America's Enduring Reliance on Life Imprisonment* (The Sentencing Project, 2021), 4, https://www.sentencingproject.org/.

These figures are down significantly following a series of recent decisions by the US Supreme Court. In 2010, the court ruled that a juvenile sentence of life without parole for a non-homicide crime is unconstitutionally disproportionate in violation of the Eighth Amendment given the "diminished moral culpability" of children.[41] Two years later, the court ruled unconstitutional sentencing laws that *mandate* life without parole for juveniles who commit homicide offenses, instead requiring that courts make case-by-case determinations as to whether that sentence is appropriate. The court noted its expectation that "appropriate occasions for sentencing juveniles to this harshest possible penalty will be uncommon."[42]

Prison Conditions

By design, prison denies people the ability to provide for their own needs. Given their confinement, they can neither hold a job to earn a living nor bear a weapon to defend themselves. They are entirely dependent on the state for provision and protection. As a result, the US Supreme Court has ruled that the Eighth Amendment's prohibition against cruel and unusual punishments imposes on prison officials an obligation to "provide humane conditions of confinement," meaning they "must ensure that inmates receive adequate food, clothing, shelter, and medical care, and must take reasonable measures to guarantee the safety of the inmates." As the court explained, given that prisoners have been "stripped . . . of virtually every means of self-protection and foreclosed . . . access to outside aid, the government and its officials are not free to let the state of nature take its course."[43]

Prison conditions, however, vary widely in terms of safety, security, control, sanitation, and overcrowding. At the most extreme end of the spectrum are the "Super Max" facilities housing those prisoners who pose the most extreme threats, including terrorists, spies, and drug lords. Given the risks they pose, prisoners in these facilities are held in individual cells for twenty-three hours per day. Other prisons vary in their security levels,

---

41 Graham v. Florida, 560 U.S. 48 (2010).
42 Miller v. Alabama, 567 U.S. 460 (2012). The Supreme Court subsequently held that the ruling in *Miller* applies retroactively to sentences already imposed prior to that decision. Montgomery v. Louisiana, 577 U.S. 190 (2016).
43 Farmer v. Brennan, 511 U.S. 825, 832–33, 837 (1994).

ranging from maximum security prisons (where prisoners are housed in cells) to minimum security prisons (where prisoners may be held in open barracks-type halls). Gangs are a common presence in prisons. Strip searches and body cavity searches are a daily part of prison life. Privacy, even for the most intimate of activities, is nonexistent. Some inmates are held in solitary confinement for months (and even years) on end, even though studies show that confinement of this sort dramatically increases suicide rates and causes severe mental health issues.[44] Overcrowding is a perennial problem, as politicians are keen on increasing prison sentences to appeal to their constituents as "tough on crime" but far more reluctant to raise taxes to expand prison facilities to house those being more severely punished.

A common threat faced by prisoners is rape at the hands of fellow inmates and (especially in the case of female prisoners) prison guards. Though these incidents are notoriously underreported, prisoners in the United States nonetheless reported nearly 28,000 incidents of sexual victimization in 2018.[45] It is estimated that juveniles are "5 times more likely to be sexually assaulted in adult rather than juvenile facilities—often within the first 48 hours of incarceration."[46] In an effort to address this crisis of sexual assault in prisons and jails, Congress in 2003 passed the Prison Rape Elimination Act. The act called for the establishment of standards designed to eliminate prison rape and a minor reduction of federal grant funding to states that failed to comply with those standards.[47]

Biblical Justice?

Sentencing is hard. But justice requires sentencing. Justice is achieved not only by rendering an accurate verdict as to who the wrongdoer was but also by acting on that verdict, making a declaration about the severity of the wrong done and responding with kind harshness toward the wrongdoer for

---

44 Hannah Pullen-Blasnik, Jessica T. Simes, and Bruce Western, "The Population Prevalence of Solitary Confinement," *Science Advances* 7, no. 48 (2021): https://doi.org/10.1126/sciadv.abj1928.

45 Laura M. Maruschak and Emily D. Buehler, *Survey of Sexual Victimization in Adult Correctional Facilities, 2012–2018—Statistical Tables* (US Department of Justice, Bureau of Justice Statistics, June 2021), 1, https://bjs.ojp.gov/.

46 34 U.S.C. § 30301(4).

47 34 U.S.C. § 30301, et seq.

the good of the wronged, the wrongdoer, and the community at large. What that kind harshness should look like in a given case was, for me, always a vexing question. To answer wrongly is to commit an injustice in the pursuit of justice. Even if the verdict is true, sentencing can pervert that justice, either because the sentence is unduly harsh or unduly lenient. The time may not fit the crime. Doing justice in sentencing means appropriately calibrating the physical force employed with the seriousness of the offense committed.

Accuracy. Sentencing practices in the United States raise concerns about the accuracy of convictions. As we saw in chapter 11, the disparity in how we sentence after trial versus pursuant to a plea bargain can cause wrongful convictions by coercing even the innocent to plead guilty. Conversely, plea bargaining creates false convictions of a different sort by allowing defendants to plead guilty to crimes far less serious than the crime actually committed.

The biblical justice principle of accuracy is also implicated by the practice of sentencing defendants for acquitted conduct. Requiring proof beyond a reasonable doubt to convict is one way in which we take all reasonable means to avoid a false conviction and its corollary of imposing unjust punishment. But if we nonetheless punish defendants for crimes of which they were acquitted (by enhancing the punishment for another crime beyond what we would otherwise impose) and do so based on a lower standard of proof (preponderance of the evidence), we increase substantially the risk of punishing defendants for crimes they did not commit. A preponderance of the evidence requires that the judge be only 51 percent certain that the defendant committed the crime for which he was acquitted. Imposing enhanced prison terms when there is such substantial (as much as 49 percent) doubt as to the defendant's guilt will, over time and under the law of averages, result in a significant number of enhanced sentences based on inaccurate assessments of guilt.

Proportionality. Even when the defendant is accurately convicted of a crime that aligns with the wrong done, the justice of the conviction can be undermined by the injustice of the sentence. Sometimes that injustice takes the form of a lenient sentence that trivializes the seriousness of the wrong and does little to correct the offender. Other times, the injustice is a harshness that is not kind and a severity that is more vindictive than benevolent. Rigid sentencing guidelines, mandatory minimums, and "three strikes" laws can, in too many cases, work injustices. To be just, sentences must be proportionate.

When I refer to proportional sentencing, your mind most likely turns to the *length* of the sentence. And sentence duration is certainly an element of the proportionality analysis. A sentence of fifty years to life in prison for stealing five videotapes is wildly disproportionate, and this is true regardless of whether the crime is the defendant's first or his third. We may be frustrated, even angry, with the defendant's refusal to comply with society's laws. The sentiment is understandable, as is a fear of what that repeated wrongdoer may do in the future. But none of that renders human lives disposable. A financial harm of $153.43—the equivalent of less than forty hours of work at the minimum wage in 1994—does not permit those of us bound by the biblical principle of proportionality to banish someone to a cage for five decades. We have no authority to wield the sword against our fellow image bearers in that way.

For some crimes, extended incarceration is harsh yet kind, serving the good of the prisoner (by preventing him from doing more wrong) and society (by protecting potential victims from further wrong). But Scripture does not authorize us to incapacitate and deter by means of punishments disproportionate to the crime committed. If incapacitation and deterrence were alone sufficient to justify a punishment, then poking out both eyes of one who harms one eye would be an acceptable response. If I poke out both my neighbor's eyes, I certainly increase the chances that he will never again harm someone else's eyes. For that matter, poking out both his eyes and cutting off his hands would almost certainly incapacitate him from ever harming again. But this type of incapacitation and deterrence is not what Scripture authorizes. What God permits is a measured response commensurate with the wrong done. To do more (or less) is unjust, regardless of what utilitarian ends it might serve. Once we understand this, we should tremble at our role in a criminal justice system that at times unjustly subjects people to mandatory minimums and three strikes laws that regard them as less than worthy of our love, that treat them differently than we would wish to be treated, that do them wrong in the name of doing justly.

But proportionality bears not only on the length of the sentence imposed but also the *type* of sentence imposed. Once we rightly understand that to impose a prison sentence at all is to apply physical force to another person, we then must grapple with the question whether physical force of that sort is *ever* the proportionate sentence for the crime at issue. Scripture speaks of an eye for an eye, to be sure. But it nowhere speaks of an eye for a dollar.

And imprisonment raises an additional issue. Prison is inherently the application of physical force against prisoners to limit their freedom. But when prison officials fail to maintain a just order in prisons, they expose those prisoners to additional assaults (including sexual assaults) while incarcerated. This may not be an outcome we wish on the inmates. But if it is a foreseeable outcome that the authorities do not take all reasonable means to prevent, then it is an outcome for which those authorities are, under the doctrine of double effect, morally accountable. Preventing assaults of this type is a moral imperative for those who embrace a biblical concept of justice, and we must use all reasonable means to prevent it.

When concerns are raised about unduly harsh sentencing or inhumane prison conditions, I have not infrequently heard people respond, "If you can't do the time, then don't do the crime." This jingle is catchy, but jingles do not define justice for the Christian. The sentence may be legal and the defendant may have committed the crime with knowledge of the sentence the law provides. But neither of those is enough to render a sentence just. The justice of a sentence depends on whether the law aligns with biblical principles, including proportionality. If the sentence is disproportionate to the crime, then the defendant shouldn't have to "do the time."

Impartiality. If justice entails treating similar cases similarly and dissimilar cases dissimilarly, then the sentence imposed should turn on the facts of the crime, not the personality of the sentencing judge. Sentencing guidelines can serve this end and protect against the injustice of partiality. To the extent that guidelines eliminate sentencing disparities attributable to the idiosyncrasies of the judge rather than the seriousness of the offense, this is something Christians should welcome. But we can, in our pursuit of justice (impartiality), commit injustice (disproportionality). Sentencing guidelines are a prime example of this phenomenon. Justice in sentencing cannot be entirely reduced to points, calculations, and charts. Guidance is useful to channel the sentencing discretion of judges. Rigid mandates, however, can at times yield an injustice of their own by requiring a sentence out of line with the true severity of the crime.

Accountability. When the authorities fail to render proportionate punishment, justice demands that they be held accountable. In the United States, at least, this duty falls in part on the electorate given the moral proximity of the governed to the governors. The governing officials act on our behalf. They wield power that we have conferred on them. When they misuse that power, when they become (to use Augustine's words) a band of robbers wreaking havoc on our neighbors, we have a moral obligation to love the officially abused neighbors by using the democratic tools at our disposal to hold the renegade officials accountable. At a minimum, this means we must vote. Not every Christian across the ages has had that tool of love at his or her disposal. But at this place and moment in time, American believers do. And it is a stewardship. We must use it for justice. To do otherwise is the criminal justice equivalent of passing by on the other side. To look away is to be the Levite rather than the Samaritan.

"Mass incarceration" has been a hot topic of conversation in recent years. Incarceration rates in the United States vastly exceed those of other Western nations, and it is not uncommon for those concerned with this mass incarceration phenomenon to blame it on a single root cause. It's racism. It's sentencing guidelines. It's over-criminalization. It's inadequate educational opportunities. It's bail practices. It's poverty. It's the war on drugs. It's mandatory minimums. It's individual choices. It's fatherlessness. The list of supposed primary causes that people offer goes on and on.

But in a fallen world in which sin has infected everything, mono-causal explanations for the tragedies we observe are rarely the best ones. Incarceration rates in the United States are several multiples of those in Western European countries. But the violent crime rate in the United States is also multiples of the rates in those countries.[48] Racism does still infect the criminal justice system in some respects. But not every racial disparity in the

48 Franklin E. Zimring and Gordon Hawkins, *Crime Is Not the Problem: Lethal Violence in America* (New York: Oxford University Press, 1997), 6–8.

criminal justice system is attributable to racial bias.[49] There is a tendency in the United States to over-criminalize. But even if we imprisoned only those charged with violent crimes, our rate of imprisonment would remain exceedingly high.[50] People are responsible for their choices to engage in crime. But we would be foolish to ignore the effect the social environment has on those choices. Sentencing is hard because life in a fallen world is hard.

At the same time, some sentencing injustices are right before our eyes. Some victims of those injustices lie right in our path. Will we look away from the Gary Ewings of the world? Will we walk past the Leandro Andrades? Will we shield our eyes from—or, worse yet, joke about—the victims of prison rape? They are all our neighbors. Will we love them?

49 James Forman Jr., *Locking Up Our Own: Crime and Punishment in Black America* (New York: Farrar, Straus and Giroux, 2017).

50 John F. Pfaff, *Locked In: The True Causes of Mass Incarceration and How to Achieve Real Reform* (New York: Basic Books, 2017), 187–88.

18

Death Penalty

DONALD HENRY "PEE WEE" GASKINS JR. was a serial killer. He confessed to dozens of murders, is known to have killed at least fifteen
people, and in May 1976 was sentenced to death for the murder of one
of eight people whose bodies were discovered in shallow graves near
his home in Prospect, South Carolina. But Gaskins's death sentence
was handed down just a month before the Supreme Court's decision
in *Furman v. Georgia* (see chap. 7) and was subsequently overturned
as unconstitutional. He was instead sentenced to life in prison.[1]

In September 1982, while serving his prison sentence, Gaskins, who
was White, murdered a fellow death row inmate, Rudolph Tyner, who
was Black. Gaskins had been hired by a relative of the victims of Tyner's
crime to kill him. When Gaskins failed in his effort to poison Tyner, he
instead built a small bomb that he convinced Tyner was an intercom.
When Tyner placed the fake intercom to his ear, Gaskins detonated it.
For this murder, Gaskins was tried, convicted, and again sentenced to
death.[2]

Nine years later, in the early morning hours of September 6, 1991,
Donald Gaskins was electrocuted by the state of South Carolina. His
execution was widely reported, with articles appearing in the *New York*

1 "Pee Wee Gaskins: Prospect's Notorious Serial Killer," Johnsonville South Carolina History,
   accessed March 3, 2022, https://www.johnsonvilleschistory.org; State v. Gaskins, 242 S.E.2d
   220 (S.C. 1978).
2 State v. Gaskins, 326 S.E.2d 132 (S.C. 1985) (per curiam); Donald Gaskins and Wilton Earle,
   Final Truth: The Autobiography of a Serial Killer (Atlanta: Adept, 1992), 199–204.

Times, Baltimore Sun, and *Los Angeles Times.* But the media interest in Gaskins was not that he was a serial killer. Gaskins's execution was noteworthy because it was the first time since 1944 that a White man or woman was put to death in the United States for killing a Black person.[3] In the intervening forty-seven years, more than 1,700 executions had been carried out across the country.[4] Not one of those executions was for a White-on-Black murder.

Donald Gaskins was executed only two years after DNA technology was first used in the United States to exonerate someone who had been wrongly convicted.[5] In the years that followed, statistical evidence of racial bias in the administration of the death penalty combined with the exonerations of dozens of innocent men and women condemned to death has led many Americans to change their view about the morality, or at least advisability, of the death penalty.

But the death penalty has a long and deep history in the United States, and even today most Americans still support its usage.[6] In this chapter, I briefly survey that history, describe the legal process by which death sentences are imposed, and then conclude by addressing some ethical questions that Christians should consider in evaluating the justice of the death penalty as it is administered today in the United States.

A Brief History

The first known execution in the American colonies was carried out in Virginia in 1608 when George Kendall was shot for espionage. It would be another fourteen years before the second execution—a hanging for theft, also in Virginia—followed two years later by an execution for the crime of

3   David Margolick, "Murderer in S.C. Is First White since '44 to Be Executed for Killing a Black Victim," *Baltimore Sun,* September 7, 1991, https://www.baltimoresun.com/; "South Carolina Executes Man for Murder," *New York Times,* September 6, 1991, https://www.nytimes.com/; "Man Executed for Killing Death Row Inmate with Bomb," *Los Angeles Times,* September 8, 1991, https://www.latimes.com/.
4   Chris Wilson, "Every Execution in U.S. History in a Single Chart," *Time,* July 24, 2014, updated April 25, 2017, https://time.com/.
5   Rob Warden, "First DNA Exoneration: Gary Dotson," Center on Wrongful Convictions, Bluhm Legal Clinic, Northwestern Pritzker School of Law, accessed April 18, 2022, https://www.law.northwestern.edu.
6   Jeffrey M. Jones, "Death Penalty Support Holding at Five-Decade Low," *Gallup,* November 18, 2021, https://news.gallup.com/.

sodomy and an execution for rape two years after that, both also in Virginia and both on the gallows.[7]

Today, we think of the death penalty as a sentence imposed exclusively for murder. But in colonial America and continuing into the nation's early years, the death penalty was authorized for a wide array of criminal offenses, from murder to robbery, witchcraft to burglary, counterfeiting to arson, and, of course, slave revolt. At least fifty-one men were executed for horse stealing; all of them were hung. In 1768, North Carolina executed three men for that crime. Tennessee did the same in 1782, as did New York in 1788. The last death sentence carried out for horse stealing was in 1851. At least thirty-one people were executed for counterfeiting, the first in 1720 and the last in 1822, eleven of them in Pennsylvania and nine in New York.[8]

Not everyone, however, shared an enthusiasm for this promiscuous usage of the death penalty. In the late 1700s, Thomas Jefferson supported a bill to limit the death penalty in Virginia to the crimes of murder and treason.[9] That bill failed to pass by a single vote, a failure that James Madison attributed to "the rage against Horse stealers."[10] Jefferson's friend, John Leland, a Baptist minister in Virginia, wrote in 1830 that "there are but few crimes, if any, that should be punished with death,"[11] penning these words as a movement to abolish the death penalty was beginning to gain traction. The Congregational minister George Cheever, a vocal proponent of the death penalty, abhorred its extension to crimes other than murder. "Modern penal codes in their lavish application

7   "Executions in the U.S. 1608–2002: The Espy File," Death Penalty Information Center, accessed January 13, 2023, https://deathpenaltyinfo.org. For a short recitation of the facts surrounding Kendall's execution, see Natasha Frost, "Was the Colonies' First Death Penalty Handed to a Mutineer or Spy?," History, August 2, 2018, last modified August 24, 2018, https://www.history.com.

8   "Executions in the U.S. 1608–2002: The Espy File." As some researchers have noted, the Espy File, although widely used, is not necessarily comprehensive and may contain errors in its compilation of data regarding executions prior to the twentieth century. Paul H. Blackman and Vance McLaughlin, "The Espy File on American Executions: User Beware," Homicide Studies 15, no. 3 (2011): 209–27, https://doi.org/10.1177/1088767911418054.

9   Autobiography of Thomas Jefferson, 1743–1790 (New York: G. P. Putnam's Sons, 1914), 69.

10   Letter from Madison, February 15, 1787, in The Papers of Thomas Jefferson, vol. 11, ed. Julian P. Boyd (Princeton, NJ: Princeton University Press, 1958), 152.

11   John Leland, "The Result of Observation," in The Writings of the Late Elder John Leland, ed. L. F. Greene (New York: G. W. Wood, 1845), 595. Other ministers expressed more enthusiasm for the death penalty, some arguing for its moral and practical necessity. Seth Kotch, Lethal State: A History of the Death Penalty in North Carolina (Chapel Hill, NC: University of North Carolina Press, 2019), 57, 125.

of the last penalty of law have well merited the accusation of savageness and barbarity," he wrote in 1846, taking special aim at the death penalty for horse stealing.[12] That same year, Michigan abolished the death penalty except for the crime of treason, with Rhode Island and Wisconsin abolishing the death penalty entirely a few years later. The death penalty abolition movement continued into the mid-1800s, but mostly proved unsuccessful.[13]

Death penalty proceedings in the United States were carried out with shocking speed even well into the 1900s. One researcher has chronicled case after case in which men and women were convicted and executed within months, and sometimes weeks, of their crimes. In November 1898, Christopher Merry, a twenty-six-year-old White man, committed a murder in Illinois for which he was hanged in Chicago the following April. Henry Bailey, a Black man in North Carolina, murdered a white man in June 1906 and was hanged for that crime in August. In November 1906, Thomas Harris, a young White man, murdered an elderly White man in South Carolina, a crime for which he was hanged in April 1907. Harris Sutton, a thirteen-year-old Black boy, was legally hanged in Georgia in January 1917 for a rape in December 1916. A thirty-six-year-old Black man, Isaac Benson, was executed by the state of Maryland in July 1926 for the murder of two Black women in Baltimore that April. In Delaware, George Scott, a Black man, was hanged in November 1936 for a murder committed in July.[14]

In the earliest years of the American colonies, the racial makeup of those executed appears to have roughly mirrored the population at large. Of the 348 known executions through 1730, 71 (20 percent) were of Black men and

12 George B. Cheever, *A Defence of Capital Punishment* (New York: Wiley and Putnam, 1846), 208, 212.
13 Louis Filler, "Movements to Abolish the Death Penalty in the United States," *The Annals of the American Academy of Political and Social Sciences* 284, no. 1 (1952): 127, https://www.jstor.org/stable/1029452/; David Brion Davis, "The Movement to Abolish Capital Punishment in America, 1787–1861," *The American Historical Review* 63, no. 1 (1957): 43–44, https://doi.org/10.2307/1847110; Stuart Banner, *The Death Penalty: An American History* (Cambridge, MA: Harvard University Press, 2002), 134.
14 Daniel Allen Hearn, *Legal Executions in Illinois, Indiana, Iowa, Kentucky and Missouri: A Comprehensive Registry, 1866–1965* (Jefferson, NC: McFarland, 2016), 16; Daniel Allen Hearn, *Legal Executions in North Carolina and South Carolina: A Comprehensive Registry, 1866–1962* (Jefferson, NC: McFarland, 2015), 52, 158; Daniel Allen Hearn, *Legal Executions in Georgia: A Comprehensive Registry, 1866–1964* (Jefferson, NC: McFarland, 2016), 113; Daniel Allen Hearn, *Legal Executions in Delaware, the District of Columbia, Maryland, Virginia and West Virginia: A Comprehensive Registry, 1866–1962* (Jefferson, NC: McFarland, 2015), 13, 49.

women. But in the years that followed, the racial composition of those subjected to this ultimate penalty began to shift. Through 1750, Black people made up 34 percent of all executions. Through 1776, the figure was 38 percent. Since then, the racial makeup of those executed in the United States has remained remarkably consistent: of those executed, 48–49 percent have been Black. That statistic holds whether you consider all executions since the nation's founding in 1776, all executions since Reconstruction ended in 1877, or all executions in the twentieth century. A sentence of death is one disproportionately carried out on Black people relative to their percentage of the population.[15]

This disproportionate execution of Black Americans is especially pronounced for crimes other than murder. For those crimes, 73 percent of the men and women executed between 1776 and 1964 (the last such execution) were Black. After Reconstruction ended, it was 88 percent. In the twentieth century, 818 people were executed in the United States for non-homicide offenses. Of those, 725 (89 percent) were Black while only 76 (9 percent) were White.[16]

Especially noteworthy is whom America has executed for the crime of rape. Since the nation's founding, at least 1,012 men have been executed for rape or attempted rape. Of the 996 whose race is known, 914 (91 percent) were Black. The percentage is the same if you consider only the period since the Civil War ended.[17] Of the 126 men executed for rape in North Carolina, to take one example, 113 were Black (almost always for raping a White female) and no White man was ever executed for raping a Black woman.[18] North Carolina is not unique in this regard. The federal government acknowledged in litigation before the US Supreme Court that the data from eleven southern states in the years 1945 through 1965 "revealed that among all those convicted of rape, blacks were selected disproportionately for the death sentence."[19]

These statistics align with the racist trope about the sexual proclivities of Black men and the danger they pose to White women.[20] Relying on those

15 These statistics are through the end of 2022. "Executions in the U.S. 1608–2002: The Espy File"; "Execution List," Death Penalty Information Center, accessed January 13, 2023, https://deathpenaltyinfo.org/.
16 "Executions in the U.S. 1608–2002: The Espy File."
17 "Executions in the U.S. 1608–2002: The Espy File."
18 Seth Kotch, *Lethal State*, 46; Daniel Allen Hearn, *Legal Executions in North Carolina and South Carolina*, 8.
19 Graham v. Collins, 506 U.S. 461, 483 n.5 (1993) (Thomas, J., concurring).
20 For a disturbing discussion of how this trope was elevated into an evidentiary presumption in criminal cases as late as the 1950s, see Randall Kennedy, *Race, Crime, and the Law* (New York: Vintage Books, 1998), 90.

bigoted stereotypes, the protection of White women from rape at the hands of Black men was a commonly invoked justification for lynching in the century between the Civil War and the Civil Rights Movement.[21] As African American newspapers observed in the 1930s and 1940s, a charge of rape by a White woman against a Black man was the equivalent of a death sentence, whether at the hands of a mob or the state.[22] So prevalent in the Jim Crow era was the view that Black men were a sexual threat to White women that Reverend Francis Grimké felt compelled to rebut it at length during his summer of 1899 sermon series.[23]

Constitutionality

In 1972, against this racially tainted backdrop, the US Supreme Court ruled in *Furman v. Georgia* that the death penalty as then administered in the United States was unconstitutional. As Justice Clarence Thomas would much later observe, *Furman* "was decided in an atmosphere suffused with concern about race bias in the administration of the death penalty—particularly in Southern States, and most particularly in rape cases."[24]

Though the justices in the *Furman* majority shared a concern about racial discrimination, they were deeply divided as to the legal rationale for declaring the death penalty unconstitutional. Justice William Douglas believed that discretionary death penalty statutes, though racially neutral on their face, were in their application "pregnant with discrimination and discrimination is an ingredient not compatible with the idea of equal protection of the laws."[25] Justices William Brennan and Thurgood Marshall thought the death penalty was in all circumstances a "cruel and unusual punishment" that violated the Constitution's Eighth Amendment.[26] Justice Potter Stewart declined to rule that the death penalty was categorically cruel and unusual

---

21 For a discussion of how the trope also fueled criminal prosecutions during that era, see Danielle L. McGuire, *At the Dark End of the Street: Black Women, Rape, and Resistance—a New History of the Civil Rights Movement from Rosa Parks to the Rise of Black Power* (New York: Alfred A. Knopf, 2010), 54–63.

22 Kotch, *Lethal State*, 45, 47.

23 Francis Grimké, "Lynching: Its Causes—the Crimes of the Negro," in *Addresses*, vol. 1 of *The Works of Francis Grimké*, ed. Carter G. Woodson (Washington, DC: Associated, 1942), 305–14.

24 Graham v. Collins, 506 U.S. 461, 479 (1993) (Thomas, J., concurring).

25 Furman v. Georgia, 408 U.S. 238, 256–57 (1972) (Douglas, J., concurring).

26 Furman v. Georgia, 408 U.S. 238, 305 (1972) (Brennan, J., concurring); Furman v. Georgia, 370 (Marshall, J., concurring).

but instead concluded that it was cruel and unusual in application because there was no rhyme or reason as to who was sentenced to death. The death penalty was, in his view, "wantonly" and "freakishly imposed."[27] In a similar vein, Justice Byron White thought the death penalty cruel and unusual because it was "so infrequently imposed that the threat of execution is too attenuated to be of substantial service to criminal justice."[28]

The five justices in the *Furman* majority fully expected that their ruling would be the end of capital punishment in the United States. To their surprise, however, dozens of states responded not by abandoning the death penalty but rather by amending their death penalty statutes to address the court's various concerns. North Carolina, for example, sought to eliminate arbitrariness by mandating that all first-degree murder be punishable by death—an approach the Supreme Court subsequently ruled was unconstitutional because a "fundamental respect for humanity . . . requires consideration of the character and record of the individual offender and the circumstances of the particular offense."[29]

Most other states took a different tack, circumscribing the types of crimes for which death was an available sentence. Some states did this by narrowly describing the types of murder that would qualify as capital murder.[30] Other states developed a list of "aggravating circumstances" that would render someone guilty of a crime (not just murder, but also rape and burglary) eligible for the death penalty.[31] Either of those two approaches was constitutionally permissible, the court later ruled, because they "directed and limited" the jury's sentencing decision so as to avoid the "wholly arbitrary and capricious" imposition of a death sentence.[32]

Most of the aggravating circumstances that render a defendant death-eligible are well-defined: murder of a police officer, a prior capital murder conviction, murder-for-hire, murder during an escape from prison or while

---

27 Furman v. Georgia, 408 U.S. 238, 310 (1972) (Stewart, J., concurring).

28 Furman v. Georgia, 408 U.S. 238, 313 (1972) (White, J., concurring).

29 Woodson v. North Carolina, 428 U.S. 280, 304 (1976) (plurality). Louisiana chose largely the same approach, which the Supreme Court also ruled was unconstitutional. Roberts v. Louisiana, 428 U.S. 325, 335 (1976) (plurality).

30 Jurek v. Texas, 428 U.S. 262, 268–69 (1976) (plurality).

31 Gregg v. Georgia, 428 U.S. 153, 165 n.9 (1976) (plurality); Proffitt v. Florida, 428 U.S. 242, 248 n.6 (1976) (plurality).

32 Gregg v. Georgia, 428 U.S. 153, 189, 206-07 (1976) (plurality).

avoiding arrest, and murder during a rape or burglary.[33] One last category of death-eligible murders, however, is less than clear-cut: murder that is "outrageously or wantonly vile" or "heinous, atrocious, or cruel."[34] But the Supreme Court concluded that this too is sufficiently specific to narrow the category of first-degree murder cases for which a death sentence could be imposed.[35]

Though the constitutionality of the death penalty was settled as a general matter by 1976 in *Gregg v. Georgia*, the Supreme Court thereafter limited the crimes for which the death penalty could constitutionally be imposed. In 1977, the court ruled that a death sentence for the rape of an adult woman is a "grossly disproportionate and excessive punishment" and therefore unconstitutional.[36] In 1986, the court ruled that a defendant who was mentally competent at the time he or she committed the crime and at trial may not be executed if he or she is mentally incompetent at the time the death sentence is to be carried out.[37] In 2002, the court ruled it unconstitutional to execute someone who is mentally retarded.[38] In 2005, the court ruled that a state may not execute someone for a crime committed as a child, meaning under the age of eighteen.[39] And in 2008, the court ruled that the death penalty is unconstitutional for the crime of raping a child.[40]

Despite this narrowing of the death penalty's availability, 8,790 people have been sentenced to death in the United States since 1973. Initially, the number of death sentences handed down each year grew quite rapidly. By 1996, 315 death sentences were handed down that year, the highest annual total since 1973. But in the ensuing years, the numbers began to wane, and nearly a dozen states repealed the death penalty. As of 2022, twenty-seven states (along with the federal government and the military) still authorize capital punishment, down from thirty-eight states in 2000. But in 2020 and 2021, only 18 people each year were sentenced to death, with only a slight uptick to 20 death sentences in 2022.[41]

33 Gregg v. Georgia, 428 U.S. 153, 165 n.9 (1976) (plurality).
34 Gregg v. Georgia, 428 U.S. 153, 165 n.9, 193 n.44 (1976) (plurality).
35 Gregg v. Georgia, 428 U.S. 153, 201 (1976); Proffitt v. Florida, 428 U.S. 242, 248 n.6, 255–56 (1976) (plurality).
36 Coker v. Georgia, 433 U.S. 584, 592 (1977) (plurality).
37 Ford v. Wainwright, 477 U.S. 399, 409–10 (1986).
38 Atkins v. Virginia, 536 U.S. 304, 321 (2002).
39 Roper v. Simmons, 543 U.S. 551, 568 (2005).
40 Kennedy v. Louisiana, 554 U.S. 407, 413 (2008).
41 These figures are as of December 31, 2022. "2022 Death Sentences by Name, Race, and County," Death Penalty Information Center, accessed January 13, 2023, https://deathpenaltyinfo.org;

Only a fraction of those sentenced to death have ultimately been executed, whether because their sentences (or convictions) were later overturned (or are still being litigated) on appeal, their sentences were commuted by governors, the death penalty was abolished in their state, a state-wide moratorium on executions was imposed, or the prisoner died of other causes while on death row. As of the end of 2022, 1,558 people have been executed since the Supreme Court's decision in *Furman*. But only 11 people were executed in 2021, the fewest in a single year since 1988.[42] Approximately 2,400 men and women remained on death row in the United States as of the end of 2021.[43]

Litigation Procedure

As noted earlier, in the first half of the twentieth century death sentences were often imposed and carried out swiftly. But since the death penalty was reinstated after *Furman*, those condemned to death are executed only after a trial and lengthy appeal process. The procedures governing capital murder trials and appeals differ slightly in each jurisdiction, but all largely follow the same general format.

A capital murder trial begins with the selection of a jury in much the same way as juries are selected in other felony cases. The principal difference in the selection of a capital jury is that the jurors must be "death qualified," meaning that each juror must be willing to impose the death penalty if called for by the law and facts of the case. Prospective jurors who, for religious or other reasons, could not impose a death sentence are disqualified from jury service for "cause"; the prosecution need not exercise a peremptory challenge to remove them.[44] Both the prosecution and the

"Death Sentences in the United States since 1977," Death Penalty Information Center, accessed January 13, 2023, https://deathpenaltyinfo.org. The states that, as of 2022, authorize the death penalty are Alabama, Arizona, Arkansas, California, Florida, Georgia, Idaho, Indiana, Kansas, Kentucky, Louisiana, Mississippi, Missouri, Montana, Nebraska, Nevada, North Carolina, Ohio, Oklahoma, Oregon, Pennsylvania, South Carolina, South Dakota, Tennessee, Texas, Utah, Wyoming. "States and Capital Punishment," National Conference of States Legislatures, August 11, 2021, accessed March 3, 2022, https://www.ncsl.org.

42 "Executions by State and Region since 1976," Death Penalty Information Center, accessed January 13, 2023, https://deathpenaltyinfo.org.

43 "Size of Death Row by Year," Death Penalty Information Center, accessed January 13, 2023, https://deathpenaltyinfo.org.

44 Witherspoon v. Illinois, 391 U.S. 510 (1968); Wainwright v. Witt, 469 U.S. 412 (1985); Lockhart v. McCree, 476 U.S. 162 (1986).

defense can exercise peremptory challenges on those prospective jurors who are death qualified and not otherwise removed for cause. Given the higher rate of opposition to the death penalty among Black Americans as compared to White Americans,[45] the death qualification of the jury has the effect of disproportionately disqualifying Black men and women from jury service for cause in death penalty cases and shrinks the pool of Black jurors against whom a prosecutor need exercise his or her peremptory challenges.[46]

Once a death qualified jury is selected, the trial proceeds in two phases: guilt and then, if needed, penalty. The guilt phase is like that in any other criminal trial, where the government seeks to prove that the defendant committed a murder for which death is an available penalty. If the jury finds the defendant guilty of such an offense, the trial proceeds to a second phase in which the jury decides whether to impose a death sentence.[47] In the penalty phase, the jury is asked to determine whether at least one aggravating factor is present and, if so, whether those aggravating factors outweigh any mitigating factors. The defendant is constitutionally entitled to present any mitigating evidence that he or she believes is relevant.[48] If the jury's verdict is that the man or woman on trial should be sentenced to death, then the judge issues an order to that effect, typically ending that decree with the phrase, "May God have mercy on your soul."

A defendant sentenced to death can appeal both the conviction and death sentence, seeking reversal of one or both of them. This is often referred to as a "direct appeal" or "direct review." Most states provide that the direct appeal will be heard by the state's supreme court rather than an intermediate appellate court. In addition to the issues normally reviewed in a criminal appeal, an appellate court reviewing a death sentence on direct appeal will also typically examine the proportionality of the sentence. Proportionality review requires that the appellate court determine whether

45 John Gramlich, "From Police to Parole, Black and White Americans Differ Widely in Their Views of Criminal Justice System," Pew Research Center, May 21, 2019, https://www.pewresearch.org.

46 Mona Lynch and Craig Haney, "Death Qualification in Black and White: Racialized Decision Making and Death-Qualified Juries," *Law and Policy* 40, no. 2 (2018): 148–71, https://doi.org /10.1111/lapo.12099; J. Thomas Sullivan, "The Demographic Dilemma in Death Qualification of Capital Jurors," *Wake Forest Law Review* 49, no. 4 (2014): 1142, https://lawrepository.ualr .edu/faculty_scholarship/161.

47 Ring v. Arizona, 536 U.S. 584, 608 (2002).

48 Lockett v. Ohio, 438 U.S. 586, 604 (1978).

the death sentence was disproportionately harsh relative to the facts of the crime and the sentence imposed in similar cases. If the court concludes that the death sentence is disproportionate, it will vacate that sentence and the defendant will instead serve a term of life imprisonment.[49]

Contrary to public perception, an appellate court does *not* review the evidence to second-guess the jury's verdict as to the defendant's guilt. Due process includes the right to be convicted only on proof beyond a reasonable doubt,[50] but the question of whether such proof has been offered is one for the jury to make. Appellate courts will only overrule the jury's decision if the evidence could not "reasonably support a finding of guilt beyond a reasonable doubt." In other words, the appellate court will only assess whether "*any* rational trier of fact could have found the essential elements of the crime beyond a reasonable doubt." Whether the appellate judges would themselves have convicted the defendant based on the evidence presented at trial is not the question resolved on appeal.[51]

If the defendant's state court conviction and death sentence are affirmed on direct review, he or she will typically then have an opportunity for what is called "post-conviction" or "collateral" review in state court. Collateral review is usually a means to raise newly discovered issues or to raise a claim that the defense attorney's conduct was not up to the constitutional standard of competence. The post-conviction review begins again in the state trial court and proceeds up through the state appellate courts. But there is no jury during these collateral review proceedings, and the judges typically will not second-guess the jury's determination of guilt.

Once the defendant has exhausted state post-conviction review, he or she may then file what is known as a habeas corpus action in federal court. *Habeas corpus* is a Latin phrase that means "show me the body" and is a legal request (petition) that the federal court order the state to free the defendant from prison. But in a federal habeas corpus action, the defendant can only raise legal arguments under the US Constitution or other federal law.[52] For

49 Pulley v. Harris, 465 U.S. 37 (1984). In *Pulley,* the US Supreme Court held that proportionality review is not a constitutional requirement (50–51).
50 In re Winship, 397 U.S. 358, 364 (1970).
51 Jackson v. Virginia, 443 U.S. 307, 318–19 (1979).
52 In 1996, Congress narrowed the ability of a criminal defendant to bring a federal habeas corpus action, the hope being that it would streamline and accelerate habeas corpus litigation in death penalty cases by tightening the time limits for and frequency with which one can file a federal

example, the defendant could argue that he was denied a lawyer in violation of the Sixth Amendment (*Gideon*) or that jury selection was infected with racial bias in violation of the Fourteenth Amendment (*Batson*).

But can a defendant use a habeas corpus action to bring a federal constitutional claim that he is innocent? In other words, even if the defendant cannot show a procedural violation of the US Constitution in his criminal case, would it be unconstitutional for a state to execute an innocent person? You might think the answer obvious. That can't happen in America, can it? Certainly some provision of the Constitution must prohibit that, right?

In 1993, however, the US Supreme Court was equivocal on the question whether "actual innocence" is a constitutional claim that can be raised in a federal habeas corpus action. The court acknowledged that the argument that the Eighth Amendment—which prohibits cruel and unusual punishments—precludes the execution of someone who is innocent has some "elemental appeal." But the problem with the argument, the court explained, was that the defendant's claim of innocence was based on evidence he was presenting in his federal habeas petition rather than during his original state court trial years earlier. And, absent some *other* constitutional violation, "claims of actual innocence based on newly discovered evidence have never been held to state a ground for federal habeas relief." The court did "assume, for the sake of argument," that it would be unconstitutional to execute a defendant who could make "a truly persuasive demonstration of 'actual innocence'" after trial. But the court ruled that the "threshold" for making such a showing "would necessarily be extraordinarily high" and was not met in that case.[53]

Justices Scalia and Thomas, however, disagreed with that assumption that federal habeas relief would be available for an innocent defendant. In their view, "There is no basis in text, tradition, or even in contemporary practice . . . for finding in the Constitution a right to demand judicial consideration of newly discovered evidence of innocence brought forward after conviction." They chided the dissenting justices for finding such a right in the Constitution, claiming that those justices were "apply[ing] nothing but their personal opinions." In the view of Justices Scalia and Thomas, claims

---

habeas petition. Antiterrorism and Effective Death Penalty Act of 1996, Pub. L. 104–132, 110 Stat. 1214 (Apr. 24, 1996).

53   Herrera v. Collins, 506 U.S. 390, 398, 400, 417 (1993).

of actual innocence should be addressed through executive clemency, not the federal courts.[54]

Executive clemency is more commonly known as the power to "pardon" or "commute" a criminal sentence. This power is not limited to capital cases, but every state that authorizes capital punishment has some legal mechanism under which the governor, alone or in conjunction with an advisory board selected by the legislature, can either pardon someone who has been convicted or commute a death sentence to something less than was imposed at trial.[55] For example, in late 2021, the governor of Oklahoma commuted the death sentence of Julius Jones to life in prison after the state's parole board twice ruled that there were substantial doubts about Jones's guilt.[56] Unlike court proceedings, executive clemency decisions are not constrained by legal principles and rules. They are "an act of grace," the US Supreme Court has said, and whether to grant or not grant a pardon or clemency is within the executive's discretion.[57]

Biblical Justice?

The death penalty is the most significant moral issue on which I have changed my mind. In law school, I was a full-throated supporter, but I have come to the view that, as currently practiced in the United States, the death penalty is unjust as the Bible defines justice.

This is not to say that capital punishment is categorically unjust. To the contrary, Scripture expressly authorizes it.[58] A sentence of death for those who murder is part of the Noahic covenant (Gen. 9:6)—an ordinance "as universal and comprehensive, as were to be the posterity of Noah; . . . an ordinance of humanity and of civil society, the world over."[59] The penalty

---

54 Herrera v. Collins, 506 U.S. 390, 427–28 (1993) (Scalia, J., concurring).
55 Herrera v. Collins, 506 U.S. 390, 414 (1993).
56 Graham Lee Brewer, "Oklahoma Governor Commutes Julius Jones' Death Sentence Hours before Planned Execution," *NBC News*, November 18, 2021, https://www.nbcnews.com/.
57 United States v. Wilson, 32 U.S. (7 Pet.) 150, 160 (1833). For a discussion of executive clemency in the context of the death penalty, see Molly Clayton, "Forgiving the Unforgivable: Reinvigorating the Use of Executive Clemency in Capital Cases," *Boston College Law Review* 54, no. 2 (2013): 751–88, https://lira.bc.edu/work/ns/1893e157-8589-4a76-9876-8112f9ee9301.
58 Wayne Grudem, *Christian Ethics: An Introduction to Biblical Moral Reasoning* (Wheaton, IL: Crossway, 2018), 505–12.
59 Cheever, *A Defence of Capital Punishment*, 138. Cheever makes the most comprehensive and compelling exegetical, theological, and philosophical case for capital punishment that I have encountered.

is repeated in the Mosaic law (Ex. 21:14; Lev. 24:17; Num. 35:31). And Romans 13 speaks of a God-ordained government bearing "the sword," which is obviously an instrument of death. Commenting on this passage, Cheever observed that the apostle Paul is "clearly sanctioning capital punishment under the Christian dispensation, and referring it to the ordinance of God."[60] Elsewhere, Paul acknowledges crimes "worthy of death" (Acts 25:11 KJV). In sum, the biblical record is overwhelming in its affirmation of the death penalty as a just punishment for certain crimes. As Augustine concludes, if "a judge or his agent executes a convicted criminal, . . . [t]hey do not seem to me to be sinning."[61]

The threat of a penalty that severe communicates the gravity of the crime and the value of its victims (Gen. 9:6). Though the death penalty is undoubtedly harsh, holding it out as a real threat that a society will promptly administer can be an act of love if intended to dissuade people from committing the most serious of evils and to thereby protect society from harm. That some, perhaps even many, will not heed the warning does not diminish its love.

But to say that Scripture authorizes the death penalty is not to say that Scripture does so without condition. And it is those conditions that many Christian arguments in favor of the death penalty fail to consider. My concern with the death penalty is not that it is, as a categorical matter, unjust, but rather that as currently (and historically) administered in the United States, it is unjust. Whatever the theoretical possibility that a people could justly administer the death penalty, the American system of doing so falls short of that standard in at least two respects: impartiality and accuracy.

Impartiality. More than two hundred years of history and careful data analysis show that the death penalty in the United States has been deeply infected by racial bias. When Warren McCleskey brought his case to the US Supreme Court in 1986, Justice Scalia conceded what the Baldus study plainly showed—that even after *Furman*, the death penalty still bore racial

60 Cheever, *A Defence of Capital Punishment*, 151.
61 Augustine, *On the Free Choice of the Will, On Grace and Free Choice, and Other Writings*, ed. and trans. Peter King (Cambridge: Cambridge University Press, 2010), 8. Elsewhere, Augustine argues that it is right and proper to intercede for even the guilty who are condemned to death. Augustine, "Letter 153: Augustine to Macedonius," in *Letters 100–155*, trans. Roland Teske, ed. Boniface Ramsey, in *The Works of Saint Augustine: A Translation for the 21st Century* (Hyde Park, NY: New City, 2003), 390–404.

---

overtones (see chap. 7). Decisions about who is sentenced to die are tainted by the race of the person murdered. As Justice Scalia acknowledged in 1987, this was not an issue in need of "more proof."[62] But, in fact, more proof has been offered. Numerous studies since Baldus's have reached the same conclusion and some have further demonstrated that the race of the defendant likewise influences who is sentenced to death.[63]

Even more troubling is the evidence that race plays a role not only in who is sentenced to die but also in who is ultimately put to death. In 2020, two professors expanded David Baldus's data to determine whether a further racial disparity existed in who, among those sentenced to death, was ultimately executed. The conclusions were shocking: the execution rate is seventeen times greater for those convicted of killing a White victim as opposed to a Black victim.[64] Somehow, race is affecting not only prosecutorial and jury decisions but also the decisions of appellate courts and officials (whether governors or clemency boards) granting relief after conviction.

A common response I have encountered to statistics of these sorts is that, in the United States, Black people commit a disproportionate number of murders relative to their representation in the population at large.[65] What the data also shows, however, is that most murders are intra-racial, not

---

62 Memorandum to the Conference from Justice Antonin Scalia of January 6, 1987, 1, McCleskey v. Kemp, Supreme Court Case Files Collection, Powell Papers, Lewis F. Powell Jr. Archives, Washington & Lee University School of Law, Virginia, accessed November 23, 2021, https://scholarlycommons.law.wlu.edu/casefiles/249/.

63 *Death Penalty Sentencing: Research Indicates Pattern of Racial Disparities* (US General Accounting Office, February 1999), https://www.gao.gov/assets/ggd-90-57.pdf; David C. Baldus, George Woodworth, and Catherine M. Grosso, "Race and Proportionality since *McCleskey v. Kemp* (1987): Different Actors with Mixed Strategies of Denial and Avoidance," *Columbia Human Rights Law Review* 39, no. 1 (2007): 143–77, https://doi.org/10.17613/4547-jy12; David C. Baldus and George Woodworth, "Race Discrimination in the Administration of the Death Penalty: An Overview of the Empirical Evidence with Special Emphasis on the Post-1990 Research," *Criminal Law Bulletin* 39, no. 2 (2003): 194–226; David C. Baldus, George Woodworth, David Zuckerman, and Neil Alan Weiner, "Racial Discrimination and the Death Penalty in the Post-*Furman* Era: An Empirical and Legal Overview, with Recent Findings from Philadelphia," *Cornell Law Review* 83, no. 6 (1998): 1638–769, https://scholarship.law.cornell.edu/clr/vol83/iss6/6.

64 Scott Phillips and Justin Marceau, "Whom the State Kills," *Harvard Civil Rights—Civil Liberties Law Review* 55, no. 2 (2020): 585–656, https://search.informit.org/doi/10.3316/agispt.20201019038355.

65 In the most recent year for which data is available, Black people committed 56 percent of murders in the United States in which the race of the perpetrator is known. "Expanded Homicide Data Table 3: Murder Offenders by Age, Sex, Race, and Ethnicity," 2019 Crime in the United States, Federal Bureau of Investigation, accessed April 22, 2022, https://ucr.fbi.gov/crime-in-the-u.s/2019/crime-in-the-u.s.-2019/tables/expanded-homicide-data-table-3.xls.

inter-racial. In other words, most murders by Black people are of Black victims, and the same for Whites.[66] Thus, were race not playing a role in death penalty decisions, we would expect to see most of the Black defendants sentenced to death to be in cases where they murdered a fellow Black person. In fact, the statistics show precisely the opposite.[67]

Accuracy. As noted earlier, 8,790 people have been sentenced to death in the United States since 1973. One hundred and eighty-four of those men and women were exonerated as of the end of 2022.[68] They were innocent of the crimes of which they were convicted and sentenced to die. In other words, we *know* that at least 2 percent of people sentenced to death since 1973 were wrongly condemned.

Even if we have identified all of those wrongly convicted and the error rate is "only" 2 percent, that is an error rate higher than I am willing to tolerate. And I have no such confidence that we have identified all the erroneous capital convictions.[69] In a justice system that injects race into jury selection in trials before elected judges who run on "tough on crime" campaign platforms with defendants represented by overworked and underfunded defense teams while the prosecution conceals exculpatory evidence without consequence, I am unwilling to wager another man's life. I would not wager

66 In the most recent year for which data is available, 91 percent of Black murder victims were killed by Blacks, while 81 percent of White murder victims were killed by Whites. "Expanded Homicide Data Table 6: Murder: Race, Sex, and Ethnicity of Victim by Race, Sex, and Ethnicity of Offender," 2019 Crime in the United States, Federal Bureau of Investigation, accessed April 22, 2022, https://ucr.fbi.gov/crime-in-the-u.s/2019/crime-in-the-u.s.-2019/tables/expanded -homicide-data-table-6.xls.

67 Seth Kotch and Robert P. Mosteller, "The Racial Justice Act and the Long Struggle with Race and the Death Penalty in North Carolina," *North Carolina Law Review* 88, no. 6 (2010): 2097–98, https://scholarship.law.unc.edu/nclr/vol88/iss6/4.

68 "Innocence Database," Death Penalty Information Center, accessed January 13, 2023, https:// deathpenaltyinfo.org.

69 There is reason to believe that the error rate in capital cases is more than 4 percent. Samuel R. Gross, Barbara O'Brien, Chen Hu, and Edward H. Kennedy, "Rate of False Conviction of Criminal Defendants Who Are Sentenced to Death," *Proceedings of the National Academy of Sciences* 111, no. 20 (May 20, 2014): 7234, https://doi.org/10.1073/pnas.1306417111. At least twenty-one cases have been identified since *Furman* in which there are serious concerns that an innocent person was executed, one of whom is Ledell Lee who was executed in Arkansas in 2017. "Executed but Possibly Innocent," Death Penalty Information Center, accessed January 13, 2023, https://deathpenaltyinfo.org; Hannah Knowles, "Four Years after a Man's Execution, Lawyers Say DNA from the Murder Weapon Points to Someone Else," *Washington Post*, May 4, 2021, https://www.washingtonpost.com/. Nina Morrison, the Innocence Project attorney discussed in chap. 13, was one of the attorneys for Ledell Lee.

my own under those conditions. Loving my neighbor as myself demands that we use all reasonable means to clean up the system. Absent that, we have no divine authority to administer the death penalty.

———

Nineteen days after Donald Gaskins was electrocuted in South Carolina, Warren McCleskey was executed by the state of Georgia in a one-story cinder block building just off Interstate 75 in Butts County. Jack Boger, the divinity school graduate who had for years served as McCleskey's lawyer, was present for the execution. In McCleskey's final words before he was put to death at 3:13 a.m. on September 25, 1991, he told the family of Officer Schlatt that he was "deeply sorry and repentant" for his role in the robbery that ended in murder. McCleskey then expressed confidence that "this is not the end, but the beginning I hoped for—to be in the presence of my Lord."[70]

McCleskey could speak with this confidence on the verge of death because, while on death row, he had become a Christian in 1984 through the ministry of Billy Neal Moore, a fellow inmate.[71] Moore, who himself came within hours of being executed, was subsequently paroled, ordained as a minister, and wrote a book about his time on death row and close friendship with Warren McCleskey.[72]

If you too are a Christian, you will meet McCleskey in eternity. "Love your neighbor as yourself," Jesus said. McCleskey will be your eternal neighbor. In fact, he always was your neighbor.

And God indeed had mercy on his soul.

---

70 Jeffrey L. Kirchmeier, *Imprisoned by the Past: Warren McCleskey and the American Death Penalty* (New York: Oxford University Press, 2015), 189.

71 Mark Curriden, "McCleskey Put to Death after Hours of Delays, Final Apology," *Atlanta Journal-Constitution*, September 26, 1991; Kirchmeier, *Imprisoned by the Past*, 113.

72 Billy Neal Moore, *I Shall Not Die: Seventy-Two Hours on Death Watch* (Bloomington, IN: AuthorHouse, 2005). Moore now travels the country speaking to prisoners about forgiveness. Sheila M. Poole, "Forgiven," *Atlanta Journal-Constitution*, March 30, 2013, https://www.ajc.com/.

19

What Can You Do?

WHEN I SPEAK TO GROUPS OR TALK with people individually about my concerns with the American system of criminal justice, the question I inevitably receive is some version of "So what can we do?" That question, when it finally comes, is a relief to me. It tells me that the data has gotten through, that the statistics have hit their mark, that the stories of real people being wronged by their government have penetrated the heart. I've made my point. I've been heard. Or you might say, my "neighbors" have been heard. Because I want people to hear *their* stories. And it's because of their stories that I want people to act. So I am relieved when the listener wants to know how to do so.

In the story of the good Samaritan, Jesus's criticism of the priest and the Levite was not that they had harmed the traveler but that they had failed to help when they saw someone suffering. They knew the facts. But they responded as if the facts weren't their problem. They hadn't robbed the man on the roadside, and they weren't going to be bothered to assist. The neighbor love displayed by the Samaritan, however, was not love for one whom the Samaritan had harmed. The Samaritan was good because he stopped to help fix a mess he did not cause. He acted not because he was culpable but because he was close. Christ's command to the lawyer who sought to justify his own self-righteous sense of himself—and to you and me, who are all too often tempted in the same way—was to "go, and do likewise" (Luke 10:37). And that's my hope for you, that after reading this book and seeing the problems with our justice system, you won't just walk by on the other side of the road but rather will help fix a mess though you may not have caused it.

The good news is that you can act, and your actions can matter. More than that, though, we must act. Those damaged by our justice system lie battered and bruised within our moral proximity because the government officials causing the harm are doing so on our behalf. Together, we could, if we wanted to, stop them. And so neighbor love compels us to act. I'll close with four ways that you can, like that good Samaritan, bind up the wounds of your neighbors who are assaulted by the justice system.

Think Differently

The first and perhaps most important thing you can do when it comes to criminal justice is to think differently about it. The apostle Paul describes our sanctification as springing from a new way of thinking. We are to be transformed in our actions by a renewal of our minds, a change in our mindset (Rom. 12:2). Our obedient lives are the product of new hearts, new thoughts, new affections (Rom. 6:17). A sharpening of one's theology and a new awareness of the facts about our criminal justice system should change one's thinking.

Stop thinking, "They're animals." Instead, think like a Christian. Remember that those accused and even those convicted are people, fellow humans made in God's image.

Stop thinking, "If you can't do the time, then don't do the crime." Instead, think like a Christian. Ask yourself whether the time in prison to which we are consigning people aligns with the severity of the offense.

Stop thinking that simply because someone has been accused, they must be guilty. Instead, think like a Christian. Remember the proverbial wisdom that every accuser seems right until their case gets tested.

Stop thinking that we should be "tough on crime." Instead, think like a Christian. Recall that we must judge impartially and sentence proportionally as we image our heavenly Father who does so.

Stop thinking that public defenders are morally compromised merely by defending the accused. Instead, think like a Christian. Recognize that accurately distinguishing the guilty from the innocent requires a process in which both sides of the question can effectively present their case.

Stop thinking that prosecutors are above reproach. Instead, think like a Christian. Remember that Scripture speaks at length about the injustices of rulers and that accuracy demands accountability when the wrongdoer is the state.

Stop thinking that jokes about prison rape are humorous. Instead, think like a Christian. Remember that God hates the wickedness of sexual assault whether it occurs in a college dorm, a back alley, or behind bars.

And stop thinking that none of this is your problem. Instead, think like a Christian. Realize that Christ's command to love your neighbor applies to you and that you have a moral obligation to those affected by the government policies you support.

This changed way of thinking is not just a means to protect criminal defendants. It's the means to accuracy, which protects the accused and the victim alike. If we think rightly about how to design a system of justice that yields accurate results, punishing the guilty and acquitting the innocent, we are loving all our neighbors, both victims and victimizers, as ourselves.

An essential ingredient of thinking differently is learning. We each approach the discussion about the criminal justice system with our understanding of the system. But is it the correct understanding? Is it a complete understanding? Even after more than twenty-six years as a lawyer, I was startled at times by what I learned in the research and writing of this book. The selected bibliography to this book is a resource for learning more. But beyond that, be aware of news stories in your community about how your local criminal justice system is operating. What changes in the criminal law are your local politicians pushing? Whom is your state prosecuting or failing to prosecute? Whom is your state executing? Whom is your state exonerating?

Speak Differently

The second thing I hope to have facilitated is better criminal justice conversations among Christians. The theological discussion in the first half of this book can provide a framework for dialogue that all Christians should be able to affirm. The historical discussion might help you better understand the divergent perspectives that Christians of different races have regarding the justice system. And the legal discussion can make the conversations more informed and specific.

To take the example of bail and plea bargaining, I trust you will walk away from this book with a better awareness of the interplay between bail and guilty pleas—and the risk of injustice posed by that interaction. As a result, Christians of good faith can converse with one another about adjustments that could be made to bail and plea bargaining in order to promote the biblical justice principle of accuracy. That will, I suspect, be a far more fruitful conversation than many that have occurred to date.

What I have not, however, sought to do in this book is advocate for a particular policy regarding bail, plea bargaining, or any of the other features of the criminal justice system I have covered. This was intentional. There is no one-size-fits-all approach for all cultures, histories, localities, and generations—not even for all Christians. As C. S. Lewis puts it,

> Christianity has not, and does not profess to have, a detailed political programme for applying "Do as you would be done by" to a particular society at a particular moment. It could not have. It is meant for all men at all times and the particular programme which suited one place or time would not suit another.[1]

Or as Paul Ramsey put it, "Christian love is always in search of a social policy."[2]

Scripture doesn't dictate one particular bail system over another. The same is true for the jury selection process, how to choose judges, and the best way to ensure that indigent defendants are effectively represented at trial. On each of those points and many more, the particulars of how to fashion a just—that is, neighbor-loving—criminal justice system are matters on which Christians of good faith equally committed to the same principles of biblical justice can disagree. I seek to bind no one's conscience by prescribing particular methods as biblically mandated. I have no such authority and no such wisdom. What I have tried to prompt and frame is better discussion about how to achieve biblical justice, and I hope to have equipped you to be a more effective participant in that discussion.

For those of you who are parents, I encourage you to have these discussions with your children. Initiate dinner conversations with them about this topic. Share with them what you have learned and are learning. Let them know what you believe about God's justice. Communicate to them your commitment to that justice. It took us centuries to get into this mess. Hate and ignorance were passed down across dinner tables and on family

1   C. S. Lewis, *Mere Christianity* (New York: HarperCollins, 2001), 82.
2   Paul Ramsey, *Basic Christian Ethics* (Louisville: Westminster John Knox, 1950), 326.

vacations. Truth, justice, and love of neighbor can be too. Commit to break that cycle and to pass on to your children an awareness of where we as a nation have gone wrong and a commitment going forward to justice for all.

Work Differently

For those readers who work in the criminal justice system—whether as police officers, prosecutors, judges, or wardens—you will every day be forced to answer whether you will follow the law or Jesus. Sometimes you will be able to do both; sometimes you won't. Perhaps you started with idealistic notions of truth and justice. The danger is that over time you may come to see the criminal defendant whose fate is in your hands as simply "the usual man in the usual place."[3] You may fail to see him or her as an image bearer, precious to God, due your love, and one to whom you must do justly. You may fall prey to the notion that doing legally is the same thing as doing justly. But it's not, or at least not necessarily.

The law may permit you to detain that defendant without bail. Biblical justice may not. The law may permit you to seek a mandatory minimum or a "three strikes" life prison sentence. Biblical justice may not. The judge may accept your supposedly race-neutral explanation for why you struck that juror. But God may not. The jury may believe the implausible story of that jailhouse snitch you called as a witness. God knows the truth. The voters may prefer a "prosecution-oriented person" as judge. The biblical justice principle of impartiality may demand otherwise. The courts may not hold you to account for a failure to diligently discharge your *Brady* obligations. God might. You may have qualified or absolute immunity for your violations of constitutional rights. Those legal doctrines are of no force or effect in the court of the only just Judge.

Here's the hard truth: some of you need to quit. In some jurisdictions, under some supervisors, before some judges, with the demands of some voters, you cannot help but commit injustice by doing your job. Sometimes you can follow Jesus and be a police officer, prosecutor, judge, or warden. Sometimes you can follow the law *and* do justly. Sometimes you can push for and achieve change. But sometimes you can't. Sometimes you have to choose.

---

3   G. K. Chesterton, "The Twelve Men," in *Tremendous Trifles* (New York: Dodd, Mead and Company, 1920), 86.

Sometimes, enforcing the law of man is breaking the law of God. Sometimes, criminal justice is a biblical injustice. Sometimes you need to leave.[4]

Vote Differently

One final step that a Christian can—and I think must—take with respect to criminal justice is to vote and, in particular, vote differently from those who hold to an unbiblical conception of justice. In the United States, the right to vote comes in two forms: in elections and on juries. Both require that we apply the biblical concept of criminal justice.

Elections

I recognize, of course, that voting in elections is a multi-issue exercise, and many if not all the issues one must consider in deciding for whom to vote are issues of biblical justice. A candidate's approach to criminal justice is one of many issues that a voter must both evaluate and weigh. How will a particular candidate approach the death penalty? Education? Transportation? Taxation? Occupational safety? Homelessness? Abortion? National defense? Public health? Labor? Energy? Each of these presents issues of biblical justice. So even if you accept that, all things being equal, Christians should vote for the candidate who more closely aligns with a biblical conception of criminal justice, all things aren't equal. In the real world, with myriad issues that must be considered when casting a vote, what priority should a Christian give to criminal justice among all these competing justice issues?

As a general matter, criminal justice should be an issue of high moral priority for the Christian voter because it is an issue of when and under what circumstances you will empower the state to use physical force, even deadly force, against other people. Criminal justice is quite literally a matter of life and death, both for citizens who are the victims of crime and the accused who are punished for it.

At the same time, how much I prioritize criminal justice in a given election will depend in part on the office at issue in the election. At one end of the spectrum, my vote for a member of the US House of Representatives will

---

4   Recent press reports suggest that the moral qualms of young lawyers with the conduct of district attorneys is making it increasingly difficult to recruit people to fill entry-level prosecutor roles. Disha Raychaudhuri and Karen Sloan, "Prosecutors Wanted: District Attorneys Struggle to Recruit and Retain Lawyers," *Reuters*, April 13, 2022, https://www.reuters.com/.

have minimal impact on criminal justice policy. Most criminal prosecution occurs at the state level, not the federal level. The executive branch, not the legislative branch, is responsible for criminal prosecutions. The confirmation of judges who will preside over criminal cases occurs in the US Senate not in the US House of Representatives. And while US Representatives will occasionally vote on criminal justice-related legislation, a US Representative is only one of 435 members of the House. These practical realities all bear on the relative priority I should assign criminal justice policy in deciding how to vote in the election of a US Representative.

At the other end of the spectrum is my county's district attorney election. This is as close to a single-issue election as possible. Obviously, criminal justice is a multifaceted topic, and a district attorney might hold a just view on bail and an unjust view on the death penalty. But at least when it comes to the district attorney election, I can exclude from consideration dozens of other issues that complicate other voting decisions. A candidate's beliefs about national defense, policy, teacher pay, or numerous other issues are not implicated by the duties of the district attorney.[5] The district attorney election is an election about criminal justice policy.

On top of that, criminal justice is highly fragmented. As law professor John Pfaff has observed, we don't have a single criminal justice system in the United States; we have 3,144 criminal justice systems—one for each county in the United States, each with its distinct features, priorities, strengths, and weaknesses.[6] Your vote may be of miniscule significance in a statewide race. But a small band of highly motivated people could literally change the criminal justice policy of a county by turning out the vote for the district attorney election. And that provides a meaningful opportunity for change.

In recent years, for example, several localities across the country have seen reform-minded candidates run against and unseat established district attorneys. In Los Angeles, George Gascón defeated the district attorney who had held office for eight years after initially running as a "tough on crime"

---

5 I recognize that the importance of abortion to the district attorney's duties has changed in some jurisdictions in which prosecutors have vowed not to enforce laws criminalizing abortion in the wake of the US Supreme Court's decision overturning *Roe v. Wade*. Ryan Jeltema, "Genesee County Prosecutor Won't Issue Charges Based on 1931 Anti-Abortion Law," *ABC12 News*, April 7, 2022, https://www.abc12.com/.

6 John F. Pfaff, *Locked In: The True Causes of Mass Incarceration and How to Achieve Real Reform* (New York: Basic Books, 2017), 15–16.

candidate.[7] In Philadelphia, civil rights lawyer Larry Krasner bested a raft of candidates to win the city's district attorney job in 2017, and then four years later he beat back a challenger backed by the local police union.[8] Candidates promising to reform the criminal justice system likewise won races in Detroit, Orlando, Chicago, and Colorado.[9] This isn't to suggest that I agree (or disagree) with the policies of the reform candidates in these elections. The point is that district attorney candidates promising to address criminal justice issues from a different perspective are winning, and this presents an opportunity for Christians to vote in a way that disrupts the status quo and more faithfully aligns with a biblical view of justice in their local district attorney elections.

Do you know who your district attorney is? Do you know when his or her next election is? If not, go look it up. Is he or she holding a town hall during the next election cycle? You could attend and maybe even ask some questions: How many *Brady* violations has the district attorney's office had during the last four years? What training have you offered to ensure that your prosecutors are not striking jurors on the basis of race in violation of *Batson*? What is your policy for pretrial bail for people charged with nonviolent offenses? How do you ensure that the plea bargains you strike are not unduly lenient? Getting answers to questions like these will make you a more informed voter as you play your role in holding your district attorney accountable.

Jury Service

As I noted, elections are not your only opportunities to vote differently when it comes to criminal justice. You can also vote differently as a juror. In fact, some legal scholars have concluded that the original intent of the US Constitution's jury trial clause was as much to secure an individual right of the defendant as it was to guarantee a right of the people—through jurors—to govern.[10]

---

7   James Queally, "George Gascón Will Be L.A. County's Next District Attorney, Promises Swift Changes," *Los Angeles Times*, November 6, 2020, https://www.latimes.com/.

8   Brian X. McCrone and Lauren Mayk, "Philly DA Krasner Wins Democratic Primary over Challenger Vega," *NBC10 Philadelphia*, May 18, 2021, https://www.nbcphiladelphia.com/.

9   Caren Morrison, "Progressive Prosecutors Scored Big Wins in 2020 Elections, Boosting a Nationwide Trend," *The Conversation*, November 18, 2020, https://theconversation.com/.

10   Akhil Reed Amar, "The Bill of Rights as a Constitution," *Yale Law Journal* 100, no. 5 (1991): 1185, 1188–89, https://doi.org/10.2307/796690; Stephanos Bibas, "Originalism and Formalism

And governing is precisely what you do as a juror. As judges frequently instruct jurors, "You are impartial judges of the facts,"[11] and in that judicial role the jurors administer the government's fact-finding function. As discussed in chapter 18, appellate courts generally will not and do not second-guess the jury's finding of guilt. An acquittal is not appealable by the prosecution at all. You, as a juror, will for all intents and purposes render the final decree as to the defendant's factual and legal guilt.

If you are called for jury service, both the victim and the accused are at that moment within your moral proximity. You are quite literally "going down that road" (Luke 10:31) of people in need of justice. Don't pass by on the other side. Be like the good Samaritan and be a neighbor. The French political philosopher Alexis de Tocqueville (1805–59), after observing the American political system, concluded that through jury service "every man learns to judge his neighbor as he would himself be judged."[12] If presented with the opportunity to govern as a juror and deliver justice, don't seek to evade it. Accept the responsibility and execute it justly. Love your neighbors by judging their case as you would want your case judged.

When you serve on a jury, demand evidence that ensures the biblical principle of accuracy is achieved. Refuse to vote for a conviction on the testimony of a single witness. According to Scripture, neither you nor your fellow jurors have the moral authority to convict on such flimsy evidence. If the prosecution calls a cooperator or a jailhouse snitch as a witness, demand compelling corroboration before you credit that witness's testimony. Love your (accused) neighbor as yourself, Jesus said.

Your vote as one of twelve jurors could make more of a difference—and certainly not less of a difference—than your vote as one of thousands of voters in any election ever will. Because criminal jury verdicts must now be unanimous in the United States,[13] you could single-handedly stop a life-wrecking injustice to someone falsely—or questionably—accused. You

in Criminal Procedure: The Triumph of Justice Scalia, the Unlikely Friend of Criminal Defendants?," *Georgetown Law Journal* 94, no. 1 (2005): 196–97, https://scholarship.law.upenn.edu/faculty_scholarship/76/.

11 "How Courts Work," American Bar Association, December 30, 2021, https://www.americanbar.org/.

12 Alexis de Tocqueville, *Democracy in America*, vol. 1, trans. Henry Reeve, ed. Francis Bowen (Cambridge: Sever and Francis, 1863), 364.

13 Ramos v. Louisiana, 140 S. Ct. 1390, 1395 (2020).

could, if the evidence warrants it, work together with your fellow jurors to grant some measure of earthly justice to the victim of a horrific crime. These are enormous privileges—stewardships, even—afforded American citizens to do justly for their fellow countrymen. As a Christian, don't squander that stewardship. Embrace it, and vote wisely. Accept it, and do justly. If you don't, then less biblically just people will act in your place.

"But I'm busy," you say. So was the Levite. The priest also had matters to attend to. So they passed up the opportunity to love. Christ called us to something different. He told us to go and be like the Samaritan who inconvenienced himself for the one in his path in need of love. Something far more than a complaint about inconvenience is needed to evade that command.

———

The American author, historian, and minister Edward Everett Hale (1822–1909) is credited with this short poem:

> I am only one,
> But still I am one.
> I cannot do everything,
> But still I can do something;
> And because I cannot do everything
> I will not refuse to do the something that I can do.[14]

This is, I think, a good way to envision your role in criminal justice. You and I are not individually entrusted by God with responsibility for correcting an entire system of justice operated by tens of thousands of actors. No one person can set it straight. We need only do what we can. But we must do what we can.

Each and every one of us can, starting even today, think differently about justice, speak differently in our sphere of influence, work differently if need be, and vote differently when the opportunity presents itself. You are only

---

14 James Dalton Morrison, ed., *Masterpieces of Religious Verse* (New York: Harper and Brothers, 1948), 416.

one, but you are still one. And while you can't do everything, you can do those things.

And a society full of people, or even just a motivated group of Christians with their minds set on justice, might change the justice system as a whole for the better. By God's grace, I know they can.

Conclusion

MY GOAL IN WRITING THIS BOOK is both to tell a history and to offer a hope. I have sought to recount accurately and fairly the legal history of my nation's struggle toward justice, and, against the backdrop of that history, I want to leave you with hope for justice.

While writing, I frequently discussed with my family what I was finding through my research and what I was thinking about my discoveries. One night at dinner, my younger son, then in eighth grade, was telling us of his day at school in which his civics class had studied the Thirteenth and Fifteenth Amendments to the US Constitution—a topic that he and I had discussed during my writing.

"Why do we study history?" I asked him. He paused, uncertain.

"So we don't make the same mistakes," I interjected, answering my own question.

America's history is complicated, and revisiting it can be uncomfortable. For many of us, returning to examine events long past can seem unnecessary, like picking at scabs we think have healed. But "the past is never dead," William Faulkner observes. "It's not even past."[1] The past's events are closer than we think, and their effects linger longer than we wish. If we ignore that past, we risk repeating its mistakes, including its theological ones.

One oft repeated motto of the Protestant Christian tradition is *ecclesia reformata, semper reformanda secundum verbum Dei*—that is, the church reformed, always reforming according to the word of God. Reformation— a refinement of our theology to conform with God's word—is never a completed task, not because Scripture changes but because we are its fallible

---

1   William Faulkner, *Requiem for a Nun* (New York: Random House, 1951), 73.

interpreters. We now see through a glass darkly, our vision shaded by the hue of our culture and circumstances. To acknowledge that reality is not to deny the absolute truth of Scripture but rather to humbly acknowledge our qualified comprehension of it.

The faith of our fathers has much to commend it. Christianity is a faith passed down. Paul was encouraged by Timothy's sincere faith that spanned back generations through his mother and grandmother (2 Tim. 1:5). Paul likewise urged Timothy to pass on to reliable messengers the faith that Paul had passed on to Timothy (2 Tim. 2:2). And yet at the same time we must be always reforming, correcting for blind spots made plain at times only by the light of history shed on Scripture. Absent that continuing reformation, we will repeat our forefathers' mistakes.

It is easy today to see the glaring errors of many who claimed the name of Christ in decades gone by and yet uncomfortably close. But have we really escaped all the theological errors of an American church that reared our parents and grandparents? Are the cultural currents of today misdirecting our theology of justice as they did those earlier generations of American Christians? Have we, like them, constructed a theology of justice built on a foundation other than love?

This book cannot resolve those questions for you because the answers for each of us are as different as our circumstances. What I offer is a map, not a destination. A guide, not an answer key. A question, not a conclusion. And the question is this: Is this the justice system that you would design if you did not know in advance which of the system's two neighbors you would be? Only when the answer is "yes" have we designed a system that loves our neighbors—both victim and accused—as ourselves.

The Christian doctrine of sanctification offers hope that tomorrow this world and our administration of justice can be, if we want it to be, more just than it is today. We can love more. We can, as Dr. King said, "determine to use the weapon of love."[2]

But ultimately, whatever justice we obtain in this life will be relative. It will be incomplete. It will be imperfect. The justice of this life, like our love

---

2   Ralph E. Luker, Penny A. Russell, Peter Halloran, eds., *Rediscovering Precious Values: July 1951–November 1955*, vol. 2 in *The Papers of Martin Luther King, Jr.* (Berkely, CA: University of California Press, 1994), 198.

in this life, will fall short. We are Christians, and so we are also realists. Our hope for justice must ultimately be an eternal one.

For nearly two millennia, Christians have confessed each Sunday that, in the end, there will be justice: "He shall come again, with glory, to judge the living and the dead; whose kingdom shall have no end."[3] Those words from the Nicene Creed form a central tenet of the Christian faith. No tyrant, no abuser, no Supreme Court Justice, no celebrity pastor, no police officer, no churchman, no murderer will have the last word. Not even death itself will speak definitively. In the end, God will have the final say. He will sort it all out. And he will set all wrongs right. "God will bring every deed into judgment" (Eccl. 12:14) and with greater justice than we ever could.

So we hope for that day when, as God assured, he will make all things new (Rev. 21:5). We look for the promised new heaven and new earth in which justice, and only justice, will dwell (2 Pet. 3:13). That land, Augustine writes, is one "whose king is truth, whose law is love, and whose limit is eternity."[4] It is a city "where the just alone have a place, the wise alone leadership, and those who are there possess what is truly their own."[5] The history could make a stone weep.[6] The hope is that every tear will be wiped away (Rev. 21:4).

If our hope were only in this life, we as Christians would, of all people, be most miserable (1 Cor. 15:19). But our hope does not consist of this life only or end with death. Our longing for justice does not turn on the events of today, tomorrow, next week, or next year. Our hope does not die even when this life does. In the end, we will—we will!—have perfect justice. In the end, his kingdom of justice will have no end.

Which brings me to one last question that I would like to leave you with if you are reading this book but are not a follower of Jesus Christ. When he comes again with glory, how will you fare when you stand before the

---

3 "The Nicene Creed," in *Creeds, Confessions, and Catechisms: A Reader's Edition*, ed. Chad Van Dixhoorn (Wheaton, IL: Crossway, 2022), 17.

4 Augustine, "Letter 138: Augustine to Marcellinus," *Letters 100–155*, trans. Roland Teske, ed. Boniface Ramsey, in *The Works of Saint Augustine: A Translation for the 21st Century* (Hyde Park, NY: New City, 2003), 235 (3.17).

5 Augustine, "Letter 153," in *From Irenaeus to Grotius: A Sourcebook in Christian Political Thought*, ed. Oliver O'Donovan and Joan Lockwood O'Donovan (Grand Rapids, MI: Eerdmans, 1999), 131 (5.26).

6 Marilynne Robinson, *Gilead: A Novel* (New York: Picador, 2004), 190.

only just Judge? It is easy, after surveying history, to feel a sense of self-righteousness. "Thank God," you may think, "I am not like those unjust people from our nation's past and present" (see Luke 18:11). That would, tragically, be the wrong conclusion to take from all of this.

The only correct response is to acknowledge that we, too, are like them. The proper response is repentance. "I am a man of unclean lips," the prophet Isaiah admitted about himself when he saw the one holy and just God, "and I dwell in the midst of a people of unclean lips" (Isa. 6:5). One day you and I, too, will stand before that Judge whom Isaiah saw those many years ago. We will all, in the end, appear before his judgment seat (2 Cor. 5:10).

What, then, must we do to be saved on that day? Jesus's answer to that question was simple and yet profound: "Come, follow me," he beckons. He pardons all who come.

May God, in Christ, have mercy on your soul.

Selected Bibliography

Books

Allen, James. *Without Sanctuary: Lynching Photography in America.* 15th ed. Santa Fe, NM: Twin Palms, 2021.

Austin, John. *The Province of Jurisprudence Determined.* Edited by Wilfrid E. Rumble. Cambridge: Cambridge University Press, 1995.

Ayers, Edward L. *Vengeance and Justice: Crime and Punishment in the 19th-Century American South.* New York: Oxford University Press, 1984.

Baldus, David C., George G. Woodworth, and Charles A. Pulaski Jr. *Equal Justice and the Death Penalty: A Legal and Empirical Analysis.* Boston: Northeastern University Press, 1990.

Barkow, Rachel Elise. *Prisoners of Politics: Breaking the Cycle of Mass Incarceration.* Cambridge, MA: Harvard University Press, 2019.

Bavinck, Herman. *Created, Fallen, and Converted Humanity.* Vol. 1 of *Reformed Ethics.* Edited by John Bolt. Grand Rapids, MI: Baker Academic, 2019.

Berg, Manfred. *Popular Justice: A History of Lynching in America.* Lanham, MD: Ivan R. Dee, 2011.

Bibas, Stephanos. *The Machinery of Criminal Justice.* New York: Oxford University Press, 2012.

Biggar, Nigel. *In Defence of War.* New York: Oxford University Press, 2013.

Blackmon, Douglas. *Slavery by Another Name: The Re-enslavement of Black Americans from the Civil War to World War II.* New York: Anchor, 2008.

Burnham, Margaret A. *By Hands Now Known: Jim Crow's Legal Executioners.* New York: W. W. Norton, 2022.

Cheever, George B. *A Defence of Capital Punishment.* New York: Wiley and Putnam, 1846.

Cohen, William. *At Freedom's Edge: Black Mobility and the Southern White Quest for Racial Control 1861–1915.* Baton Rouge, LA: LSU Press, 1991.

Dray, Philip. *A Lynching at Port Jervis: Race and Reckoning in the Gilded Age*. New York: Farrar, Straus and Giroux, 2022.

Dray, Philip. *At the Hands of Persons Unknown: The Lynching of Black America*. New York: Modern Library, 2003.

Du Bois, W. E. B. *Black Reconstruction in America*. New York: Free Press, 1935.

Faber, Eli. *The Child in the Electric Chair: The Execution of George Junius Stinney Jr. and the Making of a Tragedy in the American South*. Columbia, SC: University of South Carolina Press, 2021.

Fisher, George. *Plea Bargaining's Triumph: A History of Plea Bargaining in America*. Stanford, CA: Stanford University Press, 2003.

Foner, Eric. *Reconstruction: America's Unfinished Revolution, 1863–1877*. Updated ed. New York: Harper and Row, 2014.

Forman, James, Jr. *Locking Up Our Own: Crime and Punishment in Black America*. New York: Farrar, Straus and Giroux, 2018.

Fuller, Lon L. *The Morality of the Law*. Rev. ed. New Haven, CT: Yale University Press, 1969.

Garrett, Brandon L. *Convicting the Innocent: Where Criminal Prosecutions Go Wrong*. Cambridge, MA: Harvard University Press, 2011.

Goodman, James. *Stories of Scottsboro*. New York: Vintage Books, 1995.

Gregory, Eric. *Politics and the Order of Love: An Augustinian Ethic of Democratic Citizenship*. Chicago: University of Chicago Press, 2008.

Griffith, Aaron. *God's Law and Order: The Politics of Punishment in Evangelical America*. Cambridge, MA: Harvard University Press, 2020.

Grotius, Hugo. *The Law of War and Peace*. Translated by Francis W. Kelsey. Indianapolis, IN: Bobbs-Merrill, 1925.

Grimké, Francis. *Addresses*. Vol. 1 of *The Works of Francis Grimké*. Edited by Carter G. Woodson. Washington, DC: Associated, 1942.

Guelzo, Allen C. *Reconstruction: A Concise History*. New York: Oxford University Press, 2018.

Hart, H. L. A. *The Concept of Law*. Oxford: Oxford University Press, 1962.

Hessick, Carissa Byrne. *Punishment without Trial: Why Plea Bargaining Is a Bad Deal*. New York: Abrams, 2021.

Holloway, Pippa. *Living in Infamy: Felon Disenfranchisement and the History of American Citizenship*. New York: Oxford University Press, 2014.

Horne, Jed. *Desire Street: A True Story of Death and Deliverance in New Orleans*. New York: Farrar, Strauss and Giroux, 2005.

Kaemingk, Matthew, ed. *Reformed Public Theology: A Global Vision for Life in the World*. Grand Rapids, MI: Baker Academic, 2021.

Kamel, Onsi Aaron, Jake Meador, and Joseph Minich, eds. *Protestant Social Teaching: An Introduction*. Landrum, SC: Davenant, 2022.

Keller, Timothy. *Forgive: Why Should I and How Can I?* New York: Viking, 2022.

Keller, Timothy. *Generous Justice: How God's Grace Makes Us Just*. New York: Viking, 2010.

Kennedy, Randall. *Race, Crime, and the Law*. New York: Vintage Books, 1998.

Kirchmeier, Jeffrey L. *Imprisoned by the Past: Warren McCleskey and the American Death Penalty*. New York: Oxford University Press, 2015.

Kotch, Seth. *Lethal State: A History of the Death Penalty in North Carolina*. Chapel Hill, NC: University of North Carolina Press, 2019.

Leeman, Jonathan. *How the Nations Rage: Rethinking Faith and Politics in a Divided Age*. Nashville: Thomas Nelson, 2018.

Leeman, Jonathan. *Political Church: The Local Assembly as the Embassy of Christ's Rule*. Downers Grove, IL: IVP Academic, 2016.

Lewis, Anthony. *Gideon's Trumpet*. New York: Random House, 1964.

Lynching in America: Confronting the Legacy of Racial Terror. 3rd ed. Montgomery, AL: Equal Justice Initiative, 2017.

Malloy, Edward A. *The Ethics of Law Enforcement and Criminal Punishment*. Washington, DC: University Press of America, 1982.

Mancini, Matthew J. *One Dies, Get Another: Convict Leasing in the American South, 1866–1928*. Columbia, SC: University of South Carolina Press, 1996.

Manuel, Ian. *My Time Will Come: A Memoir of Crime, Punishment, Hope, and Redemption*. New York: Pantheon, 2021.

Marshall, Christopher D. *Beyond Retribution: A New Testament Vision for Justice, Crime, and Punishment*. Grand Rapids, MI: Eerdmans, 2001.

Matz, Brian. *Introducing Protestant Social Ethics: Foundations in Scripture, History, and Practice*. Grand Rapids, MI: Baker Academic, 2017.

McGuire, Danielle L. *At the Dark End of the Street: Black Women, Rape, and Resistance—a New History of the Civil Rights Movement from Rosa Parks to the Rise of Black Power*. New York: Alfred A. Knopf, 2010.

Meilaender, Gilbert C. *Friendship: A Study in Theological Ethics*. Updated ed. Notre Dame, IN: University of Notre Dame, 1981.

Messenger, Tony. *Profit and Punishment: How America Criminalizes the Poor in the Name of Justice.* New York: St. Martin's, 2021.

Mitchell, Jerry. *Race against Time: A Reporter Reopens the Unsolved Murder Cases of the Civil Rights Era.* New York: Simon and Schuster, 2020.

Moore, Billy Neal. *I Shall Not Die: Seventy-Two Hours on Death Watch.* Bloomington, IN: AuthorHouse, 2005.

O'Donovan, Oliver. *In Pursuit of a Christian View of War.* Bramcote, UK: Grove, 1977.

O'Donovan, Oliver. *Resurrection and Moral Order: An Outline for Evangelical Ethics.* 2nd ed. Grand Rapids, MI: Eerdmans, 1994.

O'Donovan, Oliver. *The Ways of Judgment.* Grand Rapids, MI: Eerdmans, 2005.

O'Donovan, Oliver, and Joan Lockwood O'Donovan, eds. *From Irenaeus to Grotius: A Sourcebook in Christian Political Thought.* Grand Rapids, MI: Eerdmans, 1999.

Ogletree, Charles L., Jr., and Austin Sarat, eds. *From Lynch Mobs to the Killing State: Race and the Death Penalty in America.* New York: New York University Press, 2006.

Oshinsky, David M. *"Worse than Slavery": Parchman Farm and the Ordeal of Jim Crow Justice.* New York: Free, 1997.

Outka, Gene. *Agape: An Ethical Analysis.* New Haven, CT: Yale University Press, 1977.

Pfaff, John F. *Locked In: The True Causes of Mass Incarceration and How to Achieve Real Reform.* New York: Basic Books, 2017.

Pfeifer, Michael J., ed. *Lynching beyond Dixie: American Mob Violence outside the South.* Champaign, IL: University of Illinois Press, 2013.

Philips, Elizabeth. *Political Theology: A Guide for the Perplexed.* London: T&T Clark, 2012.

Ramsey, Paul. *Basic Christian Ethics.* Louisville: Westminster John Knox, 1950.

Ramsey, Paul. *War and the Christian Conscience: How Shall Modern War Be Conducted Justly?* Durham, NC: Duke University Press, 1961.

Rawls, John. *A Theory of Justice.* Rev. ed. Cambridge, MA: Harvard University Press, 1999.

Rothchild, Jonathan, Matthew Myer Boulton, and Kevin Jung, eds. *Doing Justice to Mercy: Religion, Law, and Criminal Justice.* Charlottesville, VA: University of Virginia Press, 2007.

Skotnicki, Andrew. *Conversion and the Rehabilitation of the Penal System: A Theological Rereading of Criminal Justice.* New York: Oxford University Press, 2019.

Stott, John R. W. *Christian Mission in the Modern World.* Downers Grove, IL: InterVarsity Press, 1975.

Stuntz, William J. *The Collapse of American Criminal Justice.* Cambridge, MA: Belknap, 2011.

Waldrep, Christopher, ed. *Lynching in America: A History in Documents.* New York: New York University Press, 2006.

Whitman, James Q. *The Origins of Reasonable Doubt: Theological Roots of the Criminal Trial.* New Haven: Yale University Press, 2008.

Winright, Tobias. *Serve and Protect: Selected Essays on Just Policing.* Eugene, OR: Cascade, 2020.

Wolterstorff, Nicholas. *Justice in Love.* Grand Rapids, MI: Eerdmans, 2015.

Wolterstorff, Nicholas. *The Mighty and the Almighty: An Essay in Political Theology.* New York: Cambridge University Press, 2014.

Wright, Christopher J. H. *Old Testament Ethics for the People of God.* Downers Grove, IL: IVP Academic, 2004.

Zehr, Howard. *The Little Book of Restorative Justice.* Rev. ed. New York: Good Books, 2015.

Zimring, Franklin E., and Gordon Hawkins. *Crime Is Not the Problem: Lethal Violence in America.* New York: Oxford University Press, 1999.

Journal and Magazine Articles

Alschuler, Albert W., and Andrew G. Deiss. "A Brief History of Criminal Jury in the United States." *University of Chicago Law Review* 61, no. 3 (1994): 867–928. https://doi.org/10.2307/1600170.

Baldus, David C., George Woodworth, and Catherine M. Grosso. "Race and Proportionality since *McCleskey v. Kemp* (1987): Different Actors with Mixed Strategies of Denial and Avoidance." *Columbia Human Rights Law Review* 39, no. 1 (2007): 143–77. https://doi.org/10.17613/4547-jy12.

Baldus, David C., and George Woodworth. "Race Discrimination in the Administration of the Death Penalty: An Overview of the Empirical Evidence with Special Emphasis on the Post-1990 Research." *Criminal Law Bulletin* 39, no. 1 (2003): 194–226.

Baldus, David C., George Woodworth, David Zuckerman, and Neil Alan Weiner. "Racial Discrimination and the Death Penalty in the Post-*Furman*

Era: An Empirical and Legal Overview, with Recent Findings from Philadelphia." *Cornell Law Review* 83, no. 6 (1998): 1638–1770. https://scholarship.law.cornell.edu/clr/vol83/iss6/6.

Baughman, Shima Baradaran. "How Effective Are Police? The Problem of Clearance Rates and Criminal Accountability." *Alabama Law Review* 72, no. 1 (2020): 47–130. https://dc.law.utah.edu/scholarship/213/.

Bica, Camillo C. "Interpreting Just War Theory's Jus In Bello Criterion of Discrimination." *Public Affairs Quarterly* 12, no. 2 (April 1998): 157–68. https://www.jstor.org/stable/40441189.

Boger, John Charles. "*McCleskey v. Kemp*: Field Notes from 1977–1991." *Northwestern University Law Review* 112, no. 6 (2018): 1637–88. https://scholarlycommons.law.northwestern.edu/nulr/vol112/iss6/13.

Brigham, John C., and Robert K. Bothwell. "The Ability of Prospective Jurors to Estimate the Accuracy of Eyewitness Identifications." *Law and Human Behavior* 7, no. 1 (1983): 19–31. https://doi.org/10.1007/BF01045284.

Clayton, Molly. "Forgiving the Unforgivable: Reinvigorating the Use of Executive Clemency in Capital Cases." *Boston College Law Review* 54, no. 2 (2013): 751–88. https://lira.bc.edu/work/ns/1893e157-8589-4a76-9876-8112f9ee9301.

Colbert, Douglas L. "Prosecution without Representation." *Buffalo Law Review* 59, no. 2 (2011): 333–453. https://digitalcommons.law.buffalo.edu/buffalolawreview/vol59/iss2/2.

Forman, James, Jr. "Juries and Race in the Nineteenth Century." *Yale Law Journal* 113, no. 4 (2003): 895–938. https://doi.org/10.2307/4135685.

Garrett, Brandon L. "Judging Innocence." *Columbia Law Review* 108, no. 1 (2008): 55–142. http://www.jstor.org/stable/40041767.

Garrett, Brandon L. "The Substance of False Confessions." *Stanford Law Review* 62, no. 4 (2010): 1051–1118. https://www.jstor.org/stable/40649624.

Gershowitz, Adam M. "Prosecutorial Shaming: Naming Attorneys to Reduce Prosecutorial Misconduct." *University of California-Davis Law Review* 42, no. 4 (2009): 1059–1105. https://lawreview.law.ucdavis.edu/issues/42/4/articles/42-4_gershowitz.pdf.

"The *Gideon* Effect: Rights, Justice, and Lawyers Fifty Years after *Gideon v. Wainwright*." Symposium Issue, *Yale Law Journal* 122, no. 8 (June 2013). https://www.jstor.org/stable/i23527836.

Gross, John P. "The Right to Counsel but Not the Presence of Counsel: A Survey of State Criminal Procedures for Pre-Trial Release." *Florida Law Review* 69, no. 3 (2017): 831–85. https://scholarship.law.ufl.edu /flr/vol69/iss3/4.

Gross, Samuel R. "Errors in Misdemeanor Adjudication." *Boston University Law Review* 98, no. 3 (2018): 999–1011. https://www.bu.edu/bulawreview /files/2018/06/GROSS.pdf.

Gross, Samuel R., Barbara O'Brien, Chen Hu, and Edward H. Kennedy. "Rate of False Conviction of Criminal Defendants Who Are Sentenced to Death." *Proceedings of the National Academy of Sciences* 111, no. 20 (2014): 7230–35. https://doi.org/10.1073/pnas.1306417111.

Karakatsanis, Alec. "The Punishment Bureaucracy: How to Think about 'Criminal Justice Reform.'" *Yale Law Journal Forum* 128 (March 28, 2019): 848-935. https://www.yalelawjournal.org/pdf/Karakatsanis_vahc 6bgb.pdf.

Kassin, Saul M. "The Social Psychology of False Confessions." *Social Issues and Policy Review* 9, no. 1 (2015): 25–51. https://doi.org/10.1111/sipr.12009.

Lackey, Jennifer. "False Confessions and Testimonial Injustice." *The Journal of Criminal Law and Criminology* 100, no. 1 (2020): 43–68. https://www.jstor .org/stable/48572214.

Lynch, Mona, and Craig Haney. "Death Qualification in Black and White: Racialized Decision Making and Death-Qualified Juries." *Law and Policy* 40, no. 2 (2018): 148–71. https://doi.org/10.1111/lapo.12099.

Mayeux, Sara. "What *Gideon* Did." *Columbia Law Review* 116, no. 1 (2016): 15–103. https://scholarship.law.vanderbilt.edu/faculty-publications/748/.

Meisner, Christian A., and John C. Brigham. "Thirty Years of Investigating the Own-Race Bias in Memory for Faces: A Meta-Analytic Analysis." *Psychology, Public Policy and Law* 7, no. 1 (2000): 3–35. https://doi. org/10.1037/1076-8971.7.1.3

Morris, Phillip. "Sentenced to Death but Innocent: These Are Stories of Justice Gone Wrong." *National Geographic*. February 18, 2021. https://www.national geographic.com/.

Phillips, Scott, and Justin Marceau. "Whom the State Kills." *Harvard Civil Rights—Civil Liberties Law Review* 55, no. 2 (2020): 1–69. https://search .informit.org/doi/10.3316/agispt.20201019038355.

Puddifoot, Katherine. "Re-evaluating the Credibility of Eyewitness Testimony: The Misinformation Effect and the Overcritical Juror." *Episteme* 17, no. 2 (June 2020): 255–79. https://doi.org/10.1017/epi.2018.42.

Rainbow, Jonathan H. "Double Grace: John Calvin's View of the Relationship of Justification and Sanctification." *Ex Audito* 5 (1989): 99–105.

Redlich, Allison D., and Gail S. Goodman. "Taking Responsibility for an Act Not Committed: The Influence of Age and Suggestibility." *Law and Human Behavior* 27, no. 2 (2003): 141–56. https://doi.org/10.1023/A:10 22543012851.

Rosen, Richard A. "Disciplinary Sanctions against Prosecutors for *Brady* Violations: A Paper Tiger." *North Carolina Law Review* 65, no. 4 (1987): 693–744. https://scholarship.law.unc.edu/nclr/vol65/iss4/2/.

Scalia, Antonin. "God's Justice and Ours." *First Things*. May 2002. https://www .firstthings.com/.

Sukhatme, Neal, and Jay Jenkins. "Pay to Play? Campaign Finance and the Incentive Gap in the Sixth Amendment's Right to Counsel." *Duke Law Journal* 70, no. 4 (2021): 775–845. https://scholarship.law.duke.edu /dlj/vol70/iss4/2.

Sullivan, J. Thomas. "The Demographic Dilemma in Death Qualification of Capital Jurors." *Wake Forest Law Review* 49 (2014): 1107–72. https://law repository.ualr.edu/faculty_scholarship/161.

Taylor, Elizabeth A. "The Origin and Development of the Convict Lease System in Georgia." *The Georgia Historical Quarterly* 26, no. 2 (1942): 113–28. https://www.jstor.org/stable/40576830.

Tonry, Michael. "Federal Sentencing 'Reform' since 1984: The Awful as Enemy of the Good." *Crime and Justice* 44, no. 1 (September 2015): 99–164. https:// doi.org/10.1086/681666.

Tonry, Michael. "Prosecutors and Politics in Comparative Perspective." *Crime and Justice* 41, no. 1 (2012). https://doi.org/10.1086/666975.

Venema, Cornelius P. "Calvin's Understanding of the 'Twofold Grace of God' and Contemporary Ecumenical Discussion of the Gospel." *Mid-American Journal of Theology* 18 (2007): 67–105. https://www.midamerica.edu/uploads /files/pdf/journal/venema18.pdf.

Waldron, Jeremy. "Who Is My Neighbor? Humanity and Proximity." *The Monist* 86, no. 3 (July 2003): 333–54. https://doi.org/10.5840/monist20 0386324.

Wilson, John Paul, Kurt Hugenberg, and Michael J. Bernstein. "The Cross-Race Effect and Eyewitness Identification: How to Improve Identification and Reduce Decision Errors in Eyewitness Situations." *Social Issues and Policy Review* 7, no. 1 (2013): 83–113. http://dx.doi.org/10.1111/j.1751-2409.2012.01044.x.

Wright, Ronald F., Kami Chavis, and Gregory S. Parks. "The Jury Sunshine Project: Jury Selection Data as a Political Issue." *University of Illinois Law Review* 2018, no. 4 (2018): 1407–42. https://www.illinoislawreview.org/wp-content/uploads/2018/10/Wright.pdf.

Miscellaneous

Brown, Ketanji Onyika. "'The Hand of Oppression': Plea Bargaining Processes and the Coercion of Criminal Defendants." Senior thesis, Harvard College, 1992. Accessed November 14, 2022. https://www.judiciary.senate.gov/imo/media/doc/Jackson%20SJQ%20Attachments%20Final.pdf (thesis begins on p. 104 of the file).

Committee on Identifying Needs of the Forensic Science Community (National Research Council). *Strengthening Forensic Science in the United States: A Path Forward.* Washington, DC: National Academy of Sciences, 2009. https://www.ojp.gov/.

Death Penalty Information Center. "Death Sentences in the United States since 1977." Accessed January 13, 2023. https://deathpenaltyinfo.org/.

Death Penalty Information Center. "Executions by State and Region since 1976." Accessed January 13, 2023. https://deathpenaltyinfo.org/.

Death Penalty Information Center. "Executions in the U.S. 1608–2002: The Espy File." Accessed January 13, 2023. https://deathpenaltyinfo.org/.

Heaton, Paul. *The Effects of Misdemeanor Bail Reform.* Quattrone Center for the Fair Administration of Justice. University of Pennsylvania Carey Law School. August 16, 2022. https://www.law.upenn.edu/.

Memorandum to the Conference from Justice Antonin Scalia of 6 Jan. 1987. McCleskey v. Kemp, Supreme Court Case Files Collection, Powell Papers, Lewis F. Powell Jr. Archives. Washington & Lee University School of Law, Virginia. Accessed November 23, 2021. https://scholarlycommons.law.wlu.edu/casefiles/249/ (memorandum found on p. 147 of the scanned file).

The National Registry of Exonerations. University of Michigan. Accessed April 8, 2023. https://www.law.umich.edu.

US Supreme Court Cases

Atkins v. Virginia, 536 U.S. 304 (2002).

Atwater v. City of Lago Vista, 532 U.S. 318 (2001).

Barron v. Baltimore, 32 U.S. (7 Pet.) 243 (1833).

Batson v. Kentucky, 476 U.S. 79 (1986).

Brady v. Maryland, 373 U.S. 83 (1963).

Brady v. United States, 397 U.S. 742 (1970).

California v. Hodari D., 499 U.S. 621 (1991).

Callins v. Collins, 510 U.S. 1141 (1994).

Connick v. Thompson, 563 U.S. 51 (2011).

Dred Scott v. Sandford, 60 U.S. (19 How.) 393 (1957).

Ewing v. California, 538 U.S. 11 (2003).

Ex parte Virginia, 100 U.S. 339 (1879).

Flowers v. Mississippi, 139 S. Ct. 2228 (2019).

Ford v. Wainwright, 477 U.S. 399 (1986).

Furman v. Georgia, 408 U.S. 238 (1972).

Georgia v. McCollum, 505 U.S. 42 (1992).

Gideon v. Wainwright, 372 U.S. 335 (1963).

Giglio v. United States, 405 U.S. 150 (1972).

Gregg v. Georgia, 428 U.S. 153 (1976).

Herrera v. Collins, 506 U.S. 390 (1993).

Hunter v. Underwood, 471 U.S. 222 (1985).

Imbler v. Pachtman, 424 U.S. 409 (1976).

In re Winship, 397 U.S. 358 (1970).

Jackson v. Virginia, 443 U.S. 307 (1979).

Jurek v. Texas, 428 U.S. 262 (1976).

Kennedy v. Louisiana, 554 U.S. 407 (2008).

Lafler v. Cooper, 566 U.S. 156 (2012).

Lockett v. Ohio, 438 U.S. 586 (1978).

Lockyer v. Andrade, 538 U.S. 63 (2003).

Marbury v. Madison, 5 U.S. (1 Cranch) 137 (1803).

McCleskey v. Kemp, 486 U.S. 279 (1987).

Miller v. Alabama, 567 U.S. 460 (2012).

Missouri v. Frye, 566 U.S. 134 (2012).

Monell v. New York City Dept. of Social Servcs., 436 U.S. 658 (1978).

Norris v. Alabama, 294 U.S. 587 (1935).

North Carolina v. Alford, 400 U.S. 25 (1970).

Powell v. Alabama, 287 U.S. 45 (1932).

Pierson v. Ray, 386 U.S. 547 (1967).

Proffitt v. Florida, 428 U.S. 242 (1976).

Richardson v. Ramirez, 418 U.S. 24 (1974).

Roper v. Simmons, 543 U.S. 551 (2005).

Rummel v. Estelle, 445 U.S. 263 (1980).

Santobello v. New York, 404 U.S. 257 (1971).

Solem v. Helm, 463 U.S. 277 (1983).

Strauder v. West Virginia, 100 U.S. 303 (1880).

Strickland v. Washington, 466 U.S. 668 (1984).

United States v. Ruiz, 536 U.S. 622 (2002).

United States v. Salerno, 481 U.S. 739 (1987).

Woodson v. North Carolina, 428 U.S. 280 (1976).

General Index

Abel, 146
abortion, 24n33, 29–30, 347n5
absolute immunity, 122, 277
accountability
    in assistance of counsel, 261
    and boomerang effect, 110–13
    in exculpatory evidence, 280, 281
    and finding fault, 113–16
    in jury selection, 235
    vs. "just following the law," 120–24
    and reasonableness, 116–20
    in sentencing, 320
    of witnesses, 300–301
accuracy
    and actual guilt, 72–75
    in assistance of counsel, 260
    in the death penalty, 338
    of evidence, 266, 279, 281
    and judges, 246
    in jury selection, 234
    and just laws, 85–88
    in plea bargaining, 215–17
    in sentencing, 317
    and true verdicts, 75–85
    of witnesses, 298
acquitted conduct, 307–9
acquitting the guilty, 94
"act of grace," 335
actual guilt, 72–75
Adam, 16–17, 136
Adams, John, 238
African Americans
    crime statistics of, 337–38

as excluded from juries, 225, 226, 231, 332
    executions of, 106–7, 182–83, 326–28
    imprisonment of, 3, 110n2
aggravating circumstances, 329
Aguilera-Mederos, Rogel, 209–10
all reasonable means, 98–103, 105, 116, 216, 217
Ambrose, 25, 44
American Bar Association, 257, 258
American criminal justice system
    as biblical, 279
    cross-examination in, 104
    evolution of, 165
    failings of, 4, 8, 341
    guilty pleas in, 201
    utilitarianism of, 97–98
America's Got Talent, 235
Anabaptists, 43n23
Andrade, Leandro, 312, 313, 321
Andrus, Terence, 243
anger, 136
animals, 136
appellate court, 265, 333
Arbery, Ahmaud, 1
armed bank robbery, 309–10
arrests, 39–40, 159–60, 190
Ashford, Bruce Riley, 29n52
assault, 3, 46, 319. *See also* sexual assault
assistance of counsel, 249–62
audio recordings, 276
Augustine of Hippo, 8, 33, 43, 51, 52, 53, 66, 86, 93, 102n21, 124, 137,

Christian realism, 93n4, 101
church discipline, 81
circumstantial evidence, 83
civil law, 190–91
Civil Rights Act of 1866, 176
Civil Rights Act of 1875, 176
Civil Rights Movement, 87, 328
Civil War, 169, 172, 184, 225, 229, 327, 328
clemency, 335
Clinton, Bill, 312
collateral review, 333
"color-blind" language, 178
common grace, 49–50
communal happiness, 96
compassion, 61
compensation rate, 256
Compromise of 1877, 177
Confederate monuments, 182
confessions, 289–92
consequentialist ethic, 95
Constitution of Delaware, 168
Constitution of Massachusetts, 167
Constitution of North Carolina, 167
conviction, 115. *See also* wrongful
    conviction
cooperating witnesses, 287–89
cooperation, 298
correction, 152, 155
Council of Trent, 32n59
crack cocaine epidemic, 199
crimes, 63, 187–200, 237
criminal history category, 306
criminal justice
    criticism of, 2
    and Scripture, 1–2
    as social justice, 35–55
    theology of, 14
criminal law, 2, 35, 38–41, 57, 190–91,
    194, 198, 200
cross-examination, 103–5, 262, 284, 295,
    299
crossing paths, 65
cruel and unusual punishment, 153, 167,
    313, 315, 328–29, 334
"*CSI* effect," 292n34

data points, 63
*Daubert v. Merrell Dow Pharmaceuticals,
    Inc.*, 293
deadly force, 38n13, 40, 42, 46, 160, 346.
    See also physical force
death, 16, 17
death penalty
    and *Batson* violations, 231
    and biblical justice, 335–39
    and *Brady* violations, 270–71
    brief history of, 324–28
    constitutionality of, 127, 264, 328–31
    and judges, 243
    litigation procedure of, 331–35
    morality of, 123
    partiality of, 138
    and plea bargaining, 212, 213
    and proportionality, 145
    and right to counsel, 253
death sentence, 76, 234
deception, 266–67, 298
Declaration of Independence, 67, 166,
    171n29
defense attorneys, 91–92, 104, 244–45,
    246
defense witnesses, 296–98
dehumanizing theology, 144
democracy, 28, 67, 68–69, 195, 221
deontological system, of ethics, 96
deterrence, 57, 152, 155–57, 192, 307,
    313
Dever, Mark, 7
discrimination, 98–99
distributive (economic) justice, 142
district attorney elections, 347
DNA evidence, 83, 105, 215, 265, 267,
    270, 277, 285, 294, 298, 324
domestic violence, 217
dominion, 16, 19, 49, 136
Dondeyne, Albert, 96n10
Dorin, Dennis, 130n21
double effect, 99–100
Douglas, Stephen, 171
Douglas, William, 328
Dred Scott v. Sandford, 171

Scripture Index

UNITED?
we pray

"It is a serious matter . . . when any
body of people, however few, betake
themselves not to revolt but to prayer."

— *REV. FRANCIS GRIMKÉ, 1898*

Taking racial struggles to the throne of
grace, United? We Pray is a ministry to help
Christians pray and think about racial strife.

Learn more about our work at uwepray.org.